D1600416

The Presidency, Congress, and Divided Government

Richard S. Conley

The Presidency, Congress, and Divided Government
A Postwar Assessment

Texas
A&M
University
Press
College Station

Library of Congress Cataloging in Publication Data

Conley, Richard Steven.

 The presidency, Congress, and divided government : a postwar
assessment / Richard S. Conley.—1st ed.

  p. cm.—(Joseph V. Hughes, Jr., and Holly O. Hughes series in
the presidency and leadership studies ; no. 12) Includes bibliographical
references and index.

 ISBN 1-58544-211-9 (cloth : alk. paper)

 1. Political parties—United States. 2. Divided government—United
States. 3. United States—Politics and goverment—1945–1989. 4. United
States—Politics and goverment—1989– I. Title. II. Series.

 JK2261 .C696 2002

 973.92—dc21

                                                    2002005961

To my parents and my wife

"We have different gifts, according to the grace given us. If a man's gift is prophesying, let him use it in proportion to his faith. If it is serving, let him serve; if it is teaching, let him teach; if it is encouraging, let him encourage; if it is contributing to the needs of others, let him give generously; if it is leadership, let him govern diligently."

(ROMANS 12:6–10, NIV)

Contents

Illustrations

Tables

Tables

Acknowledgments

THE GENESIS FOR THIS PROJECT began during my graduate studies at the University of Maryland in the mid-1990s. More than any other event, the dramatic impact of the 1994 elections on President Clinton's relations with Congress stimulated my interest in examining the consequences of divided government on the modern legislative presidency. Two distinguished scholars in particular challenged and encouraged me to take up the question. I owe a heartfelt and enduring debt of gratitude to Eric Uslaner—scholar, mentor, and friend—who is both my toughest critic and strongest supporter. His indefatigable faith in my research, first as my dissertation chair, and now as a colleague in the profession, helped in immeasurable ways to bring this manuscript to fruition. His methodological guidance and dedication in reading and commenting on countless drafts of this manuscript over the past five years proved indispensable. I am also indebted to Roger Davidson, who cochaired my dissertation research. Our many discussions on presidential–congressional relations, his unmatched grasp of congressional history, and his steadfast encouragement were invaluable. Paul Herrnson and Jim Gimpel also provided many insights and assistance with this research.

For helpful comments, suggestions, and encouragement on the manuscript I thank my colleagues at the University of Florida. My many in-depth conversations with Larry Dodd helped tremendously in refining elements of the theoretical framework, as he continually prompted me to "think outside the box." Richard Scher's steadfast friendship and optimism about the project during the many arduous revisions were inestimable. Many other colleagues, including Steve Craig, Jeff Gill, Michael Martinez, Beth Rosenson, and Ken Wald contributed to the project—from hallway conversations to departmental brownbag lunch talks.

I would also like to acknowledge the scholars who reviewed my manuscript. Bruce Oppenheimer's insights and detailed, substantive comments greatly improved the work. I also thank several anonymous presidency scholars who reviewed earlier drafts of the book.

Acknowledgments

Finally, I wish to thank my parents and my wife, Stacey, for their enduring support of my scholarship throughout the years. The many pages of this book reflect my family's love, encouragement, and patience. Thanks as well to my feline companions, Badger and Belle, for keeping me company and brightening my days at the computer with their playful antics—including the occasional trek across the keyboard.

The Presidency, Congress, and Divided Government

Introduction
Party Control and Presidential Leverage in Political Time

Split-party control of the presidency and Congress—divided government—has occurred just over six out of every ten years since 1946. Surely the permanence of divided government for all but two short years between 1981 and 2000 argues for the need to theorize about the impact of party control of Congress on the modern presidency. As Paul Quirk and Bruce Nesmith assert: "Whether the president and the majority in Congress have compatible ideological and electoral goals or conflicting ones almost certainly matters somehow. The question is how."[1]

Scholars have not sufficiently explored or analyzed how presidents have approached leadership of Congress under single- or split-party control of national institutions. Analyses of the impact of divided government have tended to focus either on the electoral causes or on questions of legislative productivity without a thorough specification (or consideration) of the president's role in lawmaking.[2] Allegations that split-party control naturally contributes to policy deadlock have not withstood empirical scrutiny. Yet the scholarly preoccupation with gridlock has obscured an appreciation for the precise ways in which party control of Congress has affected the exercise of presidential legislative leadership differently across time.

This book attempts to fill this void, using a close comparative analysis with an emphasis on presidents who have faced divided government since 1945. The analysis focuses on presidential strategies and successes in the domestic policy realm. The domestic and foreign policy realms are sufficiently different to warrant separate examination.[3]

Party control of Congress *does* matter for the legislative presidency, but the impact has been highly uneven in the postwar era. The central argument of this book is that electoral contexts and institutional circumstances in Congress have produced substantial variation in presidential leadership strategy and success in the legislative realm. The conceptual framework for the study lays emphasis on the considerable differences in the exercise of legislative leadership not only *between* periods of unified and divided government but also *within* cases of single- and split-party control. The contrast in presidential strategy, and the form of legislative influence presidents have been able to wield over Congress, is most visible when early periods of the postwar era are contrasted to the closing decades of the twentieth century. In particular, presidential reliance on the veto power when faced with divided government in the 1980s and 1990s bore little resemblance to presidents' frequent coalition-building activities during periods of split-party control spanning the 1950s through the early 1970s.

In the years following World War II through the early 1970s, presidents were typically able to engage in cross-party coalition building in Congress for their legislative goals, whether party control was unified or divided. Shifting voting alignments in Congress necessitated brokering legislative support across party lines. Weak organizational structures and lack of leadership coordination in Congress prompted members to look to the president for policy leadership. Stronger presidential electoral resources—"coattails"—enhanced presidents' *coalition-building leverage.* Depending upon the interplay of the institutional setting in Congress, presidents' electoral resources, and the overlap in agenda objectives between the branches, presidents facing unified and divided conditions could influence individual members and leaders in both parties and frequently build sufficient support to carry their legislative slates to victory. Winning coalitions translated into high floor success rates, which was important because significant domestic legislation of the day was frequently linked to the president's stated policy objectives.

Changes in Congress' structural dynamics and weakening electoral resources have altered the nature of presidential influence and the type of legislative success to which chief executives have been able to lay claim since the 1970s. Stronger partisan voting cohesion in Congress, better leadership coordination, and less deference to the president's policy objectives have combined with tenuous presidential electoral resources to diminish the basis for strong executive influence and independent policy success. These factors produced a subtle yet important distinction in the type of legislative leadership presidents were able to exercise under unified conditions compared to the 1950s and 1960s. The contrast has been most stark, however, when presidential strategy and success in early periods of divided government are compared to the nearly permanent situation of split-party control in the 1980s and 1990s.

Presidents facing unified conditions in recent decades have increasingly derived most of their support from loyal partisans. As party labels became meaningful in Congress, presidents were less able to marshal—or were compelled to seek—cross-party support. Party control engendered greater reciprocity in policy goals between the branches and yielded high floor success rates for occupants of the Oval Office. Nevertheless, better-organized partisan majorities in Congress have showed less deference to presidents' independent policy goals. Presidents have had few or nonexistent coattails. Their copartisans' strong incumbency advantage has eroded electoral connections and diminished a sense of shared electoral fate between the White House and the majority on Capitol Hill. These factors were pivotal in moderating presidents' basis for considerable *autonomous* policy success. Most of the presidents' efforts and greatest policy successes entailed reinforcing support for *continuing party objectives* in Congress.

The incidence of divided government since the 1980s has significantly recast presidents' legislative strategies. Compared to earlier periods of split-party control, presidents run behind and are less popular in electoral terms than members of the opposition majority in Congress. The geographic realignment of the southern electorate sharpened the ideological divide between presidents and the opposition majorities they confronted.[4] Assertive congressional leaders undertook organizational reforms aimed at challenging presidents' policy leadership and pursued agendas with little or no overlap with the White House's policy objectives.[5] Party-line voting has robbed presidents of the ability to garner reliable support from opposition legislators. These factors have militated against the type of cross-party coalition building presidents once routinely engaged in when faced with divided government.

Presidents not only lost far more frequently on their legislative stands, they also were driven to seek alternative means to influence legislative outcomes. They sought to ensure partisan support for their legislative stands and endeavored to turn narrow margins in Congress to their advantage. Unable to persuade congressional majorities to give attention to their own policy priorities or construct winning legislative coalitions for their policy stands, presidents turned to *veto leverage* to defensively ward off the most objectionable elements of the majority's agenda and delimit the range of acceptable outcomes. Vetoes and preemptive veto threats became the presidential weapon of choice in an era of party unity in which opposition majorities in Congress typically lacked the necessary votes for successful overrides. This set of circumstances posed far more significant challenges to presidents' bids to claim credit for significant legislative outcomes compared to the 1950s, 1960s, or early 1970s. This policy-making context also increased the potential for considerable disagreement and stalemate between the branches.

Beyond Gridlock: The Presidency and Party Control of Congress

The impact of unified and divided government on the legislative presidency has been variable, and occasionally quite volatile, in the postwar era. This book's focus on the electoral and institutional contexts that have shaped presidential legislative strategies in the last half century moves the debate about the consequences of party control of national institutions beyond the basic question of legislative productivity. It is imperative to "bring the presidency back" into the debate about party control of national institutions in order to grasp how presidents have chosen to adapt strategically to changing political contexts. Only then is it possible to fully gauge the effect of single- and split-party control on legislative leadership, policy outcomes, and credit-claiming opportunities.

David Mayhew's assertion that party control matters little because "System production should be the final test, not whether presidents happened to get what they wanted" obviates the question of presidential strategy and where chief executives have fit into "significant" legislative outcomes.[6] Gridlock must not be the *only* criterion used to assess the impact of divided government. A "tandem institutions" perspective on executive-legislative relations does not preclude recasting the question of legislative output to inquire about the president's role and success in the legislative sphere and the range of strategies presidents may employ under unified and divided government across time.[7]

The yardstick of legislative productivity to measure the effect of party control of national institutions fails to account for popular expectations of presidential leadership. Such expectations of American chief executives may, alas, exceed institutional capacity.[8] Whether control of the presidency and Congress is unified or divided means little to voters, who continue to expect the president to act as "chief legislator."[9] Contemporary presidents thus rely on their legislative achievements to win reelection. Their policy legacies are the principal criterion against which voters and historians judge their success or failure. Modern presidents cannot escape the "shadow" of Franklin Delano Roosevelt's early legislative accomplishments.[10]

While we may take solace from the systemic perspective that legislative output is not inevitably that much lower under conditions of split-party control, Mayhew's "important contention that divided government does not matter very much in the long run offers very little comfort to presidents or to opposing congressional majorities."[11] Presidents oppose more significant legislation and veto more legislation under divided government.[12] Powerful electoral motives may discourage cooperation between the branches.[13] There may be incentives at both ends of Pennsylvania Avenue for what John Gilmour calls "strategic disagreement," or the conscious choice by the president and Congress to delay policy decisions until more favorable conditions for partisan credit-claiming arise.[14] It becomes essential to analyze how presidents who have confronted opposition majorities in Congress have failed or succeeded in adjusting their strategic behavior to surmount such obstacles to legislative leadership under different political contexts.

Contemporary proponents of a "responsible party government" system, such as James Sundquist and Lloyd Cutler, contend that unified control of the presidency and Congress is vital for presidential policy leadership.[15] Harmonious relations between the president and Congress, though rare, have always occurred when the same party has controlled both the White House and Capitol Hill.[16] Many scholars stress that unified government is more responsive to public demands and have shown that more partisan legislation passes under unified government.[17] These studies do not, however, provide a precise analysis of the president's legislative leadership role under unified government. At the same time, several instances of unified government in modern times—including the Kennedy, Carter, and Clinton presidencies—have not proven a panacea for presidents in the legislative sphere. It thus is critical to examine more closely the factors that either buttressed presidents' abilities to successfully pursue autonomous policy objectives or moderated their basis for influence and prompted them to concentrate on the advancement of "continuing legislative agendas" in Congress.[18]

A broader view of the impact of party control of national institutions, then, must consider presidents' strategic responses to differing governing contexts and their impact on policy outcomes. One major task of this book is to test the normative claims of contemporary "party government" advocates about the advantages of unified government for presidential leadership. Another central objective is to detail why divided government has had such a profound impact on presidential success and the *type* of influence presidents have been able to wield in recent decades compared to the early postwar period.

Presidential Leverage in Political Time

The theoretical perspective of presidential leverage in "political time" developed in this book stresses the sources of variation in the impact of party control of Congress on the legislative presidency as political contexts changed during the postwar era.[19] The empirical analysis in subsequent chapters investigates presidents' floor success, influence over individual legislators, and strategies and involvement in nationally significant legislation. The main argument pivots on the ways in which unified or divided government has interacted with voting alignments and organizational structures in Congress, policy activism by the governing majority in Congress, and the breadth of the president's own policy objectives to shape executive strategy and influence, or *leverage,* differently over the last fifty years.

Analyzing presidential leverage across periods of unified and divided control represents an extension of the scholar's quest for an understanding of periodicity and its impact on American national institutions.[20] The basic premise is that recurring cycles of presidential influence and strategy are evident under single- and split-party control in the postwar era. This is not to suggest that individual presidents and their styles do not matter. Presidents can most certainly aid their legislative efforts through organizational choices, legislative liaison, and timing of proposals.[21] Rather, the perspective stresses how the merger of electoral forces, the internal setting of Congress, and the policy-making environment frame presidential influence, strategy, and success in predictable ways when party control of national institutions is unified or divided.

Presidential leverage over Congress is best conceptualized by degree along a bounded scale. At one end of the spectrum is Richard Neustadt's ideal of assertive presidential direction of congressional lawmaking and cross-party *coalition-building leverage* or "positive" leverage.[22] At the other extreme is a defensive strategy of partisan coalition building and *veto leverage*—"negative" leverage—to forestall congressional activism. Where presidents fall between these endpoints of types of leverage depends in large measure on how party control interacts with the agendas of the two branches, the president's electoral resources, and internal dynamics on Capitol Hill.

When the same party holds both the presidency and Congress, a "shared policy agenda" is much more likely to emerge and engender a closer working relationship between the branches. The president and the governing majority in Congress are more prone to join together as "legislative partners" to pass policies that will prove mutually beneficial in electoral terms. When divided government prevails, the president and the congressional majority are often likely to develop an adversarial relationship. The relative degree of contention depends on the extent to which policy objectives between the branches conflict. Divided government yields a much larger potential space for a "contested agenda."

When government is divided, presidents may frequently intervene in the legislative process to build legislative majorities *in opposition to* the congressional leadership. When they are not successful in achieving floor outcomes consonant with their policy preferences, they may be compelled to turn to the veto power to halt legislation and force compromise. Presidents are thus more likely to act as legislative combatants who fend off elements of the governing majority's agenda with which they most strongly disagree, settling for less legislative success relative to their own agenda preferences or preferences shared by their copartisans in Congress.

The electoral and institutional context presidents face in Congress shapes the type of leverage they can exert. When presidents confront electorally vulnerable members, poorly organized leadership structures among partisan majorities in Congress, and less stability in the composition of legislative coalitions, they can then use their electoral resources and institutional position to exercise persuasive power over congressional leaders and rank-and-file members to build majority policy coalitions for their legislative stands. Popular presidents with strong electoral victories are likely to be more successful in achieving high levels of floor success and steering the congressional majority toward their independent policy objectives.

If presidents face electorally secure members, well-coordinated leadership structures, and party cohesion among the congressional majority, they are less likely to have the same level of autonomous influence over legislative outcomes. Their success will depend considerably on the extent of shared policy agreement with the congressional majority. In cases of high levels of agreement under unified government, presidents can reinforce majority party support for the "shared agenda," which may derive more or less from their own preferred agenda and historical agendas in Congress that carry over from one period to another. The result may be high levels of executive-legislative concurrence on floor votes and legislative outcomes, with the president frequently lending support from the bully pulpit for the majority's continuing legislative objectives. When policy agreement is lower and presidents face an opposition majority with greater independent electoral security and a strong leadership structure, they will have much more difficulty exercising persuasive influence over floor outcomes. As the range of the "contested agenda" expands vis-à-vis policy-focused congressional majorities, a president's ability to build winning coalitions decreases. A lack of electoral resources weakens coalition-building leverage and may impede both the president's floor success rate and his ability to turn congressional attention to his policy priorities. He may be compelled to rely on vetoes and preemptive veto threats to negotiate legislative outcomes.

Figure I.1 illustrates the potential for variation in the types of leverage

Party Control	
Unified	Divided

High	Unified	Divided
	Weak leadership structure in Congress	Weak leadership structure in Congress
	Electoral vulnerability in Congress	Electoral vulnerability in Congress
	Shifting legislative coalitions in Congress	Shifting legislative coalitions in Congress
	Strong electoral victory for the president/coattails	Strong electoral victory for the president/coattails
	Presidential leadership role	*Presidential leadership role*
	Setting the shared agenda	Setting shared agenda
	Cross-party coalition-building leverage	Negotiating contested agenda
		Cross-party coalition-building leverage
Low	Centralized leadership structure in Congress	Centralized leadership structure in Congress
	Incumbency advantage for members of Congress	Incumbency advantage for members of Congress
	Shifting voting coalitions or party cohesion in majority	Party cohesion in the opposition majority
	Weak presidential electoral linkages to majority party	Weak presidential electoral victory/few linkages to opposition majority
	Presidential leadership role	*Presidential leadership role*
	Variably setting/reinforcing support for shared agenda	Selective legislative engagement
	Partisan coalition building	Partisan coalition building
		Negotiating contested agenda through veto leverage

President's Leverage

Fig. I.1.
Presidential Leverage: Party Control, Congressional Organization, and Electoral Factors

presidents are able to exert, and the legislative leadership role they are able to play, as party control interacts with the strength of their electoral resources and institutional position. The framework is such that when the president sustains a strong electoral victory and faces an auspicious setting in Congress, he will generally have greater resources to independently and positively influence legislative outcomes. The factors contributing to such a favorable environment in Congress include a decentralized leadership structure, frequent cross-party alliances in the composition of legislative coalitions, and low incumbency advantage for members. The latter provides the president with a basis for "coattail effects," defined as bringing more members of his own party into Congress at the time of the presidential election and/or outpacing the electoral margins of members in their districts. In times of unified government, these key resources can enable the president to set the basic contours of the shared legislative agenda with his partisan majority in Congress and exercise stronger leadership in mapping the direction of domestic policy. Lyndon Johnson's overwhelming victory in 1964, strong coattails, and resultant success in Congress stands out as the unique postwar example of exceptional positive presidential leverage from this perspective.

When divided government prevails, an electorally popular president who confronts a favorable environment in Congress may also be able to wield considerable influence. Much depends on the breadth of the shared policy agenda between the branches and policy activism championed at either end of Pennsylvania Avenue. In the context of overlapping policy objectives, the president may be able to persuade the congressional majority to accept his priorities. In cases of less correspondent legislative goals between the president and the governing majority in Congress, he may still be able to proactively influence elements of the contested agenda by dint of his electoral resources. Dwight Eisenhower's experience with divided government bridges these scenarios. Eisenhower was enormously popular in the 1952 and 1956 elections. He and the Democratic Congresses he faced from 1955–60 had relatively limited legislative objectives that restricted the development of an expansive contested agenda. Eisenhower, facing a decentralized environment on Capitol Hill, was able to ally himself with shifting legislative coalitions and influence leaders and members of both parties to produce preferable outcomes, obviating the need to rely frequently on vetoes to force compromise.

The president's capacity and strategy to influence legislative outcomes will vary more considerably by party control of Congress when his electoral resources and institutional position are weak. Incumbency advantage in Congress negates the coattail influence when presidents "run behind" members who face little or only weak opposition in their home districts. Candidate-centered presidential campaigns may only exacerbate the weakened linkage between the president and members of Congress. Members and leaders whose electoral fortunes do not overlap with the president's may show less deference to his policy objectives.

Congress' organizational features are pivotal when a better-organized majority meets a president with few electoral resources. A centralized leadership structure provides party leaders with the machinery for self-sustained policy-making capacity and diminishes the president's independent influence over the legislative branch. The foundation for a stronger internal leadership structure can stem from external sources in the electorate when parties play a critical role in the recruitment of candidates and there is a strong constituency basis to the elected membership. Alternatively, stronger leadership structures may emerge when rank-and-file members perceive that the benefits of leadership coordination outweigh the costs of a loss of individual autonomy.[23]

Under unified government, a stronger congressional organization is less likely to defer to presidential directorship of the legislative agenda. The president may have more frequent cause to extend support for an agenda shared with his congressional majority rather than pursue his own independent policy agenda. Bill Clinton, for instance, reinforced efforts to pass longstanding Democratic initiatives blocked by George Bush, such as family leave and "motor voter" legislation, and claimed credit for the accomplishments in 1993–94. Clinton's weak electoral links to the Democratic majority in Congress, the incumbency advantage for members of both parties, and stronger independent congressional leadership in the 103d Congress were significant factors in his inability to push through the more controversial elements of his own agenda, including the economic stimulus plan, crime legislation, and, most notably, comprehensive health care reform.

Presidents face the most limiting conditions for proactive coalition building, high floor success rates, and independent policy leadership when unfavorable institutional and electoral resources merge with divided government. This is particularly true when midterm elections reverse party control of Congress. The president has far fewer opportunities to advance his own policy preferences or persuade the opposition majority to shirk the party line when intraparty cohesion prevails, a centralized opposition leadership takes forceful control of the legislative agenda, and there is minimal overlap between presidential and congressional electoral constituencies. He will be forced to engage selectively in the legislative process and will frequently be in the position of reacting to, or preempting, the opposition majority's agenda if he cannot build cross-party coalitions for his legislative positions. As the range of the contested agenda expands, his principal bargaining chip for negotiating with the governing majority is the veto power. The credibility of this trump card in the legislative game will be largely contingent upon the combination of the party balance in Congress and the ability of his copartisans to successfully fend off override attempts.

Bill Clinton's experience with divided government points to the power— and the limitations—of veto leverage as a legislative strategy when the president has little sway to engage in coalition building with an opposition majority. Clinton turned his copartisans' unity in opposition to the Republican

"Contract with America" to his advantage in his standoff with Speaker Newt Gingrich and GOP leaders in 1995–96. His repeated vetoes of spending bills that originally passed by narrow, partisan votes forced the Republicans to compromise and move legislative outcomes closer to his preferences. The stability of voting coalitions in Congress buttressed Clinton's veto power, even while party unity and divided government lowered his floor success rate to all-time lows in the postwar period and dashed his hope of any considerable advances of his—and his copartisans'—preferred agenda.

The Presidency, Party Control, and Political Contexts: Electoral Resources, Congressional Organization, and Agenda Control

In the early postwar period, a president's ability to persuade members of Congress was typically greater in the legislative sphere because of the weakness of the internal organization of the legislature and stronger presidential coattails. Presidents more frequently fell into the "high positive leverage" category. The lack of well-organized leadership structures and members' own electoral vulnerability pressed them to look to the president for agenda leadership in the domestic realm.[24] Presidents Eisenhower and Johnson, in particular, had relatively hardy bases from which to exercise positive leverage over Congress, set the legislative agenda, and build coalition support for their independent policy objectives. Under divided party control, Eisenhower and even Richard Nixon had far less recourse to veto leverage than recent presidents.

The defining feature of the last quarter of the twentieth century has been the uniformly weaker positive leverage of presidents over Congress. The political context for Presidents Jimmy Carter, Ronald Reagan, Bush, and Clinton differed significantly from chief executives in the decades immediately following World War II, and the impact on presidential strategy and policy success was more or less substantial depending on the configuration of party control. Under unified conditions, Presidents Carter and Clinton did not possess the electoral resources and strong institutional position commensurate with those of Eisenhower or Johnson. Carter and Clinton consequently found their congressional copartisans far less deferential to their independent policy objectives.

The effect of weaker positive leverage was much more dramatic under divided party control. Factors far less prevalent in early periods of split-party control—including intense partisan polarization in Congress, assertive opposition leaders, and little connection between the constituencies of the president and members of the opposition majority—left Presidents Bush and

Clinton with quite limited opportunities to influence the structure of voting coalitions and control legislative outcomes through cross-party coalition-building activities. As a result, they relied on veto leverage far more than earlier presidents facing an opposition majority in Congress.

Presidential influence in Congress is, of course, complicated by other factors that are both idiosyncratic and unique to individual presidents. A landslide electoral victory like Johnson's in 1964 or Reagan's in 1980 can surmount, at least temporarily, some of the regular impediments to leadership of Congress. Presidents intent on passing an extensive program are advised to act quickly, as influence in Congress is greatest at the beginning of their term and tends to wane over time.[25] The scope of presidents' agendas, their interest in domestic policy, and their mastery of legislative politics in Congress and "going public" are just a few of the additional elements worthy of consideration.[26] However, when the larger trends of the last half century are examined, it is remarkable how well the dual dimensions of party control of Congress and the relative level of presidential electoral and institutional resources interact to account for the lion's share of the variation in influence in Congress across fairly distinct historical periods. A brief examination of developments in electoral and congressional politics that have cut across the postwar period, and their effect on presidents' floor success rates and agenda-setting potential, aids in placing individual presidents more exactly on the continuum of leverage in political time under single- and split-party control.

Declining Electoral Resources and Presidential Leverage

The long-term decline in presidential electoral resources is a key factor in the increasingly fragile basis for positive presidential leverage during the last quarter century. The variability of presidential electoral resources in the early postwar period was replaced by a general loss of coattail strength.[27] Candidate-centered "outsider" candidacies and narrow victories robbed presidents of electoral legitimization of their agendas. Competitive presidential races merged with the growth of the incumbency advantage for members of Congress.[28] These developments undermined the interinstitutional electoral linkages vital to strong, positive leverage in the legislative realm.

The president's electoral popularity in Congress members' home districts is an essential ingredient in persuasion and coalition building. A strong margin of victory in legislators' districts thus forms a key component of a president's political "capital."[29] Electoral popularity is qualitatively different from aggregate public approval as a source of presidential influence over Congress. In the case of highly visible votes of great controversy and conflict that involve presidential preferences, national approval trends are less relevant to legislators in either party than cues from their perceived reelection constituencies. The president's district-level electoral popularity provides a firmer basis from which to rally members of Congress to his legislative stands than shifting trends in his job approval, which have much to do with economic conditions or short-term events in the foreign policy sphere.[30] The president's electoral performance validates constituents' basic support for his legislative preferences and lends legitimacy to his appeals to members of Congress for support of his agenda and policy priorities.

The president's electoral popularity consolidates partisan bonds and can be instrumental in gaining the support of members of the opposition party. When the president runs ahead of members in their districts and/or brings more members of his own party into Congress, his coattails amplify a shared partisan linkage in the electorate and can contribute to greater party cohesion on the president's agenda.[31] As James Campbell and Joe Sumners contend, "candidates receiving coattail votes may be a bit more positively disposed, out of gratitude, to side with a president who had helped in their election."[32] Support of a popular president thus may aid legislators' reelection chances.[33] In times of divided government, the president's electoral popularity in opposition members' districts is not a complete substitute for a shared partisan electoral bond. Members of the opposition majority may, however, fall under greater pressure to back an electorally popular president's legislative stands if they fear electoral retaliation. Legislators are acutely concerned with their voting records because they believe constituents pay attention.[34]

There are several ways to measure presidential coattails. One measure is simply the number of seats the president's party gains at the time he is elected. A second measure is the extent to which the president's district margin of victory outpaced members' own electoral margins. Using both measures to analyze coattails highlights variability in presidential electoral popularity in the early decades of the postwar period and a significant dwindling of coattail resources for presidents who faced nearly constant opposition party control of Congress since 1980.

Figure I.2 traces "seat-gain coattails" from 1948–96. Harry Truman's narrow election in 1948, Eisenhower's victory in 1952, and Johnson's landslide in 1964 ushered in unified government with significant congressional seat gains for the president's party. Other presidents, however, failed to bring a sizable contingent of copartisans to Capitol Hill on the heels of their electoral victories. The lack of coattails has frequently left Republican presidents with opposition control of Congress. Save for Eisenhower's strong victory in 1952,

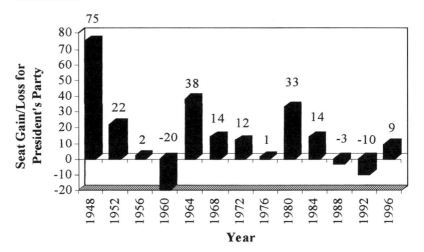

Fig. I.2
Seat Gains for the President's Party in the House of Representatives, 1948–96
Source: *Congressional Quarterly Almanacs,* 1948–96.

Republican presidents' coattails have been insufficiently long to yield a GOP majority in Congress. George Bush has the dubious distinction of being the first postwar Republican president to be elected to the presidency with a net *seat loss* for the GOP in the House.

Recent Democratic presidents elected alongside a majority of their copartisans have failed to achieve Truman's and Johnson's strong seat-gain coattails. Jimmy Carter's election in 1976 yielded a net increase of just a single Democratic seat in the House in a very narrow contest with incumbent Gerald Ford. Bill Clinton's election in 1992, like John Kennedy's in 1960, produced "negative coattails," meaning that congressional Democrats lost seats in the House. The absence of coattails challenged their claims to a policy "mandate," thus eroding the basis for considerable positive leverage.

An alternative conceptualization of coattails is whether the president's share of the two-party vote in House districts exceeded or lagged behind members' own share of the two-party vote. In other words, regardless of whether presidents carry more members of their party into office on their coattails, this measure of "marginal coattails" shows how their electoral victories stack up to the victory margins of members who are elected alongside them. In terms of potential presidential leverage over legislators, members with victory margins less than the president's can expect to experience more pressure to back his legislative stands. Figure I.3 reports the percent of legislators in the president's party and the opposition party who had margins of

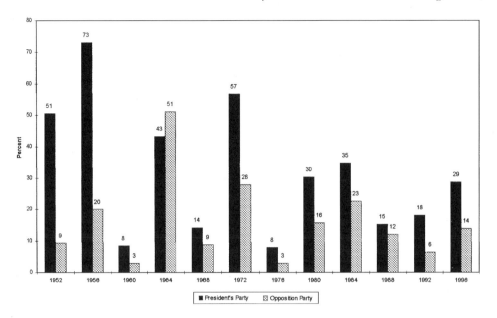

Fig. I.3
"Marginal Coattails": Presidents' Share of the Two-Party Vote
Compared to House Members', 1952–96
Source: Calculated by the author from the *Congressional Directory, Congressional Quarterly Almanacs, Congressional Quarterly Weekly Reports,* and *Almanac of American Politics.* The author thanks Gary C. Jacobson for data on presidents' district-level margins for the 1950s and 1960s.

victory less than the president. The data are unequivocal. This contingent of legislators, particularly in the opposition party, shrank rather considerably throughout the postwar period.

In assessing the potential for presidential leverage through the lens of coattail strength, several trends are noteworthy. All presidents except Johnson (1964) have run ahead of a greater percentage of members *of their own party* compared to the opposition party. Electoral coattails thus are a potentially powerful catalyst for shoring up partisan support. However, the absence of coattails in the opposition party suggests that presidents have a harder time attracting the congressional majority's needed support in times of divided government. It is ironic that Republican presidents' coattails have been the greatest upon reelection, but that each of those elections yielded split-party control. Eisenhower (1956), Nixon (1972), and Reagan (1984) ran ahead of large numbers of their copartisans at the district level, but no more than just over a quarter of House members in the opposition majority. These second-term presidents confronted an opposition membership whose electoral victories owed little to their popularity.

Lyndon Johnson's coattail leverage was indeed exceptional. Not only did a sizable contingent of liberal Democrats ride to victory on his coattails when he defeated Barry Goldwater, his victory margin also exceeded the margins of 40 percent of all Democrats and just over half of all Republicans elected to the 87th Congress. Johnson's electoral victory thus yielded the potential for substantial influence over members of both parties.

Democratic presidents have typically not been in a strong position in terms of electoral resources. John Kennedy (1960), Jimmy Carter (1976), and Bill Clinton (1992) had scarce marginal coattails despite being elected alongside a partisan majority in Congress. The 1960 and 1976 elections were among the most narrowly decided races in the postwar period in terms of the popular vote. And the three-way race between incumbent George Bush, Bill Clinton, and Ross Perot—in many ways reminiscent of the three-way split between Nixon, Hubert Humphrey, and George Wallace in 1968—prevented Clinton from claiming a majority of the popular electoral vote and robbed his election of substantial coattails. Most Democratic candidates for Congress ran ahead of Clinton, complicating the president's bid for legislative leadership on an expansive set of objectives. Paul Light quotes an assistant to President Kennedy who noted: "If the President runs behind in your district, he becomes a liability. If the President can't help you, why help him?"[35] Such was the nature of Clinton's predicament. He lacked the strong electoral base needed to build a case for consistent congressional support of his agenda in either party during the fleeting return of unified government in 1993–94.

The weakening of marginal coattails has been most pronounced during periods of divided government in the 1980s and 1990s. No president since Reagan has outpaced the victory margins of more than a quarter of all House members. Presidents Bush and Clinton not only had few coattails relative to their own party base in Congress, they also had much more limited electoral leverage over opposition members. Bush ran ahead of only an eighth of all Democrats elected in 1988, while Clinton achieved coattail effects in less than a tenth of GOP districts in 1992.

Implicit in the "marginal coattail" analysis in figure I.3 is the increased incumbency advantage for members of Congress. Incumbents' seat safety eclipses presidential coattail effects. The potential for presidential coattails decreases proportionately as electoral vulnerability among congressional incumbents abates and competition in presidential races heightens. The incumbency advantage for members of Congress began to increase in the 1960s.[36] The effects became more fully apparent by the mid-1980s, when the proportion of House incumbents winning reelection with 60 percent or more of the two-party vote share reached nearly 90 percent.[37] With members' increased ability to develop competent campaign organizations and fund-raising operations independent of the political parties, incumbency may serve as a better cue for voting in congressional elections than party affiliation or the popularity of presidential candidates.

Incumbency advantage is an important factor buttressing the split-ticket voting that is the proximate cause of divided government (figure I.4).[38] Ticket-splitting reduces the probability that presidents will run ahead of Congressmen from either party or carry members of their own party to victory in presidential election years.[39] Explanations proffered to account for split-ticket voting, including the rise of candidate-centered presidential and congressional campaigns, are beyond the scope of this discussion and have been detailed elsewhere.[40] It is worth noting, however, that the number of split districts has declined since the 1960s and 1970s as a result of stronger party-line voting by the electorate.[41] A smaller number of key "swing" districts have been responsible for robbing presidents of partisan majorities in Congress in the last two decades as the electoral coalitions supporting the president and members of the opposition majority have increasingly diverged.

In sum, the significant decline in presidents' electoral resources as a source of influence is one of the distinguishing features of executive-legislative relations since the 1970s that has placed presidents in the "low leverage" boxes in

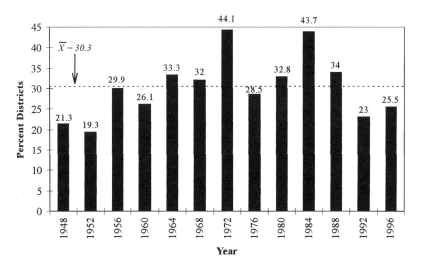

Fig. I.4
Percent of Split Districts, House of Representatives, 1948–96
Source: Calculated by the author.

figure I.1 under unified *and* divided control. Yet diminishing electoral resources must be weighed against the development of greater organizational strength, leadership coordination, and party cohesion within Congress. It is not the lack of coattails that has single-handedly transformed the contours of presidential influence in the legislative realm, but the convergence of weak electoral resources *and* organizational change in Congress that have had remarkable effects on presidential leverage.

The Internal Configuration of Congress and Presidential Leverage

Presidency research has failed to focus adequate attention on the ways in which structural change in Congress has affected executive-legislative relations.[42] The context of the few brief interludes of unified government since the 1970s and the quasi-permanent condition of divided government that has befallen presidents since the 1980s entailed fewer electoral resources for chief executives at a time when opposition majorities in Congress became better organized, more internally homogeneous in ideological terms, and more policy and constituency focused. The coincidence of these factors has been most damaging to positive presidential leverage under divided government since the 1980s, but it also limited the influence Presidents Carter and Clinton had over Congress under single-party control.

The shift toward stronger institutional parties in Congress has been a progressive, if gradual, process. Several factors, including presidential politics, the realignment of the southern electorate, and enhanced leadership coordination in Congress culminated in greater partisan cohesion on Capitol Hill in the last two decades. The Nixon and Reagan presidencies marked critical turning points. Nixon's confrontational approach to Congress and the Democrats' response in his second term was one pivotal juncture in "congressional political time." Reagan's early policy successes and the Democrats' second round of leadership reforms formed another crossroads. Over the course of two decades, the Democratic majority sought to redress the weakness of congressional policymaking capacity by instituting measures squarely aimed at challenging presidents' legislative influence. The sum of organizational changes yielded internal structures in Congress that outlasted Democratic legislative majorities in the House. When the Republicans gained majority status in Congress in the 1994 elections, GOP leaders continued the centralization trend.

Party unity replaced the more fluid voting coalitions of the early postwar period that presidents had successfully employed. Operating in tandem with organizational transformations in the national legislature were the long-term effects of the Voting Rights Act, which had precipitated a gradual geographic realignment in the two parties' core electoral constituencies. This realignment produced greater parity in the electorate, differentiated the parties' basic policy positions, and solidified institutional partisanship. Republicans' steady electoral gains in the South eroded the strength of the conservative wing of the Democratic Party in Congress and resulted in much more stable voting alignments. Partisan voting, at all-time lows in the 1950s and 1960s, increased dramatically and became commonplace. The decline in consensus among party leaders in Congress produced policy debates more frequently cast in terms of zero-sum conflicts across policy areas.[43] The evolution of these changes and their consequences for presidential legislative leadership merit closer scrutiny.

Congressional Organization and Voting Alignments in the Early Postwar Period

The lack of intraparty cohesion and weaker leadership coordination in Congress from the end of World War II through the early 1970s provided presidents with more opportunities to intervene proactively in the legislative process and forge supporting coalitions for their policy preferences. Presidents were more frequently in the "high leverage" categories depicted in figure I.1. As the discussion of electoral contexts suggested, presidents could attempt to marshal legislative support on the basis of their electoral popularity. Yet much depended on the predominant configuration of voting alignments and the structure of cross-party coalitions, which did *not* always work to their advantage. Democratic presidents were often frustrated by the paucity of support they were likely to receive from southern conservatives in the party. When southern Democrats allied with Republicans, the "conservative coalition" periodically thwarted liberal policy goals, even under nominally unified party control of the presidency and Congress.

However, like their Republican counterparts—such as Eisenhower, who faced divided government and internal fissures among his own copartisans—Democratic presidents with a fractious majority in Congress were forced to solicit support for their legislative agendas and policy positions on both sides of the aisle.[44] The general weakness of congressional organization aided this effort by prompting members to look to the president for policy leadership. All told, the decentralized setting within Congress, while clearly not a boon to presidents in every instance, frequently facilitated their task of coalition building across party lines. Their legislative success was contingent upon the extent to which they could ally themselves with elements in both parties on Capitol Hill.

From the beginning of the postwar period through the 1960s and early 1970s, voting alignments in Congress were variable and subject to broad, cross-cutting conflicts. The diffusion of power among senior committee members eroded the Speaker's influence and militated against strong party leadership.[45] To diminish the uncertainty of legislative outcomes legislators engaged in "logrolling" on distributive issues that undercut partisan voting.[46] To the degree that presidents could read the political landscape on Capitol Hill, link with key power brokers, and wed their policy objectives to alternating congressional coalitions, they could claim a modicum of legislative success in times of both unified and divided government.

Party control of national institutions was less salient for presidents because fewer votes consistently pitted a majority of one party against a majority of the other from 1954–72 as compared to later decades (fig. I.5). The "conservative coalition" of southern Democrats and conservative Republicans formed a de facto policy majority on many issues spanning economic policy to civil rights. In other cases, moderate Republicans and liberal Democrats joined together to carry the day. James MacGregor Burns's classic formulation of "four-party" politics captured the essence of the variable composition of legislative coalitions in Congress in this early postwar period. Liberal Democrats and conservative Republicans faced an important contingent of their copartisans, whose ideological stance was often more closely aligned with the other party.

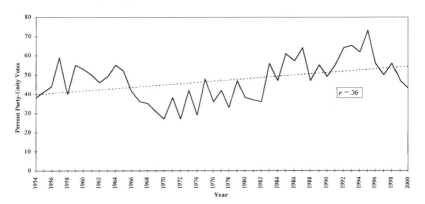

Fig. I.5
Percent Party-Unity Votes, 1954–2000
Source: Congressional Quarterly Almanacs and Congressional Quarterly Weekly Reports.

Weak parties with large numbers of moderates holding the balance over outcomes produced broad, shifting policy coalitions composed of lawmakers on both sides of the aisle.[47]

Presidents had periodic opportunities to lobby individual members and party leaders and craft supporting voting blocs in this contextual environment that lasted through the 1970s. To be sure, the union of southern Democrats and conservative Republicans could and did hamper elements of the progressive domestic agendas of Democratic presidents Roosevelt, Truman, and Kennedy.[48] Nevertheless, the conservative coalition was not monolithic. Room still existed for Democratic presidents to forge favorable cross-party coalitions because of the numbers of moderates in both parties, even if it required both a good bit of creativity and credit sharing with members of the opposition party. Lyndon Johnson's astute and judicious leadership in guiding the Civil Rights Act of 1964 through Congress despite southern Democrats' staunch opposition is perhaps the best-known example.[49]

Republican presidents could occasionally turn the conservative coalition to their advantage, but reaching out to members of different ideological persuasions on both sides of the aisle remained essential. Eisenhower, for example, who was popular both electorally and in terms of job approval, had a moderate and limited agenda and negotiated with members of both parties largely behind the scenes.[50] He was sometimes able to marry southern Democratic support with GOP backing to prevail on issues of domestic spending. In other instances, he turned to different congressional factions on issues like civil rights and foreign policy that divided his copartisans.

The lack of strong intraparty conflict through the early 1970s was not solely due to the ubiquity of the conservative coalition in Congress. President Johnson's sweeping domestic agenda, the "Great Society," and its consolidation during the Nixon and Ford presidencies, also contributed to a lack of intraparty cohesion on floor votes. Much of the legislation over this period was passed by large, bipartisan coalitions that reflected enhanced interest group activism and broad congressional agreement on the contours of public policy.[51]

Low intraparty cohesion continued into Nixon's first term (1969–72), and the continued weakness of congressional organization enhanced his institutional position to selectively negotiate policy coalitions to his advantage. Nixon was pulled in Congress's direction by the momentum of the consolidation of the Great Society. The shifting policy coalitions in the 91st and 92d Congresses sometimes allowed him to ally himself with broad policy issues and exercise some influence over the particulars of legislation that emerged primarily from the Democrats' continuing legislative agenda.

Critical Turning Points: Nixon II and Reagan

Nixon abandoned his conciliatory strategy of participating in broad congressional policy coalitions by his second term. The short- and long-term consequences were substantial. The executive-legislative conflict that existed prior to his resignation left a lasting imprint on Congress's internal structure and had a far-reaching impact on the potential for positive presidential leverage in the future. The congressional response to Nixon initiated a trend toward more stable, partisan voting blocs. Along with the organizational reforms Democrats pursued a decade later in light of Ronald Reagan's threat to the party's domestic objectives, the greater organizational strength and partisan cohesion of congressional majorities increased Congress's independent policy-making capacity. While this shift was at least partially responsible for placing greater barriers to forceful legislative leadership for Democratic presidents Carter and Clinton under unified conditions, the most pronounced impact has been visible during the periods of divided control that have dominated since 1980. In a more structured congressional environment exemplified by centralization around the Speaker and an extended party leadership apparatus, Presidents Reagan, Bush, and Clinton found far fewer opportunities to influence opposition members of Congress on floor outcomes.

Nixon's extensive impoundment of funds for domestic programs and the Watergate scandal set in motion conditions supportive of stronger party leadership and intraparty cohesion among Democrats prior to substantial shifts in the two parties' geographic electoral alignments. Liberal Democrats sought to check the monopoly of power of conservative committee "barons" in their party as early as Nixon's first term. Action began with the Hansen reforms in 1971, which limited the number of committees a member could chair and rescinded the seniority rule as the basis for committee assignments.[52] The "Watergate babies" who rode to victory in the 1974 elections in the aftermath of Nixon's resignation went much farther. The Democratic Caucus adopted the "subcommittee bill of rights," ensuring a floor vote on committee chairs, increasing the number of subcommittees, and securing subcommittee chairs' access to staff and resources. The result was not only a wide dispersal of power in the House, but also greater stability and increased party loyalty on partisan votes by committee chairs after 1974.[53]

The diffusion of power and authority in the House coincided with reforms that strengthened the party leadership's ability to control policy outcomes. While loosening the conservatives' grip on the committee system, Democrats reasoned that an extended whip system and a strengthened Speakership were essential to battle Nixon's antipathy to the party's domestic policy goals. "Nixon's landslide victory in 1972, his vetoes of major Democratic legislation, and his impoundment of appropriated funds created a crisis atmosphere among congressional Democrats that solidified the desire for stronger party leadership."[54] The enlargement of the whip system co-opted members into the leadership structure and allowed the Speaker and majority leader to keep a finger on the pulse of the rank-and-file membership. Party whips gather and transmit information to and from leaders, count votes and attempt to convert recalcitrant members, and engage in coalition building to ensure that floor outcomes correspond to party goals.

Democrats also moved to increase the Speaker's formal authority over policy outcomes during the Nixon and Ford presidencies. "Sixty years after the downfall of Speaker Cannon," James Sundquist notes, "liberal reformers had come, if not full circle, surely no little distance back toward finding merit in the centralized system they had cast aside."[55] Achieving liberal policy goals necessitated a responsive and more powerful leadership structure. In the early 1970s, Democrats restored the Steering and Policy Committee to a position of importance in setting the party's legislative goals.[56] The gradual movement toward a stronger Speakership included granting the Speaker stricter control over committee appointments, greater authority over the referral of legislation to committees, and the ability to create select committees. The sum of these reforms produced a more structured legislative environment that limited President Nixon's and President Ford's ability to set the legislative agenda and marshal support among Democratic leaders, committee chairs, and rank-and-file members in Congress.

Ronald Reagan's policy successes in 1981–82, which caught the Democratic leadership off guard, represent a second critical turning point in congressional organization and party cohesion. Democrats reinvigorated the whip operation and renewed efforts to centralize leadership. Their logic for reform was consistent with thinking in the early 1970s. Reagan, like Nixon, posed a considerable threat to the party's liberal agenda. The president's electoral popularity in 1980 provided substantial leverage in Congress, making legislation vulnerable both to Republican challenges on the floor and defections by southern Democrats facing constituency pressure to support his fiscal and defense policies.[57] Just as the Democratic leadership reforms in the early 1970s had been a reaction against Nixon's confrontational tactics, organizational restructuring in the early 1980s was vital to shore up party unity and minimize Reagan's ability to control the domestic agenda.

Democrats found that the benefits of further centralization of authority in the Speakership outweighed the costs, particularly as the party base in the electorate grew more solidly liberal. The bolstering of the Speakership under Thomas P. "Tip" O'Neill and Jim Wright included renewing the strength of the whip system to ensure greater party cohesion.[58] Multiple referrals of legislation and the adoption of rules restricting floor amendments buttressed the Speaker's control over legislative outcomes.[59] In the short term, heightened centralization contributed to a sharp decline in President Reagan's legislative success rate after 1981. In the longer term, the reforms supported a more active agenda-setting role for the House Democratic leadership.[60] The reforms contributed to President Bush's extensive use of the veto from 1989–92 to block Democratic legislation in a period of intense leadership and policy stalemate between the president and Congress. President Clinton also faced a more independent and self-assured majority that was less willing to follow his policy lead during the brief period of unified government in 1993–94.

The Constituency Bases of Congressional Voting and Organizational Strength

The development of better organized leadership structures and greater intraparty cohesion in Congress from the 1970s through the 1990s was subtended by an incremental change in the constituency bases of the two parties and the intensification of party competition in the electorate. As southerners shifted their support to the GOP and northern Democratic constituencies became more solidly liberal, the parties became more evenly matched nationally. "Party strength," Joseph Cooper and David Brady contend, "is rooted in polarized constituency configurations."[61] As legislators and leaders search for resources in a more competitive electoral environment, they are pushed away from the center to the poles.[62] The result is that they look less to the concerns of the "median voter" and instead take their voting cues from their perceived "reelection constituency": the staunch partisan backers whose votes are essential for reelection.[63] This set of voters may, in fact, be a small proportion of the total eligible electorate, but the low turnout endemic to American elections heightens the pressure on legislators to safeguard the interests of these core constituents.

The gradual Republicanization of the South has had a tremendous impact on national electoral alignments and, consequently, the internal dynamics in Congress. The initial fissures in white southerners' staunch support of the Democratic Party can be traced to Strom Thurmond's bid for the presidency in 1948 under the Dixiecrat banner. Two decades later, Lyndon Johnson failed to carry five of the eleven states of the old Confederacy—due in no small part to his stand on civil rights. Six states in the "Solid South" then turned a cold shoulder to Democratic presidential candidate Hubert Humphrey in 1968 and threw their support to Alabama governor George Wallace's independent candidacy.

Republicans also made progressive gains in congressional representation in the South in the 1970s and 1980s. Turnover and generational replacement linked both to redistricting in the 1990s and congressional scandals in the late 1980s and early 1990s culminated in the party's breakthrough of 1994. The shifting geographical balance of power between the parties was central to the GOP's winning control of Congress. The conservative themes outlined in the Republican "Contract with America" formed a consistent campaign message that resonated particularly well with southern voters. The GOP's targeted financial assistance to candidates gave the party sixty-four of the 125 seats in eleven southern states and a majority in the House of Representatives for the first time in four decades.

The electoral realignment of the South affected dynamics within Congress and between the president and Congress by shrinking the contingent of right-ward-leaning southern Democrats, dissolving the basis of the conservative coalition, and yielding more stable, partisan voting blocs. The growing homogeneity of the Democratic Party's electoral constituencies narrowed the gap in ideological stances that traditionally divided southern and northern Democrats.[64] Democrats elected from the South—particularly African Americans—now share their northern colleagues' policy goals to a much greater degree than in prior decades.[65] As the two parties' ideological positions grew wider, party labels became increasingly significant.

The fluid coalitions of yesteryear thus grew scarce by the mid-1980s, leaving presidents facing divided government with far fewer opportunities to successfully engage in strong agenda leadership and cross-party coalition building. When the Republicans captured Congress after forty years of quasi-permanent minority status, the electoral forces that contributed to more ideologically cohesive parties continued to bolster the trend toward stronger party government in the House. The principles outlined in the Contract with America on which GOP candidates campaigned served as the basis for Republican unity in the 104th Congress in much the same way that Democratic Caucus rules "bonded" members and conditioned their party support in the 1980s.[66] To make good on election promises to bring sweeping policy change to Washington, Barbara Sinclair posits that "House Republicans have given their leaders many of the same tools that Democratic leaders utilized when they were in the majority."[67] Consequently, the Contract with America supplanted

Clinton's domestic agenda in Congress and relegated the president to the sidelines—at least until he resorted to veto leverage to halt and reshape important elements of the GOP's policy program.

Presidential Support and Success in Political Time

How have the dual developments of diminished electoral resources and stronger parties in Congress affected presidential support and success on legislative outcomes? What empirical evidence is there to substantiate classifying recent presidents in the "weak leverage" boxes in figure I.1 across instances of unified and divided control in the last quarter century? A multifaceted approach is necessary to ferret out the subtleties across time. To this end, basic roll call and agenda-setting measures corroborate fundamental assertions of the theoretical framework of presidential leverage in political time.

The impact of weak electoral resources, increased congressional partisanship, and better organized governing majorities had the most visible effect on presidents' legislative influence over floor outcomes under divided government. Presidents were far less able to attract the support of members of the opposition party, they more frequently lost on position votes, and they controlled less of the agenda in Congress compared to the early postwar era. In the rare instances of unified government since the 1970s, presidents received consistent support from their copartisans and garnered high floor success rates, but they faced stiffer competition in their bid to steer congressional activity toward their independent policy objectives. The opportunity structure was more suitable for latching on to what William Lammers and Michael Genovese call "promising issues" typically linked to continuing agendas in Congress.[68] Presidents' high success rates more often reflected the "facilitation" of shared agendas between the branches rather than "directorship" of congressional lawmaking, to put it in George Edwards's terms.[69] Compared to select periods of unified government in the early decades of the last half century, the basis for presidential credit claiming was narrowed. An examination of presidential position votes and agenda-setting data bears out the changed basis of presidential legislative strategy and success over time.

Roll-call measures convey basic levels of presidential-congressional "concurrence" and are useful in identifying fundamental changes in presidential influence in Congress across time.[70] Roll-call votes are a key decision point in the legislative process.[71] Presidents take stands on legislation prioritized by one or both branches, not simply on their own agendas. The president is one of the most important cue givers to members of Congress. A president's public stands communicate an issue's priority status to the White House and signal resolve to legislators.[72]

Figure I.6 shows unambiguously that presidents *do* have a much easier time building support for their legislative stands under single-party control. Across the postwar era, presidents' copartisans supported them an average of 73 percent, with a small standard deviation of just over 6.5 percent. "Party," as Thomas Cronin and Michael Genovese posit, "is a bridge linking the institutional divide between the president and Congress."[73] Presidents' policy preferences are inherently ideological. The president's copartisans thus are far more likely to share his policy goals and be positioned closer to him in ideological terms than opposition members. Although legislative support and success on roll calls are not synonymous, they are interrelated dynamics. Under unified government, stronger consistent support will translate into high success on floor outcomes. Presidents can also enlist the aid of party leaders to shore up support for their legislative stands and agenda and use procedural levers governing debate, amendments, and the timing of votes.[74] They can also employ the extended leadership organization, such as the whip office, to verify members' positions and engage in partisan lobbying.[75] Presidents can maximize these advantages of party control with an experienced legislative liaison team.[76]

When the opposition party controls Congress, presidents are left without commensurate procedural and organizational benefits. The absence of these advantages, particularly in light of the centralization of authority in leaders

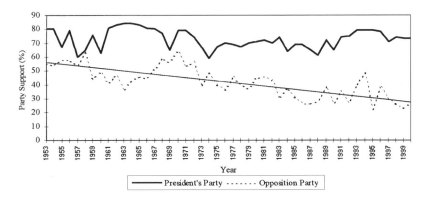

Fig. I.6
Aggregate Party Support for the President's Positions, 1953–2000
Source: *Congressional Quarterly Almanacs* and *Congressional Quarterly Weekly Reports.*

and partisan polarization in the last quarter century, is evident in figure I.6. Support for the president's positions among opposition party members was highly variable, averaging just below 42 percent (with a standard deviation of just over 11 percent) from 1953–2000. The trend line shows the steady decline in opposition support over time ($r = -.73$). Using a 50 percent threshold as a benchmark, Presidents Eisenhower (1953–58), Johnson (1967–68), and Nixon (1969–72) were fairly successful in reaching across the aisle. But in the post-Watergate period (1973–2000) *no president has attracted the opposition party's support in Congress more than half the time.* The data are particularly significant in light of nearly continuous divided government since 1980. Aggregate party support scores for presidents facing an opposition majority in the last two decades of the twentieth century were an average of 11 percent lower compared to the entire postwar period. The Democratic majority supported George Bush's legislative stands only 33 percent of the time from 1989–92. Opposition support reached its nadir when Republicans supported Clinton only 22 percent of the time in 1995. Without vital opposition support, these presidents encountered an onerous set of obstacles to legislative success.

Presidential success on floor outcomes diminished considerably during periods of divided government at the century's end. Figures I.7 and I.8 show

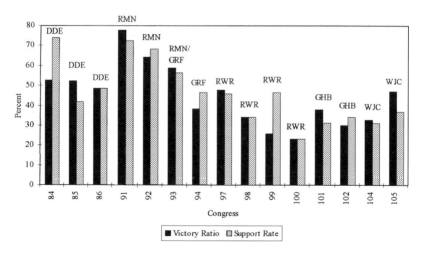

Fig. I.7
Divided Government: Presidential Floor Success and Positions in Support of Legislation, House of Representatives
Source: Calculated by the author from *Congressional Quarterly Almanacs.*

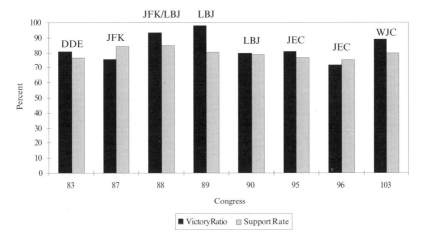

Fig. I.8
Unified Government: Presidential Floor Success and Positions in Support of Legislation,
House of Representatives
Source: Calculated by the author from *Congressional Quarterly Almanacs.*

presidential-congressional concurrence rates on single-issue domestic policy
votes for divided and unified government, respectively.[77] The percentage of
presidents' positions in support of legislation reaching the floor is also reported. The contrast in presidential floor success, and positions in favor of
legislation, is stark between early periods of divided control and the 1980s and
1990s. Presidents Eisenhower and Nixon maintained respectable annual victory ratios of 50–70 percent and higher, and typically supported legislation
that made it to the floor more than half the time. Ronald Reagan's 48 percent
mark in the 97th Congress (1981–82) tops the floor success rates of all presidents who have faced divided government since 1980. Growing ideological
conflict between presidents and opposition majorities, increased party cohesion in Congress, and party leaders' authoritative control over the legislative
agenda took its toll on presidential influence over roll-call outcomes. During
the last two decades, presidents opposed bills reaching the floor far more than
they supported them. By the end of Reagan's second term, he opposed more
than three-quarters of the bills on which he took a stand, and his position carried the day only about a quarter of the time. Similarly, Clinton opposed over
two-thirds of votes taken after the Republicans captured Congress, and his
position prevailed only about a third of the time.

Presidents elected earlier in the postwar era found far more common ground with the opposition majorities they confronted and could maneuver publicly and behind the scenes to build winning policy coalitions for their legislative stands. With the exception of the 85th Congress, Eisenhower favored half or more of bills reaching the floor, and his success rate hovered around 50 percent across six years of sustained split-party control. Nixon's success rate of 78 percent—the highest for any president under divided government—was linked to his support of almost three-quarters of the votes taken in the 91st Congress (1969–70).

Party control of Congress *is* the best predictor of consistently high levels of presidential-congressional agreement. Figure I.8 shows that even when the president's "natural" decline in influence is discounted, presidents under unified government had, without exception, success rates of 70–90 percent. Presidents supported by a partisan majority are better able to influence legislation reaching the floor. On average, presidents expressed their support for 80 percent of the votes on which they took a position in the last half century. As the next section clarifies, this does *not* imply that these presidents universally controlled legislative outcomes or that those outcomes always reflected their independent agendas. Rather, the data highlight the greater mutuality of legislative objectives between the White House and Capitol Hill that single-party control engenders.

Presidential and Congressional Agendas in Political Time: Linkages to Presidential Success

The breadth of presidential and congressional policy objectives, whether such policy objectives are shared or contested between the branches, and the strength of the president's institutional position have important implications for floor success rates and the type of leverage chief executives can ultimately wield over legislative outcomes. Two points deserve immediate elaboration. The first concerns the weaker leverage of Presidents Carter and Clinton compared to their counterparts in earlier periods of unified government. Embedded within the high legislative success and support rates in times of single-party control are important distinctions in presidents' *independent direction* of the legislative agenda and *facilitation* of "historical" or continuing agendas in Congress. Second, the early and later periods of divided control are clearly differentiated by the extent to which the legislative agenda reflected presidential policy priorities. A central feature of divided government in recent decades is the dwindling proportion of the legislative agenda set by presidents as opposed to assertive opposition majorities in Congress. The development

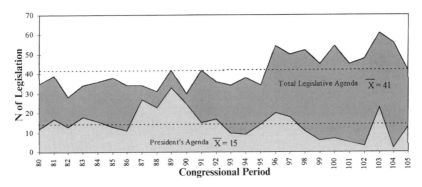

Fig. I.9
Presidential Agenda Setting in Proportion to the Total Legislative Agenda of Congress, 80th–105th Congresses (1947–98)
Source: Adapted by the author from Andrew J. Taylor, "Domestic Agenda Setting, 1947–1994." *Legislative Studies Quarterly* 23 (1998): 373–97.

of a much larger contested agenda driven by the governing majority on Capitol Hill explicates presidents' low floor success rates and steadfast stands *in opposition* to bills reaching the floor since the 1980s.

Figure I.9 shows presidents' agendas in relation to Congress' total agenda. Andrew Taylor supplied the agenda-setting data, which were updated to include the 104th and 105th Congresses.[78] Taylor researched *Congressional Quarterly's* annual listing of "major" legislation on domestic policy alongside presidents' State of the Union addresses and congressional leaders' speeches to determine whether initiatives were linked to the president's agenda or that of the majority party in Congress. The definition of the national legislative agenda is consequently limited to either the president or Congress. To qualify for inclusion, initiatives needed only to receive congressional attention, they did not have to pass.[79]

The data show that Congress plays an essential, if sometimes underestimated, role in setting the national legislative agenda.[80] On average, Congress sets about two-thirds of the total agenda and the president sets the rest. Yet congressional policy activism varied considerably. Presidents Reagan, Bush, and Clinton fixed far less of the agenda compared to Presidents Eisenhower and Nixon under earlier periods of divided control (84th–86th Congresses and 91st and 92d Congresses), and congressional agenda setting increased considerably. In times of unified government, the Kennedy-Johnson years (87th–90th Congresses) were exceptional in terms of agenda setting. Ninety percent or more of the legislative calendar reflected presidential priorities.

Presidents Carter (95th and 96th Congresses) and Clinton (103d Congresses) set much less of the agenda than their copartisans in the majority.

The Kennedy-Johnson period of unified government is clearly unique. Single-party control translated into many more *presidentially led* initiatives compared to any other point since 1947. Much of what was placed on the congressional docket was derived initially from Kennedy's "New Frontier."[81] The subsequent legislative charge was wedded to Johnson's "Great Society." Johnson's electoral resources and the decentralized setting in Congress provided an exceptionally favorable set of circumstances to steer congressional lawmaking toward his policy agenda. The data suggest that Johnson's success rate, and to a lesser extent Kennedy's (fig. I.8), reflected an emphasis on their independent policy objectives.

Carter and Clinton had more limited agendas and struggled to fit them into the congressional calendar. They also faced more independent and internally homogeneous congressional majorities. Both had weak electoral resources and faced periods of economic recession and uncertainty. They shifted attention toward the consolidation of existing programs rather than emphasize grand policy departures, including elements of "historical" or continuing party agendas in Congress.[82] Carter focused on adjusting "Great Society" programs to the realities of federal budget restraints, whereas Clinton championed elements of the Democratic agenda blocked under George Bush, such as family leave, "motor voter" legislation, and gun control. The data convey a fundamental point about the more limited basis for independent policy success in light of these presidents' weaker leverage: Their legislative successes derived much more from lending support to issues that carried over on the congressional docket from earlier years, and their independent objectives often met with controversy and conflict in Congress.

Figure I.9 points to the cementing of a much larger contested policy space as a regular feature of divided government in the last twenty years. One of the central reasons presidents opposed legislation more frequently and lost more consistently on their roll-call stands is that assertive opposition majorities drove the legislative agenda and pursued policies that had little appeal to presidents. Barbara Sinclair explains that "as party polarization increased in the late 1980s and 1990s, so did party leaders' agenda-setting. Furthermore, during the latter years the congressional majority party's agenda became even more clearly a direct challenge to the president's agenda. The Republican agenda in the 104th Congress is the best known example. . . . But the Democratic agenda in the 100th Congress also consisted mostly of items the president opposed, as did the Republicans' agenda in the 105th Congress."[83] It is also the case that recent presidents have not had burgeoning domestic agendas, in part due to economic constraints and their own ideological preferences. Reagan's "activist" first-year agenda in 1981 was aimed at *scaling back* rather than expanding the role of government. After achieving his most important legislative goals in the 97th Congress, Reagan's interest in advancing legislation diminished significantly. George Bush's legislative agenda focused largely on ensuring the continuity of Reagan's legacy by *halting* Democratic proposals rather than promoting new programs.

"Proposing legislation," Wayne Steger reminds us, "gives presidents a means of influencing the legislative process that does not exist when the administration fails to propose legislation."[84] Reagan and Bush found themselves in a much more reactive situation in the legislative realm due to their own limited policy objectives and to congressional Democrats' attempts to fill a perceived agenda gap. Clinton had few electoral resources and was in an inferior institutional position to influence agenda setting in the Republican controlled Congresses from 1995–2000. As chapter 1 shows, these presidents frequently shifted their legislative strategy to mediating, selectively preempting, or fending off the most disagreeable elements of the majority's agenda through vetoes and veto threats.

Interpreting Individual Presidents' Leverage across "Eras of Congress": An Integrative Approach

Presidents must discern what they can and cannot achieve within the temporal boundaries of their term in office.[85] The objective of the framework of presidential leverage in political time is to account for presidential legislative strategy, success, and forms of influence throughout the postwar period. The theoretical foundation emphasizes how presidential leverage has been fundamentally shaped by two predominant factors in the last half century. The first is party control of Congress—unified or divided government. The second is the nature of the electoral context and organizational setting in Congress surrounding party control of national institutions. The framework stresses how the interaction of these factors shaped presidents' agenda-setting capacity, coalition building and legislative success, and the basis for strong, moderate, or weak levels of independent policy success across time.

Attention to broad developments in electoral and institutional politics facilitates classifying modern presidents on the continuum of positive and negative leverage over Congress according to the criteria elaborated earlier in figure I.1. The interplay of the factors stressed by the framework suggests that the postwar period can be broken into distinguishable "eras" marked by decisive turning points. The matrix in figure I.10 simplifies the nexus between party control, presidential electoral resources, institutional dynamics in Congress, and each president's relative "positive" leverage across time.

Borrowing from Roger Davidson's typology of "congressional eras" in the postwar period according to voting alignments and organizational features in Congress, figure I.10 arranges individual presidents' leverage by party control. The classification extends Davidson's typology to include presidents' electoral resources, party cohesion and leadership strength in Congress, incumbency advantage, and agenda magnitude and mutuality between the branches. Presidents' leverage may be grouped within the three distinct eras that define the postwar period. Unified and divided government have occurred within the "bipartisan conservative era" (1947–64), the "liberal activist era" (1965–78), and the "postreform/party-unity era" (1979–2000).[86] The schema underscores the essential point that congressional "time" does not tick on the same clock as presidents' quadrennial terms. Continuity marks voting coalitions and organizational features in Congress. Let us examine the political contexts in which presidents sought to govern under unified and divided conditions across the three eras and the type of leverage—positive and negative—they were able to wield.

The Truman, Eisenhower, and Kennedy presidencies fall into the bipartisan conservative era. The central feature of this period was weak congressional organization and significant variation in presidential coattails. Pervasive intraparty divisions in Congress gave the "conservative coalition" of

	Bipartisan Conservative Era (1947–64)	Liberal Activist (1965–78)	Postreform/ Party-Unity (1979–2000)
Unified Government	*Moderate/High Leverage* Eisenhower (1953–54) *Low Leverage* Truman (1949–52) Kennedy (1961–63)	*Moderate/High Leverage* Johnson (1965–68) *Low Leverage* Carter (1977–78)	*Moderate/High Leverage* N/A *Low Leverage* Carter (1979–80) Clinton (1993–94)
Divided Government	*Moderate/High Leverage* Eisenhower (1955–60) *Low Leverage* Truman (1947–48)	*Moderate/High Leverage* Nixon I (1969–72) *Low Leverage* Nixon II (1973–74) Ford (1974–76)	*Moderate/High Leverage* Reagan I (1981–82) *Low Leverage* Reagan I, II (1983–88) Bush (1989–92) Clinton (1995–2000)

Fig. I.10
"Positive" Presidential Leverage in Political Time: The Eras of Congress

southern Democrats and Republicans the upper hand over policy making. Power and coordination of legislative business generally resided in a cadre of conservative southerners who chaired the committees responsible for fiscal policies. Congress's internal configuration combined with presidents' electoral popularity and the scope of their policy objectives to delimit leverage in the legislative sphere in different ways under unified and divided government.

The import for Democratic presidents under unified government was indisputable in the bipartisan conservative era. "This Capitol Hill regime proved a hostile environment for activist presidents and their ambitious legislative agendas."[87] A strong incumbency advantage allowed southerners to thwart attempts at forceful legislative leadership by Truman and Kennedy, who had expansive agendas. Both presidents fall into the "weak positive leverage" category. Unified government was a tenuous arrangement between activist presidents and an entrenched conservative de facto policy majority that undermined any basis for "party government."

Nor did the period of single-party Republican rule in 1953–54—the only such period from 1945–2000—resemble party government. Dwight Eisenhower had moderate to high leverage based on his coattails and popularity, but chose to intervene selectively in lawmaking. His circumscribed agenda defied the typical FDR model of unified government that Democratic presidents hoped to emulate, but it meshed fairly well with a congressional policymaking environment averse to action and geared toward maintenance of the status quo. The significant policies that emerged were largely a product of the president's priorities and his support for continuing GOP initiatives that had been stifled by years as the minority on Capitol Hill.

The eight years of split-party control in the bipartisan conservative era yielded contrasting experiences between the Democratic Truman and the Republican Eisenhower. Truman had the lowest positive leverage of all presidents in the period—and little veto leverage. Divided government proved a volatile and unique arrangement not repeated in the postwar period. Because he assumed the Oval Office upon Franklin Roosevelt's death, Truman had no electoral resources. He faced an assertive Republican Congress in which the conservative coalition gained near-supermajority status in the midterm elections of 1946. The swelling of the ranks of the conservative coalition in the 80th Congress (1947–48) enabled GOP leaders to trample his vetoes of major legislation on numerous occasions.

The policymaking context for Eisenhower under divided government from 1955–60 proved far more favorable to cross-party coalition-building leverage. Eisenhower sustained moderate to high positive leverage because of his strong electoral resources in 1952 and again in 1956, and because the range of the contested agenda between the branches remained relatively small until the closing years of his second term. Unlike the GOP majority Truman faced in the 80th Congress, the Democratic majority had *not* been relegated to quasi-permanent minority status in prior decades and did *not* regain the majority with an active policy program in 1954. Eisenhower used the combination of his electoral popularity and popular approval to influence policy making on an occasional basis, drawing from different partisan factions to build legislative support.

The liberal activist era from approximately 1965–78 comprised substantial legislative innovation and internal reform in Congress over an extended period. Lyndon's Johnson's landslide electoral victory ushered in the liberal activist era. One of the chief features of the period is that "Legislative activity soared by whatever measure one chooses to apply—bills introduced, hearings, reports, hours in session, floor amendments, recorded floor votes, and measures passed."[88] This era spanned the presidencies of Lyndon Johnson, Richard Nixon, Gerald Ford, and a portion of Jimmy Carter's term, with presidential leverage varying rather significantly.

The Johnson and Carter experiences under unified government are contrasting cases of positive presidential leverage in this era. Lyndon Johnson's decisive defeat of Barry Goldwater in 1964 set the stage for considerable executive-legislative synergy on the "Great Society." Johnson's strong coattails enhanced his institutional position to take charge of a decentralized Congress that turned to him for policy leadership. He possessed what neither Truman nor Kennedy had: a working legislative majority of liberal Democrats in Congress, many of whom owed their electoral victories to his coattails. By contrast, Jimmy Carter came to the White House with exceedingly weak electoral resources. His "outsider" campaign created a tenuous electoral connection to the Democratic majority. Moreover, Congress's internal organization and mood were hardly conducive to strong deference to the president after eight years of combative relations with President's Nixon and Ford. Carter had a much more limited basis for independent policy success.

The incidence of split-party control in the liberal activist era presents a somewhat anomalous set of circumstances. "Nixon may have been a conservative president," Davidson observes, "but the legislative record compiled during his administration was expansive and liberal."[89] Nixon's floor success rate was high and his support of legislation strong (fig. I.7). This enigmatic finding continues to leave scholars in search of a satisfactory explanation.[90] His high floor success rate is somewhat deceptive, however, as it depended upon a willingness to collaborate with Democrats and make changes at the margins of legislation. Nixon did not have the requisite electoral resources to halt the Democrats' march on the domestic front following his narrow victory in 1968. But the fluidity of legislative coalitions during this period did create limited opportunities to build some support for his legislative stands. Nixon's first term fits uncomfortably between the opposite poles of a shared and contested agenda between the branches, although further analysis reveals clearly that his preferred agenda did not drive the legislative charge in Congress. His "moderate to high" leverage over Congress in his first term thus requires qualification.

Nixon's positive leverage dwindled to low levels by his second term, which was truncated by Watergate and the certainty of impeachment that forced his resignation. His rather imperious tactics to halt policy activism by the majority rekindled the Democrats' desire for a stronger leadership organization. A series of institutional reforms centralized authority in party leaders in order to combat the executive threat to the consolidation of the Great Society. It was into this environment that Gerald Ford was thrust in 1974. Unelected, Ford had no electoral resources with which to persuade Congress. Often unable to build viable legislative coalitions, Ford turned to the veto power as a legislative strategy.[91] However, low party cohesion, broad policy coalitions in Congress, and constituency pressures on GOP members to address growing economic problems made it difficult to retain his fragile minority based on override challenges.

Nearly sustained divided control has defined the postreform/party-unity era. The structure of divided government has varied, pitting Republican presidents Reagan and Bush against a Democratic Congress, while Democratic president Clinton faced a Republican Congress for six years. The common feature of the period is the rise of the contested agenda between the branches, scarce fiscal resources, and far lower positive presidential leverage to persuade the opposition majority—Reagan's first two years notwithstanding. Reagan, unlike Bush and Clinton, had strong electoral resources upon his victory in 1980 and faced Congress at a critical juncture. The last strong appearance of the conservative coalition in the closing decades of the century enabled Reagan to forge narrow majority support for his early agenda. Yet, just as Democrats responded to Nixon's threat to the party agenda in the 1970s with leadership reforms, a resurgent liberal majority vowed to minimize Reagan's influence in subsequent years. Stronger congressional leadership coordination followed Reagan's first term, and his positive leverage declined dramatically. Weak coattails for his successors and the continuation of strong, well-organized governing majorities in Congress seriously hamstrung Bush's and Clinton's cross-party coalition-building potential. Frequently thwarted in their bid to influence the congressional agenda or build support for their own policy preferences, the defensive politics of vetoes came to play a central role in their experiences with split-party control. Bush and Clinton had a stronger foundation, then, for partisan coalition building and veto leverage.

Two brief years of unified government intervened in the postreform/party-unity period with Bill Clinton's election in 1992, and far greater agenda synergy developed between Clinton and the Democratic Congress. Yet Clinton's electoral victory by a plurality yielded weak leverage to direct congressional lawmaking. The return to unified government did not represent an electoral legitimization of Clinton's agenda, and Congress's institutional setting was far more centralized than in prior eras. The constant battles of nearly twelve years with a Republican president in the White House had strengthened the Democrats' independent policy-making capacity. The context of unified government was better suited to the president's facilitation of more modest and shared goals with the governing majority. Some of Clinton's most notable successes, from social policy to international trade, were on legislative items linked to Congress's carryover agenda.[92]

The classification in figure I.10 places into sharp relief the unequal impact of party control of Congress for presidential leverage across "eras" in the last half century. The framework of presidential leverage in political time elaborated in this chapter has laid the groundwork for closer analysis in subsequent chapters. This theoretical framework emphasizes how the development of electoral and institutional forces beyond presidents' control has affected legislative strategy, success, and credit claiming.

The Road Ahead: Organization of This Book

Subsequent chapters are organized chronologically around comparative case studies of presidential-congressional relations in the bipartisan conservative, liberal activist, and postreform/party-unity eras. A comparative case study approach surmounts elements of the "small N" problem common in presidency research.[93] The focus on individual presidents across time complements the next chapter's integrative and systematic analysis of aggregate data on presidents' legislative strategy and success.

Chapter 1 applies the theoretical perspective of presidential leverage in political time to floor success rates and types of presidential involvement on nationally significant legislation over the last half century. The chapter also closely examines presidents' use of vetoes and veto threats. The empirical analysis validates the utility of the "eras" perspective in accounting for the considerable variation in presidents' floor success and the *type* of legislative leadership they have been able to exert under unified and divided government. The deconstruction of Mayhew's significant laws reveals that divided government has translated into many more congressionally led policy achievements in the last two decades and frequent use of the veto and veto threats by presidents. The result has been qualitatively different forms of presidential involvement in lawmaking that have changed the dynamics of, and opportunities for, credit claiming. Furthermore, analysis of presidents' agenda leadership and legislative strategy on significant domestic legislation in periods of unified control shows how weaker presidential leverage since the 1970s has entailed a limited basis for presidential direction of congressional lawmaking.

Chapters 2–7 present case studies of presidents' relations with Congress under divided and unified government in each of the three eras. The case studies provide a more in-depth analysis of the nature of presidential involvement in significant legislative outcomes. Additionally, the case studies introduce systematic analysis of individual-level congressional support for the president's legislative positions. The model of legislative support complements the aggregate-level analysis in Chapter 1 by accentuating how electoral and institutional forces, in conjunction with party control of Congress, conditioned presidential leverage.

Chapter 2 explores the contrasting experiences of Truman (1947–48) and Eisenhower (1955–60) under divided government in the bipartisan conservative era. The 80th Congress was one of the more productive periods of divided government, but what passed was largely opposed by Truman or adopted over his objections.[94] By contrast, Eisenhower's limited legislative agenda and moderate positions were more suited to building cross-party support in Congress, and he was largely successful on the legislative front due to his personal influence and electoral popularity.

Chapter 3 takes up the puzzle of Nixon's first term (1969–72) in the liberal activist era. Nixon's position vote success rate is enigmatic in light of the impressive legislative output of the period and the large Democratic majorities in Congress. The chapter shows how Nixon's reelection incentive 1972 prompted him to *cooperate in*—but not necessarily lead—the shifting policy coalitions of which the highly decentralized 91st and 92d Congresses were susceptible.

Chapter 4 details Reagan's bout with divided government (1981–88) in light of a second congressional resurgence and geographic electoral realignment between the parties. Reagan's early policy victories were striking but short-lived. Paradoxically, Reagan's masterful success was the source of his lower positive leverage after 1982. Democratic leadership reforms curtailed his coalition-building potential in Congress, and Reagan set far less of the domestic agenda.

Chapter 5 examines the experiences of George Bush (1989–92) and Bill Clinton (1995–96) under divided government during a period of intense partisan polarization in Congress during the postreform/party-unity era. Although the two had different domestic agendas, Bush and Clinton have the poorest floor success rates in the analysis. Most of the significant legislation originated from the congressional opposition's endeavors, and both presidents wound up opposing much more legislation than they favored. The chapter traces why they resorted to wielding the veto and issuing veto threats to excise the most objectionable provisions from the legislation that emerged from the majority's agenda.

Chapter 6 examines periods of unified government by contrasting the experiences of Kennedy (1961–62) and Johnson (1965–68) in the bipartisan conservative and liberal activist eras, respectively. Although Kennedy faced an entrenched conservative majority in Congress following a narrow electoral victory in 1960, close analysis of his relations with the 87th Congress shows that the limited amount of significant legislation that passed in the two-year period evidenced a direct connection to his activist agenda. Yet, in terms of the quantity and scope of initiatives passed, Lyndon Johnson is the only postwar president whose policy successes approximate the model of FDR's legislative leadership in the domestic policy realm. Analysis of Johnson's term accentuates the importance of a massive electoral victory and strong coattails as factors legitimizing the president's agenda.

Chapter 7 compares the experiences of Jimmy Carter (1977–80) and Bill Clinton (1993–94) under unified government in the late liberal activist period through the postreform/party-unity era. The chapter emphasizes how Carter and Clinton endured trying times in dealing with their congressional majorities. The analysis reveals that the significant domestic legislation passed generally had a direct connection to the president's stated policy objectives. Nonetheless, some of Carter's and Clinton's most notable successes were in support of historical and continuing party objectives in Congress rather than their own independent policy goals. Unified government facilitated proactive presidential leadership, just not to the degree or in the same way that it did for Lyndon Johnson.

Chapter 8 concludes by emphasizing how the framework of presidential leverage in political time helps us to grasp the impact of party control of national institutions on presidential legislative influence and strategy. The chapter reinforces why it is that presidents like Nixon and Bush or Truman and Clinton, who faced similar partisan constellations of divided government, responded differently and employed different strategies of legislative leadership. The chapter also stresses the commonality in the experiences of Kennedy, Carter, and Clinton in terms of a shared agenda between the branches. These Democratic presidents did not profit from the extraordinary convergence of environmental, electoral, and institutional factors that followed Lyndon Johnson to the Oval Office in 2964. The constraints each of these presidents faced across different eras did not yield the type of executive-legislative synergy coveted by responsible party government advocates. At the same time, unified government did furnish many more opportunities for these presidents to reinforce support for a shared party agenda in Congress, engage in joint credit claiming with their congressional copartisans, and lay the groundwork for future policy innovations. The significance of this difference in legislative leadership is not trivial to presidents' policy legacies when compared to the type of influence they have been able to exercise during recent periods of divided government.

1 The Legislative Presidency and Eras of Congress
A Longitudinal Analysis

FROM THE PERSPECTIVE OF POLITICAL TIME, several qualitative changes in presidential leverage are evident in the modern era. First, compared to the early decades following World War II, divided government entailed a considerable decline in presidential-congressional concurrence in the closing decades of the twentieth century. Second, not all periods of single-party control have produced equal opportunity for strong presidential policy leadership and influence over Congress, despite consistently high levels of executive-legislative agreement. Thus, while there are fundamental differences in presidents' leadership potential *between* periods of divided and unified control, there are also important differences *within* periods of single- and split-party control in the bipartisan conservative, liberal activist, and postreform/party-unity eras. The objective of this chapter is to test the impact of these postwar governing contexts on presidential success and explore more fully the implications for legislative leadership and strategy.

The first half of this chapter develops a longitudinal model of presidential floor success in Congress. The analysis shows how party margins and interparty conflict in Congress, mutuality in ideological positions between the president and the congressional majority, and the president's coattails and popular approval have affected position-vote success rates. The model clearly reveals the basis for the more pronounced effect of divided government on the legislative presidency since the 1980s. Presidential and congressional agendas are increasingly less compatible. As presidents and opposition majorities in Congress parted ways on domestic policy objectives, heightened intraparty cohesion and centralization around the leadership weakened positive presidential leverage substantially. Presidents Reagan, Bush, and Clinton had far less freedom to maneuver to build supporting legislative coalitions under divided government in the postreform/party-unity era compared to their predecessors in the bipartisan conservative and liberal activist eras.

The second half of this chapter examines the implications of declining floor success and stronger institutional parties for presidential leadership strategy and involvement in landmark legislation in the three postwar eras. A reexamination of Mayhew's set of innovative laws offers a fresh account of the salience of party control of Congress for the legislative presidency.[1] The analysis connects presidential floor success and agenda setting with the larger question of the *type* of leadership presidents can exert as their electoral resources and institutional position have changed vis-à-vis governing majorities on Capitol Hill.

The striking effect of divided control is unmistakable in the reassessment of Mayhew's laws. As presidential floor success has diminished across eras in times of divided control, so too has the proportion of innovative legislation with linkages to presidents' stated policy objectives. Opportunities for presidents to garner independent policy successes and claim credit for significant legislation became far more restricted in the postreform/party-unity era. Congressional majorities set more of the national policy-making agenda and displaced presidential objectives. Presidents chose between "staying quiet" in the legislative realm or selectively engaging the congressional majority on nationally important legislation.[2] Presidents turned more frequently to veto leverage—from preemptive threats to sending legislation back to Congress—to force opposition majorities to negotiate on the White House's terms. The proportion of Mayhew's laws subject to presidential vetoes and veto threats in the last two decades far exceeds veto use by presidents in the bipartisan conservative and liberal activist eras.

The common feature of unified government across eras is the steadfast connection between Mayhew's significant legislative outcomes and presidents' policy objectives. Just as presidents prevail more regularly on floor outcomes under single-party control, the proportion of significant legislation linked to the president's agenda is high and relatively invariable in the postwar period. The result is that presidents consistently have had more opportunities to claim credit for innovative legislation under single-party control.

Embedded within the rare cases of single-party control in the last half century, however, are important differences in presidential *direction* and *facilitation* of congressional policy making.[3] The longitudinal analysis of floor success and presidential involvement in significant legislation sheds light on nuances in presidents' leverage when single-party control has prevailed. Lyndon Johnson's extraordinarily strong institutional position provided an unparalleled foundation for independent policy success in the liberal activist era. Other Democratic presidents have not been so advantaged. Jimmy Carter and Bill Clinton worked in collaboration with assertive and better-organized congressional majorities in a time of fiscal restraint. In the last quarter century, the character of Democratic presidents' involvement on nationally significant legislation was tied much more to the continuing congressional agenda that had been blocked by their GOP predecessors.

To test the merits of the framework of presidential leverage in political time, this chapter's analysis begins by systematically examining the factors that account for the variation in presidential floor success. The second section surveys the frequency of presidential veto politics to highlight how chief executives have adapted to the new institutional setting of divided government in the postreform/party-unity era. The final section presents a detailed reexamination of presidential involvement in Mayhew's set of innovative legislation from 1947–96. This analysis confirms the consequential yet variable effect of party control for presidential leadership in the postwar era.

Presidential Floor Success and Eras of Congress

Figure 1.1 shows presidential floor success rates for single-issue votes on an annual basis in the House of Representatives. Consistent with the biennial data depicted in the introduction (figs. I.7 and I.8), executive-legislative concurrence is consistently higher in periods of unified government, although time takes a toll. Presidential influence in Congress tends to decline over time.[4] Eisenhower (1953–54), Johnson (1965–68), Carter (1977–80), and Clinton (1993–94) sustained mildly lower success rates following their first year in office, though none dropped below the 70 percent threshold. "Presidents," as Lyn Ragsdale notes, "must build new legislative coalitions among independent partisans for each bill on which they take a position, bill after bill."[5] As their resources for influence decay over time, presidents are likely to limit their position-taking activity to issues of greatest importance to them.[6]

A similar, though less consistent, pattern emerges for presidents faced with divided government. Richard Nixon's success rate was slightly higher his second year in office compared to his first, but then fell in subsequent years. George Bush's success rate, which never surpassed 50 percent, declined steadily throughout his term. Ronald Reagan's yearly success rate soared in 1981, but fell precipitously in 1982 and never recovered. After reaching a nadir in 1995, when the Republicans captured Congress, Clinton's success rate mounted somewhat in the following two years, only to drop again in 1998. The peaks and valleys in Eisenhower's floor success do not adhere to a temporal path.

How much more damaging has divided government been to presidential success since the 1980s compared to the entire postwar period? Table 1.1 presents the results of a time-series regression model of yearly presidential floor

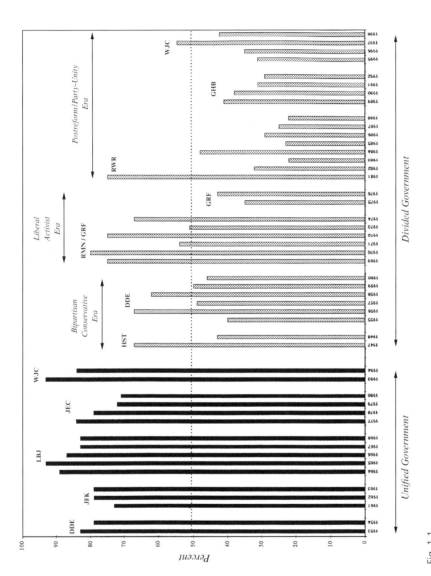

Fig. 1.1
Annual Presidential Floor Success Rates by Party Control, House of Representatives

success rates on annual single-issue votes in the House from 1953–98.[7] This model is purposefully limited in terms of the explanatory variables employed in the analysis. The goal of this simplified model is to capture long-term trends in presidential floor success across the three eras while controlling for presidents' "natural" loss of influence over time. A more elaborate regression model that considers specific electoral and institutional factors follows.

Since presidential influence in Congress is thought to be greatest at the outset of the president's term and progressively diminishes over the course of the administration, year in the president's term (coded 1–8) is included as a control variable in the model.[8] The other three variables are dummy terms for years of divided government within the bipartisan conservative, liberal activist, and postreform/party-unity eras (coded 1 for each year of divided government, 0 otherwise). Because each of the three eras comprises years of unified and divided government, this methodology allows for a comparative assessment of the relative impact of divided control across broad temporal periods.

As time marches on, presidents are apt to watch their success rates diminish by just under 2.4 percent for every year in their term. The model predicts that the success rate of a one-term president will be slightly more than 9 percent lower his fourth year compared to his first year. The data confirm the con-

Table 1.1
Yearly Presidential Success Rates in the House:
The Impact of Divided Government by Era

Variable	B coefficient
Bipartisan Conservative Era × Divided Government (1953–64)	–21.48**** (6.71)
Liberal Activist Era × Divided Government (1965–78)	–21.81**** (4.99)
Postreform/Party-Unity Era × Divided Government (1979–98)	–41.25**** (4.61)
Year in President's Term	–2.37** (1.11)
Constant	86.83**** (3.68)
Number of Cases	46.00
Adjusted R^2	.74
Durbin-Watson	2.05

Coefficients are ordinary least squares (OLS) estimates.
Standard errors are in parentheses.
**** $p < .001$ *** $p < .01$ ** $p < .05$ * $p < .10$ (one-tailed)
The dependent variable is the president's annual, single-issue, yearly roll-call success rate from 1953–98, calculated by the author.

ventional scholarly wisdom about the need for presidents to "hit the ground running" before influence naturally diminishes.[9]

Controlling for the year in a president's term, however, the coefficients for the three eras leave little doubt about the progressively negative impact of divided government on presidential success in Congress. Critical, longer-term forces in the last half of the twentieth century have indeed been at work to undermine presidential-congressional agreement. The constant in the model estimates that a first-year president under unified control would achieve a success rate of 84 percent. The incidence of divided government diminishes that success rate, but in an uneven way across time. Divided control in the bipartisan conservative era under Eisenhower has a comparatively modest effect on presidential success. The model predicts a decline of 21 percent over unified conditions, from 84 to 63 percent. Even when the president's proclivity to lose influence over time is considered, the data forecast a first-term success rate for Eisenhower of well over 50 percent—56–65 percent, to be exact. The impact of divided government in the liberal activist era is scarcely stronger overall. The model forecasts a net decrease in yearly presidential floor success of slightly less than 22 percent compared to unified government. Recalling Nixon's relatively high floor success rate in 1969 and 1970, his expressive support for some elements of the consolidation of the Great Society compensates for Gerald Ford's lower success rate in 1974–76 (fig. 1.1).

The coefficients for the bipartisan conservative and liberal activist periods pale in comparison to recent presidents' experience with divided conditions. The negative impact of split-party control nearly doubles compared to the liberal activist and bipartisan conservative eras. Presidents Reagan, Bush, and Clinton could expect annual success rates to drop by nearly half—41 percent—compared to unified conditions. Combined with the "natural" loss of influence across presidents' terms, the model forecasts success rates of less than 50 percent when divided government prevails in the postreform/party-unity era. Divided government *does* impact upon presidential success. The message of the analysis in table 1.1, however, is that it matters by degree in the modern period.

The dummy variables for the three eras are surrogates for the electoral and institutional developments traced in the last chapter. As such, the coefficients provide only a "stylized" account of the effect of divided government for each broad era and cannot convey underlying contextual forces. An enhanced model of presidential floor success must consider specific factors stressed by the theoretical framework, including the effects of internal party cohesion in Congress, the ideological compatibility in policy goals between the president and the majority party in Congress, and the president's electoral resources and public approval.

The model emphasizes a "multiple perspectives" approach to presidential success.[10] Several of the measures employed in a more elaborate model, including annual levels of party unity and the ideological composition of the governing majority, comport with a "Congress-centered" perspective on presidential success in Congress.[11] The model also tests the president's annual job approval as a resource posited by a "presidency-centered" perspective. Some analysts, including Terry Sullivan, have argued that the president's job approval can prove instrumental early in his term.[12] The model also accents the president's electoral resources as a factor in legislative success. A search of the quantitative literature on presidential-congressional relations fails to uncover models that fully consider presidents' coattails and electoral popularity, although several studies take note of their importance.[13] Let us detail the rationale for the measures and how they pertain to the core theoretical argument.

The three variables that tap the features of the internal setting in Congress include the seat margin between the parties in Congress, the yearly percentage of partisan votes in Congress, and the president's ideological placement relative to the governing majority. The coding of the seat margin variable is the number of seats for the president's party minus the number of seats for the opposition party. A surplus of seats for the president's party (unified government) is coded positively; a deficit of seats for the president's party (divided government) is coded negatively. While a partisan majority should enhance a president's success rate, the expectation is that the seat margin should matter most to presidents when there is a significant imbalance. For example, the dearth of Republicans Ford confronted in the 94th Congress (1975–76), and the significant working majority of Democrats for Lyndon Johnson in the 89th Congress, should have had a dramatic impact on presidential success.

The framework of presidential leverage in political time contends that it is the interaction of institutional features of Congress—such as party cohesion and the overlap in presidential-congressional ideological positions—that should carry a stronger effect on presidents' success rates than party balance, per se. As the Introduction documented, party-unity in Congress varied widely across the postwar period. Mounting policy discord in Congress in the closing decades of the century should negatively affect the president's ability to influence legislative outcomes and build cross-party support. The measure of policy conflict internal to Congress is the annual percentage of party-unity votes, defined as those votes that pit a majority or more of one party against a majority of the other party.

Ideological conflict between the president and governing majority in Congress is another key determinant of presidential success. Presidents' legislative preferences are inherently ideological. The closer the president and the majority party are in ideological terms, the greater the likelihood of high presidential success and inter-branch agreement. The challenge is to construct a measure that adequately captures the president's ideological distance from the governing majority, while taking into account the relative homogeneity of preferences in the majority party. The measure of presidential-governing majority ideological distance employed in the model is derived from Poole and Rosenthal's DW-NOMINATE scores. This index of ideology places the president and members of Congress in a common issue space from Eisenhower through Clinton on a scale ranging from +1 to –1 (positive scores indicate conservatism, negative scores liberalism).[14]

Presidents who face a diverse majority are more likely to be able to influence supporting coalitions for their stands under divided control. With unified control, on the other hand, presidents' floor success rates should increase the closer their ideological position is to the mean of their congressional co-partisans. It thus is essential to gauge the president's ideological position relative to the majority party and the consistency in the ideological positions of the governing majority in Congress. A standardized score of the presidents' relative ideological distance from the governing majority was calculated using each president's DW-NOMINATE score and the corresponding average and standard deviation of the score for the majority party. To simplify the measure, the absolute value of the distance was used.[15]

As figure 1.2 illustrates, presidents are consistently positioned much closer to the governing majority in times of unified government. Eisenhower was slightly more moderate than the Republican majority of the 83d Congress (1953–54). Democratic presidents have been somewhat more to the left of their congressional majorities. Reagan's election in 1981 (97th Congress) marks an important upswing in the ideological distance between presidents and the opposition majority that continues into the Bush and Clinton presidencies in the postreform/party-unity era. The growing breach between presidents and the majority opposition parties they have faced is most likely a product of the greater differentiation of the parties' policy positions and a stronger constituency basis to congressional voting. The wider gap in ideological stances between presidents and the opposition majorities should account for a

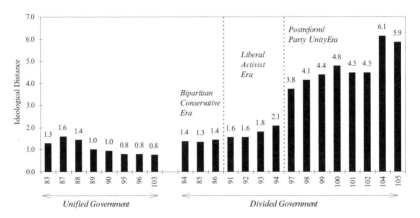

Fig. 1.2
Ideological Distance Scores Between the President and Majority Party in the House of Representatives, by Party Control and Congressional Period
Source: Calculated by the author from the NOMINATE scores in Keith T. Poole and Howard Rosenthal, *Congress: A Political–Economic History of Roll Call Voting.*

considerable share of the declining presidential success rates in the 1980s and 1990s. By contrast, the ideological distance between Presidents Eisenhower, Nixon, and the Democratic majorities in Congress is much less pronounced. This factor should explicate a large share of these presidents' higher success rates in the bipartisan conservative and liberal activist eras.

Coattail effects and the president's average annual job approval rating are integrated in the model to test the effect of resources that may strengthen the president's positive leverage over floor outcomes. Scholarly analyses of the impact of public opinion on presidential success in Congress are decidedly mixed. A number of methodologically sophisticated studies have found that the correlation between presidential fortunes on legislative outcomes and job approval is limited, at best.[16] However, as Brad Lockerbie, Stephen Borelli, and Scott Hedger contend, "if anything, the impact of mass approval should be increasing in recent years as centralized bargaining is no longer possible and members of Congress are increasingly responsive to constituent pressures."[17] This is the message of Samuel Kernell's thesis of presidents' frequent decisions to "go public."[18] Presidents will attempt to marshal grassroots opinion behind their agenda preferences—a task that is easier when their job approval is high. Sullivan finds some evidence that public approval can, in fact, influence members initially not supportive of the president's positions, but the effect is fleeting.[19] While the inclusion of the president's job approval in the model surely cannot resolve this ongoing scholarly debate, higher public approval of a president's job performance should be positively related to presidential success.

Some of the confusion surrounding the impact of public approval on presidential success may stem from a lack of consideration of the electoral context. Public opinion is likely to matter most when conditions in Congress are conducive to a combination of bargaining and going public, especially when the president has stronger electoral resources. This is a difficult set of conditions to tap in an aggregate model of presidential success that relies on yearly averages of job approval. Reagan's skillful control of the legislative agenda in his first term probably best reflects the convergence of these factors in his high success rate in 1981 (see chapter 4).

The decline of presidential coattails and the concomitant rise of incumbency advantage in Congress should disadvantage presidents' success in recent decades. The president's "marginal coattails" among the governing majority are brought to bear in the analysis in order to capture, within the limits of an aggregate model, the import of the electoral context. The data employed include the percentage of legislators in the governing majority whose share of the two-party vote was less than the president's at the district level (fig. I.3). The expectation is that strong coattails and weak incumbency advantage should boost the president's floor success rate. Interaction terms are employed to gauge the effect of coattails in the president's first year and fifth year for two-term presidents. Coattails should have the strongest effect during the president's first-year honeymoon with Congress. Two-term Republican presidents should have less leverage over opposition majorities, despite fairly large electoral victories. The majority opposition has fewer incentives to follow the lead of a "lame duck" in the White House, so legislators may seek to distinguish their policy stances from the administration in anticipation of the next election. Finally, consistent with the previous model, the year in the president's term is employed in order to measure the anticipated decline of influence and success over time.

Table 1.2 presents the results of the detailed time-series regression models of presidential success in the House of Representatives, using the Cochrane-Orcutt method to remove serial correlation. The first equation includes a dummy variable for divided government with controls for the year in the president's term, public approval, and interparty conflict in Congress. The analysis shows that throughout the postwar period, the overall effect of divided government translates into a net decrease of approximately 32 percent in presidents' annual success rates. The passage of each year yields a decrease of just over 2 percent. The simplified model in equation 1 points to heightened

Table 1.2
Institutional and Electoral Factors:
Yearly Presidential Success Rates in the House of Representatives, 1953–98

Variable	Equation 1 B Coefficient	Equation 2 B Coefficient
Seat Margin for the President's Party[a]	———	.11**** (.02)
Ideological Distance between the President and the Governing Majority	———	−5.76**** (1.12)
President's Marginal Coattails in the Governing Majority × First Year	———	.29** (.17)
President's Marginal Coattails in the Governing Majority × Fifth Year (Two-Term Presidents)	———	−.34* (.24)
Divided Government (1=yes, 0=no)	−31.75**** (4.61)	———
Year in President's Term	−2.07** (1.04)	−1.47* (.89)
Yearly Party-Unity Votes	−.71**** (.18)	−.30** (.16)
President's Annual Public Approval	.35** (.18)	.13 (.14)
Constant	99.02**** (13.85)	84.61**** (9.65)
Number of Cases	45.00	46.00
Adjusted R^2	.67	.82
Durbin-Watson	1.35	1.99
Durbin *h* (after correction for serial correlation)	1.95	———
Rho	.36	———

**** $p < .001$ *** $p < .01$ ** $p < .05$ * $p < .10$ (one-tailed)
Entries for equation 1 are Cochrane-Orcutt iterated estimates.
Entries for equation 2 are ordinary least squares (OLS) regression estimates.
Standard errors are in parentheses.
The dependent variable is the president's annual, single-issue yearly roll-call success rate from 1953–98.
[a] The seat-margin data were coded positive (+) for unified government and negative (−) for divided government.

internal conflict in Congress as a key factor in the more pronounced impact of split-party control on legislative success in the postreform/party-unity era. Each 4 percent increase in party-unity votes reduces annual success rates by 3 percent. As partisan voting in Congress mounted from annual averages of 40 or 50 percent in the bipartisan conservative and liberal activist eras to 60 and 70 percent in the postreform/party-unity era, presidents' success rates were a casualty. The president's job approval rating has little mitigating effect. As the president's approval rises from 50 to 60 percent, the estimated increase in success is only 3.5 percent.

The more complex model in equation 2 taps how the fusion of the institutional setting within Congress and the president's ideological proximity to the governing majority most heavily conditions levels of success across eras. Partisan conflict within Congress and clashing policy objectives between the branches—not the lack of party control per se—have been responsible for the precipitous decline in presidential success in the postreform/party-unity era. Equation 2 brings to bear the seat margin of the president's party in Congress, the ideological distance between the president and the governing majority, and the president's marginal coattails. All told, the model accounts for 82 percent of the variance in presidential success in the House of Representatives.[20]

The House seat margin for the president's party is a more subtle measure of the net effect of party control for presidential success. While party balance in Congress is a statistically significant predictor of annual presidential victory rates, it has only marginal *substantive* impact. A nine-seat majority increases presidential success by only one percentage point. Seat margin matters most when there is a significant imbalance between the parties under unified or divided control. Of the presidents operating under unified government since World War II, Lyndon Johnson benefited most from Democratic strength in the House. The model predicts that the 155-seat majority in 1965 bolstered Johnson's annual success rate by over 17 percent. Several presidents have faced a substantial paucity of partisan strength under divided conditions. Eisenhower (1959–60), Ford (1975–76), and Reagan (1983–84) faced opposition majorities with surpluses of 100–130 seats. The model estimates that such seat deficits drive down annual success rates from 11–13 percent.

Party balance itself cannot explain the dramatic decrease in presidential success in recent decades. Reagan was the last president to confront an opposition party with a margin of a hundred seats or better. As the parties have become more competitive in the electorate, however, party seat margins in the House have narrowed. This development did not aid recent presidents because the opposition majorities they faced were more internally cohesive and more firmly in control of the legislative calendar. Clinton, for example, squared off against a Republican majority with a thirty-nine-seat margin in the 104th Congress (1995–96), which diminished to just a ten-seat margin in the 105th Congress (1997–98). The model predicts that a nine-seat deficit alone would decrease the president's annual victory ratio by about 1 percent. Yet Clinton's success rate was a paltry 54 percent in 1997 and 42 percent in 1998. Clinton's predecessors operating under divided government faced much larger opposition majorities but maintained higher success rates. Eisenhower, for example, faced a shortfall of 120 seats but achieved a success rate in 1959 and 1960 of 56 and 53 percent, respectively. Gerald Ford began the 94th Congress with a 145-seat deficit and was the most disadvantaged president in the model in terms of numerical partisan strength, yet his success rate in 1975–76 never sank to Clinton's low of 31 percent in 1995.

The results stress that party balance does not matter nearly as much as ideological compatibility between the president and the governing majority. This critical variable explains a large share of the variation in presidential success under divided government across time. If divided government seemed less consequential to Eisenhower or even Nixon in his first term, it is because of the modest ideological distance between these presidents and the opposition majorities they faced and the greater heterogeneity in preferences in the governing majority. The regional divide among Democrats in the 1950s yielded a wide diversity in ideological positions in Congress. Eisenhower was positioned about 1.4 standard deviations to right of the Democratic Party mean from 1955–60. The model forecasts a net decrease in Eisenhower's success rate of about 8 percent based on his ideological position from the majority. Similarly, the ideological diversity in the Democratic majority and Nixon's moderate stances did not entail a substantial decline in presidential success. Nixon's position of 1.6 deviations from the Democratic mean translates into a predicted annual decrease of just over 9 percent.

The ideological breach between presidents and governing majorities under divided conditions in the postreform/party-unity era is the principal culprit in declining success rates. At the beginning of Reagan's first term, the president was positioned 3.8 deviations from the Democratic Party mean. By the end of his second term, the gap had grown a full standard deviation as the Democratic base in Congress became more internally homogenous (fig. 1.2). The regression model predicts a steady loss in legislative success for Reagan, ranging from about 22 percent in the 97th Congress (1981–82) to 28 percent by the 100th Congress (1987–88), based on the presidential-governing majority ideological distance.

The ideological distance between postwar presidents and opposition majorities reached a zenith in the 104th Congress. Clinton was positioned a full 6.1 deviations from the mean position of GOP legislators. The model estimates a net loss for Clinton's annual success rate of over 35 percent—*nearly four times the impact for Eisenhower under divided government.* Clearly, the ideological divide between Clinton and the Republican majority—long relegated to the minority in the postwar era—was the chief cause of his dismal success rate in 1995 and beyond.

The regression model reiterates that it is not the incidence of divided government per se, or even the magnitude of seat margin deficit, that is a bane to presidential success. Rather, it is the lack of mutuality in ideological preferences between presidents and governing majorities in the postreform/party-unity era that distinguishes presidential-congressional relations in this period from others. To argue that divided government is irrelevant to national policy making, or that it is somehow an unimportant "analytical category," is to overlook the severe burden split-party control now imposes on our chief executives' ability to construct supporting coalitions.[21]

Unified control yields consistently stronger ideological compatibility between presidents and the governing majority across time. All Democratic presidents under unified government have been to the left of the governing majorities they faced in Congress, but the gap has narrowed in the most recent instances of single-party control. Kennedy was the furthest from his party base, some 1.6 deviations to the left—twice as far as Carter and Clinton. The model anticipates a net decrease in Kennedy's success rate of about 9 percent. From this perspective, Kennedy was the most disadvantaged of Democratic presidents, struggling as he did to shake a seemingly immovable and entrenched southern conservative wing of the party. Interestingly only Eisenhower, in the single instance of unified Republican control in the last half a century, was nearly as far from his governing majority in Congress. The GOP began with only a four-seat margin in the House in 1953–54, and Eisenhower was 1.3 standard deviations *to the left* of the Republican majority. If party control of Congress seemed to matter less in the 1950s, it is because "Ike's" moderate stances and diversity in the ideological preferences in the ranks of both parties—regardless of partisan control of Congress—typically curbed strong interbranch friction across his two terms, with only occasional bumps along the path such as the economic recession in 1957 and somewhat heightened Democratic activism in the 86th Congress.

Policy conflict within Congress continues to have a spillover effect on presidential success rates in the more elaborate model. The percent of yearly party-unity votes is negatively related to presidential success. However, the substantive impact decreases by over half compared to the simplified model when the ideological distance between the president and the majority party is included. Each increase of 1 percent in the level of party unity diminishes presidential success by 3.4 percent. Presidents in the postreform/party-unity era have been most disadvantaged by the rise in party cohesion. Not only did the ideological divide between presidents and the majority oppositions they faced cause success rates to plummet, but internal conflict in Congress further injured their bids to forge cross-party support.

Heightened interparty conflict may also increase the cross-pressures on members of the president's party and complicate the president's task of constructing supporting coalitions under unified government. Clinton, for example, was somewhat more disadvantaged under unified conditions compared to his Democratic predecessors. Party unity ranged from 65 percent in 1993 to 67 percent in 1994. This level of interparty conflict compares to a high of 55 percent in 1965 to a low of 35 percent in 1968 for Lyndon Johnson, and cohesion levels never surpassed 47 percent during Carter's term. When the congressional minority is intransigent in its resistance to the president's policy preferences, media and constituency attention to controversial legislative issues is likely to cause internal cleavages in the governing majority. Clinton's difficulty in winning support for his economic stimulus package and associated tax increases in 1993, and the Republicans' steadfast opposition to those proposals, serve as a pointed example.

Coattails and public approval enhance presidential success, although the decline of presidential-congressional electoral linkages and the near-permanence of divided government have diminished the impact of these vital resources for recent presidents. Coattails are most important in the president's first year. Running ahead of 10 percent of governing majority's members yields a net increase of about 3 percent in annual success rates. The stronger the president's coattails, the stronger is his capacity to prevail on floor outcomes. The model confirms that Eisenhower and Johnson profited the most from strong coattails under unified government in the bipartisan conservative and liberal activist eras. Eisenhower ran ahead of just over half of Republicans elected to the 83d Congress, a figure that boosts his expected first-year success rate by an estimated 14.5 percent. Johnson ran ahead of 43 percent of Democrats elected in 1965, yielding an anticipated increase of about 12.5 percent in his first-year success rate. As later sections in this chapter make clear, Johnson made the most of his coattails to push an expansive agenda of innovative legislation with long-term policy impacts. Eisenhower had much more limited policy objectives and shunned offering a legislative program to Congress in 1953.

The evaporation of coattails and the rise of incumbency advantage have disadvantaged other presidents in the postwar era. Kennedy ran ahead of only 8 percent of Democrats elected in 1960, due in large part to southerners' lack of electoral vulnerability and the extremely close presidential contest. No president since Johnson has run ahead of more than 20 percent of the governing majority in Congress. In sum, since Nixon's election in 1968, marginal coattails have increased presidents' success rates by no more than 5 percent. The data confirm the importance of making the most of coattail effects in a president's first year in office. Two-term presidents do not derive leverage over the congressional majority based on their second electoral showing. Indeed, their coattails are *negatively* related to legislative success at the beginning of a second term and lame duck status. The model predicts that running ahead of 10 percent of the membership of the governing majority yields a net decrease in the president's fifth year success rate of just over 3 percent.

The impact of public approval in the simple model vanishes when ideological positions between the president and the majority party are included. The detailed model, on the other hand, forecasts that the difference in the annual victory rate for the extremes in presidents' job approval ratings from 1953–98—Eisenhower's average of 78 percent approval in 1955 and Bush's average of 40 percent in 1992—is less than 5 percent. To borrow from Edwards's characterization, public approval is "at the margins" of presidential legislative success in the aggregate.[22] When it matters most is early in the president's term, and in conjunction with the president's electoral resources and the policy context of the election.[23]

The model stresses that presidents are unlikely to garner substantially higher success rates based on their attempts to manipulate public approval trends. Public evaluations have much to do with fluctuating economic trends over which presidents have little influence.[24] As Paul Brace and Barbara Hinckley explain, "People apparently do not respond to their own personal hardships or well-being but judge the national economy and the president's ability to cope with these national problems."[25] The Bush and Clinton experiences are cases in point. Some observers charged that George Bush failed to utilize his high public approval, which approached 90 percent at the end of the Gulf War, to advance a domestic legislative agenda. But Bush's ephemerally high public approval had little ostensible impact on his legislative success rate, which languished well below 50 percent for the duration of his term. Clinton, benefiting from robust economic growth, won reelection handily in 1996, and his average annual job approval ranged between 57 percent in 1997 and 66 percent in 1998. Yet this high level of approval did little for his floor success rate.

The time-series models in table 1.2 accent how institutional and electoral changes that culminated in the postreform/party-unity era have militated against the type of coalition building in which presidents once more routinely engaged in early decades of the modern era. The data clarify that a stronger constituency basis to congressional voting, presidents' weak electoral resources, and the considerable gap in ideological preferences between presidents and the opposition majorities they faced were countervailing forces that limited their legislative success.

Political Time and Presidential Success in the Senate

The discussion and data analysis of the impact of divided government on presidential success in Congress has been simplified by focusing on the House of Representatives. The framework of presidential leverage is not, however, solely applicable to the lower chamber. The factors posited by the perspective of political time weigh in similar fashion on presidents' success rates in the Senate.

There are important contrasts in structural features between the House and Senate. "Process partisanship" is weaker in the Senate compared to the House because of the individualistic nature of the upper chamber. Leaders cannot set rules governing floor debate without unanimous consent. Other antimajoritarian features of the Senate, including the filibuster (unlimited debate) and nongermane amendments, render strong party leadership much more problematic compared to the House.[26]

Yet the forces of change that have resulted in centralization and a rise of partisanship in the House in recent decades also affected internal dynamics in the Senate to disadvantage presidential success more heavily in the post-reform/party-unity era. "There is little question," Burdett Loomis writes, "that the Senate has grown more partisan since the 1970s, under Democratic and Republican regimes alike."[27] The proportion of party-unity votes has risen more slowly than in the House, but intraparty cohesion reached new heights by the 1990s. Sixty-nine percent of recorded votes in the Senate in 1995 pitted a majority of Republicans against a majority of Democrats, the high-water mark of unity since 1954.[28] The Senate has also witnessed an incremental transformation of the role of party leaders and expectations of leaders by their copartisans.[29] More assertive, partisan leaders in the Senate in recent decades, including George Mitchell, Bob Dole, Trent Lott, and Tom Daschle have not removed the essential facets of individualism in the upper chamber, and majority and minority leaders have continued to play visible and central roles in managing legislative affairs. Finally, competition in the electorate has narrowed party margins in the Senate as in the House. The ideological divide between presidents and the majority opposition has widened for the Senate under divided government in a fashion similar to the lower chamber.

The central claims of the perspective of presidential leverage in political time are borne out in a time-series analysis of presidents' floor success in the Senate using single-issue annual domestic policy votes. To maintain consistency with the House data, cloture votes and nominations were excluded in

Table 1.3
Divided Government and the Senate:
Yearly Presidential Success Rates, 1953–98

Variable	Equation 1 B Coefficient	Equation 2 B Coefficient
Seat Margin for the President's Party[a]	———	.007**** (.002)
Ideological Distance between the President and the Governing Majority	———	–2.55* (1.87)
Divided Government (1=yes, 0=no)	–30.16**** (4.96)	———
Year in President's Term	–1.45 (1.26)	–1.31 (1.30)
Yearly Party-Unity Votes	–.128 (.257)	.098 (.271)
President's Annual Public Approval	.002 (.002)	.001 (.002)
Constant	78.11**** (17.93)	61.02**** (18.62)
Number of Cases	46.00	46.00
Adjusted R^2	.53	.51
Durbin-Watson	1.94	1.94

**** p < .001   *** p < .01   ** p < .05   * p < .10 (one-tailed)
Entries are ordinary least squares (OLS) regression estimates.
Standard errors are in parentheses.
The dependent variable is the president's annual, single-issue yearly roll-call success rate from 1953–98.
[a] The seat-margin data were coded positive (+) for unified government and negative (–) for divided government.

the calculation of the aggregate annual success scores. In the simplified model in equation 1, the net impact of divided government on presidential success over the whole of the postwar period is commensurate with the House. Table 1.3 shows that the incidence of opposition control of the Senate diminishes annual success rates by just over 30 percent. Year in term, public opinion, and interparty conflict do not reach statistical significance, although each coefficient is signed in the expected direction. One may surmise that the more insular nature of the Senate stemming from less frequent elections and longer terms may downplay the importance of the president's public approval and year in term.[30]

Divided government has had a stronger impact on presidential success in the Senate in recent decades for reasons consistent with the House analysis. The more elaborate model in equation 2 substitutes the seat margin of the president's party for the divided government dummy. The model also includes the ideological distance between the president and the majority, using DW-NOMINATE scores and the same calculation used in the House model.

Table 1.3 shows that seat margin matters, but it has a weak substantive effect. Each increase of three seats for the president's party augments annual success by just under 2 percent. Given the size of the Senate membership relative to the House, the effect is roughly equivalent in absolute terms. Presidents have been advantaged or disadvantaged only when there has been a significant imbalance in party strength. The model predicts that the Democrats' thirty-eight-seat edge over Republicans in the 89th Congress boosted President Johnson's success rate by nearly 25 percent. Since 1981, however, neither party has held more than an eleven-seat margin in the Senate.

As in the House of Representatives, it is the growth of the ideological divide between presidents and the majority opposition that has had the most damning effect on recent presidents' success rates. In the bipartisan conservative and liberal activist eras, Presidents Eisenhower, Nixon, and Ford were no more than 2.8 absolute deviations from the Democratic Party mean under divided government. Eisenhower's position is about average for the three presidents. In 1959–60 he was 2.2 deviations from the mean of the Democratic 86th Congress—a distance predicted to decrease presidential success by only about 6 percent. The developing breach in presidential and congressional policy preferences across eras left an indelible imprint on presidential success in the Senate in the postreform/party-unity era. For each case of divided control that has occurred from 1987–98, presidents were positioned between 4.5 and 5.4 deviations from the mean of the majority opposition.[31] Although Reagan was slightly to the right of his GOP majority in the Senate in 1985–86 (less than 1 deviation), when Democrats recaptured the upper chamber in 1987 he found himself some 4.6 deviations from the new majority. The model forecasts a drop in his annual success rate of over 12.5 percent. The high-water mark for ideological conflict between the branches was George Bush's term. Bush was 5.4 deviations from the activist Democratic majority in the Senate, a figure that decreased his predicted success rate by just under 14 percent. Consistent with the House model, presidents' public approval has no significant effect on aggregate annual success rates.

Institutional factors play a larger role in shaping presidential success on floor outcomes. The more elaborate model in table 1.3 underscores that dynamics similar to those in the House underlay the decline in presidential success rates in the Senate in recent decades. Opposition control of the upper chamber, combined with the lack of overlapping ideological preferences between the branches, has brought the expected rate of presidential success to well below the 50 percent threshold in the postreform/party-unity era.

The application of a political time approach to presidential floor success has clarified the key factors weighing on executive-legislative concurrence in the postwar period, whether the House or the Senate is the focus. Governing contexts surrounding party control account very well for the dramatic variation in presidential floor success. The analysis affirms why divided government has *not* had a uniform effect on presidential success. The lack of consonance in the ideological positions of presidents and governing majorities, heightened internal conflict within Congress, and the dearth of presidential electoral resources stress the extent to which the basic features of split-party control in the postreform/party-unity era are unique from the perspective of political time.

Presidential Adaptation to the New Era of Divided Government: Veto Leverage

Surely the formidable constraints on recent presidents under divided government are evident from the analysis of floor success rates over time. Presidents with weak coalition-building leverage have thus turned to veto leverage to influence legislative outcomes. They have opted for selective intervention in the legislative realm and exercised persuasion through postpassage veto politics or veto threats. Narrowed seat margins in Congress and the greater ability to sustain unity in the ranks of their copartisans give presidents a powerful tool in the form of vetoes and veto threats.

Table 1.4 extends Sinclair's cataloguing of veto threats on major legislation (as defined by *Congressional Quarterly*) for selected periods of divided government dating to the 1950s.[32] Arranging the congressional periods by era, the use of veto threats as a bargaining tool is a far more frequent phenomenon in the postreform/party-unity era. Presidents had less cause to rely heavily on veto politics in the bipartisan conservative and liberal activist eras because they could often fashion cross-party support. The lack of veto threats fits very well with the time-series analysis of annual presidential roll-call success rates. Eisenhower, for example, rarely issued veto threats in the period of extended divided government from 1955–60 during which his floor success rate exceeded or hovered around 50 percent.

Nixon used veto threats more frequently in the beginning years of his first and second terms to win compromises from the activist Democratic Congresses he confronted. But Nixon's was a highly varied legislative strategy reflective of the governing context of the liberal activist era. He employed a mixed bag of tactics ranging from support of the congressional agenda to veto threats

Table 1.4
**Veto Threats and Vetoes Cast on Major Legislation,
Selected Periods of Divided Government**

Era	Congress	President	Veto Threats	Vetoes*
Bipartisan Conservative	84th	Eisenhower	0%	0
	85th	Eisenhower	3%	3
	86th	Eisenhower	0%	3
Liberal Activist	91st	Nixon	14%	5
	92d	Nixon	1%	4
	93d	Nixon/Ford	21%	4
	94th	Ford	1%	8
Postreform/Party-Unity	97th	Reagan	23%	4
	99th	Reagan	<1%	2
	101st	Bush	52%	9
	104th	Clinton	60%	10
	105th	Clinton	69%	5

* Pocket vetoes excluded.
Source: Data for the 91st, 97th, 101st, 104th, and 105th Congresses are from Barbara Sinclair, "Hostile Partners: The President, Congress, and Lawmaking in the Partisan 1990s," in *Polarized Politics: Congress and the President in a Partisan Era,* ed. Jon R. Bond and Richard Fleisher; data for all other years were researched by the author using *Congressional Quarterly* bill histories.

in his first term. After his reelection, however, he chose outright confrontation with the Democratic majority through the heavy-handed impoundment of appropriated funds for domestic programs. The essential point here is that the shifting legislative coalitions he confronted in his first term precluded the need for a reliance on veto threats because he was frequently able to draw advantage from cross-party alliances in Congress.

Reagan also did not use the veto power excessively. He threatened to veto roughly a quarter of the major bills under congressional consideration in his first two years. Like Nixon, Reagan employed a mixed strategy. He focused on excising disagreeable provisions of legislation and employed veto threats as a means of shaping the policy debate. At the same time, he was better placed to influence floor outcomes than would be the case later in his term or for his successors, Bush or Clinton, because of the greater ideological heterogeneity in the opposition majority and his strong electoral victory in 1980.

What distinguishes the Bush/Clinton experiences under divided government is the rather remarkable growth on the reliance of veto threats *as a general legislative strategy.* Bush threatened vetoes on over half of the major legislation considered in his first two years in office. Clinton used veto threats on three-fifths and over two-thirds of legislation in the 104th and 105th Congresses, respectively. The dependence on negative leverage is unquestionably a product of the opposition majority's seizure of the legislative agenda and restrictive procedures that minimized the ability of the president and the minority party in Congress to influence roll-call outcomes. With far fewer opportunities to craft supporting coalitions for their stands, presidents came full circle to rely on veto threats as *an alternative mode of influence* in the late 1980s and 1990s.

It is important to note that the actual number of vetoes cast shows no consistent pattern of increase in the Bush and Clinton periods. As Barbara Sinclair notes, "Often the purpose of a veto threat is not to kill the legislation, but to extract concessions from an opposition majority that has major policy differences with the president but lacks the strength to override his vetoes."[33] Such a legislative strategy, in other words, constitutes presidents' adaptation to the new landscape of institutional politics in Congress. They have turned narrow party margins and intraparty cohesion to their advantage. A president's application of veto leverage today reflects a very different form of legislative influence than earlier chief executives were typically able to exercise.

Divided government in recent decades has redefined the connotation of presidential legislative leadership. Split-party control has altered the means by which presidents seek to negotiate the national legislative agenda. While a president's veto leverage is aimed at "reframing" the legislative debate and setting limits on acceptable outcomes, it inverts the traditional expectation that "the president proposes and the Congress disposes." Credit-claiming opportunities are arguably much more difficult to achieve and require a good bit of creativity. Presidents must attempt to make the case to voters that they have ameliorated legislation that is derived far less regularly from their own set of policy objectives than from the opposition majority's agenda. Alternatively, presidents may simply choose to "stay quiet" and not draw public attention to legislation passed by opposition majorities. Either way, presidents face a "tough sell" to voters, and frequently to their own congressional copartisans, in the bid to claim credit for significant domestic policies.

Significant Legislation, Party Control, and Presidential Leverage in Political Time

Consolidating our understanding of the impact of party control on the legislative presidency necessitates an integrative approach that moves beyond roll-call analysis. The regression analyses presented in the first half of this chapter validated the utility of the eras framework for explaining the considerable decline in presidential-congressional agreement in episodes of divided government at century's end. The growth of veto threats under divided government in the postreform/party-unity era further points to a transformation of presidential legislative strategy in light of new constraints presidents confront in the legislative sphere. There is also an important distinction in the degree to which presidents under unified conditions have been able to direct or manage the shared agenda with Congress that deserves closer scrutiny.

The final step in testing the merits of the eras approach to presidential leverage calls for a different methodology that complements roll-call analysis and taps subtle variations in the form of legislative leadership that presidents have been able to exert in times of both unified *and* divided control. Of paramount interest is not only the overlap of significant legislation with presidents' policy objectives but also the degree to which presidents support, oppose, threaten to veto, or stay quiet on major initiatives that emanate from the congressional agenda. A reexamination of Mayhew's set of innovative laws melds the focus on agenda setting between the branches, floor outcomes, and presidential strategy. Mayhew's collection of important laws provides a nearly ideal list of legislation to test the effect of party control on the legislative presidency. Using historical sweeps of newspaper and scholarly accounts of legislation that general observers and specialists retroactively regard as having significant and lasting impacts on public policy, Mayhew assembled more than three hundred laws from 1947–96. His authoritative study is a basic reference point in discussions of divided government.

The rationale for a reexamination of presidential involvement on these "landmark" policy outcomes is that the impact modern chief executives are able to make on history through their legislative presidencies has become an important benchmark of success. It is not presidents' stands on routine legislative matters or their legislative failures for which they are most often remembered. Rather, it is the bold, innovative legislation passed during their administrations that voters and historians are most likely to recall. The heart of the matter goes to presidents' ability to claim credit for significant policies, whether for their reelection bids or for the policy legacies they leave behind.[34]

Recategorizing Mayhew's laws to explore how much significant legislation overlaps with the president's priorities, and the president's leadership role in passing this body of laws, brings into sharper focus the impact of party control of national institutions that scholars have missed. Mayhew and others elegantly make the case that lawmaking under unified government is no more productive compared to periods of divided control. However, they do not test the degree to which the president or the governing majority in Congress drove such output in the postwar era or what precise role the president played in significant domestic lawmaking. Applying the framework of presidential leverage in political time to Mayhew's laws fills this considerable void.

The 252 significant domestic laws on Mayhew's updated list form the basis for the empirical analysis spanning 1947–96.[35] As with the roll-call analysis, foreign affairs, trade, military/defense, and immigration issues were excluded to retain a focus on domestic affairs. The list of the laws is in appendix A. The objective is to test the degree to which significant legislation had at least some correspondence to the president's objectives across eras and to gauge presidents' support of congressionally inspired legislation. The question of the origination of legislative ideas is of less interest to the analysis. For the purpose of recategorizing Mayhew's laws, and consistent with prior studies, agenda setting is limited to either the president or Congress.[36]

Identifying the number of significant laws in each two-year congressional period with a connection to the president's stated policy objectives followed two tracks. First, presidents' mentions of specific policies in their annual State of the Union addresses and other major policy speeches were compared to Mayhew's laws. This methodology is consistent with scholarly convention. The president's State of the Union message is widely regarded as a key forum for drawing national attention to his agenda priorities. The goal is to verify, at a minimum, the proportion of the important legislation passed in each congressional period in some way linked to the president's agenda. To qualify for inclusion as a "presidential priority," the president needed only to mention the legislation once in the two-year congressional period. Second, the bill history of each law was researched using *Congressional Quarterly* sources to determine if the legislation was linked to a presidential proposal. These criteria for juxtaposing major legislation that passed within each congressional period with presidential priorities were purposefully liberal in order to give the maximum benefit of the doubt to the alternative thesis—or null hypothesis—that party control has had little impact on presidential involvement in the legislative realm across time.

For important legislation not part of presidents' stated objectives and for which the research of bill histories showed no substantive presidential involvement, their positions on the final conference bill (or last recorded vote) were verified—either in favor of the bill, in opposition to the bill, or no position on the bill. For legislation adopted without a recorded vote, presidents' stance on the legislation was ascertained using bill histories in *Congressional Quarterly* and *Congress and the Nation* sources. Research of bill histories also identified the number of congressionally inspired laws that were subject to veto politics—including threats, prior vetoes, and successful veto overrides.

Table 1.5
Autoregression of Significant Laws on the President's Agenda and Subject to Veto Politics

Variable	President's Agenda	Veto Politics
First Two Years of President's Term	−2.40	−2.80
	(5.90)	(4.10)
Divided Government × Bipartisan Conservative Era (1953–64)	−30.50**	12.90*
	(7.10)	(6.40)
Divided Government × Liberal Activist Era (1965–78)	−51.60**	12.60*
	(6.30)	(5.70)
Divided Government × Postreform/Party-Unity Era (1979–96)	−53.30**	35.70**
	(5.30)	(4.80)
Constant	9.27**	3.00
	(4.70)	(3.90)
N of observations	24.00	24.00
Adjusted R^2	.84	.71
Rho	−.189	−.026
Durbin-Watson (original)	1.80	1.80
Durbin h (after correction for serial correlation)	2.16	1.93

** $p < .001$ (one-tailed test)   * $p < .05$
Coefficients are Cochrane-Orchutt iterated estimates. Standard errors are in parentheses.
The dependent variable for the "president's agenda" column is the percentage of Mayhew's significant laws with a connection to the president's agenda per biennial congressional period.
The dependent variable for the "veto politics" column is the percentage of Mayhew's significant laws subject to presidential vetoes, veto threats, and overrides per biennial congressional period.

Landmark Bills, Presidents' Agendas, and Veto Politics under Divided Government

Regression analysis summarizes the changing nature of presidential involvement on Mayhew's significant legislation across the three eras of divided government. The time-series models in table 1.5 replicate the analysis of annual presidential success rates (table 1.1). The dependent variable in the first equation (president's agenda) is the percentage of Mayhew's laws in each biennial congressional period with a connection to the president's stated policy objectives. The dependent variable in the second model (veto politics) is the percentage of Mayhew's significant laws subject to presidential vetoes, veto threats, or successful congressional overrides. Dummy terms for times of divided government were employed for the three eras, with a control for the president's first two years in office.

The data unequivocally show the progressive impact of split-party control on presidential involvement in nationally significant legislation. In the bipartisan conservative era, the percentage of laws linked to the president's agenda dropped only by about a third over unified government. In the liberal activist period, divided government yielded a net decrease of more than 50 percent in laws with a connection to presidents' agenda. The slightly larger coefficient and lower standard error for the postreform/party-unity era show that the trend solidified in the last quarter century. Well over half of the significant legislative outcomes from 1981–96 had no linkage to the president's agenda compared to the period of unified government in 1993–94.

The second equation for veto politics shows the consequences for presidents' weak positive leverage over significant lawmaking in the 1980s and 1990s. The model predicts that more than *one-third of all significant legislation in the postreform/party-unity era* involved negative leverage of vetoes and veto threats. Veto politics did *not* play such a central role in the bipartisan conservative and liberal activist periods. Only an eighth of all significant bills were shaped by vetoes or veto threats across these two broad periods.

The data sharply define the more problematic nature of divided control for presidents' credit-claiming opportunities at the close of the twentieth century. A dwindling share of significant laws was connected to the policy objectives of Presidents Reagan, Bush, and Clinton. They negotiated significant laws more frequently on the basis of veto leverage. Further analysis shows that they publicly opposed many bills that they decided not to veto. Credit-claiming opportunities were further diminished by their frequent choice to stay quiet and avoid taking public positions on significant legislation rather than draw attention to the opposition majority's policy accomplishments. The implications of these developments merit a closer examination of individual presidents' linkages to significant lawmaking across the three eras.

Table 1.6 provides a subtle breakdown of individual presidents' agenda leadership and veto usage across the three eras. Also included is the percentage of bills for which presidents expressed support or opposition or took no position. This detailed rearrangement of Mayhew's laws shows remarkable congruity with the tenets of the theoretical framework.

The stark contrast in leverage for Truman and Eisenhower is evident in the bipartisan conservative era. Truman was in an exceedingly weak institutional position as an unelected president facing an assertive opposition majority that had been relegated to the minority for nearly two decades. A careful researching of the bill histories reveals that *not a single domestic law* on Mayhew's list stemmed from Truman's agenda.[37] Significant ideological divisions in the Democratic base in Congress enabled Republicans to forge supermajorities with the southern wing of the party to trump Truman's vetoes. Indeed, two of the seven important laws passed in the 80th Congress were over Truman's objections: Taft-Hartley and the income tax reduction of 1948. Truman vetoed a score of other bills that did not make it onto Mayhew's list, but the result was

Table 1.6
Significant Legislation and Presidential-Congressional Agendas and Interaction, Divided Government, 1947–96*

BIPARTISAN CONSERVATIVE ERA

Congress/ No. of Laws	President	Agenda Connection and Presidential Position					Vetoes and Veto Threats		
		Presidential Priority	Agenda— Supported	Congressional Agenda— No Position	Congressional Agenda— Oppose	Congressional Priority— Veto Threat	Presidential Agenda— Veto Threat	Congressional Agenda— Prior Veto	Congressional Agenda— Vetoed/ Overridden
80th [n=7]	Truman[a]	0	0	0	0	0	0	0	2 (29%)
84th [n=4]	Eisenhower	3 (75%)	0	0	0	0	0	1 (25%)	0
85th [n=9]	Eisenhower	6 (67%)	1 (11%)	1 (11%)	1 (11%)	0	0	0	0
86th [n=5]	Eisenhower	2 (40%)	1 (20%)	1 (20%)	0	0	0	1[b] (20%)	0

LIBERAL ACTIVIST ERA

Congress/ No. of Laws	President	Agenda Connection and Presidential Position					Vetoes and Veto Threats		
		Presidential Priority	Agenda— Supported	Congressional Agenda— No Position	Congressional Agenda— Oppose	Congressional Priority— Veto Threat	Presidential Agenda— Veto Threat	Congressional Agenda— Prior Veto	Congressional Agenda— Vetoed/ Overridden
91st [n=20]	Nixon	8 (40%)	2 (10%)	3 (15%)	3 (15%)	3 (15%)	1 (5%)	0	0
92d [n=15]	Nixon	3 (20%)	3 (20%)	5 (33%)	2 (13%)	1 (7%)	0	0	1 (7%)
93d [n=19]	Nixon/Ford	4 (21%)	6 (32%)	6 (32%)	0	0	2 (11%)	0	1 (5%)
94th [n=14]	Ford	7 (50%)	0	6 (43%)	0	0	1 (7%)	0	0

Table 1.6 continued

POSTREFORM/PARTY-UNITY ERA

Congress/No. of Laws	President	Agenda Connection and Presidential Position				Vetoes and Veto Threats			
		Presidential Priority	Agenda—Supported	Congressional Agenda—No Position	Congressional Agenda—Oppose	Congressional Priority—Veto Threat	Presidential Agenda—Veto Threat	Congressional Agenda—Prior Veto	Congressional Agenda—Vetoed/Overridden
97th [n=9]	Reagan	3 (33%)	3 (33%)	1 (11%)	0	0	2 (22%)	0	0
98th [n=6]	Reagan	2 (33%)	0	2 (33%)	0	2 (33%)	0	0	0
99th [n=7]	Reagan	2 (29%)	0	2 (29%)	0	0	3 (43%)	0	0
100th [n=10]	Reagan	3 (30%)	0	1 (10%)	1 (10%)	0	2 (20%)	0	3 (30%)
101st [n=9]	Bush	2 (22%)	2 (22%)	2 (22%)	0	1 (11%)	0	2 (22%)	0
102d [n=5]	Bush	1 (20%)	0	1 (20%)	0	1 (20%)	0	1 (20%)	1 (20%)
104th [n=14]	Clinton	5c (36%)	5 (36%)	3 (21%)	0	0	0	0	1 (7%)

* Row percentages do not always equal 100% due to rounding.

a Congressional Quarterly did not begin keeping records of presidential positions until 1953; see text for discussion.

b Eisenhower vetoed the Housing Act of 1959 twice.

c Clinton vetoed welfare reform twice in the 104th Congress; he also issued prior vetoes on the budget; see chapter 5.

the same.[38] Overrides did not reflect *bipartisan* coalitions of the variety that Mayhew identifies in the liberal activist era, but *ideological coalitions* fashioned by Republican leaders who took advantage of the regional split among congressional Democrats. As chapter 2 recounts in greater detail, the 80th Congress represents an exceptional marginalization of the president in the legislative process. Truman arguably added to his weak position in the legislative realm by failing to work with the Democratic leadership and pursuing a risky reelection strategy in 1948.

Eisenhower was in a much stronger position to take a leadership role on significant legislation. Two-thirds to three-quarters of the legislation from 1955–58 was connected to his stated priorities. In terms of the proportion of the legislation with ties to the White House, no other period of divided government in the postwar era witnessed such a strong linkage between significant legislation and the president's agenda. The caveat, of course, is that policy activism was rather limited in this period. In 1955–56, for example, only four major domestic laws were passed. Nonetheless, this does not detract from the central point that what *did* pass was typically linked to Eisenhower's objectives. Eisenhower stopped short of issuing veto threats on any of the bills appearing on Mayhew's list of significant legislation. He employed a veto strategy as a last result, and was far more successful than Truman in gaining veto leverage. Whereas the conservative coalition trumped Truman's veto pen, the voting alignment sided with Eisenhower to block several override attempts.

If the 1950s are the frame of reference, it is understandable why scholars concluded that divided government seemingly had little impact on presidential-congressional relations. As Mark Peterson notes, "When a president is 'successful,' numerous members of Congress participate in the coalition and share in that legislative victory."[39] Eisenhower's amiable relations with Democratic leaders and the policy-making environment of the times afforded both the Republican president and the Democratic Congress ample opportunity to jointly derive benefit from the modest policies passed. Cooperation and compromise typically eclipsed overt interbranch conflict.

Divided government ended in 1960 with the election of John Kennedy and did not return until Richard Nixon's election in 1968. In those interceding years (discussed below), the legislative restraint of the 1950s gave way to a torrent of legislative activity that spanned Johnson's term in office. This activity continued well into the conservative Nixon and Ford administrations. Nixon was the most successful president under divided government when it comes to floor outcomes. Many innovative laws and their legacies have been attributed to his presidency.[40] There is, however, a qualitative difference between legislation *passed* during Nixon's two terms and those significant laws actually *connected* to the president's domestic policy objectives.

As chapter 3 elaborates, Nixon followed Congress much more than he led it. Few of the significant laws that emerged in the highly productive liberal activist period of divided government were tied to the president's agenda. Nixon's involvement in innovative legislation reflected a complex strategy that was driven by a reelection incentive. In his first term, Nixon attempted to preempt the Democratic majority with a string of domestic proposals. Sometimes this strategy backfired, however, and the legislation that emerged from Congress was to his dissatisfaction. He thus wound up threatening to veto legislation he had proposed. In other cases, the Democratic majority went much farther than the president desired, but Nixon threw his support behind the modified proposals.

Nixon did earn a share of the credit for major laws in his first term. However, the proportion of such legislation diminished after the 91st Congress as a prelude to the heightened conflict that would subsume interbranch relations in his second term. In the 92d and 93d Congresses, Nixon took no clear-cut position on a third of the major legislation that passed. The diverse issues spanned campaign finance reform to environmental regulation and education. These were priorities of the Democratic majority, not the Republican president. Nixon had qualms about various aspects of bills, but he was averse to risking electoral or public reprisal for opposing popular measures and instead chose to stay quiet.

Rarely did Nixon express outright opposition to legislation. The Economic Stabilization Act of 1970 was an exception. The bill, which originally set out to standardize cost-accounting practices for defense contracts, gave the president the power to impose wage and price controls that he did not want (but ultimately did use). Upon signing the bill, Nixon stated that he would have preferred to veto it but he signed it "under duress" because of the need to reauthorize several programs.[41] In fact, Nixon only vetoed a single important law, the Water Pollution Control Act of 1972, claiming that the bill was well-intentioned but too costly. The successful override of Nixon's veto was the only such instance on significant legislation during his time in office (the other successful override was on Gerald Ford's veto of the Freedom of Information Act of 1974). In many other instances, Nixon selectively threw his support behind legislation crafted by the Democratic majority. Roughly a fifth to a third of all of the major domestic laws adopted in 1970–74, ranging from agriculture to health maintenance organizations, were not part of Nixon's objectives but were sanctioned by him.

Divided government in the liberal activist era represents a unique landscape in the terrain of postwar executive-legislative relations. Nixon's role alternated from occasionally leading on some domestic laws of national import to lending support for congressionally inspired legislation, to taking no position on bills about which he had reservations. Nixon's legislative strategy was partially preemptive, partially reactive, and sometimes passive. There is evidence of a shared and contested agenda, and Nixon was occasionally able to influence supporting coalitions for his domestic stands. All told, however, his engagement in the legislative realm was a reflection of the centrifugal pull of the consolidation of the Great Society. This agenda was largely inspired by the governing majority, drawing Nixon to follow Congress, and not vice versa.

Gerald Ford suffered a dearth of leverage over Congress rivaled only, perhaps, by Harry Truman. Ford was widely hailed as a skilled legislative leader given his experience as minority leader from 1965–73.[42] Nevertheless, he faced huge Democratic majorities and an assertive opposition leadership after the 1974 elections. He suffered a lower success rate on position votes than any of his postwar predecessors in the last years of divided government in the liberal activist era (fig. 1.1). Despite the daunting governing context of his brief term in office, when the focus shifts to innovative legislation there is some evidence of Ford's leadership in domestic affairs. Half of the fourteen significant laws adopted in 1975–76 were connected to the president's policy objectives. The energy crisis, unemployment, and inflation dominated Ford's stay in the White House, and he focused his efforts on the economy. Legislation concerning energy policy, tax reduction and reform, unemployment compensation, and railroad regulatory reform can be traced to Ford's agenda.

However, Ford did stay quiet on much of the other legislation passed by the 94th Congress. Nearly two-thirds of the bills on which Ford took no position concerned environmental affairs as the Democratic majority in Congress sought to assure the legacy of the Great Society. Ford opposed elements of some of the bills, but he ultimately took no solid position on a host of others adopted in 1976.[43] Despite Ford's heavy reliance on the veto, he subjected none of the laws on Mayhew's list to a presidential veto or override. Ford publicly threatened to veto only one bill: the New York City financial bailout of 1975. Initially opposed to rescuing the nation's largest city, he reversed course and offered his own bailout plan, much of which Congress adopted.[44]

It may be argued, nonetheless, that Ford's veto pen implicitly loomed large over policy making in the 94th Congress. Ford called on Congress to reduce taxes and make steep cuts in domestic social spending to revitalize the economy.[45] When Democrats balked, he prioritized passing energy legislation and settled on a veto strategy designed "to deal with legislation that the administration found objectionable, which included most of the other legislation that Congress was moving at the time."[46] While Ford's vetoes of bills that did not make it to Mayhew's list were sometimes overridden, his tough stance on domestic spending and his willingness to exercise the veto prerogative may have given him some additional sway to negotiate with Democrats on his priority issues. Ford could claim more than a modicum of credit for the important economic legislation of the mid-1970s, but apparently not enough to win election in 1976.

Presidential leadership on significant legislation in the postreform/party-unity era underscores limited policy activism in a period of budget deficits. Several common threads run throughout the terms of Reagan, Bush, and Clinton. These include a far greater contested agenda, an increase in vetoes threatened and cast, and more restricted opportunities for presidential credit claiming. From the 97th to the 104th Congresses, typically one-third or less of Mayhew's significant laws were connected to the president's policy objectives—a figure that is consistently lower than for periods of divided government in either of the two preceding eras. Congress, not the president, determined the lion's share of the limited innovative lawmaking in the postreform/party-unity period.

Of the presidents who faced divided government in the postreform/party-unity period, Reagan had the strongest leverage in his first term. His electoral victory in 1980 and the greater heterogeneity in the Democratic membership of the House were key factors, as chapter 4 details, in setting the agenda, forging supporting coalitions, and passing his essential priorities by the end of his second year. Three laws, the Economic Recovery Tax Act and Omnibus Reconciliation Act (1981), and the Tax Equity and Fiscal Responsibility Act of 1982, were top presidential policy priorities. These sweeping bills had substantial impact on domestic programs and precipitated massive federal deficits. In subsequent years, several other important laws were linked to Reagan's policy priorities, including tax reform in 1986, catastrophic health insurance, and antidrug-abuse legislation. By Reagan's second term, however, most legislation emanated from the Democratic majority in Congress, forcing him to depend frequently on veto leverage. His record of success thus was mixed.

Whereas Reagan was able to accomplish bold objectives early in his term, Bush and Clinton were rarely responsible for significant domestic laws adopted during their bouts with opposition majorities in Congress. For Bush, part of the reason stemmed from his limited domestic focus. For Clinton, the Republican congressional agenda displaced his policy goals. All told, only four of the fourteen important domestic laws passed from 1989–92 had any connection to George Bush's policy priorities. Similarly, only five of the fourteen measures adopted by the Republican 104th Congress reflected Clinton's policy priorities. Several bills, including welfare and the budget, fit uncomfortably in the classificatory scheme because of Clinton's prior vetoes of these measures and his attempts to preempt the GOP agenda.

Dependence on the veto as a form of defensive and occasionally preemptive leverage "of last resort" indubitably narrowed credit-claiming opportunities for Reagan, Bush, and Clinton. If, as Charles Cameron asserts, significant legislation is most likely to draw presidential vetoes, the dynamic is more a product of divided government in the postreform/party-unity era.[47] Reagan frequently employed veto threats on legislation emanating from the Democratic congressional agenda after 1982. His goal was to halt legislation or wrest concessions on new spending for domestic programs. Reagan threatened a veto of the antirecession jobs measure in 1983, the Food Security Act of 1985, the cleanup of toxic waste dumps in 1986, the Housing and Community Development Act of 1987, and reparations for surviving Japanese-Americans who had been interned during World War II.

Reagan faced several challenges to his vetoes of significant laws. Three of the ten important measures adopted in the 100th Congress (1987–88) were passed over Reagan's veto pen: the Water Quality Act of 1987, the Surface Transportation Act of 1987, and the Grove City civil rights bill in 1988. It is not a coincidence that these overrides took place in his final two years in office, when his political capital had declined rather considerably in the wake of the Iran-Contra controversy and Democrats sought to challenge the president with their own agenda.

Bush issued relatively few veto threats, but he did cast vetoes on several important measures. He won compromises from Democrats on three bills, none of which is traceable to his domestic objectives. As chapter 5 documents, Bush vetoed prior minimum wage legislation in 1989, as well as deficit reduction and civil rights legislation in 1990, before these significant measures were ultimately enacted. The Democratic majority was able to trump only one of his forty-six vetoes—cable television reregulation—a tribute to Bush's ability to turn the party cohesion that defined the 101st and 102d Congresses to his advantage through veto politics.

Clinton's use of the veto power and veto threats does not come through as clearly when the universe of laws is narrowed to Mayhew's list. The several appropriations bills he vetoed in late 1995 and 1996 that brought budget conflict to a head with GOP leaders did not make it to Mayhew's list, but welfare reform did. Clinton vetoed Republican welfare reform efforts twice in the 104th Congress. What ultimately emerged was a compromise bill acceptable to the president, although many of his copartisans opposed it. Like Bush, Clinton was overridden only once on significant legislation. As chapter 5 recounts, a peculiar turn of events led to congressional Democrats joining with Republicans to override Clinton's veto of shareholder lawsuits.

When the vantage point on significant legislation is shifted to modes of presidential involvement, closer analysis of Mayhew's laws underscores how few bills were tied to presidents' policy objectives in the postreform/party-unity era. Few of the laws on Mayhew's list that were part of the congressional agenda won the backing of Reagan or Bush, and presidents chose to stay quiet on important legislation anywhere from a third to a fifth of the time. Clinton, on the other hand, publicly supported five of the fourteen measures enacted by the 104th Congress that were not part of his agenda, including congressional workplace compliance, the line-item veto, the Kennedy-Kassebaum health insurance portability bill, and environmental regulation. His support represented a type of "bandwagon" effect in an effort to claim some level of credit for what passed in 1995–96 as he eyed reelection. However, the lack of laws in the "presidential priority" column belies the intense conflict and preemptive politics that Clinton employed through veto leverage to try to gain the upper hand over the GOP majority.

Mayhew is correct to emphasize that scholars have endeavored to "identify presidential leadership with party control through arguments about 'deadlock,' 'stalemate,' and 'party government.' Regardless of its theoretical merits, that effort runs into an empirical problem. At least since the 1930s, the real world has refused to follow the script."[48] Indeed, moving the debate beyond gridlock is critical to grasp the consequences of divided government for the legislative presidency. It is imperative to shift analytical perspective from systemic output to the fundamentally changed nature of presidents' involvement in, and negotiation of, significant laws. Only then is it possible to appreciate the more limited credit-claiming opportunities that characterized the closing decades of the century. Presidents' efforts to stave off or remold the governing majority's agenda in the postreform/party-unity era contrast mightily to the context of divided government in the early postwar years.

The claim that divided government is of no consequence does not withstand empirical scrutiny from the standpoint of political time. "Presidents," Charles Jones asserts, "must fit themselves into an ongoing lawmaking process. They may be key actors in this process, but it can, and often does, operate without or alongside them."[49] The weight of evidence presented in this chapter—from presidential success on floor outcomes, veto threats, and lead-ership on significant legislation—accentuates how much more the lawmaking process has, in fact, operated *without* the president's cooperation under divided control in the last two decades. Moreover, the ways that presidents have been able to "fit themselves into" the lawmaking process have more frequently involved veto leverage.

Significant Legislation and Unified Government

Defenders of the "legislative productivity" argument have also failed to recognize how unified government has, in fact, facilitated qualitatively different types of presidential leadership on significant lawmaking. The president's electoral resources and institutional position affect congressional deference to his policy objectives. These factors also condition the extent to which he can direct activity toward his preferred agenda or reinforce support for continuing party agendas that constitute a larger, more consistently shared agenda between the branches. Yet, unified government yields a qualitatively different type of leadership than the veto leverage that characterizes the postreform/party-unity era of divided government because of typically stronger agenda mutuality between the branches. Veto politics, as a closer look at Mayhew's laws reveals, have not played a role in times of single-party control since 1950.

Only a single domestic law on Mayhew's list was subject to a presidential veto under unified government. Congress overrode Truman's veto of the McCarran Internal Security Act of 1950, which among other things required members of the Communist Party to register with the government at the height of the "red scare." A careful study of each bills history reveals not a single incidence of a presidential veto threat since.

What distinguishes unified government from *all* periods of divided government in the postwar era is the proportion of significant legislation that is connected with the president's expressed policy priorities. Eighty percent or more of significant laws reflected the president's priorities. Presidents fully supported other initiatives generated by the governing majority, Truman's objections to the McCarran bill notwithstanding.

Ferreting out the subtleties in presidential direction or facilitation of the shared agenda between the branches requires a discriminating analysis, which is provided in the case studies in chapters 6 and 7. Still, several observations about presidential involvement in significant legislation across the three eras can be gleaned from table 1.7. Johnson's presidency stands out among periods of unified government not only because *all* significant laws were linked to his priorities, but also because the 89th and 90th Congresses were the most pro-

Table 1.7
Significant Legislation and Presidential–Congressional
Agendas and Interaction, Unified Government, 1947–96*

Era	Congress	President	Presidential Agenda	Congressional Agenda— Supported	Congressional Agenda— Vetoed/ Overridden
Bipartisan Conservative	81st [n=8]	Truman	7 (88%)	0	1 (13%)
	82d [n=2]	Truman	2 (100%)	0	0
	83d [n=8]	Eisenhower	7 (88%)	1 (13%)	0
	87th [n=10]	Kennedy	10 (100%)	0	0
	88th [n=11]	Kennedy/ Johnson	10 (91%)	1 (9%)	0
Liberal Activist	89th [n=22]	Johnson	22 (100%)	0	0
	90th [n=15]	Johnson	15 (100%)	0	0
	95th [n=11]	Carter	8 (73%)	3 (27%)	0
Postreform/ Party-Unity	96th [n=9]	Carter	8 (89%)	1 (11%)	0
	103d [n=11]	Clinton	10 (91%)	1 (9%)	0

* Row percentages do not always equal 100% due to rounding.

ductive biennial periods for innovative lawmaking in the postwar era. Two to three times as many significant laws traceable to the president's priorities passed under Johnson than under all the other presidents who profited from unified government.

Johnson's substantial leverage in the legislative realm translated into an unrivaled ability to manage and direct the congressional calendar. As chapter 6 details more thoroughly, much of the legislation that emerged in this period was the product of Johnson's initiative, from voting rights and programs linked to the "war on poverty" to environmental and consumer safety regulation. If the "public mood" of activism was apparent in the mid-1960s, it was the White House that capitalized on public sentiment to initiate the vast majority of the legislative surge. Following the electorate's legitimization of Johnson's activist platform in 1964, a largely deferential majority of Democrats stood poised and willing to pass his priority legislation at the other end of Pennsylvania Avenue.

Significant legislation adopted during other interludes of unified government shows a marked link to the president's policy objectives, but the quantity pales in comparison to the early liberal activist period. Kennedy had weak electoral resources and confronted a less than favorable leadership structure and configuration of voting coalitions in Congress. Nevertheless, his leadership is evident on the ten significant domestic laws that were enacted in the 87th Congress as the ancien régime of the conservative coalition began to crumble. As chapter 6 highlights, Kennedy spent much time trying to advance a shared agenda with the liberal base of his copartisans in Congress over the objections of the de facto policy majority of Republicans and southern Democrats. In view of the constraints he faced, Kennedy's accomplishments were many—ranging from housing, Social Security, and minimum wage legislation in 1961 to manpower training and public welfare in 1962. The amount of significant legislation passed in the 87th Congress was far less compared to the record of the Great Society, but what *did* pass under Kennedy's watch was largely driven by the president's policy priorities.

On the other side of the historical continuum, Carter and Clinton faced situations similar to Kennedy in terms of a dearth of electoral resources. Both presidents confronted a more autonomous majority of copartisans in Congress. The policy-making environment was one of economic constraint. These factors translated into less independent agenda success for both presidents.

A total of twenty significant laws were enacted during Carter's presidency, of which sixteen were deemed presidential priorities. Four laws—the Surface Mining Control and Reclamation Act of 1977, the Clean Water Act of 1977, the Clean Air Act amendments of 1977, and Alaska Lands Preservation in 1980 were not part of the president's stated objectives. These laws were fully supported by Carter, but represented the *renewal* of programs spearheaded a decade earlier or the extension of regulatory efforts begun in the Great Society. These are clear-cut cases of the president lending support for the continuing legislative agenda in Congress. Carter also prioritized policy issues requiring adjustment to the status quo that carried over from the prior administration. He was forced to confront both the Social Security deficit issue and the minimum wage, and refashioned President Ford's proposed Social Security tax increase in 1976. He also worked with labor groups and his copartisans in Congress to reach a compromise on an indexing arrangement for the minimum wage.

Much of the significant legislation prioritized by Carter involved responses to the economic troubles that dominated the mid- to late 1970s. Carter found the federal government in the position of needing to "rescue" a private corporation, Chrysler, whose financial ruin represented a threat to workers around the country. The federal loan guarantees to Chrysler did not constitute a new federal social program or the extension of an existing one, but rather rapid governmental action to forestall the serious economic consequences of a failing industry. Several of the important bills connected to Carter's agenda reflected attempts to deal with the energy crisis, including his 1978 energy package, legislation on windfall profits on oil producers, and the development of synthetic fuels to reduce reliance on foreign production.

Carter did see several independent policy initiatives achive success, but his weak leverage often necessitated compromise with the Democratic majority. Arguably his greatest policy triumphs involved regulatory relief for the transportation industry. Several of the bills did not go as far as Carter wished, and involved at least some compromise with congressional leaders. All told, however, the basic contours of the president's plans were adopted relative to trucking, airline, and railroad deregulation. Like Civil Service Reform in 1978, these bills stemmed from Carter's agenda focus on spurring economic growth through competition in the private sector.

A similar dynamic of lending support for the continuing congressional agenda and "fine-tuning" existing programs emerges on the eleven significant laws adopted during Clinton's first two years in office. A single bill, California desert protection in 1994, was not a stated presidential objective, but Clinton publicly backed it. At least four of the significant laws Clinton prioritized were clearly linked to the carryover agenda of the party in Congress. His Republican predecessor had blocked Democratic efforts to pass family leave and voter registration legislation. Moreover, Democrats had been unable to enact gun control legislation over Bush's objections. With the White House in Democratic hands, vetoes and threats of vetoes vanished. Clinton lent strong support to the Family Leave and Medical Act, the Motor Voter Act, and tougher handgun control legislation (Brady Bill and Omnibus Crime Act), all of which Democrats in Congress had championed for some time.

Clinton, like Carter, was also not without some independent policy successes during the brief return to unified government in 1993–94. The president is credited with the Omnibus Deficit Reduction Act of 1993. Although his proposals stirred considerable controversy, the legislation wound through Congress by fits and starts, and he garnered not a single House Republican's vote for his budget. Clinton's proposals for national service (Americorps), setting national educational goals (Goals 2000), and reforming college loan financing policies were also among his greatest agenda victories.

By most accounts, Clinton's policy successes were modest in light of the failure of health care reform, which was his top priority. Yet, when the focus turns to the president's advocacy for continuing policy goals shared with his copartisans on Capitol Hill, Clinton was unquestionably able to exercise a very different form of leadership on landmark bills than proved to be the case when Republicans captured Congress in the 1994 elections. That leadership did not include the type of bold, new programs that were enacted under Johnson. Rather, the emphasis for Clinton, like Carter, was to bring existing programs into greater harmony with an economic context of constraint and/or reinforcing support for longstanding party priorities blocked by the previous administration, with only a moderate basis for autonomous policy success.

There is another underlying dynamic that draws a further distinction between Clinton's leadership mode under unified and divided government. As others have already documented, significant legislation that passed under unified conditions in the 103d Congress overwhelmingly passed by *partisan* support.[50] What is of most import to this analysis is the interrelation between the passage of this significant legislation and the president's objectives. Of the ten bills constituting Clinton's policy priorities in the 103d Congress, the passage coalitions on nine of the ten bills were composed of partisan majorities in both chambers. Several were also subject to foiled Senate filibuster attempts. Significant legislation sanctioned by the president in the 103d Congress had a distinct partisan flavor. By contrast, Clinton supported six bills in the 104th Congress that were *not* among his policy objectives, and all of these measures eventually won *bipartisan* congressional backing. The changed nature of Clinton's negotiations with the governing majority, and the altered basis for credit claiming he endured under divided government, are taken up in greater detail in chapter 5.

Summary

This chapter has presented a systematic overview of the impact of party control of national institutions across the bipartisan conservative, liberal activist, and postreform/party-unity eras. The merits of the theoretical framework of presidential leverage in political time have been elaborated along two tracks. The first half of this chapter emphasized the interplay of electoral and institutional factors that account for the sharp decline in presidential floor success in the most recent era of divided government. The second half of the chapter stressed the qualitatively different modes of presidential legislative leadership over time based upon party control of Congress. The impact of party control on the legislative presidency has been highly uneven. Presidents in the bipartisan conservative and liberal activist eras had greater opportunity to fashion supporting legislative coalitions in times of unified and divided government. Presidents have relied much more on the veto power and veto threats in the postreform/party-unity era, or they have tempered their engagement on significant legislation driven more by the opposition majority's agenda.

The analysis of floor outcomes and significant legislation also supports the assertion about the variable basis of presidential legislative influence in times of unified government. The common thread to all periods of unified government is the consistently high rate of executive-legislative concurrence and a stronger shared agenda with the congressional majority. Nonetheless, only Lyndon Johnson's term comes close to resembling the "textbook" model of legislative leadership with respect to setting and directing the national agenda. The governing contexts that Kennedy, Clinton, and Carter confronted complicated directorship of the national legislative agenda. Although not without independent successes, much of the agenda was already defined for Carter and Clinton and required adjustments to the status quo or expressions of support for longstanding party objectives blocked by their Republican predecessors.

The case studies in chapters 2–7 offer a close, comparative examination of presidential success and types of leadership across eras. Beginning with the experiences of Presidents Truman and Eisenhower in the bipartisan conservative era, each chapter presents a more in-depth account of presidential involvement in significant lawmaking. The case studies also introduce a model of individual-level legislative support for the president to cast light on presidents' legislative strategy and coalition-building opportunities. The variables in the model closely parallel this chapter's aggregate-level analysis of the importance of electoral and institutional contexts to presidential floor success. The details of the logit model of presidential support in Congress are provided in appendix B.

2 Truman, Eisenhower, and Divided Government

84   IN THE 1940s AND 1950s, whatever the partisan configuration of national institutions, the omnipresence of the conservative coalition in Congress is the common thread of the period. Presidents' ability to manage this voting alignment, set the legislative agenda, and influence legislative outcomes pivoted on the strength of their institutional position and the policy activism of the governing majority in Congress. From the perspective of presidential leverage, the experiences of Truman and Eisenhower under divided government are cases in contrast.

Truman's bout with the Republican 80th Congress is one of the most unique arrangements of divided government in the postwar period. The midterm partisan reversal of Congress in the 1946 elections yielded a cohesive opposition majority that wrenched the policy-making agenda from Truman's hands. Fragmentation among Democrats in Congress allowed the GOP leadership to override his vetoes. As FDR's unelected successor to the Oval Office, Truman had the basis for neither coalition building nor veto leverage. Significant domestic legislation was overwhelmingly the product of the Republican majority, passing without the president's involvement or over his objections. Truman's predicament conditioned his decision to disengage from legislative leadership and focus instead on campaigning for reelection against the GOP majority. His reelection effort succeeded, but it was not without substantial policy costs: He spent his next term trying, mostly unsuccessfully, to undo the policy legacy of the ephemeral Republican majority.

Eisenhower's strong institutional position and his "hidden-hand" approach to legislative affairs were uniquely suited to managing legislative outcomes in a period of legislative restraint.[1] His resounding electoral victories in 1952 and 1956, along with stable and high levels of job approval, enabled him to build cross-party support for his moderate positions in times of both unified and divided control. The ideological composition of supporting coalitions changed according to the issue at hand, and he relied heavily on congressional leaders in both parties to marshal legislators behind his positions.

Over the course of his term, Eisenhower was "increasingly placed in the position of offering scaled-down alternatives to programs launched on Capitol Hill by coalitions of activist Democrats and moderate Republicans."[2] As a result, significant legislation was typically wedded to Eisenhower's objectives, and his positive leverage over Congress saved him from having to make extensive use of the veto to achieve them.

Harry Truman and the 80th Congress: Legislative Conflict and Campaigning for Reelection, 1947–48

Truman's bout with the GOP-controlled 80th Congress stresses how the partisan configuration of national institutions within the same broadly defined era can affect presidential legislative fortunes quite differently. The pivotal factors for Truman included an agenda that was the source of considerable contention between the branches, and his weak institutional position. The combination of Republican cohesion and Democratic fragmentation limited Truman's influence in the legislative sphere. Where the conservative coalition would occasionally be an ally to Eisenhower, this voting alignment approached supermajority status in the 80th Congress and wreaked havoc on Truman's ability to negotiate significant outcomes through the veto power.

Harry Truman assumed the presidency in April, 1945, only eighty-one days into Roosevelt's fourth term. During the first two years of his presidency, Truman focused mainly on an inexorable search for legitimacy and respect as Roosevelt's successor.[3] Critics compared Truman's wily personality, connection to "machine politics," and middle-class roots to Roosevelt's polished image and inspirational vision and doubted the Missourian's leadership abilities.[4] Truman attempted to affirm his commitment to the New Deal in the summer of 1945 by launching a panoply of bold proposals aimed at completing unfulfilled reforms.[5] The president soon realized, however, that he "had no personal political base from which to operate, no public following. He knew far less about the administration's programs and plans than those who now looked to him for leadership."[6] An increasingly fragmented Democratic Party in Congress compounded Truman's difficulties. Moreover, he faced the same contingent of anti–New Deal Democrats that had frustrated Roosevelt's plans to expand social programs after 1938.[7]

Truman was the first postwar president to suffer a reversal of partisan control of Congress in the midterm elections, although the loss of seats for the president's party in Congress has since been a common occurrence. Midterm elections draw little fanfare, and turnout is generally lower than for presidential elections. Partisans of the "out party" are more likely to go to the polls to express dissatisfaction with the president. Complacent voters registered with the president's party are less likely to turn out to vote, or they may choose to "punish" congressional candidates in the president's party for what they perceive as poor presidential leadership. The interaction of economic conditions and presidential popularity can determine the extent of the president's losses in Congress.[8]

The worsening postwar economy set the stage for the Democrats' electoral demise in 1946. Republicans charged that shortages of goods were the result of Truman's incompetent handling of the economy.[9] The combined effects of apathetic Democratic voters who stayed away on election day and voters who went to the polls to reject Truman's economic reconversion policies gave birth to the Republicans' first majority in Congress in nearly two decades.

The Republican electoral landslide of November, 1946, left Truman facing a confident partisan opposition in the congressional majority. Republicans considered the election a referendum on Truman's policies and a mandate to rescind New Deal policies of the last decade and a half.[10] Democratic senator J. William Fulbright went so far as to suggest that the president appoint a Republican secretary of state, resign, and give Republicans full control of the executive and legislative branches. Low morale pervaded the administration, and Truman's advisers became persuaded "if not that all was over, at least that the postwar reaffirmation of the liberal cause had been a crashing failure at the polls—out of fashion with the public, out of date for officeholders."[11]

In the early months of 1947, Truman sent proposals on decontrol of the wartime economy that were well received by Republicans. However, the president eventually heeded the advice of his assistant James Rowe, who wrote a strategic memo entitled "Cooperation or Conflict?" The Republicans' goal, Rowe believed, was to prepare for victory in the next election and they would "pass with great fanfare any popular policies that they foresaw causing difficulties for the president, thereby daring him to veto."[12] Rowe advised Truman to distance himself as much as possible from Congress and "select the issues upon which there will be conflict with the majority" as a means to persuade voters that Republicans were to blame for poor public policies.[13] Rowe's electoral strategy, while ultimately successful in reversing the seat losses in Congress and allowing Truman to hold on to the presidency in 1948, was a risky legislative strategy that resulted in the enactment of a sizable number of laws to which the president was opposed.

Truman's experience under divided government is atypical in the postwar era because of the unique coalitional configuration of Congress that dominated the 80th Congress. None of the Republican presidents who confronted

Democratic majorities had such a fractured partisan base in Congress, save perhaps Gerald Ford. The combined effects of Truman's lack of electoral resources, Republican cohesion around a limited set of policy priorities, and disunity in the Democratic Party base in Congress realized the president's worst nightmare on the legislative front. Truman could not advance his own agenda, and he had little success fending off elements of the GOP agenda. Republican leaders used the ideological fragmentation among Democrats to forge voting blocs capable of trampling his vetoes. The irony of the 80th Congress is perhaps that this very adversity provided Truman with the opportunity to stage one of the greatest electoral comebacks of the modern presidency.

Lawmaking and Presidential Leadership under Truman

In his catalogue of important laws, Mayhew counts seven domestic measures for the 80th Congress. Legislative histories of the laws reveal that *none* of the statutes were connected to Truman's stated policy objectives. Republicans pushed forth a limited anti–New Deal program that sailed through Congress either without Truman's involvement or over his veto. Portal-to-portal pay legislation resulted from efforts begun by legislators in the 79th Congress to address the Supreme Court's decision in the Mount Clemens Pottery Company case, which had opened up a floodgate of lawsuits. Truman had little input into the legislation and somewhat reluctantly signed the bill, seizing the occasion to call upon Congress to increase the minimum wage.[14] His plea fell on deaf ears. The Federal Insecticide, Fungicide, and Rodenticide Act of 1947 (FIFRA), the Water Pollution Control Act of 1948, and the Hope–Aiken Agricultural Act of 1948 were all Republican initiatives. The president criticized the latter measure for omitting soil conservation and a panoply of issues from housing to low income diets, yet he did not provide substantive commentary until debate was well under way in Congress.[15] The Twenty-second Amendment to the Constitution, which limits the president's tenure in office to two terms, was also generated by the Republican majority. After a fiery debate in Congress, the bill passed without much comment from Truman.

As further evidence of the degree to which parts of the Republican agenda were at odds with Truman's policy objectives, two of the seven domestic laws—Taft–Hartley and the income tax reduction of 1948—were passed over the president's veto. Truman vetoed two Republican income tax bills in the first session of the 80th Congress, but GOP leaders finally managed to successfully override a third veto in 1948.

Perhaps more than any other issue to arise in the 80th Congress, Truman's stance on the Taft–Hartley Act illustrates his focus on electoral victory in 1948 rather than on substantive policy outcomes. Truman deliberately kept Congress at arm's length, and his lack of legislative leadership was part and parcel of his strategy to blame Republicans for putatively irresponsible legislation without drawing attention to the crumbling of the New Deal coalition. By disengaging from the legislative process, Truman's actions were "calculated to build a record against the Republicans for his reelection rather than to adjust to the new political alignments to gain some advances in social and economic legislation."[16] But his strategy also facilitated the Republicans' ability to construct ideological coalitions with southern Democrats to override his vetoes, not only of Taft–Hartley but also of five other bills in the 80th Congress that did not make it to Mayhew's list. These bills included interstate commerce, Social Security coverage, employment taxes, and appropriations for the Federal Security Agency.[17]

Truman did not articulate any counterproposals to the Republican legislation designed to amend the Wagner Act. He issued only general statements to the press and left the Democratic minority in Congress largely unaware of his position.[18] Once the conference report on Taft–Hartley had passed both chambers, the president and his advisers hurriedly undertook an effort to study provisions of the legislation and gauge public sentiment on the bill. Truman eventually vetoed the legislation, contending that it would only add to industrial strife. He had just vetoed an income tax reduction championed by the GOP, arguing that it was poorly timed and would benefit only the wealthy. Truman's veto of Taft–Hartley was meant to place him further "on the side of the common man" as the 1948 election neared.[19] When Republicans set out to override the president's veto, they were aided by a large bloc of southern Democrats who defected from the president's position. Truman's failure to provide direction to Democratic members during the course of the congressional debate over Taft–Hartley contributed to the successful override and exacerbated his future legislative woes, as the law proved quite difficult to amend in the future.[20]

Truman's Success and Support in the 80th Congress

Assessing Truman's floor success entails several challenges unique to his presidency. *Congressional Quarterly* and other sources did not keep records of Truman's expressed positions on floor votes. Consequently, his roll-call success rate is an approximation of the measures used for other presidents. The vote set for the 80th House includes roll-call votes on issues on which Truman made proposals or expressed an opinion. Provisions of the final legislation were compared with his public statements to determine whether the legislation corresponded or ran counter to his preferences. The nineteen House votes are listed in appendix C.

Truman did not fare too poorly on floor votes. He won two-thirds of the time on close votes for which the final outcome was 10 percent or less of members voting, and just over half the time on less controversial legislation (all other votes). Republican opposition was not consistently strong on legislation without connection to the anti–New Deal party agenda. Members of the GOP supported the president just less than half the time overall. On occasion, Truman found common ground with moderates in both parties. The passage of bills on rent control, housing, and the poll tax serve as examples.

Closer inspection of the data reveals the root causes of Truman's most significant losses. When the GOP remained cohesive on agenda priorities, southern Democrats frequently joined their ranks. Truman won a majority of Democrats on just less than half the votes in the analysis when close and nonclose votes are combined. His defeats included issues ranging from labor and antitrust legislation (Taft–Hartley and interstate commerce) to Social Security payments and housing. The president's defeats on these domestic floor votes, as on his vetoes of several of these issues, stemmed from GOP leaders' exploitation of conservative southern Democrats' support of select anti–New Deal legislation.

Republicans controlled 244 seats (56.4 percent) in the House, but as the president's mixed success rate among Democrats suggests, the Republicans' working majority was much higher. A significant proportion of southern Democrats regularly abandoned the president's positions and found more common policy ground with the congressional majority. Forty-four of the fifty House Democrats with ideological scores above the party median (meaning they were more conservative) were from the South. They bolstered the Republican leadership's working majority on crucial votes. This pivotal factor is visible in an analysis of individual support of Truman's legislative positions.

The pooled logistic regression model of legislative support emphasizes

Table 2.1
Truman's Legislative Success Rate,
80th Congress*

	Close Votes (n=3)	Nonclose Votes (n=16)
Overall	2 (66.7%)	9 (56.3%)
Democrats	0 (0%)	10 (62.5%)
Republicans	2 (66.7%)	9 (56.3%)

* Entries are the number and percentage of votes on which the president gained a majority overall and by party.

Truman's precarious position in the 80th Congress. Roosevelt's popularity in the 1944 election did not carry over to Truman after the midterm reversal in 1946.[21] Roosevelt's district-level margin had no significant impact on members of either party. Sensing their constituents' frustration with Truman's reconversion policies, all but the most liberal House Democrats were hesitant to support the president—who had not stood for election but who was widely blamed for the party's defeat at the polls in 1946.

The strong effect of ideology on Democratic support depicted in table 2.2 underscores the party's deep regional divide. The impact is most considerable on close votes. The negative sign of the coefficient shows that as Democratic members' ideological positions moved .10 to the left of the party median on the NOMINATE scale, the probability of support increased by 12 percent. The model forecasts that southern Democrats supported the president about 20 percent less than the party as a whole based on their ideological positions. Southerners were particularly averse to Truman's support of Hawaii statehood and rent control. They also parted ways with his opposition to issues such as limitations on employers' liability and Taft–Hartley.

Seat safety among southerners enhanced their independence from the president. Southerners' average margin of victory in 1946 was 74 percent ($\sigma = 34$), whereas the average margin of victory of northern Democrats was only 28 percent ($\sigma = 29$). The logit model forecasts that a Democrat who ran unopposed was over 10 percent less likely to support the president on less controversial legislation (nonclose votes). The greater levels of incumbency advantage among southerners, compared to their northern colleagues, thus proved one important impediment to Truman's ability to retain critical support among his copartisans. Southern Democrats did not fear electoral retaliation for voting against the president and joining the GOP majority.

It is no coincidence that the variable for the Democratic leadership has no significant impact on support for the president. Truman's situation vis-à-vis Democrats grew more tenuous from his failure to work for party solidarity. He did not confront a particularly hostile Democratic leadership, even though nine of the nineteen ranking committee members were southern Democrats. Rather, the president added to Democrats' fragmentation by limiting his contact with leaders and refusing to court them or rank-and-file members. For example, although Democratic floor leader Sam Rayburn supported the president more often than the party as a whole, the president's decision to avoid liaison with Rayburn and other leaders did little to assuage intraparty discord. Rayburn had been reluctant to take the minority leader post in 1947 out of fear that his involvement in partisan conflict in the 80th Congress would prove detrimental if he again became House Speaker.[22]

The negative sign of the coefficient for ideology among Republicans in table 2.2 confirms that Truman drew at least some support from liberal to moderate members of the opposition majority on a smattering of less controversial

Table 2.2
Logistic Regression Estimation of Party Support for Truman,
80th Congress

	Republicans		Democrats	
	Close Votes	Nonclose Votes	Close Votes	Nonclose Votes
Roosevelt's Margin of Victory, 1944 (%)	.761 (.618) *17.80*	.238 (.282) *4.90*	−.496 (.608) *−13.30*	.045 (.247) *1.10*
Legislator's Margin of Victory (%)	−.596 (.480) *−14.70*	−.135 (.220) *−3.30*	−.317 (.396) *−7.90*	−.430*** (.163) *−10.20*
Legislator's Terms Served	−.027 (.035) *−10.20*	.020* (.015) *7.20*	−.074 (.032) *−34.60*	−.009 (.013) *−4.50*
Republican Leaders	−.179 (.353) *−13.10*	.071 (.159) *5.00*	——	——
Committee Chairs	.209 .362 *5.20*	.063 (.064) *1.60*	——	——
Democratic Leaders	——	——	.504 (.451) *30.70*	.016 (.160) *1.20*
Ranking Minority Members	——	——	.712* (.460) *16.90*	.119 (.182) *2.80*
Ideology	−.103 (.828) *−2.10*	−1.78**** (.384) *−31.90*	−5.13**** (.906) *−42.20*	−1.70**** (.363) *26.10*
Public Approval of the President	−.339**** (.060) *−14.70*	.084**** (.004) *45.60*	.308**** (.073) *22.30*	.043**** (.005) *24.10*
Constant	18.92**** (3.30)	−3.22**** (.237)	−17.04**** (4.05)	−1.66**** (.262)
Number of Cases	619.00	3,286.00	458.00	2,383.00
−2 × Log Likelihood	815.70	4,018.12	538.14	3,062.80
Model χ^2	42.40****	470.93****	96.07****	149.99****
Pseudo-R^2	.05	.10	.15	.05
Cases Correctly Predicted	.62	.69	.68	.64

**** p < .001   *** p < .01   ** p < .05   * p < .10 (one-tailed tests)
Entries are maximum likelihood coefficients.
Standard errors are in parentheses. Mean effects are in *italics*.
The dependent variable is whether the legislator supported or opposed Truman's stand.

issues. The data also show that his dwindling job approval over the course of the 80th Congress eroded Republican as well as Democratic support. Truman's job approval rating began at 48 percent in January, 1947, peaked at 60 percent in March of that year, and then slowly declined, reaching a nadir of 36 percent in April, 1948. The impact of this decline had almost twice the impact on members of the GOP compared to Democrats. The predicted probability of Republican support diminishes by just over 20 percent as Truman's public approval fell from 46 to 36 percent. The message of this analysis is that as the president's public standing deteriorated, the Republican majority became energized to challenge Truman with its own policy priorities.

The factors subtending weak legislative support for Truman in each party help to explain both the Republicans' successful passage of a succession of limited anti–New Deal measures and Truman's ultimate decision to shun engagement in the legislative realm. As Truman purposively distanced himself from Congress, he searched for a way to turn the modest Republican legislative achievements to his electoral advantage in 1948. Calling Congress into a special "Turnip Day Session" in 1948, he made a last-minute barrage of bold domestic proposals upon which he knew Republicans would not have time to act. The strategy allowed Truman to distract voters' attention away from what the GOP had accomplished to what the party had failed, in his view, to achieve. He labeled the 80th a "do-nothing" Congress and took his message to the public in an exhaustive "whistle-stop" tour of the nation.[23]

Truman's strategy paid off, as he narrowly defeated New York governor Thomas Dewey in the 1948 election. Perhaps few pictures are more memorable in the annals of American electoral history than the one of Truman holding an advance copy of a Chicago paper with a banner headline proclaiming Dewey the winner. Truman's reelection defied the pundits' conventional wisdom. However, an evaluation of his witty electoral politics must be balanced by the Republican policies passed in the 80th Congress that were difficult to revise or repeal in subsequent years, such as Taft–Hartley and adjustments to Social Security coverage, despite the return of unified government. Truman's arguments in the fall of 1948 notwithstanding, the 80th Congress *did* engage in productive and innovative lawmaking. And that lawmaking was, by and large, without his blessing or had little association with his leadership.

Dwight D. Eisenhower and the Legislative Presidency, 1953–60

The confluence of several factors posited by the framework of presidential leverage explains why divided government was much less of a burden for Eisenhower. First, he had a limited agenda that was largely compatible with many moderate Republicans and conservative Democrats in the majority. Second, the opposition majorities he faced either did not have an activist agenda that gave rise to considerable interbranch conflict, or conservative forces in Congress operated in tandem with the administration to foreclose policy activism.[24] Third, Eisenhower profited from shifting voting alliances that provided him with frequent opportunities to work behind the scenes to build legislative support across issues. He maintained good relations with leaders of both parties while seeking to hold himself above the partisan bickering. Finally, his strong electoral popularity and high job approval ratings provided a firm basis for negotiations with Congress.

The quantity and substance of significant legislation adopted during Eisenhower's terms surely pales in comparison to that of the New Deal or Great Society. Judged by the standards of policy engagement that Eisenhower brought to the White House, however, the *absence* of far-reaching legislation must be regarded as a success in its own right. Eisenhower was less concerned with cutting domestic programs than he was with limiting growth in federal spending and maintaining fiscal responsibility—goals he largely achieved during his two terms. Importantly, though, the significant legislation that *did* pass evinced relatively consistent connections with his policy objectives.

Eisenhower was a "guardian" president, scarcely an ideologue. He noted at a press conference early in his first term that he was "not very much of a partisan,"[25] and he was uncomfortable with the role of "party leader."[26] As president, the World War II hero had twin goals in the domestic and foreign policy realms. The first was to ensure the continuation of an internationalist foreign policy vital to the security of the United States and its allies as the Cold War began to take shape. The second was to keep the growth of the federal government and spending at bay on the domestic front. Unlike many in the GOP's right wing in the 1950s, Eisenhower accepted the basic tenets of the New Deal.[27] He contended that the public would not accept the wholesale dismantling of the welfare state. "The best that could be realistically expected of a Republican president," Eisenhower believed, "was that he retard the movement toward enlarging government and that he work to change public expectations of government."[28]

Eisenhower's general disavowal of partisan politics structured his deference to congressional leaders of both parties on legislative matters. He relied on Republican leaders Charles Halleck, Joe Martin, and Everett Dirksen as much as he did on Democratic leaders Sam Rayburn and Lyndon Johnson. His approach to Congress allowed him to maintain a respectable success rate throughout his two terms, even in light of Democratic control of both chambers. Parties were less polarized compared to the 1980s and 1990s and voting structures were less consistent. Congressional Republicans were internally fractured over domestic and foreign affairs, divided as they were between the anti–New Deal, isolationist "Old Guard" and moderate to liberal and internationalist factions of the party. The regional split between liberal northern Democrats and conservative southern Democrats similarly hindered party unity on the other side of the aisle. Eisenhower had ample room to maneuver in the legislative process and build occasional supporting coalitions for his stands across issue areas. Sometimes he turned to the conservative coalition for his positions on domestic spending. At other times he drew support from liberal and moderate elements in both parties on issues such as civil rights. In combination with his legislative leadership style, Eisenhower's ability to set the agenda on significant legislation derived from his strong institutional position.

The Electoral Context of Eisenhower's Presidency, 1953–60: From Unified to Divided Government

Eisenhower was reluctant to enter politics, but his supporters' successful grassroots campaign, led by Republican Henry Cabot Lodge, ultimately convinced the General to run for president.[29] Upon winning the GOP nomination in 1952, however, Eisenhower "realized more keenly than ever before that he had become the candidate of a loose coalition including fanatics of the extreme right as well as middle-roaders and liberal elements."[30] The main cleavage in the party was between the liberal, eastern Republican establishment led by Thomas Dewey and conservative midwestern stalwarts antipathetic to big government and the New Deal, led by Sen. Robert Taft of Ohio.[31]

Although Taft persuaded Eisenhower to move more to the right on issues of fiscal policy, economy in government, and foreign policy, Eisenhower never launched appeals to scale back or do away with New Deal social programs and he was cautious on tax cuts.[32] Instead, the dual themes of ending the war in Korea and economic prosperity dominated the campaign against Democratic standard-bearer Adlai Stevenson. Eisenhower's illustrious military career and promise to go to Korea to end the conflict added to his popular appeal, culminating in his victory with over 55 percent of the popular vote in 1952.

Eisenhower's coattails were just long enough for Republicans to regain a majority in both chambers of Congress. The president ran ahead of more than half of the House Republicans elected in 1952. Yet as Chester Pach and Elmo Richardson note, "While a strong majority of Americans 'liked Ike,' they gave the Republicans a much smaller margin of victory in Congress."[33]

The party margins in Congress were slender and the nominal majority of Republicans did not promise Eisenhower a consistent working majority given the breadth of disagreement within the GOP. Republicans had only a three-seat majority in the House and a two-seat majority in the Senate in the 83d Congress (1953–54).

Eisenhower's coattails and personal popularity were not sufficient to sustain Republican control of Congress for long, however. The 1954 midterm elections clarified that the presidential election two years earlier had failed to spark a partisan realignment in the electorate. The lack of an issue-focused campaign notwithstanding, a record number of voters turned out in 1954 and a dealt the GOP a devastating setback.[34] Majority control of both chambers of Congress reverted to Democrats, who scored a net gain of seventeen seats in the House and regained control of the Senate with a gain of two seats. Old Guard Republicans contended that Eisenhower's distance from the congressional campaign trail until just a month before the election dashed the GOP's hopes. The president's reasoning was that bipartisan support for his programs would have been "seriously jeopardized if he publicly attacked the opposition."[35] Democrats wittingly used support of the popular president on the campaign trail. "The Democrats," Malcolm Moos explains, "were able to say to the electorate: 'The President really needs us. Look how we have given this popular President more support than his own party on some of the really critical votes.'"[36]

The 1956 election pitted Eisenhower against Adlai Stevenson for a second time. The campaign was conducted without overarching national policy themes. With a healthy economy, the Korean War ended, and his public approval boosted by foreign policy crises that produced a "rally-'round-the-flag" effect on the eve of the election, Eisenhower improved on his popular vote margin over 1952, defeating Stevenson by nearly 9 million votes.[37] The 1956 election did not produce the necessary coattails for the GOP to regain control of Congress, however, and the Democrats maintained their lock on both chambers. Democratic voters who had abandoned the party in 1952 over the corruption controversies connected to Truman returned to the party fold in congressional races, although Eisenhower remained personally popular.[38]

The 1958 midterm elections presaged the partisan rancor that would rock Congress in the final two years of Eisenhower's lame-duck presidency. In classic fashion, voters turned out in droves to punish the president's party for the economic recession that took shape in 1957. Poor local organization added to the Republican's losses as Democrats gained in both urban and rural areas as the economy worsened.[39] House Democrats gained a 130-seat majority over

Republicans—nearly a two-to-one advantage—and the influx of eighty-two new members promised both a more liberal policy response to Eisenhower's moderate stands and challenges to conservative forces within Congress.

As the GOP's electoral fortunes changed during his two terms, Eisenhower attempted to remain above the commotion of partisan politicking. His general stance was based on the "firm belief that a Republican president, even with a Republican Congress, could not introduce large change in public policy and programs, but must instead be content to work at the margins."[40] He did not even put forth a legislative program before Congress his first year until prompted to do so by his staff.[41] Eisenhower, his close entourage of advisers, and congressional leaders engaged in low-key negotiation on select legislation. Eisenhower's legislative approach to divided government "fared well because of the president's great popularity, his personal friendships with Democratic leaders Sam Rayburn and Lyndon Johnson, the skill of his staff, and mostly because he did not ask for a great deal."[42] A review of Eisenhower's involvement in significant lawmaking from 1953–60 elucidates his strategy and success.

Lawmaking and Leadership under Eisenhower

Eisenhower's strategy for dealing with Congress was to "defer to its coordinate status, but seek to lead it".[43] Despite the lack of an expansive domestic agenda, the president quickly established an office of congressional relations headed by his friend and personal confidant Gen. Wilton Persons and staffed with capable individuals experienced in the ways of Capitol Hill.[44] The president delegated responsibility for legislative issues to the liaison staff under Persons's tutelage and depended upon congressional leaders to work out the details of proposals. The president sought to "create a mechanism for maintaining friendly relations with Congress, point it in the right direction and let it run, taking personal control only during critical moments or during turbulence."[45] He was careful to ensure consultation with leaders before any major initiative was announced. In unified and divided government the president relied principally on Halleck in the House, and, upon Taft's death in 1953, Dirksen in the Senate, to win congressional support for his positions, and he continued to meet on a weekly basis with leaders of both parties when the Democrats regained control of Congress in 1954.[46]

There is much evidence of Eisenhower's laissez-faire style of congressional leadership in an analysis of the twenty-four significant domestic laws passed from 1953–60 that Mayhew included on his list. Eisenhower overtly opposed few laws that emanated from the congressional agenda, and he wielded the veto only as a last resort to bring about compromise. Eisenhower and Congress were generally content to share credit for the significant legislation that emerged. Congress did not bypass the president altogether, but neither did Eisenhower attempt to take the reins of Congress forcefully. Congressional deference to the president, Eisenhower's strong institutional position, and joint policy moderation between the branches precluded the development of an expanded contested agenda. Consequently, Eisenhower's two terms were typified by limited policy action on the domestic front, bipartisanship, and infrequent executive-legislative conflict. When Eisenhower chose to intervene in the legislative arena, his mixed strategy of positive leverage and occasional veto usage was typically successful in shaping significant laws.

Eisenhower's lack of a first-year legislative program is reflected in the dearth of significant legislation passed in 1953. The only important law Mayhew notes is the tidelands oil bill, which turned over control of offshore reserves from the federal government to the states. Truman vetoed a bill in 1952 that was similar to the one that passed under Eisenhower's watch. All eight of the other bills passed during the second session of the 83d Congress—the only period of unified Republican control from 1945–2000—were linked to Eisenhower's limited policy objectives. Few of the bills could pass without bipartisan support, and the president's flexibility and reliance upon congressional leaders facilitated crafting that support. Tax cut and Social Security legislation are prime examples of his reserved approach to legislative affairs.

The president called for a comprehensive revision to the tax code in his January, 1954, State of the Union address, hoping to reinforce congressional efforts begun the year before. The president favored a tax cut, but only to the degree that it would not hinder his goal of reducing the federal budget deficit.[47] The final tax reduction bill did not go as far as he wanted in slashing dividend taxes, but he was successful in warding off Democratic attempts to raise the personal exemption substantially. Eisenhower lauded the final bill's provisions as part of his larger economic program, calling the tax revision "a law which will help millions of Americans by giving them fairer tax treatment than they now receive."[48]

Eisenhower believed that Social Security was "an absolute necessity in a modern, industrialized society."[49] He repeatedly warned that any attempts by Republicans to alter the program radically would spell disaster for the party. The president proposed and won congressional approval for an extension of the old age and survivors insurance (OASI) program to over 10 million citizens. A select House committee charged with sorting through more than two hundred competing proposals completed much of the legislative work. In the final analysis, Eisenhower did not win everything he wanted in the bill. Congress exempted self-employed individuals from coverage, which the president supported. Still, much of Eisenhower's plan was adopted—including an increase in payments, an easing of restrictions on income ceilings for retirees, and revisions to the federal-state cost-sharing formula.[50] The Housing, Agriculture and Atomic Energy Acts of 1954 were important laws that reflected Eisenhower's emphasis on private initiative in sectors of the economy in which the federal government had been predominant for some time. Flexibility again marked the president's approach. He proposed giving private industry a larger share of mortgage loans while compromising with Congress on the construction of new public housing units. Eisenhower then proposed replacing farm subsidies fixed at 90 percent of parity with flexible price supports. Opposition emerged among Republicans from farm states, and the president wound up compromising with Clifford Hope of Kansas by accepting a higher ceiling on subventions. Finally, Eisenhower sought and won congressional approval for private ownership of nuclear energy reactors. The congressional debate centered on costs and controversies surrounding the Dixon-Yates contract for a power plant in Arkansas to supply electricity to greater Memphis. The president relied on congressional leaders to manage the internal debate, and was pleased with the final bill, which allowed the Atomic Energy Commission to issue licenses to private businesses.[51]

Relations between Eisenhower and Congress did not become hostile after Democrats won back and maintained control of the House and Senate after 1954. As in the brief period of unified control, the majority of laws were connected with the president's agenda, and he continued to depend on congressional leaders to take charge of specifics. Eisenhower wielded the veto on only two important laws, winning compromises with Democrats each time.

Eleven of the eighteen important laws adopted from 1955–60 emanated from Eisenhower's recommendations for legislative action, typically articulated during the State of the Union address or through special messages to Congress. The genesis for some of the bills included several presidential commissions and task forces. Perhaps the most sweeping legislation was the federal aid for highways bill in 1956, which accorded more than $31 billion over a thirteen-year period for the development of the interstate system. At the time, the bill represented the largest public works appropriation for roads in U.S. history. Eisenhower placed Gen. Lucius Clay in charge of a blue-ribbon committee to study the state of the nation's roads. Although the president failed to get Congress to issue bonds for highway construction in 1955, he reiterated his support of a large-scale highway bill in his 1956 State of the Union speech and in a special message to Congress later that year. Prodding the Democratic majority to action, the president compromised on financing and agreed to a "pay-as-you-go" plan.[52] He contended that the legislation would serve the purposes of defense transportation and improve the standard of living in rapidly growing urban areas.

Eisenhower commissioned two task forces to investigate the status of the nation's science and technology training. His special message to Congress formed the basis for the National Defense Education Act of 1958, which guaranteed over $1 billion in loans and grants to students and secondary institutions.[53] The emphasis on science training came in the wake of the launch of the USSR's *Sputnik* satellite, prompting alarm about America's relative technological advantage over the Soviets. Eisenhower had been previously unsuccessful in marshaling support for federal involvement in education in 1956 and 1957. Southern Democrats and key Republicans had opposed various elements of his proposals, and the conservative coalition united to defeat them. As Wayne Steger notes, "For three years, the administration had pitched its bill as being necessary to resolve the country's shortage of classrooms and teachers. In 1958, the administration reframed the issue as a matter of national security . . . the 'defense' rationale was a compelling argument for congressional conservatives."[54] The 1958 bill passed with the support of majorities of both parties.

The president also won adoption of legislation for space exploration and mandatory indemnification for the nuclear industry. In a special message to Congress, he proposed the idea of a National Aeronautics and Space Administration to be charged with coordinating space exploration.[55] Lyndon Johnson, the Senate majority leader, took the lead in marshaling the bill through Congress. Eisenhower's recommendation that Congress take action to require licensees of nuclear reactors to carry liability insurance culminated in the Price-Anderson amendments.[56]

Although he rarely employed the veto on important legislation, Eisenhower managed voting alliances in Congress to his advantage when he did. He vetoed two bills and was successful each time in compelling Congress to eventually compromise on provisions to which he objected. Agricultural subsidies were a particularly thorny issue. The president sent a special farm message to Congress in January, 1956, in which he proposed paying farmers not to plant on portions of their land. The "soil bank" was aimed at preventing the persistent surpluses of commodities that drove down prices. When the Democratic majority passed a bill to reinstate mandatory price controls, Eisenhower vetoed the measure. Unsuccessful in their attempt to override the veto, House leaders reworked the 1956 Agriculture Act and passed an omnibus bill that omitted most of the provisions to which the president had objected. The final bill that emerged was thus a compromise. The shortcoming for Eisenhower was that passage of the bill in late May, 1956, all but ensured that the soil bank program would not affect that year's crops.[57]

Eisenhower squared off against the Senate on housing issues and ultimately triumphed in persuading Democrats to shape a less costly bill after two vetoes. In a special budget message to Congress, the president expressed his desire to extricate the federal government from urban renewal programs and compel states and local governments to pay more of the costs. He vetoed the first rendition of the 1959 Housing Act because it called for 190,000 new public housing units and other programs he called inflationary. In this case, the conservative coalition worked to the president's advantage. Republicans and a handful of southern Democrats joined to prevent a Senate override of the first bill. When Senate Republicans failed to delete a loan program for college classrooms and Federal Housing Authority (FHA) insurance programs were expanded in a second version of the bill, Eisenhower employed the veto pen a second time. Senate Republicans and southern Democrats again prevented an override, but with a less comfortable margin. In an end-of-session rush, Congress finally amended the bill to Eisenhower's satisfaction by eliminating the college loan program, limiting FHA obligations, and spreading outlays for urban renewal programs over a two-year period.[58]

The two civil rights bills adopted in 1957 and 1960 deserve special mention in terms of presidential leadership. Eisenhower has been roundly criticized for failing to provide forceful leadership on civil rights. His public statements were often muddled, his public silence on the *Brown v. Board of Education* decision troubled many, and his stances were largely peripheral to the internal debate in Congress once the administration's bills were submitted. At worst, the limited progress on civil rights that the two laws accomplished did little to quell the tumult that would rock the South in the early 1960s. At best, they laid the groundwork for a substantial strengthening of civil and voting rights that culminated during Johnson's presidency. The two bills nonetheless provided some credit-claiming opportunities for the president and progressives from both parties.

Eisenhower was reluctant to engage the civil rights debate, consistent with his views about limiting the federal government's reach. He was loath to intervene directly in "local matters." Even as unrest fomented in the South following the *Brown* decision, the president could conceive of no situation in which federal troops would be required because the "common sense of America would never require it."[59] The intransigence of Arkansas governor Orval Faubus to desegregate schools in Little Rock would, of course, prove him wrong in September, 1957.

The Civil Rights Acts of 1957 and 1960 are best viewed as a tempered response by Eisenhower to blacks' growing demands for equality, balanced both by his general sympathy for white southerners and his hesitancy about the prospects for rapid change. At the top of his list of priorities in proposing the civil rights bills was the hope of avoiding confrontation and maintaining civil order in the South. The 1957 bill followed from Eisenhower's State of the Union proposal to create a bipartisan commission to investigate civil rights violations and expand the attorney general's powers in voting rights matters. Passed by the House, the measure largely conformed to Eisenhower's goals. But southern Democrats managed to substantially weaken provisions calling for jury trials in voting rights cases and gave short shrift to expanding the attorney general's authority. Eisenhower ardently opposed the jury trial provisions because all-white juries in the segregated South were unlikely to render judgments favoring black plaintiffs.

As adopted, the 1957 bill established an independent fact-finding commission and left voting rights enforcement to the courts. Despite its shortcomings, Eisenhower took solace that the bill was the first civil rights legislation passed since 1875. Moreover, although the president was taciturn on the *Brown* decision, the six-member commission he appointment was chaired by Stanley Reed, a former Supreme Court justice and Kentucky Democrat who supported the high court's decision.[60]

Eisenhower submitted another civil rights bill in 1959 that Senators Johnson and Dirksen maneuvered jointly through the upper chamber the following year. The bill was aimed at picking up where the 1957 legislation left off in terms of voting rights, but it ultimately fell short of the president's objectives. While the 1960 Civil Rights Act provided for greater penalties for the interstate transport of bombs, it failed to expedite desegregation efforts in school districts and create an equal employment opportunity commission. Enforcement of voting rights was again left to the courts, which could appoint referees to assist with the registration of blacks. Further progress on civil rights would await the landmark legislation of 1964–65 under President Johnson's leadership.[61]

Five of the eighteen significant laws passed between 1955 and 1960 were not part of Eisenhower's stated policy objectives, but joint credit-claiming opportunities for the president and Congress remained. The president publicly expressed support for the Alaska and Hawaii statehood bills, which were

clearly part of the continuing legislative agenda in Congress. Efforts for statehood began much earlier in the century. The Agriculture Act of 1958 and the
Kerr-Mills legislation providing medical care for the aged were compromise
bills. Eisenhower and the Democratic majority reached an agreement on agricultural price supports after a series of failed bills. The president joined with
liberal Democrats in support of a comprehensive bill for the elderly that failed,
but took no position on the final votes on Kerr-Mills after compromising on
the contours of a federal matching aid program for the states.

The only bill that Eisenhower publicly opposed but did not veto was the
Social Security increase of 1958. The president criticized Democrats on the
House Ways and Means Committee for holding closed hearings on the proposal and argued that the 1954 Social Security revisions were adequate. Congress nevertheless pushed for legislation to reduce the eligibility age from
sixty-five to fifty. Eisenhower was reluctant to challenge Democrats on the issue for fear of a popular backlash. He put the best face on the bill when he
signed it, noting that varying the federal matching amount according to states'
financial resources and other provisions were a positive step. However, consistent with his concern about deficits, he also expressed reservations about
the increase in federal expenditures.[62]

By examining a larger set of domestic issues one can gain a fuller appreciation of how the context of divided government in the 1950s provided Eisenhower with opportunities to hold sway over legislative outcomes. Analysis of
party support for Eisenhower's stands on floor votes demonstrates the link between support from congressional leaders, his moderate stands, shifting coalitional support, and his success rate under unified and divided conditions.

Eisenhower's Success and Support in the 83d and 85th Congresses

The incidence of unified government in 1953–54 boosted Eisenhower's success rate across vote categories. He received strong support from Republicans, but there were only four close votes on which the president expressed a
position in the 83d Congress. The issues hardly reflected an expansive presidential agenda. The votes ranged from agriculture appropriations to a motion
to recommit the bill on excise tax reductions.

Split-party control had only a moderately negative impact on Eisenhower's
floor success rate from 1955–60. His victory rate on close votes reached a nadir
in the 85th Congress, in large part because Republicans were divided internally over the appropriate legislative response to the recession into which the
economy had sunk by 1957. Conservatives in the party sought to cut domestic
programs dramatically, while Eisenhower and moderates favored a more tem-

Table 2.3
Eisenhower's Legislative Success Rate, Close and Nonclose Votes,
83d–86th Congresses*

Close Votes	Congress			
	83d (n=4)	84th (n=5)	85th (n=15)	86th (n=7)
Overall	3 (75%)	2 (40%)	4 (26.7%)	3 (42.9%)
Democrats	0 (0%)	1 (20%)	10 (66.7%)	3 (42.9%)
Republicans	4 (100%)	4 (80%)	4 (26.7%)	4 (57.1%)

Nonclose Votes	Congress			
	83d (n=22)	84th (n=14)	85th (n=31)	86th (n=31)
Overall	18 (81.3%)	8 (57.1%)	20 (64.5%)	14 (48.4%)
Democrats	11 (50%)	7 (50%)	21 (67.7%)	12 (38.7%)
Republicans	20 (90.9%)	10 (71.4%)	16 (54.8%)	25 (80.6%)

* Entries are the number and percentage of votes on which the president gained a majority overall and by party.

pered response. On less controversial votes, however, Eisenhower fared well. His position prevailed on generally more than half the stands he took, and he often gleaned a majority of Democrats.

The results of logistic regression analyses of presidential support for Republicans and Democrats are shown, respectively, in tables 2.4 and 2.5. Model estimations were completed for the 83d Congress (1953–54) and the 85th Congress (1957–58) in order to compare the effects of electoral and institutional variables at the beginning of each of Eisenhower's terms and under unified and divided party control. The data tap elements of the president's hidden-hand approach to fashioning legislative coalitions.[63] When he was successful in upholding his legislative stands it was often because of the support and intervention of party leaders on both sides of the aisle.

Bipartisan support is a constant feature of Eisenhower's legislative presidency. In the brief period of unified control, House Republican leaders gave the president stable levels of support. The leadership variable for close votes was excluded from the estimation because it *perfectly predicts support.*[64] On nonclose votes, members of the leadership were 10–12 percent more likely to support the president compared to rank-and-file members. Strong support from Joe Martin and Leslie Arends did not fade with the passing of unified conditions. Although some in the GOP shirked support of the president's

Table 2.4
Logistic Regression Estimation of Republicans' Domestic Policy Support for Eisenhower,
83d and 85th Congresses

	83d Congress		85th Congress	
	Close Votes	Nonclose Votes	Close Votes	Nonclose Votes
Eisenhower's Margin	.06	−.00	−.16	.74***
of Victory, 1952/1956 (%)	(.29)	(.13)	(.43)	(.31)
	1.10	*.10*	*−2.50*	*11.10*
Legislator's Margin	.02	.00	−.78***	−.74***
of Victory (%)	(.52)	(.23)	(.33)	(.24)
	.20	*.10*	*−18.80*	*−18.30*
Legislator's Terms	−.08***	−.03**	.07****	.04****
Served	(.03)	(.01)	(.01)	(.01)
	−22.80	*−7.60*	*30.60*	*18.10*
Republican Leaders	———	.36**	.25**	.03
		(.18)	(.13)	(.08)
		12.40	*23.30*	*2.70*
Committee Chairs (83d)	.31	.13	−.15	.01
Ranking Minority	(.36)	(.17)	(.16)	(.12)
Members (85th)	*4.50*	*1.80*	*−3.70*	*.40*
Ideology	−.80	−.84**	−4.82****	−5.31****
	(.89)	(.39)	(.43)	(.32)
	−7.20	*−8.70*	*−57.10*	*−61.20*
Public Approval	−.21****	−.02**	−.07****	−.10****
of the President	(.04)	(.01)	(.01)	(.01)
	−26.70	*−12.40*	*−32.30*	*−39.90*
Constant	17.27****	3.01****	5.39****	7.06****
	(2.66)	(.59)	(.37)	(.35)
Number of Cases	789.00	4,278.00	2,678.00	5,062.00
−2 × Log Likelihood	682.78	2,885.82	2,352.18	6,335.50
Model χ^2	81.83****	19.41***	350.97****	655.42****
Pseudo-R^2	.11	.01	.09	.09
Cases Correctly Predicted	.81	.83	.67	.66

**** p < .001   *** p < .01   ** p < .05   * p < .10 (one-tailed tests)
Entries are maximum likelihood coefficients.
Standard errors are in parentheses.
Mean effects are in *italics*.
The dependent variable is whether the legislator supported or opposed Eisenhower's stand.

moderate positions in 1957–58, leaders were particularly supportive of Eisenhower on close votes.

It is also telling that the mean effects for support among Democratic leaders under divided government are positive and quite strong. Support from John McCormack and Carl Albert ranged from 10–26 percent higher than rank-and-file Democrats on controversial *and* less controversial legislation in the 85th Congress. The data point to one of the core reasons why Eisenhower maintained a fairly successful record in the 85th Congress, despite the divide among Republicans over government cutbacks. Liaison with Democratic

Table 2.5
Logistic Regression Estimation of Democrats' Domestic Policy Support for Eisenhower, 83d and 85th Congresses

	83d Congress		85th Congress	
	Close Votes	Nonclose Votes	Close Votes	Nonclose Votes
Eisenhower's Margin	−.57*	.27**	.29*	.03
of Victory, 1952/1956 (%)	(.34)	(.11)	(.22)	(.15)
	−10.60	*9.20*	*7.50*	*1.30*
Legislator's Margin	−1.03***	−.17*	−.17	−.28***
of Victory (%)	(.35)	(.11)	(.14)	(.10)
	−13.30	*−4.40*	*−4.50*	*−6.90*
Legislator's Terms Served	.04	.00	−.01	.00
	(.04)	(.01)	(.01)	(.01)
	10.60	*1.10*	*−7.40*	*2.30*
Democratic Leaders	−.14	.09	.29**	.15*
	(.42)	(.15)	(.14)	(.10)
	−5.80	*9.80*	*25.90*	*13.60*
Ranking Minority	−.31	−.01	−.37**	−.14
Members (83d)	(.54)	(.16)	(.17)	(.12)
Committee Chairs (85th)	*−3.60*	*−.10*	*−9.10*	*−3.40*
Ideology	−3.49****	.77***	−3.72****	−3.44****
	(.79)	(.25)	(.28)	(.20)
	−28.20	*12.50*	*−59.10*	*−54.50*
Public Approval	.19****	.01*	.05****	.02****
of the President	(.03)	(.006)	(.01)	(.004)
	26.1	*4.2*	*21.5*	*10.6*
Constant	−15.67****	−.63	−3.33****	−1.58****
	(2.29)	(.48)	(.34)	(.31)
Number of Cases	677.00	3,605.00	3,062.00	5,878.00
−2 × Log Likelihood	581.92	4,971.60	2,811.75	7,393.40
Model χ^2	121.40****	20.78***	422.67****	587.69****
Pseudo-R^2	.17	.00	.10	.07
Cases Correctly Predicted	.76	.54	.66	.65

**** p < .001   *** p < .01   ** p < .05   * p < .10 (one-tailed tests)
Entries are maximum likelihood coefficients.
Standard errors are in parentheses.
Mean effects are in *italics*.
The dependent variable is whether the legislator supported or opposed Eisenhower's stand.

leaders paid off. Leaders consistently backed his positions and were well placed to marshal moderates' support behind his policy stances.

Eisenhower's policy moderation is also borne out in the weak impact of legislators' ideological positions as a predictor of support in the 83d Congress. The negative coefficients convey that Eisenhower drew slightly more support from Republican legislators *to the left* of the party median, but the substantive effect is modest. Among Democrats, the president drew somewhat more support from *liberal Democrats on close votes* and slightly more support from legislators *to the right of the party median on nonclose votes*. The data underscore how Eisenhower's legislative positions had the greatest level of appeal to middle-of-the-road members of both parties. Support from different congressional factions changed across issue areas. Unlike Truman, who faced a much more cohesive opposition majority on select bills, Eisenhower drew support from different wings of the parties and worked closely with leaders.

The dynamics of legislative support changed somewhat in the turbulent economic circumstances surrounding the 85th Congress. Members' ideological stances have the greatest impact on close and nonclose votes under divided government. In both instances, Eisenhower obtained substantial support from moderate to liberal Republicans *and* Democrats, and the net effects are similar. The likelihood of support among Democrats increases by just over 9 percent as a legislator's position moves just .10 to the left of the party median. Much of this effect is attributable to the president's opposition to proposals by conservative Democrats and Republicans to cut governmental programs. In particular, Eisenhower was at odds with southern Democrats and members of the Taft wing of the GOP, who proposed slashing federal salaries, unemployment compensation benefits, and outlays for the Departments of Labor and Health, Education, and Welfare. In addition, the president favored expenditures for school construction, flood insurance, and publics works programs like the Glen Canyon Dam, to which conservatives in both parties were averse as the economy slowed.

The incumbency advantage among members of both parties mattered more than Eisenhower's electoral popularity. The model does, however, point to a positive effect of Eisenhower's electoral popularity in solidifying the support of Democrats from districts where he was popular across a smattering of issues in the 83d and 85th Congresses. Nonetheless, both Democratic and Republican legislators with safe seats were more apt to shirk supporting the president. The effect is most pronounced among Republicans in the 85th Congress. A member who ran without opposition in 1956 was more than 18 percent less likely to back the president on either set of votes. In addition, Republicans who had served longer in Congress were less likely to defer to the president upon the return of unified government in 1953. Seat safety gave members the latitude to eschew supporting Eisenhower without fear of electoral reprisal. Incumbency advantage was thus one of the core challenges that Eisenhower, like Truman, faced in the legislative arena. Unlike Truman, however, Eisenhower relied heavily on congressional leaders to counteract the effect of incumbency in his bid to construct winning legislative coalitions.

Eisenhower was almost universally popular in Republican members' districts. The lack of an impact of electoral popularity in 1952 and 1956 may seem somewhat counterintuitive, but one might posit several factors in addition to incumbency advantage to account for this finding. First, the framework of presidential leverage posits that the relative influence of the president's electoral popularity is intrinsically linked to the policy focus of elections. Eisenhower had no sweeping agenda or specific policies on which he campaigned in 1952 and 1956 other than themes of peace, prosperity, and keeping federal spending in check. Second, it follows that because Eisenhower's electoral appeal was his strong personal popularity among voters, his "outsider" status vis-à-vis Old Guard Republicans did not give him an automatic claim to party leadership. Internal divisions plagued the GOP in the 1950s on issues spanning the economy to foreign policy, and Eisenhower's election did little to quell those divisions. His electoral popularity shaped the context of his legislative presidency, but in ways that the statistical model of congressional support cannot sufficiently capture. What comes through most clearly is Eisenhower's ability to read the congressional landscape of shifting voting alliances in both parties and turn it to his advantage with the aid of leaders.

Although Eisenhower's public approval rating is positively related to Democrats' support, it shows an inverse relationship for Republicans. A closer reading of the data suggests that issue-focused voting and the relative constancy in Eisenhower's approval for the votes in the analysis explain much of the effect. During the 83d Congress, Eisenhower's job approval rating never dipped below 60 percent for the votes in the analysis. Even at the height of the recession in 1957, his popularity did not drop below 48 percent. Like Reagan, Eisenhower is one of the few presidents to leave office nearly as popular as when he began his term. There is simply less variation in Eisenhower's approval for the votes in the analysis when compared to other presidents. Congressional workload was relatively modest in the 1950s compared to the present day, and Congress typically remained in session for a shorter period of time. In the 85th Congress, six of the fifteen close votes were taken *on the same day,* so there was no variation in the president's job approval for these votes. Similarly, eight of the nonclose votes were taken during months when Eisenhower's popularity was at an enviable 66 percent.

The data analysis accentuates how Eisenhower's legislative stands appealed to moderates in both parties. The shifting coalitions of the period played a central role in his floor success rate. Eisenhower's flexible approach to legislative affairs was consonant with the decentralized setting of Congress in the 1950s and was possible because of the crosscutting cleavages in both parties. Eisenhower used shifting voting alignments in Congress to his advantage—in some cases to promote legislation, in other cases to fend off legislation with which he disagreed. Most of all, though, his reliance on leaders was central to keeping himself above the fracas of partisan politics that might otherwise have detracted from his legislative success. The institutional setting that he faced in Congress, coupled with his engagement in legislative affairs, mark important contrasts to Truman's experience. Truman shunned working with opposition leaders to negotiate the legislative agenda, abstained from engaging leaders in his own party to manage intraparty divisions, and ultimately ran against Congress with much partisan rhetoric. Eisenhower's engagement in the legislative realm provided a more solid basis to jointly claim credit with legislators and leaders in both parties for significant policies of the day.

Eisenhower emerges as one of the more successful presidents under divided government, particularly when he is judged by the limited policy objectives he set for his administration. Scholars and historians have incorrectly assumed that Eisenhower's lack of an active agenda and delegation to staff meant that he was unconcerned about policy. Working outside of public view, placing a premium on good relations with leaders of both parties, and maintaining a nonpartisan image, he was able to maintain a fairly consistent success rate despite sustained split-party control after 1954. Eisenhower's approach to legislative politics did not heal the split in the Republican Party any more than Truman's 1948 campaign closed the gap in ideological cleavages among Democrats. Most importantly, however, Eisenhower's legislative presidency did not lead to frequent interbranch conflict of the type that would come to characterize subsequent periods of divided control in the twentieth century.

Summary

Placing Truman's and Eisenhower's experiences with divided government in the framework of presidential leverage emphasizes the variable impact of party control during the bipartisan conservative era. The boundaries of the contested agenda between the branches were much greater in the 80th Congress than during the six years of divided party control under Eisenhower. The brief period of divided government in 1947–48 was characterized by a congressionally driven national policy agenda. Relegated to quasi-permanent minority status in Congress for almost two decades, Republicans seized the opportunity of their ephemeral majority to pick away at elements of the New Deal. Truman's uniquely weak coalition building and veto leverage eroded the basis for much influence over congressional policy making.

Eisenhower was in a much stronger position to focus congressional attention on his policy priorities and influence legislative outcomes. Eisenhower managed the internal divide in his partisan base and drew from diversity in ideological positions among Democrats. He turned to leaders on both sides of the aisle for support. His leadership style of selective engagement and flexibility in the legislative sphere sometimes allowed him to gain support from the conservative coalition, and at other times from loose coalitions of moderates and liberals. The result was frequent credit-claiming opportunities. Eisenhower played a far more central role in shaping significant legislative outcomes than Truman.

The next chapter moves through political time to the liberal activist era to examine Richard Nixon's complex response to divided control. Nixon did not have Eisenhower's leverage, but neither was he in as weak a position as Truman to negotiate the contested agenda. Nixon's success in the legislative arena bears some resemblance to Eisenhower's strategy of allying himself with different factions across party lines to claim credit for important laws. He was aided in this effort by the shifting voting alignments prevalent in Congress in the late 1960s and early 1970s, although he faced a far more activist opposition majority than Eisenhower.

3 Nixon and Divided Government

110 SEVERAL PUZZLES ARE INHERENT in Richard Nixon's first term under divided government in the liberal activist era. The first is the extraordinary production of innovative legislation in the late 1960s and early 1970s. Nixon's presidency forms an important component of the "bulge in the middle" of lawmaking since the end of World War II.[1] A second is Nixon's high floor success rate. As the Introduction and chapter 1 showed, Nixon was one of the most successful presidents on floor outcomes. These features of his legacy are difficult to square with traditional expectations that a conservative president and a liberal, opposition-controlled Congress would produce more conflict and gridlock than far-reaching legislation.

Grasping Nixon's legislative strategy and its impact upon his floor success rate and involvement in significant legislation demands a close examination of the unique electoral, institutional, and policy context surrounding divided government from 1969–72. Nixon's reelection incentive shaped substantial, *positive* competition between the branches to lay claim to the domestic policies that emerged in the 91st and 92d Congresses. Paul Quirk and Bruce Nesmith correctly emphasize that when there is support in the electorate for action on broad, crosscutting issues, the president and Congress are more likely to struggle over credit for policy outcomes.[2] When pressure for policy activism diminishes in the electorate, on the other hand, the potential for gridlock increases.

Nixon ceded to the momentum of the Democrats' legislative agenda. He adopted a multifaceted strategy that included making changes at the margins of policy outcomes, preempting the congressional majority on select issues, and portraying himself as a fiscal conservative while expressing support for a host of "progressive" legislation. Nixon adjusted his positions to the shifting policy coalitions to which the decentralized Democratic Congress was susceptible. His limited leverage derived from multiple sources. He was able to carry some modest influence over the structure of supporting voting blocs by dint of his electoral popularity and by maximizing support from conservative

Democrats on domestic spending issues. When support fell short, he turned to veto threats to gain compromise. On other issues, he allied himself more with moderate elements in both parties as a credit-claiming strategy. The key point that emerges from an analysis of Nixon's involvement in significant legislation and explicates his high floor success rate is that he *cooperated in* policy coalitions in Congress much more than he *generated* them.

The Policy-Making Environment: Nixon, Congress, and the 1968 Elections

The rocky road leading to the November, 1968, elections was marked by civil unrest and the assassination of Rev. Martin Luther King Jr. and Robert F. Kennedy. Divided government was at least partially a product of the steep divisions within the Democratic Party.[3] The war in Vietnam dominated the Democratic convention in Chicago, deeply splitting the party faithful in an atmosphere marked by clashes between protesters and the police. Opponents of the war championed the candidacy of Eugene McCarthy, while Vice Pres. Hubert Humphrey struggled with his loyalty to President Johnson on one hand, and the need to differentiate himself from Johnson's policies in Southeast Asia on the other. Humphrey, the eventual nominee, attempted to walk a fine line, advocating a peaceful solution to the conflict but not ruling out the possibility of the resumption of bombing.[4]

Nixon focused on "law and order" throughout much of the campaign, eschewing discussion of Vietnam other than to emphasize his commitment to reach "peace with honor." He centered his campaign on issues of crime and President Johnson's putative failure to curb domestic violence. On social policy Nixon made only general statements about decentralizing power and moving the country beyond the programs of the New Deal.[5]

"The central paradox of the 1968 election," David Broder notes, "was that . . . A year that saw repeated challenges from the nation's political left- and right-wings ended with the country dividing with almost mathematical equality between two candidates of the center."[6] Nixon maintained a sizable lead throughout most of the campaign. Humphrey rebounded toward the end, however, and Nixon wound up winning a narrow plurality of the popular vote: 43.6 percent, less than a 1 percent margin over Humphrey. Alabama governor George Wallace, who mounted a third-party challenge and campaigned on a platform of racial segregation, law and order, and victory in Vietnam, could not extend his appeal beyond the Deep South, where he won five states.[7] Voters in border states and the mid-South rejected both Wallace and Humphrey. Nixon carried Tennessee, Kentucky, Virginia, North and South Carolina, Florida, and Oklahoma. Scholars have debated the extent of Nixon's "southern strategy" of appealing to white segregationists, but his frequent criticism of the Warren Court's decisions on crime and social policy (forced integration) and South Carolina senator Strom Thurmond's endorsement surely added to his gains in the region.[8]

Humphrey's near comeback in 1968 suggested that voters had rejected neither the Great Society's domestic programs nor their expansion. The congressional elections provided further evidence as Nixon failed to provide significant coattails: Republicans gained only four seats in the House and five seats in the Senate. Such meager gains contrasted sharply to the forty-seven seats Republicans won in the 1966 midterm elections.[9] In the complicated three-way presidential race, few congressional candidates owed their victory directly to Nixon, and memories of his tireless campaigning for his copartisans in 1966 began to fade. Nixon confronted a burgeoning Democratic majority, which quickly ensnared him in the continuing thrust of the consolidation of the Great Society. The Democratic majority, whatever its divisions over Vietnam, had little incentive to recede from completing work on the domestic front begun earlier in the decade. Much of the legislative "surge" during Nixon's first term may be attributed to the "public mood" that spurred governmental action. As Mayhew points out, "Among the centers of activity were interlocking civil rights, consumer, antiwar, labor, student, women's liberation, environmental and 'public interest' movements."[10]

With an eye toward reelection in 1972, Nixon realized that he could face a severe voter backlash by launching a program of massive retrenchment. The best Nixon could hope for was piecemeal reform of domestic programs. The activist penchant in Congress necessitated that he adopt a realistic approach to domestic policy change, and his policy stances encompassed both liberal and conservative dimensions. Nixon showed himself to be a moderate or "progressive-conservative" on domestic policy—more out of necessity than conviction. His positions on welfare reform and the environment—and even domestic spending—placed him somewhat left of center.[11] Realizing that he could not dismantle Great Society programs outright, Nixon sought to "rationalize" domestic spending and decentralize functions to the states.[12] Beyond this "New Federalism," Nixon failed to articulate an overarching domestic agenda.

Nixon's flexibility was visible in the policy stands he took. He chose to compromise with congressional Democrats on the broad, crosscutting domestic issues of the day rather than engage in direct conflict for fear of electoral retribution. By accepting the basic thrust of the congressional Democrats' domestic agenda, Nixon altered his positions for the political expediency of reelection in 1972, attempted to moderate policy outcomes, and consequently appeared fairly successful on roll-call votes on which he expressed a position. The lion's share of significant legislation in the 91st and 92d Congresses, however, had far stronger ties to the consolidated agenda of the congressional majority than to Nixon's policy objectives.

Lawmaking and Presidential Leadership under Richard Nixon

The scope of the domestic legislation adopted during Nixon's first term is surpassed only by Johnson's unparalleled agenda success in office. Whereas Johnson's legislative leadership was at the heart of the congressional legislative juggernaut, a similar agenda synergy between Nixon and the Democratic Congress is far less obvious on the thirty-five important domestic laws Mayhew reports for the 91st and 92d Congresses. If leadership of the national policy-making agenda may be characterized as a tug-of-war between the president and Congress, it was the Democratic legislature that was pulling Nixon most often toward its policy priorities, not vice versa.

In October, 1969, and again in September, 1970, Nixon sent special messages to Congress in which he urged the adoption of more than fifty bills under the rubric of reform and fiscal responsibility.[13] While some of Nixon's proposals were more elaborate and detailed than others—like revenue sharing and the Family Assistance Plan (FAP)—most were vague and general. His laundry list of legislation early in his term was largely an attempt to claim credit for the consolidation of the Great Society rather than to offer the blueprint for strong legislative leadership. A close examination of the bills listed by Mayhew reveals that the important laws adopted from 1969–72 can be classified into five broad categories: a handful of bills that Nixon proposed and won, bills he threatened to veto, congressionally inspired legislation that he often opposed but came to accept, compromise on legislation largely initiated by Congress, and clear-cut losses for the president. Slightly more than half of the major laws passed in 1969–70 were connected to Nixon's policy objectives, while only 20 percent of significant laws evidenced a link to his agenda in 1971–72.

Nixon did score several victories. His general revenue sharing plan was a major element of the "New Federalism" approved by Congress following a bicameral compromise on the allocation of funds to states and localities. Revenue sharing was part of his "six great goals" announced in the 1971 State of the Union address and marked an attempt to reshape parts of the Great Society by increasing governmental autonomy at lower levels. President Johnson had studied the possibility of revenue sharing, but the concept never won his approval. Revenue sharing "was a major departure from federal aid programs of the past. It meant more federal dollars with no strings attached, with no narrow purpose guidelines and promised no red tape."[14] Nixon is also credited with winning the extension of unemployment insurance coverage to 4.8 million workers in a 1970 bill, as well as the passage of legislation for funds to improve the nation's air transit system.

In assessing Nixon's involvement in significant laws, one must bear in mind, as George Edwards notes, that the president "saw himself more as an administrator and executive decision maker and not as a power broker pushing to get his bills through Congress."[15] He did not like to ask members of Congress for their votes, and he refused to reach out personally to congressional Democrats for support.[16] The president allocated primary responsibility for legislative affairs to his small staff in the Office of Congressional Relations, which "was much further removed from the process of policy making in the Nixon White House than it had been during the Johnson years. . . . Nixon was uncomfortable with the give-and-take of congressional politics. He was quite unwilling to bargain with members of Congress or to seek compromises on policy problems through the building of coalitions."[17] As the primary advocate for Nixon's policy positions on Capitol Hill, the congressional liaison staff centered much of its effort on persuading the Democratic majority to structure legislation acceptable to the president, frequently under the threat of a veto.[18]

There is evidence of Nixon's veto-threat strategy in five of the significant laws, and he was variably successful in persuading Democrats to retool the legislation to his liking. Moreover, he wound up threatening to veto several major laws that stemmed *from his own proposals* when Democrats shaped the legislation to his dissatisfaction. Such cases included coal-mine safety, the Social Security increase of 1969, and the 1969 Tax Reform Act. Nixon had requested coal-mine safety legislation in a special message to Congress, but later threatened to veto the bill over workmen's compensation issues. He ceded on the legislation when more than a thousand West Virginia miners walked off the job in protest of a potential veto.[19] On Social Security, Nixon made a major televised address to the nation in which he outlined his plan to restructure the welfare system. Along with his proposal to replace the Aid to Families with Dependent Children (AFDC) program with the Family Assistance Plan, he proposed a 10 percent increase in Old Age, Survivor, and Disability Insurance (OASDI) benefits. The House Ways and Means Committee went even farther, adopting a 15 percent across-the-board increase. Nixon threatened to veto the bill because he thought the increase was too costly, but yielded when confronted with the program's widespread popularity.[20] Finally, the groundwork for the 1969 Tax Reform Act was laid by Johnson's outgoing treasury secretary, who warned of a citizen backlash if perceived inequities in the tax system were allowed to continue. Nixon proposed a 5 percent surcharge on higher incomes, along with a tax investment credit. When Congress balked, he threatened to veto the bill, and convinced Democrats to compromise on the personal exemption but not on a 15 percent increase in Social Security benefits. The compromise bill resulted in a phase-in of Nixon's surcharge proposal.[21]

He threatened to veto several bills with no connection to his agenda. In 1971, Nixon utilized the threat of a veto to delay until 1973 a provision in the tax reduction law that provided for a checkoff on tax return forms for presidential campaign contributions.[22] The president worried that such a scheme might damage his prospects for reelection in 1972 by removing the edge Republicans held in campaign funds. Nixon also let Congress take the lead on the Rail Passenger Service Act of 1970. After rejecting the Department of Transportation's proposal as too costly, Nixon expressed dissatisfaction with Democratic legislation that sought to continue railroad subsidies. Faced with a potential veto, Senate Commerce Committee chairman Warren Magnuson compromised with the president to establish a national corporation, which Nixon favored.[23]

The bulk of legislation passed from 1969–72 was initiated by Congress or represented efforts begun in the Johnson years. Nixon accepted much of the legislation, and when he attempted to preempt the congressional majority with proposals of his own, Democrats frequently reshaped the bills. Social Security, education, consumer product safety, narcotics control legislation, and the Equal Rights Amendment (ERA) are prime examples of legislation linked to the consolidation of the Great Society. The increases in Social Security benefits in 1971 and 1972 are instances of positive competition that developed between the branches to claim credit for popular programs. In 1971, Nixon proposed a 6 percent benefits increase, but Congress lured him into agreeing to a 10 percent increase by raising the debt ceiling. The following year, Nixon opposed a congressional plan for an additional 20 percent increase with provisions for cost-of-living adjustments. Confronting Democrats over the popular program was risky in an election year, so he again accepted an increase in the national debt ceiling and signed the legislation, contending that outlays would be counterbalanced by reductions in other federal programs.[24]

The president was unwilling to challenge the Democratic majority on much legislation. He had little involvement in the culmination of the Higher

Education Act of 1972, the comprehensive bill that established Pell Grants. From afar, the president criticized the education bill for having inadequate antibusing provisions. The final bill represented nearly $400 million more than the president had sought after Congress rejected his aid proposals, but he did not chance a veto on the popular measure.[25] On consumer product safety, Nixon had called upon Congress to establish a new agency within the Department of Health, Education and Welfare (HEW) but was less than pleased with the final legislation. He refused to support creating an independent commission, but decided the bill was not worth a protracted fight with Democrats.[26] Congress fundamentally reshaped Nixon's proposal for drug abuse and control. The president emphasized law enforcement, whereas Congress favored rehabilitation and education.[27] Rather than confront Congress, Nixon again revised the proposal's provisions—in this case by distinguishing between the sale and possession of marijuana. Finally, the establishment of the Occupational Safety and Health Administration (OSHA) flowed not from Nixon's domestic agenda, but from Johnson's 1968 proposal. Nixon desired an independent board to oversee occupational safety issues, and the House passed just such a version of the legislation. The conference committee followed the Senate version, however, which gave the labor secretary authority to establish safety standards. Nixon yielded and did not challenge the bill.[28]

In select cases Nixon latched onto issues that were clearly part of Congress's continuing agenda and attempted to claim a modicum of credit. The Organized Crime Control Act of 1970, for example, was not the president's proposal. The genesis for the legislation proposed by Democratic senator John McClellan was President Johnson's Commission on Law Enforcement, which drafted over two hundred recommendations—most of which were included in the bill. Nixon lauded the legislation, and some administration requests were ultimately folded into it.[29] In addition, after failing to act on Nixon's 1969 postal reorganization proposal, Congress was spurred to action after the nation's first postal strike a year later. Although the legislation finally adopted closely followed Nixon's plan for organizational restructuring, it did not include the pay increase he had sought for postal employees.[30]

Civil rights and price control authority deserve special mention when considering Nixon's followership of Congress. His stances on civil rights have historically been the source of great controversy. In his unsuccessful 1960 campaign against John F. Kennedy, he made television commercials lauding the importance of civil rights and championing the accomplishments of the Eisenhower administration in this realm. As noted earlier, however, his stands were more ambiguous in 1968, culminating in what many viewed as a "southern strategy" to appeal to whites by criticizing the Warren Court's decisions on the forced integration of public schools. Nixon remained true to his 1968 position when the Voting Rights Act came up for renewal in 1970. He opposed extending what he called "regional legislation" aimed at the South and objected to the use of a "trigger formula" to apply the legislation to states and counties that continued to administer literacy tests where less than half the voting age population was registered to vote.[31] Nixon also favored scrapping the requirement for states to file election law changes with the attorney general. His objections were largely symbolic, however. He was loath to engage legislators on voting rights, and Congress renewed the law for another ten-year period without the president's public objection.

The passage of price control legislation is an extraordinary example of the governing majority's adoption of legislation that gave Nixon a power that he did not want. The authority to freeze wages and prices flowed from congressional renewal of the Defense Production Act, which was originally passed during the Korean War to insure adequate material resources for defense production. Among the provisions of the 1970 renewal legislation was the application of uniform accounting procedures to defense contracts. A report issued by the House Banking and Currency Committee stated that the legislation would furnish the president with "all of the necessary weapons needed to control inflation."[32] To Nixon and fellow Republicans, the authority was a Democratic ploy to give the president an unwanted tool and then blame him for the state of the economy if he did not use it. Nixon insisted that he would not use the discretionary authority and that wage and price controls were unwarranted given prevailing economic conditions. He signed the bill with great reluctance, contending he would have vetoed wage and price controls had that aspect of the bill been sent to him separately. To the astonishment of many, however, Nixon—a year after signing the bill—reversed his position and used the authority to impose controls for a period of ninety days following severe escalation in unemployment and inflation levels and unprecedented turmoil in international currency markets.[33]

Congress visibly prodded Nixon to act on legislation that manifested signs of compromise or a joint effort. When Nixon tried to preempt Congress by issuing an executive order creating an advisory commission on environmental quality, Congress responded by passing legislation that set national policy for federal, state, and local governments that, among other things, required "impact" statements. The president and Congress also compromised

on provisions of the 1970 Clean Air Act. Nixon opposed but accepted legisla-
tion lowering vehicle emissions, calling the final bill a "cooperative effort."[34]
With regard to agriculture, Nixon sought a system of flexible price supports,
Congress agreed only to impose ceilings on subsidies in passing the 1970
Agriculture Act. Finally, Nixon also compromised with congressional Dem-
ocrats on the National Cancer Act. He had wanted an independent agency
that would report directly to him, but struck a bargain with Senators Jacob
Javits and Edward M. Kennedy to establish the agency within the National
Institutes of Health.[35]

Regarding the two laws generated by the congressional majority that appear to be clear-cut losses for Nixon—the 1972 water pollution and Supplemental Security Income bills—there is still evidence of Nixon's desire to claim
credit for, or preempt, Democrats on domestic policy achievements. As the
1972 election neared, the president sought to portray himself both as a fiscal
conservative and a social progressive. He vetoed the Water Pollution Control
Act of 1972, citing the $24 billion cost as excessive and "budget-wrecking." Af-
ter Congress easily overrode his veto, Nixon announced that he would im-
pound appropriated funds because Congress had not given him the independent authority he wanted to set spending levels and make specific budget cuts.
The override may have worked to the president's advantage nonetheless:
"Nixon could have it both ways: first claim an effort to hold down spending,
inflation and taxes, then later take credit for implementing the massive pollution control program. And if anything went wrong, he could still say: 'I-told-
you-so.'"[36] The Water Pollution Act is just one example of Nixon's strategy of
calling for fiscal restraint while gravitating toward popular programs.

Congress approved Supplemental Security Income in 1972, but it dropped
Nixon's proposal for the FAP. Perhaps more than any other high-profile legislation in his first term, Nixon's plan to scrap AFDC was the penultimate example of his strategy to profit from the shifting coalitions of the 91st and 92d
Congresses. He attempted to walk a fine line between liberal and conservative
forces, offering a plan that appealed to elements in both parties. In the case of
the FAP, the strategy ultimately backfired as liberals contended that the welfare reform effort did too little to aid the poor while conservatives argued that
Nixon's proposal for a "negative income tax" went too far by shifting emphasis from services to cash payments.[37] Nixon's FAP proposal casts light on a
general strategy of attempting to build a legislative record for reelection by
participating in "floating coalitions" in Congress.[38] This strategy comes to the
fore more clearly in a systematic examination of the roll-call votes on which he
expressed a public position.

Nixon's Success and Support in the 91st and 92d Congresses

There is little doubt after examining Nixon's impact on significant legislation that he was caught up in the gravitational pull of the congressional consolidation of the Great Society. It is with this caveat in mind that one must approach his roll-call success rate. Analysis of his floor success rate and the factors underlying congressional support for his positions accentuate his strategy of attempting to appeal to different factions within each party. Nixon targeted conservative Democrats on domestic spending, and liberal Democrats on progressive domestic initiatives like welfare reform. Nixon partook in the shifting coalitions dominant in Congress, occasionally drawing support from moderates in both parties as well as from opposite wings of each party on an issue-by-issue basis.

Preliminary evidence of Nixon's floating coalition strategy emerges in a partition of his roll-call success rate overall and by party (table 3.1). In the 91st Congress, Nixon won five of the six close votes, but garnered only a bare majority of Democrats on a single vote on agriculture subsidies. Nixon took conservative stands on such high-profile issues as voting rights, cutting transportation funds, and increasing excise taxes. With strong Republican support, he received just enough votes from conservative Democrats to cross the threshold of victory. As Nixon's influence waned after the midterm elections, he found less room to maneuver and the strategy worked less well for close votes. The president took far fewer positions on congressional roll calls after 1970 as executive-legislative conflict began to mount, foreshadowing the impoundment controversy that climaxed in his second term.

To the extent that it was successful, Nixon's "floating coalition" strategy was possible because intraparty cohesion among Democrats was weak and

Table 3.1
Nixon's Legislative Success Rate,
91st and 92d Congresses*

	91st		92d	
	Close Votes [n=6]	Nonclose Votes [n=30]	Close Votes [n=9]	Nonclose Votes [n=17]
Overall	83.3% (5)	83.3% (25)	33.3% (3)	88.2% (15)
Democratic Party	16.7% (1)	66.7% (20)	33.3% (3)	70.6% (12)
Republican Party	100.0% (6)	83.3% (25)	66.7% (6)	82.4% (14)

* Entries are the number and percentage of votes on which the president gained a majority overall and by party.

few votes pitted a majority of Democrats against a majority of Republicans. Particularly early in his term, Nixon went along with the broad consensus in Congress on domestic issues. The smattering of less controversial issues—ranging from the debt ceiling and manpower training to federal pay and governmental reorganization—facing the 91st and 92d Congresses bears out the flexibility of his policy stands. Nixon won a majority of Democrats much more frequently on these votes, which were less prone to narrow passage. Democratic support, combined with strong Republican backing, edged his success rate higher overall.

Evidence of Nixon's attempt to portray himself as a conservative on high-profile issues and take credit for progressive legislation on less controversial issues is clearly evident in the pooled logit analyses of individual legislators' support presented in tables 3.2 and 3.3. The positive coefficients for ideology on close votes show that Nixon drew support from the more conservative wing of both parties. Supporting coalitions originated with legislators *to the right of the party median.* The effect for members of both parties was greatest at the outset of his term because of Nixon's posturing on spending issues. By contrast, the negative coefficients on less controversial legislation reveal that Nixon drew his greatest support from moderate to liberal legislators *to the left of the party median.* The effect is most pronounced in the 92d Congress because the president had set his sights on reelection in 1972. The data confirm the duality of Nixon's domestic policy stands, which transcended ideological rigidity in order to claim at least some responsibility for legislation on the domestic front. With the exception of just a few high-profile votes, Nixon varied his policy stances and allied himself more with northern Democrats rather than confront the Democratic agenda directly.

In order to gauge the impact of Nixon's electoral popularity on congressional support, two variables were added to the standard model to account for the three-way race between Nixon, Humphrey, and Wallace. The variables include Nixon's margin of victory over (or loss to) Humphrey in districts and states in which the two were contending candidates. In the "outer South," for districts and states in which the share of the popular vote of both Nixon and Wallace exceeded that of Humphrey, Nixon's margin of victory over Wallace was used in the models. Finally, for states and districts in the Deep South where Nixon ran behind both Wallace and Humphrey, Wallace's margin of victory over Humphrey was included to examine the electoral basis of southerners' support for Nixon.

The data point to Nixon's limited ability to shape coalition support based on his narrow victory in 1968. Democrats did not perceive a strong overlap be-

Table 3.2
Logistic Regression Estimation of Democrats' Domestic Policy Support for Nixon, 91st and 92d Congresses

	91st Congress		92d Congress	
	Close Votes	Nonclose Votes	Close Votes	Nonclose Votes
Nixon's Margin	1.22**	.04	−.09	−.00
of Victory, 1968 (%)	(.53)	(.19)	(.31)	(.22)
	26.40	*1.10*	*−2.40*	*.00*
Nixon's Margin	.46	−.00	−.54	.01
of Victory over Wallace (%)	(.85)	(.38)	(.98)	(.48)
	6.70	*.00*	*−9.60*	*.20*
Wallace's Margin	−1.13*	−.77**	1.14**	−1.35***
of Victory over Humphrey (%)	(.77)	(.34)	(.62)	(.44)
	−17.00	*−24.10*	*23.40*	*−16.50*
Legislator's Margin	.55**	−.23**	.18	−.18
of Victory (%)	(.28)	(.12)	(.20)	(.14)
	11.70	*−5.60*	*3.20*	*−4.40*
Legislator's Terms Served	.07****	.00	.03**	−.03***
	(.02)	(.01)	(.01)	(.01)
	23.90	*2.40*	*15.10*	*−18.20*
Democratic Leaders	.03	.08	.00	.21**
	(.14)	(.06)	(.12)	(.09)
	2.90	*7.30*	*1.20*	*16.80*
Committee Chairs	.03	.13	−.08	.23*
	(.28)	(.12)	(.21)	(.15)
	.60	*3.10*	*−2.00*	*5.20*
Ideology	4.65****	−.22	.98***	−.67***
	(.52)	(.19)	(.31)	(.22)
	78.10	*−5.10*	*22.60*	*−15.60*
Public Approval	−.08****	−.06****	.09****	.01
of the President	(.02)	(.01)	(.01)	(.01)
	−18.10	*−20.50*	*28.70*	*1.90*
Constant	4.21****	3.68****	−5.02****	.24
	(1.02)	(.41)	(.53)	(.37)
Number of Cases	1,231.00	5,772.00	1,954.00	3,626.00
−2 × Log Likelihood	1,271.72	7,743.60	2,495.96	4,777.36
Model χ^2	314.91****	99.69****	128.72****	73.15****
Pseudo-R^2	.20	.01	.05	.02
Cases Correctly Predicted (%)	.75	.59	.66	.62

**** $p < .001$ *** $p < .01$ ** $p < .05$ * $p < .10$ (one-tailed tests)
Entries are maximum likelihood coefficients.
Standard errors are in parentheses.
Mean effects are in *italics*.
The dependent variable is whether the legislator supported or opposed Nixon's stand.

tween their election constituencies and the president's. Nixon's electoral popularity outside the South mattered only somewhat on close votes early in his term, carrying a moderate (and approximately parallel) impact for members of the two parties. In northern constituencies, a 10 percent victory margin raises the likelihood of a Democratic members' support by about 5 percent.

.

Table 3.3
Logistic Regression Estimation of Republicans' Domestic Policy Support for Nixon, 91st and 92d Congresses

	91st Congress		92d Congress	
	Close Votes	Nonclose Votes	Close Votes	Nonclose Votes
Nixon's Margin	1.76**	.37	.40	.49
of Victory, 1968 (%)	(.77)	(.34)	(.59)	(.45)
	23.50	5.20	6.50	7.10
Nixon's Margin	4.24*	−.53	1.16	−.68
of Victory over Wallace (%)	(3.03)	(.85)	(1.64)	(1.04)
	18.50	−4.20	9.90	−9.50
Wallace's Margin	6.52*	−.49	.81	−.55
of Victory over Humphrey (%)	(4.37)	(.56)	(1.15)	(.75)
	23.20	−5.20	9.00	−6.20
Legislator's Margin	.33	.16	.15	−.53**
of Victory (%)	(.41)	(.18)	(.34)	(.25)
	6.30	3.10	3.50	−11.20
Legislator's Terms Served	−.03	.02*	−.03	.02*
	(.03)	(.01)	(.02)	(.01)
	−8.40	26.00	−3.50	8.00
Republican Leaders	.60***	.30****	.26**	.30***
	(.26)	(.09)	(.14)	(.12)
	22.00	1.60	20.50	18.10
Ranking Minority	.17	.05	.23	−.19
Members	(.32)	(.14)	(.23)	(.17)
	3.10	.10	5.00	−3.90
Ideology	3.87****	−1.49****	−.00	−2.72****
	(.66)	(.28)	(.46)	(.37)
	66.70	−2.60	.00	−42.30
Public Approval	.10****	.03***	−.13****	.03****
of the President	(.02)	(.01)	(.01)	(.01)
	19.50	.80	−39.4	5.30
Constant	−5.77****	−.42	7.07****	−.24
	(1.18)	(.52)	(.62)	(.46)
Number of Cases	1,004.00	4,716.00	1,436.00	2,670.00
−2 × Log Likelihood	1,024.32	5,429.20	1,758.68	3,150.88
Model χ^2	126.29****	69.47****	127.97****	99.17****
Pseudo-R^2	.11	.01	.07	.03
Cases Correctly Predicted (%)	.76	.73	.71	.71

**** p < .001   *** p < .01   ** p < .05   * p < .10 (one-tailed tests)
Entries are maximum likelihood coefficients.
Standard errors are in parentheses.
Mean effects are in *italics*.
The dependent variable is whether the legislator supported or opposed Nixon's stand.

Support from Democrats from the outer and Deep South had less to do with Nixon's electoral margin and more to do with ideological predispositions. Table 3.2 shows that Nixon's third-place status behind Wallace and Humphrey negatively affected the likelihood of support in the heart of Dixie. Nixon's fiscal stances appealed most to senior conservative Democrats. In the

91st Congress, for example, twenty-four Democrats with over ten terms of service in the House were from southern constituencies. Additionally, all seventy-nine southern Democrats had ideological scores above the party median. With the average southern Democrat positioned twenty-five points further to the right of the party median, the likelihood of presidential support increases by just over 27 percent. The weakened impact of both seniority and ideology on close votes in the 92d Congress reflects greater variability in Nixon's policy stances after the midterm elections. In 1971–72, the president did not draw support from conservatives as uniformly as in the preceding Congress. For instance, Nixon favored spending on manpower training, emergency loans for businesses, and equal employment opportunity legislation, but took conservative stands on agency appropriations (HEW, Labor, and related agencies) and child development programs.

The lack of consistent opposition by Democratic leaders points to Nixon's followership of elements of the majority party's agenda. Democratic leaders supported the president 52 percent of the time—about as often as all Democrats together. On the GOP side, minority leader Gerald Ford's stewardship of the minority was critical in providing the Republican unity that undergirded Nixon's legislative strategy. Across voting categories, Republican leaders looked to the president's position as a cue for voting decisions and rallied the troops. Republican leadership support was most evident on the high-profile spending issues on which Nixon took more conservative stances.

There is little evidence in either party model to suggest that Nixon's public approval was an important factor in shaping congressional voting. For Democrats, Nixon's popularity had an inverse effect during the first half of his term, and no consistent pattern is discernible for Republicans. With the legislative agenda defined by larger external forces in the electorate and institutionally by the Democratic majority in Congress, Nixon's popular approval carried little weight in Congress. Supporting coalitions were largely issue-focused and formed more frequently on the basis of ideology, with constituency factors playing a more important role among members of both parties than the president's job approval.

Nixon was variably successful in his pragmatic attempt at credit claiming. On the surface, his success rate on floor votes looks quite impressive compared to other presidents who faced divided government. His first term, however, scarcely conforms to the notion of "presidential government." His floor success rate, like his involvement in significant lawmaking, requires qualification. It is important to distinguish between the amount of legislation that *passed* during Nixon's presidency and the legislation actually *connected* with his policy objectives.

The escalation of conflict between Nixon and Democrats ultimately chased him from office under a cloud of ignominy with the revelations of the Watergate break-in and cover-up. It is the historical precedent of resignation for which Nixon is often remembered. Equally important, though, is the policy legacy over which Nixon presided in his first term and which evidenced some flexibility with Congress. His complex strategy included a moderate basis for positive leverage and occasional reliance on veto threats to negotiate the legislative agenda. These factors contributed to the appearance of a high level of presidential legislative success. His acquiescence to the Democratic agenda was indubitably shaped by his desire to win a second term. In this latter effort, he was notably successful.

Summary

For a short time during 1969–72, the "public mood" prompted Nixon and Democrats to reach some common ground on domestic policy. Nixon's re-election incentive enabled Congress to pull him in directions that were perhaps far less reflective of his true policy preferences. In the competition to attribute policy successes to their leadership, the president and Congress supervised an impressive spate of domestic legislation rivaled only by Lyndon Johnson's presidency.

Nixon was co-opted to a large degree by the continuing Democratic program in Congress. Charles O. Jones aptly sums up how the "public agenda" of Nixon's first term conditioned his approach to domestic policy making: "The Nixon administration faced the enormously complex task of consolidating the Great Society. In addition, however, were the fresh issues generated by these many programs and defined by the clienteles that had been created. In particular, there were new emphases on the environment, energy, and safety. It was not a set of issues that instinctively attracted Nixon, but as president he could not ignore their politics: they were a major part of the agenda during his administration."[39] Had Nixon chosen steadfast conflict with Congress in his first term, it is likely that he would have been bypassed in the legislative process in much the same way as Truman. He chose not to challenge congressional Democrats on popular measures or run *against* Congress in 1972. Hence, the president "acted variously as initiator, acquiescer, foot-dragger, and outright vetoer. But the bills kept getting passed."[40]

Nixon's limited leverage over Congress derived both from shifting policy coalitions in Congress and the threat of vetoes. The story of executive-legislative relations from 1969–72 is one of much presidential posturing. Nixon's positions followed from the desire to portray himself simultaneously as a conservative reformer while attempting to claim credit for popular legislation passed by the Democratic majority. Nixon's "floating coalition" strategy does bear a certain resemblance to Eisenhower's ability to draw support from different factions across issue areas in Congress. However, Nixon's weaker institutional position did not afford him the same level of autonomous influence over the congressional agenda that Eisenhower enjoyed. Nixon confronted a more assertive, policy-focused, and self-confident majority that looked less to the White House for policy leadership as time passed.

Of course, the drama of Nixon's presidency does not end with his first term. He won a landslide reelection in 1972 alongside another Democratic majority in Congress. The strain of split-party control became evident as Nixon grew increasingly less willing to follow the Democrats. Determined to halt inflationary spending and frustrated by the pace of congressional outlays, he embarked on a strategy of impounding appropriated funds that drew the ire of Congress and culminated in the passage of the Budget Control and Impoundment Act of 1974 and a host of other reforms aimed at curtailing his ability to thwart the Democrats' agenda.[41]

Nixon's legacy, as earlier chapters have shown, had a profound impact on Congress's organizational structure through the end of the liberal activist era. The far-reaching effects of the Democrats' internal reforms left Gerald Ford in an extraordinarily weak position to influence Congress and resulted in far less congressional deference to Jimmy Carter's agenda upon the fleeting return of unified government. Democrats hearkened back to this period of resurgence when they confronted a popular, conservative, and assertive president in Ronald Reagan just six years after Nixon left office.

As chapter 4 documents, Reagan came to office in 1981 with a key element that was missing from Nixon's 1968 bid for the White House: A resounding electoral victory. Reagan effectively used his landslide victory to control the domestic agenda, albeit for a brief period, as the House Democratic majority fell into disarray. Reagan's two terms marked another significant turning point in the contours of executive-legislative relations in the last half of the twentieth century. His early policy legacy fundamentally shaped enduring features of executive-legislative relations with which his successors, Bush and Clinton, would have to contend in their respective bouts with opposition-controlled Congresses in the postreform/party-unity era.

4 Reagan and Divided Government

UPON TAKING THE OATH OF OFFICE IN 1981, Ronald Reagan offered his view of the ills that beset the country. "It is no coincidence," the president contended in his inaugural address, "that our present troubles parallel and are proportionate to the intervention and intrusion in our lives that result from unnecessary and excessive growth of government." Reagan championed the drastic reduction of the role of the federal level in economic and social spheres. His goals were rooted in conservative principles that wedded the problems of a sagging economy to the dominance of "big government" programs. Reagan directly challenged the basic tenets of the New Deal—a stance that Eisenhower had rejected as imprudent in the 1950s. He took aim at the very programs that grew out of the consolidation of the Great Society on which Nixon evidenced some flexibility in his first term. Reagan was also determined to shore up America's military forces. He achieved a massive defense buildup and took a highly confrontational posture towards the Soviet Union—another stance that Eisenhower, some three decades earlier, had decried as potentially ruinous to the domestic economy and dangerous to the prospects for peace.

The impact of Reagan's domestic policy legacy on electoral politics and institutional dynamics in Congress solidified the basic traits of executive-legislative relations in the postreform/party-unity era. The tale of Reagan's two terms is one of transition, punctuated change, and resurgence by the governing majority in the House. It is also a story of the transformation of presidential leverage along the positive-negative continuum, from cross-party coalition building to reliance on the veto power. Electoral developments and organizational change in Congress robbed Reagan of the ability to draw from conservative southern Democrats to push his legislative stands across the threshold of victory as his term progressed. A close analysis both of the factors underlying his legislative success and his involvement in significant legislation highlights stellar victories, stunning defeats, and a steady decline of positive leverage over Congress. Reagan's legislative presidency accentuates the limits of electoral and personal popularity as a source of continued influence on Congress in an era of heightened partisan polarization.

Reagan and Congress, 1981–88:
The Electoral and Institutional Context

Reagan's remarkable electoral victories over Jimmy Carter in 1980 and Walter Mondale in 1984 reflected his widespread popularity with voters. However, like his Republican predecessors Eisenhower and Nixon, Reagan's personal popularity did not translate into large gains for House Republicans. His lack of coattails left Republicans forty-nine seats shy of a majority in the 97th Congress (1981–82). Consistent with tradition, Reagan's copartisans lost seats in the midterm elections of 1982. Democrats were aided both by an economic recession and the effects of redistricting following the 1980 census.[1] The off-year election produced eighty-one freshmen, fifty-seven of whom were Democrats. The infusion of new and more solidly liberal Democrats presaged greater policy activism by the majority, and reformers set out to correct the perceived power imbalance between the branches. They bolstered the Speaker's authority, supported restrictive rules aimed at curtailing Republicans' ability to challenge Democratic initiatives on the floor, and expanded of the whip organization to shore up party cohesion (see Introduction). As *Congressional Quarterly* noted after the election, "The new Democrats of 1982 will go down as the group that resurrected traditional liberal issues from the graveyard to which all but a tiny element of the party had consigned them over the course of the 1970s."[2]

Like Eisenhower in 1956, Reagan's landslide reelection in 1984 was without coattails sufficient to counteract the midterm losses in the House two years earlier. Reagan pleaded his case for reelection on the basis of his past performance in office, but his refusal to outline the goals of his second term hurt GOP candidates on the campaign trail.[3] The fact was, Reagan had largely achieved most of his legislative goals by 1982 and his focus was on "staying the course." Nevertheless, the president faced another strong contingent of liberal Democratic freshmen in his lame-duck session. In 1987–88, House Democrats maintained an eighty-one-seat advantage over Republicans. The 1986 elections thus did little else but portend greater stalemate and party conflict as Reagan commenced his final two years.[4]

Republican gains in the Senate in 1980, by contrast, were more impressive. Republican senators rode to victory on Reagan's coattails and took control of the upper chamber for the first time in almost three decades. The president could depend on a new Senate leadership that proved much more conservative than any in recent memory.[5] Republicans maintained control of the Senate until the midterm elections of 1986. As Democrats picked up a total of eight seats in an off-year election that lacked a coherent national theme, Reagan lost whatever residual bargaining advantage he had over House Democrats.[6] Stripped of a majority in the Senate, the beleaguered president squared off against an increasingly hostile and partisan Congress in his last two years as the allegations of wrongdoing in the Iran-Contra affair surfaced. The fading memory of Reagan's 1984 electoral popularity was of little help as he sought to lead a Congress firmly controlled by a more cohesive and programmatic opposition majority.

Reagan, like Eisenhower, left the details of much legislation to his skilled staff. He used the levers of the rhetorical presidency extraordinarily well to control the legislative calendar and bargain with House Democrats,[7] and scholars have noted Reagan's "strategic competence" in the handling of policy decisions, processes, and promotion early in his first term.[8] But Reagan's heavy reliance on the conservative coalition for support of his fiscal policies helped polarize the parties in Congress. He was unable to maintain long-term positive influence. As Reagan's agenda goals dissipated after 1981–82, Democrats sought to fill the void, forcing the president to guard against encroachments upon his early and ephemeral policy victories.

Lawmaking and Leadership under Reagan

Reagan recognized that his window of opportunity for swift legislative action was narrow. Congressional Democrats were in turmoil following the 1980 election, and he successfully exploited his personal and electoral popularity to gain key budget and tax cut victories in Congress in 1981. His strategy encompassed a behind-the-scenes lobbying effort launched by the White House and the use of the "bully pulpit" to win over conservative Democrats. Reagan's closest advisers—including Edwin Meese, James Baker, Howard Baker, David Stockman, and Donald Regan—were adept at coupling his conservative vision with public relations campaigns aimed at convincing the public and Congress that the president had a mandate for sweeping change.[9]

Reagan's first-year budget and tax cut victories top David Mayhew's list of the thirty-two important domestic laws passed during the "great communicator's" two terms. Yet only twelve of the thirty-two significant laws (38 percent) adopted from 1981–88 were linked to Reagan's stated policy objectives. As the president's influence waned in his second term, well over half the bills were the product of the agenda of the congressional majority, which frequently drew Reagan's public opposition and use of the veto power. This category of significant lawmaking from 1985–88 is a reflection of the intense conflict and occasional stalemate that dominated relations between Reagan and House Democrats for much of his presidency.

Mayhew lists only two domestic laws for the first session of the 97th Congress. Both were linked to the president's policy goals. In Reagan's case, it is arguably not quantity that mattered nearly as much as the substance of the legislation. A critical element in Reagan's first year agenda passed by creative, and to many Democrats, imperious means. The president used the budget "reconciliation" process to make steep budget cuts in domestic programs and simultaneously increase defense outlays. By folding spending cuts into an omnibus bill, Reagan and his advisory team undermined the Democratic leadership's leverage to veto individual program items in the budget proposal.[10] Ironically, Reagan transformed the reconciliation process, which had been devised in the 1974 Budget and Impoundment Act as a reaction to Nixon's impoundment of appropriated funds, into a powerful tool for slashing federal spending on social programs.[11]

The Omnibus Budget Reconciliation Act (OBRA) of 1981 trimmed over $130 billion from the federal budget. Not only did Reagan's use of reconciliation catch the Democrats off guard, but interest groups also had precious little time to mobilize against programmatic cuts ranging from agriculture to welfare. Reagan's budget plan was facilitated by special reconciliation procedural rules that placed time restrictions on the length of debate and precluded the possibility of Senate filibusters. What became OBRA emerged as an alternative budget fashioned by House Republicans and conservative Democrats dissatisfied with the lower level of cuts to entitlements proposed by the majority leadership. Mounting a challenge to the Democratic budget, Republicans and a contingent of mostly southern Democrats defeated efforts to bring the majority budget to the floor. The coalition then joined forces to force a vote on the substitute bill (Gramm-Latta), which prevailed by a narrow margin.[12] The alternative budget was adopted with twenty-nine Democrats—twenty-four of whom were from the South—voting in favor of the measure, which cut more than $5 billion from entitlement programs like Social Security and welfare.

The Economic Recovery Act of 1981, another major presidential victory, featured a $749 billion tax cut. The plan, originally fashioned by Republican senators Jack Kemp and William V. Roth in 1977, had stalled in Congress before Reagan latched onto it.[13] The president dickered with Congress in early 1981 on the precise contours of the tax reduction, but in his televised speech to a joint session on Capitol Hill he called for a 10 percent across-the-board cut in individual tax rates. His live television appearance yielded a significant grassroots response that gave moderate Democrats a reason to vote for the president's program without fear of alienating their constituencies.[14] Speaker "Tip" O'Neill was notably frustrated in his attempt to keep Democrats together. He noted in the days leading up to the floor vote: "We are experiencing a telephone blitz like this nation has never seen. It's had a devastating effect."[15]

The final bill slashed individual tax rates by 25 percent over three years and contained provisions for accelerated depreciation for businesses that the administration expected would spur economic growth. Reagan relied heavily on the Republican-controlled Senate to work out details of the package. Throughout negotiations with Congress, he held firm on the basics of his plan, compromising occasionally and offering "sweeteners" like tax breaks for oil producers to bring on board wary Democrats from petroleum-producing states.[16] The combination of a behind-the-scenes bargaining strategy and public appeals worked masterfully. In the opposition-controlled House, forty-eight Democrats—thirty-five of whom were from the South, where Reagan's 1980 campaign had been exceedingly popular—voted with Republicans to pass the package. In the final analysis, Treasury Secretary Donald Regan claimed the administration had gotten 95 percent of what it wanted from the bill.[17]

The budget and tax cut victories were the last hurrah for the conservative coalition in Reagan's presidency. After the Democrats' seat gains in 1982, party leaders were determined not to let the popular president outmaneuver them again. The majority leadership implemented a series of organizational reforms and adopted a variety of restrictive procedures after 1982 that effectively limited Reagan's influence in Congress and the ability of southern Democrats and House Republicans to mount floor challenges on his behalf. Indeed, the magnitude of Reagan's subsequent victories on important legislation pales in comparison to the triumphs of 1981.

Reagan did score some modest victories on economic affairs, but there were caveats. He prevailed in trimming another $17.5 billion from the budget with the Tax Equity Act of 1982. Most of the cuts came from Medicare, Medicaid, and welfare programs. Ironically, the previous year's ballooning deficit forced him to throw his support behind a $98 billion tax *increase*. "The new 'revenue-enhancing' bill was labeled a reform and focused on closing tax loopholes and increasing taxpayer compliance with laws already on the books."[18] The antideficit bills of 1984 and 1987, both of which Reagan had called for, were limited victories in an analogous fashion. In each case he was forced to accept higher taxes to offset spending for defense programs he favored. The

1984 legislation cut Medicare spending while increasing select taxes on liquor, telephones, and real estate.[19] Wrangling between the White House and Congress over the deficit continued into Reagan's second term, and by 1987 "there was a pervasive belief that the deadlock would continue until Reagan left office, because the president would block the tax increases that many influential members believed were critical to balance the budget."[20] The 1987 bill was another uneasy compromise between the branches. That legislation extended the public debt limit to some $2.8 trillion, raised an additional $19 billion in new revenues, and represented a downward revision of the deficit-reduction targets set forth by the Gramm-Rudman Act.[21]

Other significant legislation, like the 1984 anticrime package and the 1986 antidrug measure, followed from the president's proposals but were also part of continuing congressional efforts. Reagan first mentioned the crime legislation in his 1983 State of the Union address, lending his support to those who had spent nearly a decade trying to change the criminal code.[22] The bill passed by Congress in 1984 called for more uniform federal sentencing and made insanity defenses more difficult to mount in court. The measure advanced first in the Republican-controlled Senate and won passage in the House after Dan Lundgren of California attached the bill to an appropriations measure in order to circumvent the Judiciary Committee. Reagan did more than "just say no" to the nation's drug abuse problem. He went on national television to appeal to Congress for antidrug legislation, and both the president and Congress engaged in credit claiming when the measure was passed in 1986. The bipartisan effort yielded $1.7 billion in funding, more than twice what Reagan had sought, for a variety of interdiction programs.[23]

Several other bills connected to Reagan's policy objectives were anticlimactic. Passage of the catastrophic health care coverage bill in 1988 followed from Reagan's request for congressional action two years earlier. Health and Human Services Secretary Otis Brown suggested such coverage be folded into Medicare. The legislation represented the largest expansion of Medicare since the program's inception in 1965. Although Reagan took credit for the bill, he issued a stern warning to Congress to be wary of future cost increases.[24] The president also sparred with Democrats over "workfare" in the Family Support Act of 1988 (welfare reform) until a compromise on mandatory work provisions was finally reached.[25] Although Reagan had called for Social Security reform, Congress and the president were forced to turn to a bipartisan commission to study how to remedy the system's potential insolvency. The president and Speaker O'Neill could not reach an agreement on how to approach the issue. Reagan ultimately backed recommendations to raise the minimum age requirement and put off inflation adjustments. He was, however, loath to try to influence the commission's work for fear of a divisive floor battle in Congress.[26]

Nearly *two-thirds* of the important legislation adopted during Reagan's two terms had no connection to the president's stated policy objectives. He took no position on many of these congressionally inspired bills, including the Transportation Assistance Act of 1982, the Garn–St. Germain Depository Institutions Act of 1982, the Cable Communications Policy Act of 1984, and the water projects bill of 1986.

In other cases, conflict within Congress overshadowed reservations Reagan had about Democratic bills. The president was skeptical of creating another federal holiday, though he signed the bill to honor Dr. Martin Luther King Jr. North Carolina senator Jesse Helms's filibuster during the congressional debate about honoring King is what is most remembered.[27] The antidrug legislation of 1988 was essentially a joint endeavor by Speaker Wright and Majority Leader Foley. Reagan was content with the administration's "just say no" program and saw little need for further legislation. The congressional bill created the "drug czar" position in the White House. The legislation also allowed the death penalty in drug trafficking cases, but failed to include Reagan's request for an easing of the exclusionary rule for improperly obtained evidence if a "good faith" effort could be shown by authorities.[28]

A large proportion of the significant legislation that emerged during Reagan's second term showed evidence of substantial conflict between the branches that was never far from the surface. Reagan often expressed misgivings about bills linked to the Democrats' legislative agenda before reluctantly signing the laws. Voting rights, immigration reform, and homeless aid are prime examples. The extension of voting rights enforcement for twenty-five years in 1982 won only tepid presidential support. Reagan's attorney general, William French Smith, took the lead in articulating the administration's opposition to provisions of the legislation that would allow the examination of electoral results to validate discrimination claims by minority groups. In fact, administration officials boycotted congressional hearings on extending the legislation.[29] Reagan ultimately supported Republican senator Bob Dole's compromise language inserted into the bill, which more explicitly stated that nothing in the law required proportional representation for minorities.

Reagan was also skeptical of congressional immigration reform legislation that contained civil rights provisions. He took particular issue with the antidiscrimination wording in the bill and used the signing ceremony in 1986 as an opportunity to offer his own interpretation, contending that only employees who could show "discriminatory intent" could win lawsuits filed against employers. He also reinforced his belief that employers were not required to offer explanations of employee selection. Reagan's statements angered members of Congress, and civil rights attorneys were quick to dispute the president's narrow interpretation of the scope of the law.[30] Finally, Reagan did not go so far as to issue a veto threat on the McKinney Homeless Act in 1987, but he was initially opposed to the legislation when it emerged in Congress. He called it duplicative and too costly, with $725 million targeted for a variety of federal programs to reduce homelessness.[31]

Veto leverage came to play a central role in Reagan's second term as interbranch conflict mounted. Although a dozen of Mayhew's thirty-two significant laws were subject to vetoes, veto threats, or congressional overrides, only two—the 1983 jobs measure and tax reform in 1986—were bills with ties to Reagan's agenda. Eight of the bills that were vetoed or threatened with vetoes were passed in Reagan's second term and were squarely part of the Democrats' congressional agenda.

Reagan's use of veto threats was often effective. Such threats were based primarily on his concerns about a bill's price tag. The subject matter of the legislation ranged from agriculture to tax reform. In 1982, David Stockman, director of the Office of Management and Budget (OMB), signaled the inevitability of a veto of the Agriculture and Food Act if the Democratic Congress did not restructure farm loan and credit issues and increase price support programs for ailing farmers.[32] The administration threatened to veto the Job Training Partnership Act of 1982 over spending levels and restrictions on the use of funds, prompting a compromise worked out in conference. The legislation replaced the Comprehensive Employment and Training Act (CETA).[33] Reagan also called the bill for financial reparations to Japanese-Americans interned during World War II too costly. The 1987 ruling in *U.S. v. Hohri,* which the Supreme Court refused to hear, had prompted Congress to take action.[34] The president won congressional concessions in conference to spread the payments out over ten years and establish that the bill represented the final compensation for Japanese-Americans.

Two bills linked to the president's priorities were adopted under the aegis of veto threats, again because of concerns over their cost. The antirecession job measure in 1983 largely conformed to Reagan's proposal outlined in February of that year as the ranks of the unemployed grew to 11 million. Under the weight of an imminent veto, the House and Senate compromised on supplemental appropriations and accorded the president $5.2 billion in jobless benefits, up from the $4.3 billion he requested but less than the Democrats had originally proposed. Democrats also reorganized some $300 million more for various programs, prompting Reagan to oppose about a quarter of the provisions that represented new funding. They were, however, careful not to go too far and provoke an outright veto.[35]

Reagan also used veto threats to shape tax reform legislation he had requested in 1984 and proposed again a year later. The legislation that ultimately emerged from committee in 1986 caused House Republicans consternation as business groups mounted opposition. Reagan took the extraordinary step of going to Capitol Hill to lobby for the bill among reticent members of the GOP. "But the personal appeal appeared to have less influence than assurances that he would send a letter to members vowing to veto any tax bill that reached his desk without a number of changes."[36] Reagan's efforts changed enough votes to win the bill's passage in the House. Despite a number of fits and starts, Sen. Bob Packwood was able to maneuver the bill through the upper chamber. Although Reagan took credit for the ultimate passage of the Tax Reform Act of 1986, Packwood was largely responsible for the effort to keep the bill "revenue neutral" and consistent with the president's pledge.[37]

Reagan's veto threats on the Food Security Act of 1985 and the so-called Superfund in 1986 achieved mixed results. The agriculture bill contained record subsidies for farmers over a three-year period. The president at first indicated he would veto the bill if outlays were over $50 billion, but he went along with the $52 billion appropriated by Congress after persuading legislators to lower price supports. While both the president and Congress were able to claim a limited victory, "The results pleased few in Congress or the Administration, but, more importantly, they angered fewer."[38] Congressional efforts to redress the solvency of Superfund for the cleanup of toxic waste dumps resulted in another confrontation between the branches. Reagan threatened to veto the bill because of new taxes imposed on imported oil to shore up the fund. He eventually backed down when fifty-seven senators petitioned Senate Majority Leader Dole to keep the Senate in special session in case a veto override attempt was necessary.[39]

Reagan suffered a number of major defeats on significant legislation toward the end of his term that proved a counterweight to his early successes. Congress overrode three of his vetoes of significant domestic legislation in the 100th Congress (1987–88), two on spending issues, and one on civil rights. Reagan's vetoes of the spending bills were largely symbolic. The bills had widespread support in Congress, so the president's goal was not necessarily to halt the legislation, but rather to "go public" and make an issue of Congress's alleged lack of restraint.[40]

Reagan pocket vetoed the Water Quality Act in 1986. When Congress came back into session in 1987, Democrats had regained a majority in the Senate and Congress repassed the bill designed to provide grants to state and local governments for water and sewage treatment. Reagan vetoed the bill, calling it "loaded with waste and larded with pork." He appealed to Congress to reduce outlays by two-thirds, but legislators instead easily overrode the veto with an eye to various pet constituency projects. In similar fashion, Reagan objected to the Surface Transportation Act of 1987, which he regarded as wasteful spending for congressional pork barrel projects. The $88 billion bill included 120 special "demonstration" projects to which he was particularly ill disposed. The president's political capital had waned to such a degree by the end of his second term, however, that not even a personal plea to the Senate could forestall the override. *Congressional Quarterly* observed that the highway bill override was "the second major legislative defeat" for Reagan in the 100th Congress.[41]

The final blow to the president's veto efforts came in the last year of his term when Congress enacted the Grove City civil rights measure (Civil Rights Restoration Act) over his objections. The legislation effectively overturned a 1984 Supreme Court decision on civil rights by applying antidiscrimination provisions to entire institutions covered under civil rights legislation. The Court had ruled that such provisions only applied to select programs within institutions such as universities. Reagan contended that the Grove City legislation would expand federal intrusion into local matters. Congress demurred, overriding his veto and staging the last in a series of major defeats on significant legislation.

A careful reading of Reagan's involvement on significant bills shows a decidedly mixed record. A transformation is evident in his involvement in lawmaking over time. In his early presidency, Reagan engaged in coalition building with conservative forces in Congress. By the halfway point in his two terms he had turned to veto leverage to ward off the agenda of a resurgent Democratic majority, achieving some success and encountering several defeats. An examination of Reagan's roll-call success rate underscores the sources of the decline in his legislative success rate and positive leverage over time.

Reagan's Success and Support in the 97th and 99th Congresses

None of Reagan's postwar Republican predecessors—Eisenhower, Nixon, or Ford—experienced such a steep drop in legislative support in Congress after his first year.[42] The effect of the Democrats' efforts to centralize control around the leadership is clearly visible on Reagan's roll-call success rate in table 4.1. On close votes, Reagan's success rate plummeted from a high of nearly 86 percent in the 97th Congress to a paltry 11 percent in the 100th Congress, despite steady support from House Republicans. A similar, though less pronounced, decline is evident in his overall success rate on less controversial votes from 1981–88. Reagan never won a majority of Democrats on more than a third of his stands across time. As Democratic leaders staged a coordinated effort to implement procedural tools to undercut GOP floor challenges, the ongoing realignment in the electorate and generational replacement of Democratic legislators in the South eroded the basis for Reagan's early successes. No longer could he rely on the cadre of conservative southerners to carry his stands to victory.

In the 97th Congress, Reagan won six of the seven votes overall despite gaining the support of a majority of Democrats only once. The scattering of conservative Democrats who backed the president pushed his stands to victory with the strong support of Republicans. By his second term, the implicit Democratic party-unity against Reagan's stands notable in table 4.1 exacted a high toll on his floor success rate. The conservative "boll weevils" who had supported Reagan in his first year in office were a distinct minority whose abil-

Table 4.1
Reagan's Legislative Success Rate, Close and Nonclose Votes,
97th–100th Congresses*

Close Votes	Congress			
	97th (n=7)	98th (n=9)	99th (n=7)	100th (n=9)
Overall	6 (85.7%)	6 (66.7%)	1 (14.3%)	1 (11.1%)
Democrats	1 (14.3%)	2 (22.2%)	1 (14.3%)	1 (11.1%)
Republicans	7 (100%)	9 (77.8%)	6 (85.7%)	8 (88.9%)

Nonclose Votes	Congress			
	97th (n=36)	98th (n=41)	99th (n=33)	100th (n=34)
Overall	14 (38.9%)	11 (26.8%)	9 (27.3%)	9 (26.5%)
Democrats	12 (33.3%)	5 (12.2%)	8 (24.2%)	8 (23.5%)
Republicans	27 (75.0%)	31 (75.6%)	22 (66.7%)	25 (73.5%)

* Entries are the number and percentage of votes on which the president gained a majority overall and by party.

ity to play a pivotal role in legislative outcomes dramatically disappeared. Most damaging to Reagan's agenda was the short shrift House Democrats gave his budget submissions, which were considered "dead on arrival" by the majority leadership.[43]

Analysis of individual-level support for Reagan's positions underscores how his early policy stands drove a wedge between liberal and conservative Democrats. On close votes in the 97th Congress, Democrats' ideological placement carried a tremendous effect that overwhelms the model of legislative support for Reagan's positions (table 4.2). The mean effect of ideology is nearly 89 points for the 97th Congress. Taking into account the distribution of ideological positions in the party, the average southern Democrat was about 28 percent more likely to back Reagan compared to the average northern Democrat. The effect of ideology declines substantially over time, however. Although Reagan continued to draw support from rightward-leaning moderate legislators, the increased cohesion of Democrats and the replacement of southern Democrats with more liberal members shrank the president's crucial base of legislative support.

Although Reagan's electoral popularity does not carry a significant effect in the Democratic model overall, there is an embedded regional impact. It should be noted that his average percent of the two-party vote share at the district level was 5 percent higher in southern districts. There is also a moderate correlation between Reagan's victory margin and the level of conservatism of the seventy-five southern Democrats in the 97th House ($r = .37$, $p > .001$). In addition, incumbent Democrats' seat safety *increases* the likelihood of presidential support. Southern Democrats averaged a margin of victory 11 percent higher than their northern colleagues, and southerners' seat safety mitigated concerns about electoral reprisal for backing the president. All told, the model paints an intuitive picture of the key to Reagan's early but ephemeral successes on the budget reconciliation bills of 1981 and 1982 and the tax cuts of 1981. The president's positions touched a strong ideological chord with the waning contingent of older southern Democrats who fell under heightened constituency pressure to back his agenda.

Ideology does not emerge as a considerable factor for Republicans early in Reagan's term in light of the near unanimity in the GOP, particularly on the budget reconciliation and tax cut issues. Leadership and seniority carry a stronger effect. Senior House Republicans viewed Reagan's early leverage over Congress as an exceptional, if perhaps fleeting, opportunity for policy change given the party's quasi-permanent minority status since 1955. Minority

Table 4.2
Logistic Regression Estimation of Democrats' Domestic Policy Support for Reagan, 97th and 99th Congresses

	97th Congress		99th Congress	
	Close Votes	Nonclose Votes	Close Votes	Nonclose Votes
Reagan's Margin of	−.02	−.04	−.31	.15
Victory 1980/1984 (%)	(.34)	(.14)	(.38)	(.17)
	−.60	*−1.10*	*−8.90*	*4.40*
Legislator's Margin	.60***	.11	−.19	.00
of Victory (%)	(.24)	(.11)	(.28)	(.14)
	12.90	*2.30*	*−3.60*	*.00*
Legislator's Terms	.03**	−.02**	−.00	.01
Served	(.01)	(.01)	(.02)	(.01)
	14.40	*−6.60*	*−2.10*	*2.30*
Democratic Leaders	.12	−.02	.03	−.05
	(.11)	(.05)	(.13)	(.06)
	10.50	*−.17*	*2.70*	*−3.10*
Committee Chairs	.00	.14*	−.22	−.16
	(.24)	(.11)	(.29)	(.13)
	.10	*3.10*	*−4.20*	*−2.70*
Ideology	5.14****	2.04****	3.69****	1.24****
	(.40)	(.16)	(.55)	(.25)
	88.60	*48.60*	*56.70*	*17.60*
Public Approval	−.06****	.09****	.20****	.33****
of the President	(.01)	(.004)	(.04)	(.02)
	−22.40	*36.70*	*24.70*	*45.80*
Constant	2.79****	−4.44****	−12.82****	−21.77****
	(.45)	(.23)	(2.29)	(1.16)
Number of Cases	1,582.00	7,496.00	1,420.00	6,783.00
−2 × Log Likelihood	1,681.68	8,781.04	1,557.44	7,113.66
Model χ^2	328.99****	594.64****	106.13****	569.94****
Pseudo-R^2	.16	.06	.06	.07
Cases Correctly Predicted (%)	.72	.72	.73	.74

**** $p < .001$ *** $p < .01$ ** $p < .05$ * $p < .10$ (one-tailed tests)
Entries are maximum likelihood coefficients.
Standard errors are in parentheses.
Mean effects are in *italics*.
The dependent variable is whether the legislator supported or opposed Reagan's stand.

Leader Bob Michel of Illinois led the charge to keep the GOP forces united behind Reagan's agenda.

As Reagan's political capital diminished over time, however, he drew support more heavily from Republican legislators to the right of the party median. His legislative stands were increasingly in opposition to the House Democrats' agenda. He opposed five of the seven close votes in the 99th Congress, including budget and public welfare bills sponsored by Democrats. Moderates in the GOP were pressured to back the majority's proposals for social programs popular with their constituents, Reagan's objections notwithstand-

Table 4.3
Logistic Regression Estimation of Republicans' Domestic Policy Support for Reagan, 97th and 99th Congresses

	97th Congress		99th Congress	
	Close Votes	Nonclose Votes	Close Votes	Nonclose Votes
Reagan's Margin	.44	.40	.49	.38*
of Victory 1980/1984 (%)	(.57)	(.23)	(.74)	(.29)
	5.80	*7.10*	*7.40*	*8.00*
Legislator's Margin	−.03	.12	−.27	−.08
of Victory (%)	(.33)	(.13)	(.45)	(.17)
	−.60	*3.00*	*−4.70*	*−1.80*
Legislator's Terms	.080**	.01	.02	.01
Served	(.03)	(.01)	(.03)	(.01)
	15.40	*3.30*	*3.80*	*3.70*
Republican Leaders	.27**	−.02	.03	.06
	(.16)	(.05)	(.15)	(.06)
	14.10	*−1.60*	*2.00*	*5.80*
Ranking Minority	.20	.09	−.28	−.15
Members	(.31)	(.11)	(.30)	(.12)
	.60	*2.00*	*−5.00*	*−3.50*
Ideology	.73	3.80****	4.96****	3.18****
	(.58)	(.24)	(.78)	(.30)
	8.20	*53.80*	*50.60*	*43.10*
Public Approval	.10****	.06****	−.26****	−.04****
of the President	(.01)	(.01)	(.05)	(.01)
	31.40	*25.00*	*−25.90*	*−11.90*
Constant	−4.34****	−3.54****	16.21****	1.90****
	(.51)	(.27)	(2.91)	(.65)
Number of Cases	1,278.00	6,034.00	1,140.00	5,368.00
−2 × Log Likelihood	1,302.78	7,637.32	1,042.48	6,976.28
Model χ^2	134.63****	492.93****	122.02****	236.66****
Pseudo-R^2	.09	.06	.10	.03
Cases Correctly Predicted (%)	.75	.64	.77	.62

**** $p < .001$ *** $p < .01$ ** $p < .05$ * $p < .10$ (one-tailed tests)
Entries are maximum likelihood coefficients.
Standard errors in parentheses.
Mean effects are in *italics*.
The dependent variable is whether the legislator supported or opposed Reagan's stand.

ing. The eastern "Gypsy Moth" Republicans were most prone to defect from Reagan's stands. This contingent of legislators also fell under the strongest cross-pressures on override attempts of Reagan's vetoes.

The president had a tougher time holding the party together as time progressed. House Republicans' frustration in the minority mounted. Compared to their colleagues in the Senate majority from 1981–86, House GOP members were foiled in their ability to influence policy outcomes.[44] Democratic Party leaders became the instruments of order, stability, and agenda setting, endowed as they were with special rules to set the terms of floor debate, restrict amendments, and co-opt wayward members through an expanded whip system.[45] Worried about reelection, GOP moderates voted with Democrats and against Reagan's positions, particularly on less controversial issues. Bills with constituency benefits, such as public works projects, were particularly attractive to moderates. Other conservatives became furious with Democratic tactics and followed the lead of Newt Gingrich of Georgia, who orchestrated "special order" speeches to protest the Democrats' agenda. Labeled a "bomb thrower" by many, Gingrich began plotting a course to win a majority in the House through confrontation with Democratic leaders, a style that contrasted significantly to that of Minority Leader Michel.[46]

Consistent patterns are difficult to discern relative to the impact of Reagan's public approval on legislative support in the two parties. Among Democrats, his public approval carries a negative effect on close votes in the 97th Congress, but a positive and rather strong effect across vote categories thereafter. There is some evidence that the decline in Reagan's approval in 1981–82 had a negative effect on Democrats' support on nonclose votes, as well as Republican support across vote categories. His approval rating for votes in the 97th Congress peaked at 59 percent and reached a low of 41 percent as the economy faltered in 1982. Caution is nonetheless warranted in the interpretation of Reagan's popularity on legislative support in 1985–86, despite the high level of statistical significance in the models. His job approval varied little during this period and hovered around 63 percent. Reagan's job approval on a smattering of votes in the spring of 1985 was in the low 50s. He received slightly higher relative support from Democrats compared to Republicans. All told, the data patterns suggest that ideology and constituency factors, not public opinion, drove legislative support for Reagan.

Summary

Reagan's presidency may well have symbolically revitalized public perceptions of a strong presidency in the early days of his term.[47] However, his bout with divided government shows the limits of *sustained* positive leverage by dint of a landslide personal electoral victory or high levels of public approval in the changed policy-making environment of the postreform/party-unity era. Reagan could perhaps ultimately find solace in the fact that the bulk of his budget-cutting agenda was in place by the end of his first term.[48] Yet, the decline in his influence and success in Congress was more profound than for any other president in the postwar era. His polarizing agenda was a key factor in reshaping Congress's internal organization. Democratic reforms coincided with Reagan's diminished interest in agenda setting and the geographic realignment of the electorate, which yielded a more internally cohesive Democratic Party base in Congress. The president's command of the legislative agenda was thus short-lived. His early successes were contingent upon unity in the ranks of the GOP minority combined with critical support from conservative Democrats. The influential role that this waning contingent of legislators could play largely vanished by the end of Reagan's presidency, closing future windows of opportunity for much independent policy success.

Reagan's presidency marked a critical period of transition in executive-legislative relations. His successors, Bush and Clinton, grappled with the legacy of quasi-permanent structural deficits that dominated policy making in the 1990s. The competition for scarce resources left little room for new programs or the expansion of old ones, and drew even sharper distinctions between the parties' policy objectives. Reinvigorated parties in Congress, as chapter 5 elucidates, placed Presidents Bush and Clinton in much more defensive positions on the legislative front under divided government. Assertive opposition majorities pursued agendas largely antithetical to their policy preferences. The cementing of a more hotly contested legislative agenda in Congress and between the branches bolstered Bush's and Clinton's reliance on veto leverage. At the close of the twentieth century, presidents stood much more in the shadow of Ronald Reagan than that of Franklin Roosevelt.

5 Bush, Clinton, and Divided Government

GEORGE BUSH AND BILL CLINTON faced opposition majorities in Congress in the second half of the postreform/party-unity era. Although they came to the Oval Office under different party affiliations and with very different policy objectives, their general legislative strategy bore some striking similarities. Bush and Clinton had very low leverage to set the legislative agenda. Few significant laws originated with their proposals, and they struggled to claim much independent policy success. They opposed the vast majority of legislation that made it to the floor in Congress, and their success rates were among the lowest for presidents in the last half of the twentieth century. They exploited the partisan institutional setting within Congress to derive influence over legislative outcomes most consistently through veto leverage.

Bush's exhaustive battles with a Democratic majority in Congress evidenced a fair bit of continuity with Reagan's second term. Fiscal constraints defined presidential-congressional relations. Bush sought to guard the status quo and proffered no major domestic proposals in the 1988 election. The Democratic majority took the lead in setting forth an activist legislative agenda, and Bush wielded the veto and used veto threats to block important elements of that agenda. The drawback was that little of the significant domestic legislation that emerged during Bush's presidency was linked to his leadership, complicating the president's task of winning reelection in 1992 on the basis of policy accomplishments.

Clinton's reliance on veto leverage marked a far more dramatic transformation in legislative strategy. Republicans' sweep of Congress in the 1994 midterm elections forced him to shift from building primarily partisan coalitions for his domestic agenda in the 103d Congress to fending off the House leader's policy platform outlined in the "Contract with America." Clinton employed the veto power judiciously in an effort to retool Republicans' proposals and force the majority leadership to negotiate. The threat that the Republican agenda represented to his copartisans' electoral constituencies enabled him to sustain unity in the ranks of congressional Democrats and exact concessions from House leaders unable to trump his vetoes. Clinton was arguably more adept than Bush at preempting the governing majority to share at least some credit for important domestic legislation adopted in 1995–96.

Comparing Bush and Clinton under divided government stresses how the culmination of institutional and electoral developments at century's end yielded a highly unfavorable set of circumstances for presidential agenda setting, coalition-building leverage in Congress, and credit claiming for significant policies. The governing context Bush and Clinton inherited contrasted sharply to the circumstances surrounding split-party control in the bipartisan conservative and liberal activist eras.

Bush and Congress, 1989–92

The electoral context of divided government was paramount in shaping George Bush's relations with the Democratic Congress. From the outset, Democrats were ill disposed to defer to the president. They angrily blamed him and his campaign advisers for waging what they considered an ugly campaign that had devastated Democratic presidential candidate Michael Dukakis. The Bush campaign's attacks on Dukakis included portrayals of the Massachusetts governor as an extreme liberal who let dangerous criminals go free and who failed to improve environmental pollution in his state.[1]

Bush began and ended his term without much of a basis for positive leverage over Congress. Despite a substantial personal triumph over Dukakis, Bush failed to bring any Republicans into Congress, and in fact suffered from "negative coattails" as Republicans lost three House seats and one Senate seat in the 1988 elections. Accusing Bush of lacking vision, Democrats contended that the president had not received a mandate from the electorate, evidenced by the split-ticket voting that allowed them to solidify their hold on Congress.[2] But if the message voters sent in 1988 was to "stay the course" by returning divided government to Washington after Ronald Reagan's two terms, Democrats were similarly unable to claim an electoral mandate. The main problem that Bush faced as he took the helm of the presidency was how to manage a more cohesive and aggressive Democratic majority that had responded to Reagan's confrontational approach by strengthening organizational resources to shore up party unity.

The Democrats sought to advance a liberal legislative agenda while Bush's policy objectives were wedded to maintaining the status quo. Bush's leadership appeal, Dean C. Hammer writes, "was not that he had an agenda for the future but that he was better able to handle whatever situation arose."[3] Bush's chief of staff, John Sununu, defined the preferred contours of legislative activity for the second half of the president's term in late 1990 when he posited: "There's not a single piece of legislation that needs to be passed in the next two years for this president. In fact, if Congress wants to come together, adjourn, and leave, it's all right with us."[4]

Given the electoral and institutional context under which he came to the Oval Office, it is little wonder that "more emphatically than any other modern president, Bush set out to cooperate with Congress and specifically with the rival party."[5] He was careful to avoid criticizing the Democratic Congress at the beginning of his term, and his conciliatory gestures to Democratic leaders, combined with his reputation as a pragmatist, suggested there would be greater executive-legislative harmony in comparison to the bitter partisan battles during the last four years of Reagan's presidency. Although Bush promised a "kinder, gentler" America in his inaugural address and pledged himself to cooperate with the Democratic majority, bipartisanship was fleeting.

Bush increasingly turned to the veto to stifle Democratic initiatives, and his "victories" over Congress have been typecast as "negative achievement."[6] Unable to find much support for his positions among the Democratic majorities in firm control of both Houses, Bush opted to stonewall legislation, often forcing the opposition to negotiate through the veto power. He was successful in sustaining forty-five of the forty-six vetoes he cast from 1989–92.

Ironically, Bush's early attempts to hammer out bipartisan compromises may well have enhanced conflict between the branches. His equivocation sometimes undermined effective negotiations with Democrats. Moreover, his about-faces damaged relations with House Republicans, particularly when he reneged on his "no new taxes" pledge in what evolved into the 1990 budget fiasco. In an effort to retain his base of support among conservative Republicans, Bush's policy positions became increasingly rigid as he squared off against congressional Democrats in the last two years of his term. Ultimately, neither negotiation nor conflict seemed to ease his embattled relations on Capitol Hill.

It is doubtful that Bush could have used his extremely high public approval, which peaked with the Gulf War victory, to lay before Congress a sweeping agenda in 1991.[7] The "rally-'round-the-flag" effect could not fill in the gaps of an electoral context devoid of crosscutting issues. National trends in the president's public approval rating do not legitimize his policy stands the way a policy-focused election with coattails does. Bush's public approval had little bearing on Democrats' support of the policy stands he took, and there is little reason to suspect that a laundry list of domestic proposals would have met with Democrats' approbation in the 102d Congress. The quick military victory may have been popular with the public, but Democrats were much more skeptical. Bush failed to garner a majority of Democrats in support of the Gulf War Resolution.

Lawmaking and Presidential Leadership under George Bush

Bush ultimately suffered one of the lowest legislative success records of presidents in the past half century.[8] Given the partisan disadvantage with which he began his presidency—Democrats held 59 percent of the seats in the House—and in light of his own limited objectives, he did not set forth an active agenda for Congress.[9] Most of the significant laws passed in the 101st and 102d Congresses were congressionally initiated. Those linked to the president's agenda were often continuing legislative issues, proposals negotiated under the weight of veto threats, or bills that Democrats took well beyond his modest objectives. On the vast majority of congressionally inspired legislation, high-profile partisan conflict or Bush's prior vetoes of legislation overshadowed the president's efforts to engage in credit claiming.

Domestic policy making hardly got off to a quick start when George Bush came to the White House. Of the fourteen important domestic laws that Mayhew counts during Bush's term, only two—an increase in the minimum wage and the savings and loan bailout—were adopted during his first year in office. Bush's only major first-year domestic victory was the savings and loan bailout in 1989—a subject of great importance to the health of the financial industry, but hardly one that captured the minds and hearts of voters. Congress acquiesced to most of Bush's proposal to give the Treasury Department authority to oversee thrifts and create a new insurance fund under the Federal Deposit Insurance Corporation, but only after he threatened to veto the legislation. Bush sparred with Democrats over how much of the bailout would be included in the budget. The president wanted the funds to be borrowed by the Resolution Funding Corporation and not included in the general budget deficit. House Democrats, on the other hand, adopted a plan that would give the funds to the Treasury Department, potentially requiring a revision of the parameters set forth in the Gramm-Rudman deficit reduction package. A compromise was ultimately reached that spread $30 billion of the recovery costs across the fiscal 1990 and 1991 budgets.[10]

In a similar vein, Bush wound up threatening to veto highway legislation in 1991. He initially made a far-reaching proposal to improve the nation's highway transit system by spending $105 billion on the Interstate system. With the economy dipping, however, Bush and Transportation Secretary Samuel Skinner soon lost control of the congressional agenda. "In the next few months, an even more radical plan from the Senate—coupled with a gas-tax increase proposal in the House—pushed Skinner into a strategy of negotiating with lawmakers mostly through veto threats."[11] When the final bill passed, Skinner claimed the administration had been successful in securing funding and new incentives for highways. However, he deemphasized congressional pet projects to which the president was opposed, as well as the higher share of federal spending in proportion to state outlays—more than double in many cases—than what the administration had originally proposed.[12]

Several of the bills with connections to Bush's stated policy objectives were related to long-term programs that came up for renewal during his term or predated his presidency. Although the president called the 1990 Clean Air Act amendments "the most significant air pollution legislation in our nation's history," his role in getting them passed was marginal.[13] His 1989 proposal prompted congressional representatives of business, the environment, and regional concerns to resume negotiations that had previously stalled. The bill adopted a year later—which addressed air pollution, acid rain, and motor vehicle emissions—was a substitute that looked much different from the administration's original proposal and cost over $10 billion more than the president had said he would accept. However, with over sixteen months of negotiations with Congress hanging in the balance, Bush signed the law.[14]

Bush tried to derive some credit for legislation on Congress's continuing agenda but found a tough row to hoe. Although child care had emerged as an issue in the 1988 campaign, congressional initiatives predated Bush's term. Once in office, Bush called for tax credits for the poor and an expansion of the Head Start program. However, the president remained largely aloof from the internal debate in Congress about the specifics of the legislation.[15] The bill he signed expanded the Earned Income Tax Credit and went much farther than his own proposals by creating a new Social Security entitlement program at a cost of $700 million over five years. Similarly, Bush claimed the omnibus energy legislation passed by the 102d Congress contained important elements of his proposal. However, partisan conflict in Congress precluded passage of Louisiana senator Bennett Johnston's lengthy effort on a comprehensive bill. The compromise bill was marked by internal wrangling in Congress over such issues as the Yucca Mountain, Nevada, nuclear waste facility and oil drilling in the Arctic Circle in Alaska.[16]

Other attempts to claim credit for congressionally initiated legislation were also hard sells for Bush. The president publicly supported several important bills without linkages to his stated objectives. Bush steadfastly supported the Americans with Disabilities Act, which addressed issues of discrimination, public services, and access for the handicapped. Bush's only caveat was that the bill, which had strong bipartisan support in Congress, not contain provisions for monetary compensation.[17] His position stirred ample controversy in Congress. The president expressed little interest in the Immigration Act of 1990, which increased the inflow of immigrants by two hundred thousand over the next three years, as the bill wound through Congress. In signing it, Bush attempted to connect provisions for the deportation of illegal aliens and expanded authority for Immigration and Naturalization Service employees to his "war on drugs."[18]

Several other significant laws on which the president took no public position sailed through Congress. Interior Committee chairman George Miller of California was responsible for the sweeping legislation aimed at reforming water policy in the West.[19] The agriculture bill cut $13.6 billion in federal subsidies and gave the Agriculture Department greater control over the pricing of commodities. Bush had called for cuts in agricultural subsidies but omitted specifics. Similarly, Agriculture Secretary Clayton Yeutter had promoted reductions in subsidies but also failed to articulate where the cuts should come from, leaving the task to Congress.[20] Bush also tried to claim credit for the expansion of public housing programs and subsidies in the National Affordable Housing Act, although the bill did not evince much presidential involvement. Bush worked through Housing and Urban Development (HUD) Secretary Jack Kemp, whose Housing Opportunities for People Everywhere (HOPE) program was aimed at preventing sudden rent increases and awarding grants to low-income earners to buy homes. When he signed the bill, Bush pointed to the administration's role in the legislation but omitted mention that it made no provision for spending for the grants program.[21]

Bush's use of vetoes and veto threats also narrowed the potential for credit claiming on significant legislation that emerged over the course of the 101st and 102d Congresses, largely because of the uneasy economic context surrounding his term. Before the passage of the minimum wage increase in 1989, Bush had vetoed a bill that set the minimum level at $4.55 per hour to take effect over three years. When Democrats crafted a compromise bill that raised the hourly rate to $4.25 per hour over a two-year period, Bush was ambivalent, but feared that a second veto might be overridden. Democrats yielded to the president on setting the minimum wage lower for trainees in some fields, but the president could not win application of the trainee wage to all employees.[22]

Bush also got little credit-claiming mileage out of passage of the Civil Rights Act in 1991. The previous year, he became the first president to veto a civil rights law, citing the legislation for putatively setting hiring quotas for minorities. Congress began the effort to enact civil rights legislation in the wake of a series of decisions by the Rehnquist Court that made discrimination suits by employees more difficult. The controversy that developed over Bush's nomination of Clarence Thomas to the Supreme Court and allegations of sexual harassment also spurred Congress to action. Bush offered his own bill, which would have placed more of the burden on employees to prove their case and allowed businesses to use tests for prospective employees. But the congressional bill went much farther in overturning the *Wards Cove* and *Price Waterhouse* decisions. The legislation shifted the burden of proof to employers to defend hiring practices and prohibited hiring decisions for any reason on the basis of race, ethnicity, national origin, religion, or sex.

Bush tried to make the best of the civil rights bill, saying, "We worked out in a spirit of compromise a negotiated settlement where I can say to the American people, this is not a quota bill."[23] But the signing ceremony turned out to be an uncomfortable, if not embarrassing, event for the president. Bush's counsel, C. Boyden Gray, wrote a draft signing statement that would have used the occasion to direct government agencies to terminate affirmative action programs. The leak of the draft statement drew the ire of Democrats and civil rights activists. The controversy prompted Bush to profess his support for affirmative action. However, he again angered many of the bill's advocates by suggesting that the legislation's wording should be narrowly interpreted.[24]

It is ironic that the only successful congressional override of Bush's forty-six vetoes was particularly damaging, coming as it did on the eve of the presidential election. Bush had vetoed a Senate-inspired bill to reregulate the cable television industry in October, 1992, citing requirements that cable television companies provide broadcast channels as too costly to consumers and potentially damaging to investment in the telecommunications industry. As the economy sank further into recession in 1992, the president's political capital had waned to such a degree that he could not persuade enough Republicans to stick by his position. Both chambers overrode the veto by large margins. As James A. Thurber noted after the vote: "On this particular bill (Bush) had very little to trade with, other than loyalty to the party and loyalty to him. And he didn't get it."[25]

Indeed, Republican loyalty to the president was tested more than once during Bush's term. The 1990 deficit reduction package is "significant" not simply for its substantive provisions, but most notably for the degree to which it marked the quintessential turning point in Bush's relations with Congress when he recoiled from his "read my lips, no new taxes" campaign promise.[26] The process leading to the failed budget agreement of October, 1990, was marked by Bush's inconsistency on whether he would accept new taxes as part of a compromise deal. The president's prime-time televised speech on a budget accord reached through summitry with congressional leaders, which included a variety of new taxes and spending cuts without a capital gains tax cut that he had championed, had the reverse effect of rallying public opinion *against* the agreement.[27]

The budget accord was defeated by a majority of House Democrats *and* Republicans. Rank-and-file members of both parties called the budget summit process flawed because it had excluded their concerns for months as moderates attempted to hammer out a compromise. On one hand, Democrats were rankled by proposed cuts to Medicare. On the other hand, Republicans were irate over new taxes. Just before the vote, the House Republican Conference—stunned by Bush's tax pledge reversal—adopted a resolution that called increased taxes unacceptable. House Republicans contended that the president had damaged their electoral prospects for the midterm elections in November, 1990. However, Bush's "flip" on taxes reflected a fundamental dilemma he faced under divided government. As Jon Bond and Richard Fleisher note: "The president's reversal of this campaign pledge generated a great deal of anger and hostility from conservative Republicans. But without support from Democrats, there was no hope of passing a budget to meet the targets mandated by Gramm-Rudman. Unable to generate majority support for his own budget, Bush was forced to give Democrats the major concession that they wanted or to suffer the economic and political consequences of Gramm-Rudman's automatic cuts."[28]

With the threat of a government shutdown hanging in the balance following the flopped budget vote, the House passed a continuing budget resolution that Bush promptly vetoed. House leaders failed to override the veto and were stirred to action on a compromise resolution that the president ultimately signed in early November. Bush called the bill "a compromise that merits enactment" and tried to put the best light on the deficit reduction package, pointing out that the new bill was in the spirit of the original budget agreement. But the final bill was less consistent with the president's goals than the summit agreement. The package increased tax rates on the wealthiest taxpayers and lowered exemptions for the top wage earners. Roughly half of the new revenues to be devoted to deficit reduction came in the form of new excise taxes on gasoline, spirits, tobacco, and airline tickets. Moreover, the cuts to Medicare and other entitlement programs were less compared to the original agreement, and there was no provision for the 15 percent capital gains tax cut Bush had long championed.[29]

The budget imbroglio was symbolic of the exhaustive conflictual relations and veto politics that characterized presidential-congressional interactions during much of Bush's tenure. The deficit reduction package may have been historic for its long-term provisions, but the more immediate effect of the process by which it was reached was to intensify conservatives' mistrust of and alienation from Bush. The president's desire not to estrange his the base of his party further resulted in more rigid stands and use of the veto rather than compromise with Democrats after the midterm.

Bush's Success and Support in the 101st and 102d Congresses

Frustrated by the Democrats' liberal agenda and hamstrung by the dearth of Republican strength in the House, Bush cast nearly four times as many vetoes as Nixon had in his first term. Bush's paltry success rate on floor votes highlights why he turned to the veto so frequently. Across vote categories, Bush never won more than half the stands he took. Even on less controversial votes, Bush had difficulty mustering a majority of Democrats a quarter of the time.

In similar fashion to his role on significant legislation, Bush's floor-vote positions were largely reactive. In the 101st and 102d Congresses, 67 percent and 65 percent of the stands he took, respectively, on the annual single-issue votes in the analysis were *in opposition* to legislation. Party unity shaped Bush's success rate even on votes that were less controversial. Seventy-four percent of all votes on which Bush took a public stand from 1989–92 pitted a majority of Democrats against a majority of Republicans. The slight variations in the president's success rate among his copartisans hint at House Republicans' frustration with his occasional vacillation on policy stands. On the whole, however, party unity was the rule—not the exception.

There is little evidence to suggest that Bush's district electoral margin in

Table 5.1
Bush's Legislative Success Rate,
101st and 102d Congresses*

	101st Congress		102d Congress	
	Close Votes [n=9]	Nonclose Votes [n=50]	Close Votes [n=9]	Nonclose Votes [n=59]
Overall	44.4% (4)	38.0% (19)	11.1% (1)	33.9% (20)
Democratic Party	11.1% (1)	26.0% (13)	11.1% (1)	22.0% (13)
Republican Party	88.9% (8)	72.0% (36)	55.6% (5)	78.0% (46)

* Entries are the number and percentage of votes on which the president gained a majority overall and by party.

the 1988 election carried sway over Democrats. In each vote category and across time, Bush's electoral popularity has no significant influence on Democratic support. In fact, the data imply that Democrats viewed support of the president—in opposition to the party line—as risky. Only members with safer seats were somewhat more willing to take that risk, but the impact is slight. A Democrat who ran without opposition in 1988 was only 7 percent more likely to support Bush on close votes in the 101st Congress. The data accentuate that Democrats did not perceive a shared electoral connection with Bush. The lack of a policy focus in the 1988 election damaged Bush's already

Table 5.2
Logistic Regression Estimation of Democrats' Domestic Policy Support for Bush, 101st and 102d Congresses

	101st Congress		102d Congress	
	Close Votes	Nonclose Votes	Close Votes	Nonclose Votes
Bush's Margin of Victory 1988 (%)	−.09 (.32) *−2.70*	−.02 (.13) *−.60*	−.37* (.26) *−12.30*	−.05 (.12) *−1.50*
Legislator's Margin of Victory (%)	.31* (.20) *7.00*	.20*** (.08) *4.10*	−.020 (.17) *−.60*	.13** (.07) *3.30*
Legislator's Terms Served	.01 (.01) *6.60*	.00 (.01) *.40*	.03*** (.01) *19.30*	−.00 (.00) *−2.40*
Democratic Leaders	−.11 (.11) *−1.20*	−.05 (.04) *−4.00*	−.03 (.09) *−.50*	−.03 (.03) *−2.70*
Committee Chairs	.08 (.22) *1.20*	−.03 (.09) *−.70*	−.34 (.19) *−7.40*	.01 (.08) *.10*
Ideology	4.98**** (.47) *67.80*	2.57**** (.19) *37.00*	1.27*** (.41) *21.70*	2.76**** (.18) *41.10*
Public Approval of the President	−.07**** (.01) *−30.00*	−.06**** (.00) *−27.40*	.007**** (.002) *9.70*	.005**** (.001) *5.40*
Constant	4.79**** (.53)	3.59**** (.25)	−.50*** (.20)	−.39 (.08)
Number of Cases	2,073.00	11,767.00	2,270.00	14,818.00
−2 × Log Likelihood	2,396.98	13,749.70	3,098.36	18,176.26
Model χ^2	300.03****	627.90****	29.42****	530.80****
Pseudo-R^2	.11	.04	.01	.03
Cases Correctly Predicted (%)	.70	.70	.55	.68

**** $p < .001$ *** $p < .01$ ** $p < .05$ * $p < .10$ (one-tailed tests)
Entries are maximum likelihood coefficients.
Standard errors are in parentheses.
Mean effects are in *italics*.
The dependent variable is whether the legislator supported or opposed Bush's stand.

Table 5.3
Logistic Regression Estimation of Republicans' Domestic Policy Support for Bush, 101st and 102d Congresses

	101st Congress		102d Congress	
	Close Votes	Nonclose Votes	Close Votes	Nonclose Votes
Bush's Margin	1.81****	.60***	−.55	.31
of Victory 1988 (%)	(.55)	(.21)	(.45)	(.19)
	30.30	*11.30*	*−9.30*	*6.30*
Legislator's Margin	−.05	.13	−.05	−.13*
of Victory (%)	(.29)	(.11)	(.19)	(.08)
	−1.10	*3.10*	*−1.30*	*−2.70*
Legislator's Terms	.09****	.03***	.05***	.02
Served	(.02)	(.01)	(.02)	(.01)
	22.30	*10.60*	*20.50*	*8.60*
Republican Leaders	.00	.19****	−.04	.04
	(.14)	(.05)	(.10)	(.05)
	.00	*14.70*	*−4.50*	*3.60*
Ranking Minority	.06	.00	−.22	.01
Members	(.25)	(.09)	(.20)	(.08)
	.80	*.20*	*−6.40*	*.3*
Ideology	4.85****	3.11****	.97**	3.02****
	(.62)	(.23)	(.54)	(.23)
	55.20	*42.60*	*15.70*	*40.90*
Public Approval	.11****	−.02****	−.005**	−.003***
of the President	(.01)	(.00)	(.003)	(.001)
	41.20	*−9.50*	*−7.20*	*−3.90*
Constant	−8.07****	1.08****	.03	−.05
	(.70)	(.30)	(.25)	(.11)
Number of Cases	1,458.00	8,085.00	1,416.00	9,302.00
−2 × Log Likelihood	1,489.46	9,997.28	1,946.44	11,416.94
Model χ^2	255.87****	376.32****	12.89**	280.27****
Pseudo-R^2	.15	.04	.01	.02
Cases Correctly Predicted (%)	.75	.68	.55	.68

**** $p < .001$ *** $p < .01$ ** $p < .05$ * $p < .10$ (one-tailed tests)
Entries are maximum likelihood coefficients.
Standard errors are in parentheses.
Mean effects are in *italics*.
The dependent variable is whether the legislator supported or opposed Bush's stand.

minimal "marginal coattails." With an eye to the preferences of their own reelection constituencies, Democrats pushed forth their own legislative agenda and feared little retaliation for opposing the president.

Bush's electoral popularity mattered more to congressional Republicans. Particularly on close votes early in his term on such issues as the budget, the environment, and Democratic efforts to raise the Environmental Protection Agency to a cabinet-level department, the president's electoral margin helped shore up unity among Republicans. Significantly, however, Bush's electoral margin loses importance in the second half of his term. Part of the effect is connected to the natural decline in political capital presidents suffer. But in Bush's case, it is also potentially due to the residual effect of the 1990 budget fiasco. Republicans kept a keen eye on their own reelection prospects after the midterm elections. Trepidation in presidential support among junior Republicans is also evident, suggesting that Bush's early attempts at accommodation with Democrats made younger members uncomfortable. On close votes in the 101st Congress, a ten-term Republican was nearly 15 percent more likely to support Bush's stand than a freshman. The impact is almost identical on close votes after the midterm.

For members of both parties, ideology had the greatest impact on presidential support. The data paint a picture of considerable party polarization over the stands that Bush took. He consistently drew support from members of both parties situated to the right of the party median. Among Democrats, most of his support came from the few remaining conservative southerners, but their backing was generally insufficient to build minimum winning coalitions against the Democratic leadership—even when coupled with a strong majority of Republicans. The erosion of the conservative coalition's strength reflected the realignment of the southern electorate. There were far fewer cross-pressured Democrats on whom Bush could rely. Southerners were ideologically much closer to their copartisans than in the bipartisan conservative or liberal activist eras. When Nixon faced divided government in his first term, the average southern Democrat was about twenty-five points to the right of the party median. In the 101st Congress, the average southern Democrat was about fifteen points to the right of the party median. On close votes in the first half of Bush's term, southern Democrats were 18 percent more likely to support the president. The problem for Bush was that even with their backing, support from southern conservatives translated into an average pool of only twenty-eight votes.

Could George Bush have used his exceedingly high public approval following the military victory in the Persian Gulf to win over Democrats on domestic policy? The data do not convey much optimism. Following the general pattern for presidents who face a majority opposition in Congress, table 5.2 shows an inverse relationship between Bush's public approval and opposition support, at least in the first half of his term. It was, of course, after the midterm elections that Bush's approval soared on the wings of the victory against Iraq and then plummeted dramatically against the backdrop of a sagging economy. But the wild variation in popular support had seemingly little substantive impact in Congress. Bush's approval rating ranged from a high of 87 percent in 1991 to a low of 32 percent in 1992 for the nonclose votes in the analysis. For close votes, the high was 84 percent and the low 34 percent. Thus, his national approval had only a meager positive impact on Democratic support. The expected change in individual support for the 55-point difference on less controversial issues is only about 5 percent and just under 10 percent for close votes.

Members of Congress do not alter their basic policy predispositions on the basis of shifts in national trends of the president's popular approval. Public evaluations of Bush's job performance could not bridge the gap of an electoral context devoid of policy issues. Nor did Bush's electoral victory necessarily translate into positive leverage over Congress. The incumbency advantage in Congress robbed him of coattails, and his own lack of agenda objectives, coupled with the Democrats' centralization of authority in party leaders, limited his ability to shape floor outcomes.

The Bush presidency will be remembered for partisan conflict, gridlock, and uneasy accommodation between the branches. If elections are a compass for policy action, in 1988 the electorate gave neither the president nor Congress a clear direction to follow. Without broad issues that required immediate attention, Bush and Congress were frequently unable to find common ground for policy agreement. They followed the cues of their partisan electoral constituencies. The president's precarious situation forced a reliance on veto politics to halt or alter legislation, with rather limited credit-claiming opportunities for domestic policies of national import.

Bill Clinton and Divided Government, 1995–96

Bill Clinton's bout with an opposition-controlled Congress began with the midterm elections in 1994 and continued for the next six years. Unlike Bush, Clinton commenced his term in 1993 with a much larger agenda for change. A key difference between Clinton and his predecessor is that the intervention of split-party control impeded making significant progress on his active agenda. Like Bush, however, Clinton wielded the veto and veto threats to block and moderate the majority's agenda. Clinton was arguably more savvy at preempting the majority on budget and social issues.

The partisanship and intense conflict between the branches that characterized the 104th Congress precluded passage of much of the Republicans' Contract with America, save for select elements with bipartisan backing. Clinton adapted to the new condition of divided government by carefully supporting such legislation and engaging in credit claiming where possible. At the same time, Clinton used the veto to either block most major elements of the GOP agenda or reshape significant outcomes like welfare reform. In this manner, Clinton was able to portray himself as a centrist reformer willing to work with Congress and simultaneously fortify his partisan base as he and fellow Democrats depicted the Republican agenda as "extreme." Although Clinton failed to garner much independent policy success in the 104th Congress, some scholars have suggested he may well have been more successful in his manipulation of institutional and electoral politics in 1995–96 than he was in pushing forth an expansive agenda two years earlier under unified conditions.[30]

Clinton, the 1994 Elections, and Divided Government

Short-term factors—including Clinton's policy failures, controversy over early cabinet appointments, and congressional scandals in the brief interlude of unified government in 1993–94—furnish much of the explanation for the 1994 electoral earthquake.[31] In November, 1994, Republicans captured the House of Representatives for the first time in forty years and regained control of the Senate, which they had lost in 1986. Although the rate of incumbents reelected surpassed 90 percent, dissatisfaction with Clinton's leadership hurt Democratic candidates in both national and state elections.[32] Clinton's "honeymoon" with Congress had been curtailed by the polemic over cabinet nominations and the president's plan to allow homosexuals to serve openly in the military. Controversy over his failed economic stimulus plan, the 1993 budget, and the North American Free Trade Agreement (NAFTA) contributed to Clinton's legislative woes. By 1994, health care reform, the cornerstone of the president's 1992 election campaign, had failed to materialize despite the White House's full-scale effort to redesign the American health care system—which in turn precluded action on other administration priorities such as welfare reform (see chapter 7).

The Republicans' Contract with America nationalized the 1994 midterm elections.[33] Even if the Contract itself drew scant attention from voters, the policy platform gave GOP candidates common themes on which to campaign. The items outlined in the Contract—including a balanced budget, term limits, welfare reform, tax cuts, and crime control—galvanized support from districts that had generally voted Republican in previous presidential elections but often returned Democrats to Congress. "Republicans," as James Gimpel notes, "had deliberately crafted their campaign appeals to attract the independent voters who wanted change."[34] Only 38 percent of eligible voters turned out for the November, 1994, elections, and many of those who did were supporters of Ross Perot's "antiestablishment" presidential candidacy in 1992. Independents, "swing voters," and backers of Perot in 1992 were more prone to support Republicans in 1994. As a result, the same volatile portion of the electorate that had helped defeat George Bush in 1992 turned on many incumbent Democrats.[35] While Republicans had generally suffered from a lack of competitive candidates in the past, "quality challengers"—many with political experience and financial advantages over Democratic incumbents— captured seats that had been highly competitive in 1992.[36] Interpreting the re- sults of the 1994 elections as a signal that voters had rejected Clinton's policy agenda, House Speaker Newt Gingrich stood poised to profit from strong Republican unity within a highly centralized legislative structure. Gingrich pushed the Contract with America through the House of Representatives with lightening speed, but Senate Republicans, who were not signatories to the policy program, greeted it with less enthusiasm or sense of immediacy.

Clinton first approached the 104th Congress with pledges of bipartisan- ship, but ultimately wound up engaging in high-profile conflict with Republi- cans. The discord that developed over budget issues produced two shut- downs of the executive branch. Clinton's legislative strategy was predicated upon the greater party unity on which he could count among congressional Democrats. His repeated vetoes of appropriations bills eventually forced the Republicans' hand in a game of budgetary brinksmanship as the tide of public opinion shifted to the White House's advantage.

Lawmaking and Presidential Leadership under Clinton

Clinton's strategy on significant lawmaking was complex. At key points he wielded the veto power to force negotiation and compromise. In other cases he preempted the majority's agenda and backed bipartisan legislation for the purposes of credit claiming. Few of the significant laws in the 104th Congress, however, derived from Clinton's stated policy objectives.

Of the fourteen significant domestic laws Mayhew identifies in 1995–96, five were linked, albeit rather tenuously, to Clinton's agenda. They include the minimum wage increase, the 1996 budget, lobbying reform, health insurance portability, and welfare reform. At first glance, some of the legislation's subject matter, like lobbying and welfare reform, appears to have a direct connection to the president's agenda from the 103d Congress. Such outcomes, however, did *not* reflect independent policy successes for the president or even his pre- ferred agenda. In several cases, Clinton engaged in a politics of preemption reminiscent of Nixon's dealings with an opposition majority. Most of the pol- icy issues had already been targeted for action by the Republican majority in their Contract with America, so the president sought to use the levers of the presidency and his institutional position to define the parameters of accept- able legislative outcomes. He was highly successful in this regard with the budget and welfare reform.

The budget agreement merits special attention. After Clinton's repeated vetoes of spending bills in late 1995 and early 1996, failed override attempts by the House Republican leadership, and two government shutdowns for which the public ultimately held the GOP accountable, the president had strengthened his hand considerably by 1996. Clinton essentially preempted the Republican agenda and called for a balanced budget by 2002, based on Congressional Budget Office forecasts. In the give-and-take that followed, the White House proposed considerable spending cuts to offset outlays for education and the environment. Although Republicans roundly criticized the president's budget proposal for suspect accounting methods, the basic contours of Clinton's proposal were adopted—and without the cherished across-the-board tax cut Republicans had championed.[37]

The welfare reform bill fits uncomfortably in the classification of significant laws. Per the coding rules, the legislation is grouped in the "presidential priority" column (chapter 1), although it arguably forms a category unto itself. After failing to act on welfare reform in the first half of his term, the president returned to the issue in his 1995 State of the Union address, presumably to win as much leverage as possible over Republicans' plans to radically alter the system as outlined in the Contract with America. But his stance on welfare reform was highly inconsistent and shifted over time.[38] Clinton vetoed Republican welfare legislation twice in the 104th Congress, and was ultimately successful in his bid to force GOP leaders to drop Medicare reform from the bill. Signing the bill, although with some trepidation, gave the president an opportunity to argue that he had made good on his 1992 campaign promise to "end welfare as we know it."

The welfare bill—which terminated the sixty-year-old federal guarantee of benefits, mandated work requirements, and gave sweeping control to the states—was at best a mixed victory for Clinton, and it brought scathing rebukes from members of his own party. Congressional Democrats critical of the law viewed Clinton's ultimate acceptance of the Republican plan as a miscarriage of traditional party principles. Influential Democrats in both chambers chided provisions of the bill. Representative Charles Rangel of New York was indignant that "my president will boldly throw 1 million into poverty,"[39] and fellow New Yorker Sen. Daniel Patrick Moynihan similarly condemned what he considered to be the bill's premise: that "the behavior of certain adults can be changed by making the lives of their children as wretched as possible."[40]

Lobbying reform and health insurance portability were two other significant laws representing considerably scaled-down versions of legislation that had failed in the 103d Congress. Clinton again called for congressional action and attempted to claim credit for the passage of the bills. Republicans had effectively blocked lobbying reform the president had championed during his first two years, foreclosing the success of any bill with a filibuster strategy in 1994.[41] The GOP version of lobbying reform passed by the 104th Congress, which included the restriction of gifts and registration requirements, did not represent the comprehensive approach that Clinton had proposed.[42] Similarly, Clinton supported legislation on the portability of health care coverage, dubbed Kassebaum-Kennedy for the bill's cosponsors. The legislation was "miniature in scope" compared to the president's earlier plans for sweeping reform that never came to a vote in the 103d Congress.[43] Clinton's involvement on Kassebaum-Kennedy was evident primarily in his opposition to medical savings accounts originally floated in the bill. A bipartisan agreement produced a pilot program to his satisfaction.[44]

The 1996 minimum wage increase was as close to an independent policy success as Clinton—and his minority copartisans—were able to garner in the 104th Congress. A year earlier, the president had called for a hike in the wage floor, but the plea fell on deaf ears in the GOP-controlled Congress. The 1995 request was "less a serious legislative proposal than an effort by Democrats to draw a clear distinction between themselves and Republicans in the minds of working-class voters."[45] With the 1996 elections looming on the horizon, Senate Democrats forced the issue to the forefront by attaching amendments to increase the minimum wage to every bill that emerged on the legislative calendar. Republicans ultimately ceded to the pressure. House leaders appended the minimum wage increase to the Small Business Protection Act of 1996, which began as a bill targeting tax cuts as part of the Contract with America.[46] In this manner, the president and congressional Democrats were successful in drawing attention away from a central feature of the Republican agenda. Upon signing the law, Clinton was careful to point out elements of the legislation with which he disagreed while taking credit for the passage of the first minimum wage increase since 1991. He called the increase "long overdue" and essential for the "millions of Americans and their families who struggle to make ends meet while working at the minimum wage."[47]

Clinton was not involved in several of the important bills of the 104th Congress, including pesticides, safe drinking water, and telecommunications. He did, however, lend support to several elements of the Contract with America in the bid to overshadow the GOP majority's policy accomplishments. Unfunded mandates, congressional accountability, and line-item veto legislation sprang forth not from the president's agenda but from the Republican policy program. In these cases, the president publicly agreed with and accepted portions of the Contract. Although Republican Dirk Kempthorne of Idaho led the effort on unfunded mandates legislation, Clinton attempted to steal some of the GOP's thunder by issuing two executive orders promoting consultation between executive branch departments and state and local governments.[48] The president left it to Congress to decide whether to apply federal labor and antidiscrimination laws to the legislative branch, but he commended the effort to ensure that "all laws that apply to the rest of the country also apply equally to Congress."[49] Finally, every president in the past quarter century had sought the authority to veto individual budget items. Clinton, being no different, praised the GOP's efforts to pass the line-item veto. Although the Republicans ultimately made good on their promise to enact the statute—if somewhat begrudgingly with a Democrat in the White House—the president had few opportunities to test the waters because the law was later ruled unconstitutional.[50]

Clinton achieved less success with his efforts to claim credit for other innovative legislation with no connection to his agenda. Interest groups that insisted, as did Clinton, that the issues of legal and illegal immigration be separated, blasted Republicans seeking comprehensive immigration reform. The legislation provided funding for more agents to patrol the southwestern border, provided for more expeditious deportation of illegal aliens, and stripped away most of the provisions governing legal immigration. But if the exclusion of restrictions on public benefits to legal immigrants was consistent with Clinton's position, the GOP's softening was less the result of pressure from the White House than it was the urgency to return home to campaign at the end of the 1996 legislative session.[51]

The antiterrorism law enacted by the Republican majority was a more clear-cut loss for the president. Clinton tried to overtake the GOP by outlining his own proposal to combat domestic terrorism in February, 1996—a month after Republican leaders introduced their bill. The president's legislation stalled, and the shape of the statute adopted was not consistent with Clinton's request for expanded wiretapping and chemical identification provisions.[52]

The president's sufferings under divided government were also evident in other significant bills. Clinton showed considerable ambivalence for agriculture reform, and congressional Democrats became frustrated with his veto of legislation to curb unwarranted shareholder lawsuits. The Republican deregulation of agriculture, which replaced subventions with declining fixed payments, drew criticism from Clinton. The president vowed to propose legislation to reinstate an agricultural safety net, and congressional Democrats pledged to reverse the law if they won back a majority in Congress.[53] There was visibly less solidarity between the president and his copartisans on the subject of shareholder lawsuits. In Trumanesque fashion, Clinton distanced himself from the public debate. Democratic senator Christopher Dodd believed that he had worked out a compromise on details of the legislation that were acceptable to the president, but Clinton, much to the Dodd's dismay, vetoed the bill on the basis of narrow technical issues. Democrats responded by overwhelmingly overriding the president's veto. While the president's copartisans were careful to note that their actions were not meant as an affront, "Privately . . . many were angered at the way Clinton handled the matter, directing his veto at issues that the Administration had not previously emphasized and embarrassing Dodd, a Clinton loyalist."[54]

Clinton's record on significant legislation in the 104th Congress was mixed. On one hand, his prior vetoes of GOP-sponsored legislation had allowed him to exact considerable concessions on issues such as the budget and welfare. Clinton also adeptly engaged in preemptive politics on several occasions in order to upstage the congressional majority as the 1996 elections approached. He may have been more successful in this regard than George Bush. Nonetheless, Clinton was in a particularly weak position to define the national agenda. His engagement in the legislative realm was reactionary and occasionally preemptive. A closer analysis of the president's floor success rate underscores his symbolic and substantive displacement as "chief legislator" in the 104th Congress.

Clinton's Support and Success in the 104th Congress

In the opening days of the 104th Congress, Clinton struggled to remind the new congressional majority and the American people that the president was still "relevant" because of the veto power. The Republicans' Contract with America emulated a party platform typical of a bygone era, and the promise to hold floor votes on a set of key domestic policy issues in the first hundred days arrogated a powerful symbol of presidential leadership. House Republicans' remarkable cohesion, and the willingness of freshmen to defer to the leadership, enabled Speaker Gingrich to pass all of the "Contract" items, save for a constitutional amendment on term limits, on schedule.[55]

Party-unity voting structured executive-legislative relations for Clinton in the 104th Congress, just as it had for Bush in the 101st and 102d Congresses. All of the close votes in the analysis pitted a majority of Democrats against a majority of Republicans, and nonclose votes were scarcely less partisan. As

Table 5.4
Clinton's Legislative Success Rate,
104th Congress*

	Close Votes [n=13]	Nonclose Votes [n=36]
Overall	30.8% (4)	33.3% (12)
Democratic Party	100.0% (13)	94.4% (34)
Republican Party	0% (0)	22.2% (5)

* Entries are the number and percentage of votes on which the president gained a majority overall and by party.

House Republicans commanded floor proceedings on issues spanning abortion and environmental issues to the budget, the president scored few victories overall.

The analysis of roll-call votes provides critical insight as to why Clinton was ultimately successful in halting considerable policy reversals. He had a strong electoral base from which to lead his party in Congress *against* the Republican agenda. The GOP agenda of domestic programmatic cuts threatened core Democratic constituencies. His congressional copartisans stood firm in opposition. House Republicans attempted four overrides on budget matters, but their search for the sixty to seventy Democratic votes needed to produce a supermajority proved a futile task. So, although Clinton could not move his preferred agenda and scored few legislative victories on floor votes, he was successful in "winning the war" against the Republican platform.[56]

The Democrats' noteworthy unity in support of the president's opposition to the Republican agenda did not mean that they did not encounter difficulties adjusting to minority status. Some House Democrats suffered from what Charles O. Jones described as the "minority mentality."[57] Minority party members may be tempted to vote with the majority to seek personal gain or to act responsibly to produce public policies. The problem is that cooperation may result in a perpetuation of their minority status. A small contingent of moderate to conservative "Blue Dog" Democrats from the South were particularly frustrated by their minority status and worried about having only a record of obstructionism against Republicans on which to campaign in the next election. Powerless to halt the march of the initial Republican legislative onslaught, they gravitated toward the Republicans' positions. "For southern Democrats," Gimpel explains, "many of the Contract items were popular issues that they had championed in years past. The Democratic party remained insensitive to the sensibilities of its conservative wing as President Clinton launched his own full scale assault on the Republicans' proposals."[58] Nonetheless, Clinton did not face the dramatic defections that Truman did when he encountered a similar partisan configuration. The smaller contingent of southern Democrats did not play a pivotal role on legislative outcomes.

The Republicans' midterm election victory and Clinton's lack of "marginal coattails" in GOP districts in 1992 diminished his positive leverage over the opposition majority. The president's electoral popularity had no effect on Republicans, but it was strong and positive for Democrats. The data in table 5.5 were analyzed via two separate equations, altering Democratic members' ideological positions and Clinton's district-level margin of victory because of collinearity. The intercorrelation between ideology and the president's electoral popularity is –.73, and reflected the dramatic changes in the Democratic

Table 5.5
Logistic Regression Estimation of Democrats' Domestic Policy Support for Clinton, 104th Congress

	Close Votes		Nonclose Votes	
Clinton's Margin of Victory 1992 (%)	6.52**** (.53) *54.20*	———	2.82**** (.19) *45.90*	———
Legislator's Margin of Victory (%)	-1.24*** (.36) *-9.20*	-.78** (.40) *-3.80*	-.75**** (.15) *-14.60*	-.54**** (14) *-10.10*
Legislator's Terms Served	-.02 (.02) *-3.10*	-.00 (.02) *-.10*	.007 (.008) *2.90*	-.001 (.008) *-.50*
Democratic Leaders	.50*** (.16) *6.00*	.31* (.20) *3.30*	.24**** (.06) *13.40*	.11** (.06) *6.90*
Ranking Minority Members	-.05 (.33) *-.30*	-.44 (.40) *-2.20*	-.02 (.13) *-.40*	-.11 (.13) *-2.00*
Ideology	———	-11.71**** (.72) *-86.30*	———	-5.11**** (.24) *-64.70*
Public Approval of the President	-.05**** (.02) *-5.30*	-.06**** (.01) *-4.20*	3.23**** (.65) *10.20*	3.36**** (.67) *10.60*
Constant	4.44**** (.84)	6.61**** (.92)	-.90*** (.33)	-.26 (.33)
Number of Cases	2,500.00	2,505.00	6,833.00	6,846.00
–2 × Log Likelihood	1,371.82	1,169.40	7,376.18	7,126.38
Model χ^2	218.14****	443.82****	292.71****	572.01****
Pseudo-R^2	.14	.28	.03	.07
Cases Correctly Predicted (%)	.91	.92	.75	.76

**** p < .001   *** p < .01   ** p < .05   * p < .10 (one-tailed tests)
Entries are maximum likelihood coefficients.
Standard errors are in parentheses.
Mean effects are in *italics*.
The dependent variable is whether the legislator supported or opposed Clinton's stand.

constituency base in the previous three decades. Democratic districts that gave Clinton a larger margin of victory over George Bush in 1992 tended to elect more liberal members of Congress. A Democrat from a district where Clinton's margin of victory over Bush was 5 percent was 10.4 percent more likely to support the president on close votes compared to a Democrat from a district where Clinton lost to Bush by the same margin. The magnitude of the impact of the president's electoral popularity underscores the importance of the electoral connection between the president and members of his party in Congress as a rallying mechanism against the GOP agenda.

For both parties, the effect of ideology was most prominent on close votes.

Table 5.6
Logistic Regression Estimation of Republicans' Domestic Policy Support for Clinton, 104th Congress

	Close Votes	Nonclose Votes
Clinton's Margin	1.12*	.14
of Victory 1992 (%)	(.71)	(.31)
	6.10	*1.60*
Legislator's Margin	.09	.07
of Victory (%)	(.28)	(.12)
	.80	*1.30*
Legislator's Terms	−.09****	.00
Served	(.02)	(.01)
	−8.80	*.40*
Republican Leaders	−.18*	−.02
	(.14)	(.05)
	−4.8	*−1.80*
Committee Chairs	−.11	.08
	(.25)	(.10)
	−.90	*1.50*
Ideology	−12.08****	−3.08****
	(.74)	(.29)
	−97.50	*−48.40*
Public Approval	−.00****	3.21****
of the President	(.01)	(.58)
	−.30	*10.60*
Constant	−1.86****	−2.83****
	(.67)	(.30)
Number of Cases	2,993.00	8,237.00
−2 × Log Likelihood	1,999.90	8,972.11
Model χ^2	481.51****	193.29****
Pseudo-R^2	.19	.02
Cases Correctly Predicted (%)	.86	.75

**** p < .001   *** p < .01   ** p < .05   * p < .10 (one-tailed tests)
Entries are maximum likelihood coefficients.
Standard errors are in parentheses.
Mean effects are in *italics*.
The dependent variable is whether the legislator supported or opposed Clinton's stand.

The eighty-six-point effect on close votes underscores that Clinton marshaled exceptional support from liberal Democrats. Conservative Democrats, on the other hand, were uncomfortable in the minority and were sometimes caught between constituency pressures to support the Contract with America and the White House's stand against the GOP agenda. The forty-six southern Democrats tended to rank among the more conservative, with ideological scores averaging 17 percent above the party median. The rest represented a smattering of more conservative Democrats primarily from the Midwest and Pacific Coast. Blue Dog southern Democrats were about 19 percent more likely to defect from the president's positions.

Incumbency advantage gave some moderate Democrats more latitude to defect on popular issues. The support model shows that there was a slight tendency for Democrats with wider victory margins in the previous election to defect from the president's positions across vote categories. Although Democratic defections did not alter the outcome of floor votes because of the Republicans' strong unity, issues that resonated with their constituencies—like votes on the repeal of assault weapons legislation and a ban on partial-birth abortions—were a natural magnet. Nevertheless, it is essential to emphasize that widespread Democratic defections from the president's positions were rare. Using Truman's relations with the 80th Congress as a point of comparison, the Republican leadership had no real opportunities to construct ideological coalitions capable of overriding the president's vetoes.

Ideology was the driving factor behind Republican positions for close and less controversial votes. The remarkable ninety-seven-point impact on close votes highlights Republican unity in favor of the issues outlined in the Contract. Only a smattering of moderate Republicans were willing to occasionally shirk the party line. Republicans worried more about electoral reprisals for failing to deliver on campaign pledges. Clinton's opposition to two-thirds of floor votes was largely irrelevant in their view.

The president's job approval does not mitigate constituency pressures on Republicans to adhere to the party line. Support for Clinton was about 10 percent more likely at the height of his public approval in 1996, but only on nonclose votes. The trend of Clinton's job approval contradicts normal expectations of a decline over time. His job approval rating early in the 104th Congress stood squarely below 50 percent, but it increased rather steadily and moved into the mid-50 percent range for votes in the second session. Much to the Republicans' chagrin, the budget showdown may have solidified this trend in early 1996 as the public came to side with the president. As for Bush, Clinton's job approval rating does not appear to have been a key factor in gaining the legislative support of the opposition majority in Congress under highly partisan conditions.

Summary

Divided government in the latter half of the postreform/party-unity era has been marked by stability in voting alliances in Congress, policy-focused and better-organized majorities, and the growth of a contested agenda between the White House and the opposition majority in Congress. These conditions have been less conducive to presidential agenda leadership. Bush and Clinton were in weak institutional positions to set the national legislative agenda. The dearth of overlap in the election constituencies of these presidents and members of the majority opposition ossified the ideological divide between the branches and severely limited cross-party coalition building.

For Bush and Clinton, their role in the legislative sphere was recast to fending off the most objectionable elements of the majority's agenda and placing limitations on outcomes through the use of the veto and veto threats. This weapon in the president's arsenal has become more powerful in recent times as party margins in Congress have narrowed and intraparty cohesion has increased. The opposition leadership has been unable to forge coalitions capable of trumping the president's veto. Veto leverage transformed the meaning of presidential "success" from independent policy accomplishments or support for a shared agenda with Congress to halting legislation or frequently reshaping the majority's agenda through the veto power.

The circumstances of divided government in the postreform/party-unity era place a premium on a chief executive's ability to defend his veto record and selectively preempt the congressional agenda. Savvy presidents must also seek opportunities to take a leadership stance on—or lend support for—whatever legislative issues are likely to draw bipartisan support. In this regard, the experiences of Bush and Clinton offer a marked contrast. Bush was less deft at preempting or modifying the contested agenda that developed in the 101st and 102d Congresses in ways that could aid his reelection effort in 1992. His focus on the management of current problems in what amounted to a "procedural presidency," as Kerry Mullins and Aaron Wildavsky describe it, haunted the campaign as the economy worsened.[59] Bush was frequently accused of lacking vision, and the dearth of positive domestic accomplishments of which he could boast contributed to his electoral demise. His high popular approval following the Gulf War victory was insufficient to fill the void.

Clinton, by contrast, was able to skillfully exploit the condition of divided government as the 1996 election approached. He did not "steal" the

Republican agenda as much as he moderated it, preempted it, and retooled it at key junctures. To this end, he frequently wielded the veto and adroitly exploited public relations to eclipse the opposition majority's accomplishments. Clinton seems to have understood early what Republicans leaders learned too late: When Congress challenges the president, public opinion tends to shift to the president's side.[60] Democratic Party cohesion gave Clinton a vital edge in negotiating with GOP leaders, who lacked the votes to override his vetoes. The president forced compromise on spending levels and ultimately placed himself in a position to co-opt a central element of the Contract with America by calling for a balanced budget in 1996. As the economy strengthened toward the end of his first term, Clinton attempted to make the case that his "centrist" approach was vital for continued economic growth.

Divided government for Bush and Clinton—even when the difference in the scope of their policy objectives is considered—scarcely resembled the idealized "FDR model" of presidential leadership of Congress. The decline of coattails and the development of stronger parties in Congress have had a significant impact on the legislative presidency. The current policy-making context of divided government favors a strategy of veto leverage. This is a fundamental difference in the exercise of legislative leadership compared to prior eras in which divided government occurred. Such a strategy contrasts even more starkly with the type of legislative leadership presidents exerted in the few postwar incidences of unified government that are explored in the next two chapters.

Kennedy, Johnson, and Unified Government at the Crossroads of Eras

6

THE TYPE OF LEGISLATIVE LEADERSHIP John Fitzgerald Kennedy and Lyndon Baines Johnson were able to exert diverged wholly from presidents who faced opposition majorities in the postreform/party-unity era. Their agenda leadership—not efforts to block congressional initiatives or wield the veto power to alter legislation—defined their legislative presidencies. The significant legislation that emerged over the course of their terms thus was unanimously linked to their stated policy objectives.

Yet Kennedy and Johnson did not have an equivalent basis for positive leverage over Congress. The electoral and institutional contexts of unified government differed considerably. What varied most for Kennedy and Johnson was the magnitude of lawmaking, the *dimensions* of the shared agenda between the branches, and the strength of their resources to persuade the congressional majority. Unified government mattered for both presidents, but by degree.

Kennedy began his term with weaker positive leverage over Congress. His thin electoral victory and the unfavorable institutional setting in Congress during the closing years of the bipartisan conservative era restrained his activist approach to governance. Kennedy, who defeated Republican challenger Richard Nixon in 1960 by one of the most narrow popular vote margins in the twentieth century, suffered from negative coattails: twenty-two Democrats, mostly liberals who otherwise shared his "New Frontier" agenda, lost their seats. He faced a Democratic majority on Capitol Hill composed of a large number of conservative members who occupied important leadership positions and had safe seats. Southerners maintained a lock on the most important committees, and the strength of the conservative coalition promised that the 87th Congress would be ill disposed to grand departures from the status quo. As a result, Kennedy spent much time trying to *forge* a shared agenda with his regionally bifurcated congressional majority. His efforts centered on goading recalcitrant leaders into action. The conservative coalition in Congress often proved an important, though not consistently insurmountable, hindrance to Kennedy's legislative objectives.

The 1964 election legitimized Johnson's "Great Society" agenda in a way that Kennedy's election four years earlier had not for the New Frontier. It also gave Johnson what his predecessor had failed to obtain: A *working* legislative majority of liberal Democrats in Congress. Johnson's coattails broke the seemingly intractable hold of conservatives on policy making and ushered in the liberal activist era. There is little doubt that Johnson's familiarity with and passion for the legislative process, the product of his many years as Senate majority leader, facilitated his direction of much of Congress's legislative business on the domestic front from 1965–68. But equally, if not more important, than Johnson's reputed skill was the interplay of strong electoral resources over members of both parties, coupled with a weak organizational structure on Capitol Hill. These circumstances provided an exceptional basis for Johnson to set and manage the contours of the shared agenda with a receptive governing majority composed of many members who owed their electoral victories to the president. The policy-making environment of the mid-1960s also lacked the tentativeness and restraint of the 1950s or early 1960s. The policy activism called for by the public, as evidenced by the panoply of interest groups that emerged to demand redress of various social and economic issues in the mid- to late 1960s, was nothing less than remarkable.

A closer inspection of executive-legislative relations under Kennedy and Johnson emphasizes the differing environmental context of unified government in the bipartisan conservative and liberal activist eras in terms of positive leverage over Congress. Although Kennedy had some independent policy victories, the majority of his successes were merely the expansion of existing domestic programs. Johnson's far stronger leverage resulted in greater autonomous control of the congressional agenda and the establishment of many new programs.

The Electoral and Policy Context: Kennedy and Congress, 1961–62

The composition of Congress mirrored the electorate's sharp division in the 1960 presidential election, portending some of the considerable obstacles to Kennedy's activist agenda. As James L. Sundquist contends, "the fundamental trouble in the Eighty-seventh Congress was not presidential leadership, just as it was not House organization. The trouble was the ambiguity of the 1960 election."[1] Kennedy defeated Republican rival Richard Nixon by one of the most narrow margins for elections in the last half of the century. Less than half a million votes separated the two presidential contenders. As a result, many in Congress were much less convinced than Kennedy that activist government was either essential or desirable in the domestic sphere. The new president had a vision of where he wanted to lead the country. But congressional followership was far from certain.

The 1960 election returned a majority of Democrats to Capitol Hill, but it was the first time in the twentieth century an incoming president's party lost seats in Congress—two in the Senate and twenty more in the House. The House losses were particularly troubling. Republicans replaced progressive Democrats who had been narrowly elected in 1958. Kennedy's marginal coattails were regionally based.[2] His electoral edge at the district level surpassed the margins of only twenty-two Democratic House members, mostly from liberal constituencies in the northeast. He had no coattails elsewhere, and failed to run ahead of a single southern House Democrat. His lack of popularity in Dixie reflected Southerners' mistrust of his domestic agenda and bias against his religious affiliation, which may have cost him votes in other regions of the country.[3]

Because the Democrats had only a nominal majority in Congress, Kennedy, Carroll Kilpatrick notes, "learned early in his Administration that his fundamental weakness as leader is that he heads a party which is not united behind him."[4] Despite Democratic margins of 262-174 in the House and 65-35 in the Senate, a tenacious contingent of southern Democrats could join with conservative Republicans to impose a formidable blocking majority against Kennedy and liberal Democrats. Theodore Sorensen, counselor to the president, underscored the quandary in which the conservative coalition placed Kennedy: "The meaning was clear. No bill could pass the House of Representatives without somehow picking up the votes of 40 to 60 Southerners or Republicans, or a combination of the two, out of the 70 or so Southerners who were not intransigent on every issue."[5]

Neither the congressional committee system nor the congressional leadership mitigated Kennedy's predicament. The seniority system in both chambers, which gave southern Democrats chairmanship of the most powerful committees, reduced the probability that controversial domestic proposals would be reported out to the full House. Kennedy also could not depend on the Democratic leadership in either chamber to bring about congressional support for his agenda, particularly on nonincremental policies. Vice President Johnson emphasized the Democratic leadership's thin support for Kennedy by noting that the president "had the minnows, but not the whales."[6] Both venerable Speaker Sam Rayburn, who died in 1961, and John McCormack, his successor, were generally supportive of the president's agenda—although McCormack and Kennedy were rivals in Massachusetts politics and had sparred over local issues when Kennedy served in the House.[7]

Republicans, on the other hand, were not predisposed to cooperate with the new president. Voting irregularities in the 1960 election, particularly in Chicago, prompted the GOP to launch inquiries into alleged Democratic fraud. The campaign controversies only added to the potential for partisan conflict in Congress.[8]

Lawmaking and Presidential Leadership under Kennedy

Kennedy's attempts to establish a shared agenda with a refractory majority in Congress were marked both by tenacity and compromise. The president pushed an expansive agenda, but conservatives tempered legislative action. He was forced to make concessions on many major agenda items, for which he was roundly criticized. "Some of these compromises," Carroll Kirkpatrick posits, "may have resulted in improvements, some may have been no more than the normal give-and-take expected in a free society. But all represented retreat on the president's part."[9] When the details of legislation are juxtaposed with the administration's proposals, some of the bills adopted did indeed fall short of the president's goals.

Kennedy's real triumph, however, may have been that he *was able to obtain any action at all* on his priorities. He doggedly pursued an activist agenda, using his institutional position to force consideration and debate of his priority issues—most of which were scarcely intuitive to many in Congress. From this vantage point, George Edwards and Andrew Barrett observe, "whoever decides what is debated is more important than who wins the debate."[10]

Party control of Congress afforded Kennedy some advantages that proved essential to the passage of his policy objectives. The president and liberal forces failed in their bid to revise Rule 22 in the Senate to facilitate halting filibusters (unlimited debate).[11] But Kennedy waged a successful battle at the beginning of the 87th Congress to break the conservatives' lock on the House Rules Committee, chaired by Howard Smith of Virginia.[12] With Speaker Rayburn's help, the expansion of the Rules Committee from twelve to fifteen members curbed the ability of the conservative coalition to impede Kennedy's agenda from consideration on the House floor. While not a cure-all in light of the conservative coalition's entrenched power as a voting bloc, this key change in 1961 was crucial to the fate of many of the president's legislative objectives in the House. When he and his supporters succeeded in extricating pending legislation out of committee, a floor vote dramatically increased the likelihood of a favorable outcome.

The president's steady efforts and willingness to compromise with Congress produced a variety of innovative, far-reaching policies in a short time period. Each of the nine important domestic laws that Mayhew identifies for the 87th Congress was clearly linked to the president's stated policy objectives. The fruits of Kennedy's endeavors were borne out in the passage of area redevelopment, a minimum wage increase, housing, manpower development, and public welfare amendments. These laws formed the core of the president's New Frontier agenda.

Area redevelopment, housing, and manpower development are manifest examples of policies Kennedy championed during his 1960 campaign. Urban blight was a particular focus at the outset of the new administration. Kennedy's area redevelopment proposal initially encountered resistance from southern Democrats opposed to federal spending. However, through steadfast lobbying, the president co-opted their support by showing how the various loans, grants, and vocational programs would benefit their districts.[13] The comprehensive Housing Act of 1961 was also part of the president's plan to redress urban decline. The main provisions covered urban renewal, community planning, and mass transportation. As with many bills in 1961–62, the Housing Act was subject to substantial internal dissension in the 87th Congress. Nevertheless, steady lobbying and some compromise enabled Kennedy to get the bill passed with most of the provisions he had sought.[14] Finally, Kennedy's special economic message to Congress prompted consideration of the Manpower Development and Training Act. The bill sought to raise the skills of displaced workers and represented the most comprehensive effort in employment legislation since 1946.[15]

The president's willingness to compromise in order to procure congressional action when legislation became delayed or embroiled in conflict was clearly evident on several other bills. Kennedy sent a draft proposal for drug regulation to the House but ultimately threw his support behind Tennessee senator Estes Kefauver's bill, which contained some of the same provisions, to get action.[16] Congress adopted a minimum wage bill that extended coverage incrementally to some 3.6 million workers. Kennedy, however, preferred more far-reaching provisions. As a senator, he had sought an increase in coverage in 1960, but could not push the bill out of conference committee. He commented that the 1961 bill "doesn't finish the job, but it is an important step forward."[17]

Kennedy's stances on Social Security and tax reform are further indications of his preference for getting action on his agenda priorities even if the specifics required backing away from a nonincremental approach. The president had championed higher benefits for retirees as well as a larger increase in wage taxes than Congress was willing to accept.[18] The Social Security amendments adopted his first year in office represented a more moderate step, as Congress reduced the eligibility age from sixty-five to sixty-two and increased benefits for retirees and widows. Congress also worked over the president's tax reform bill. Still, the administration considered the sweeping changes to the tax code and investment tax credits for businesses a considerable success. As on the vast majority of bills, the president's call for action had been the impetus for reform efforts in which Congress might not otherwise have engaged.[19]

Kennedy's significant policy successes included both new programs designed to address urgent problems, such as urban decay, and modifications and expansions of existing programs like the minimum wage and Social Security. All told, nearly twice as many significant laws were passed in 1961–62 as during the last two years of Eisenhower's presidency and despite the fact that the bias in the ideological balance in Congress was similar for the two periods. Why, then, have scholars frequently viewed Kennedy's record as poor or mediocre and given short shrift to the advantages of unified government?

Such reactions may stem from several causes. First, critics have often focused on measures that did *not* pass during the period rather than on those that did. Congressional conservatives wielded a disproportionate amount of influence. The conservative coalition joined forces to defeat Kennedy's proposals for the creation of a new Department of Urban Affairs and federal aid to education in 1961. The untimely failure of the education bill was particularly damaging to the president's prestige. Kennedy had given substantial weight to education during the 1961 campaign and staked his personal reputation on the bill, the controversial nature of which he had greatly underestimated.[20]

Second, Kennedy generated high public expectations for his legislative presidency with which he could not keep pace.[21] Kennedy made 220 policy declarations during the 1960 campaign, two-thirds of which related to domestic policy.[22] The sheer number of legislative requests Kennedy made in his first two years—653—is remarkable. But only 10 percent of his legislative requests had been acted upon four months into his term,[23] and by the end of the 87th Congress, only 46.7 percent had received congressional attention. While the energetic president inundated Congress with proposals, the sluggish pace of action on the New Frontier legislation frustrated many liberals.[24] "Once presidents stop 'thinking small' and move toward nonincremental policies,"

Paul C. Light reminds us, "they face higher political costs."[25] One cost is that Congress remains more disposed to scrutinize, change, or reject presidential proposals in the domestic sphere.

Party control of Congress did furnish, albeit narrowly at times, essential resources for Kennedy to influence congressional lawmaking and steer activity toward his policy objectives. What is true for Kennedy is true for other Democratic presidents who have benefited from single-party control: Legislative support from copartisans increases in proportion to the strength of shared electoral and ideological bonds between the president and his governing majority. In Kennedy's case, his electoral popularity among liberal Democrats shored up unity in the party's base and helped surmount the recalcitrance of southern conservatives on many occasions.

Kennedy's Success and Support in the 87th Congress

Kennedy had a strong record of success with congressional roll-call votes on which he expressed a position. The close votes are of particular importance, as they concerned the core of the president's agenda. Most of these votes, including area redevelopment, the minimum wage increase, tax revisions, and agriculture were significant laws identified by Mayhew. Kennedy prevailed on all of these issues and was also successful in warding off challenges to various cabinet reorganization plans.

Kennedy's domestic roll-call stands touched a strong ideological chord in both parties. Among copartisans, his attempts to secure support for his domestic policy objectives were as much a struggle between "two different generations of politicians" as between regional factions in the Democratic Party.[26] Kennedy's stands across vote categories exposed the ideological rift among Democrats. Nearly three-quarters of the conservative Democrats with ideological scores above the party median were from southern constituencies. Based on ideological placement within the party, the likelihood that the average southern Democrat would support the president was 17 percent lower

Table 6.1
Kennedy's Legislative Success Rate,
87th Congress*

	Close Votes [n=13]	Nonclose Votes [n=32]
Overall	76.9% (10)	81.3% (26)
Democratic Party	84.6% (11)	93.8% (30)
Republican Party	15.4% (2)	40.6% (13)

* Entries are the number and percentage of votes on which the president gained a majority overall and by party.

compared to the average northern Democrat. Kennedy drew the bulk of his support from younger, more liberal Democrats with districts situated in the North, and from a handful of moderate Republicans from constituencies scattered around the country.

The impact of incumbency on Democratic support for the president is also telling of the party's regional divide. Seventy percent of southern Democrats had electoral margins of at least 60 percent over their rival candidate, and about half faced no opposition in the 1960 election. Northern Democrats typically faced much more competitive races. Fewer than 10 percent ran unopposed. Incumbency advantage was most damaging to presidential support on

Table 6.2
Logistic Regression Estimation of Democrats' Domestic Policy Support for Kennedy, 87th Congress

	Close Votes	Nonclose Votes
Kennedy's Margin of Victory 1960 (%)	.82***	.25*
	(.27)	(.18)
	13.80	*3.90*
Legislator's Margin of Victory (%)	−.94****	−.59****
	(.16)	(.11)
	−15.30	*−8.90*
Legislator's Terms Served	−.00	−.00
	(.02)	(.01)
	−2.00	*−.90*
Democratic Leaders	.21	.24**
	(.17)	(.11)
	10.40	*10.30*
Committee Chairs	−.21	−.43***
	(.21)	(.14)
	−2.50	*−7.00*
Ideology	−4.87****	−4.66****
	(.33)	(.22)
	−73.90	*−69.40*
Public Approval of the President	.05****	.015****
	(.01)	(.005)
	15.90	*4.10*
Constant	−1.55	−.87**
	(.55)	(.41)
Number of Cases	2,914.00	6,933.00
−2 × Log Likelihood	2,654.50	6,195.02
Model χ²	596.03****	1,018.18****
Pseudo-R²	.18	.14
Cases Correctly Predicted (%)	.78	.79

**** p < .001   *** p < .01   ** p < .05   * p < .10 (one-tailed tests)
Entries are maximum likelihood coefficients.
Standard errors are in parentheses.
Mean effects are in *italics*.
The dependent variable is whether the legislator supported or opposed Kennedy's stand.

controversial votes. Compared to a Democrat engaged in a highly competitive race in 1960 (that is, a race determined by 1 percent or less), an unopposed member was just over 15 percent less likely to support the president's position on close votes. Seat safety bolstered conservative southern Democrats' latitude to oppose the president openly on more contentious elements of his domestic agenda.

Kennedy's electoral popularity carried a moderate, positive impact on members of both parties, particularly on close votes. His electoral popularity mattered most among northern Democrats. A Democrat from a district in which Kennedy prevailed over Nixon by 10 percent was about 3 percent

Table 6.3
Logistic Regression Estimation of Republicans' Domestic Policy Support for Kennedy, 87th Congress

	Close Votes	Nonclose Votes
Kennedy's Margin of Victory 1960 (%)	1.74***	.82***
	(.57)	(.30)
	13.30	*11.50*
Legislator's Margin of Victory (%)	.29	.17
	(.45)	(.24)
	4.20	*4.10*
Legislator's Terms Served	.04**	.05****
	(.02)	(.01)
	12.1	*24.20*
Republican Leaders	−.19	.08
	(.18)	(.07)
	−8.00	*8.40*
Ranking Minority Members	.20	−.19*
	(.22)	(.12)
	2.60	*−4.50*
Ideology	−2.16****	−3.50****
	(.45)	(.26)
	−33.40	*−67.00*
Public Approval of the President	−.02	.00
	(.09)	(.01)
	−8.00	*2.10*
Constant	−.34	−.82**
	(.68)	(.40)
Number of Cases	2,057.00	4,948.00
−2 × Log Likelihood	1,817.50	6,448.29
Model χ^2	65.31****	311.16****
Pseudo-R^2	.03	.05
Cases Correctly Predicted (%)	.83	.61

**** $p < .001$ *** $p < .01$ ** $p < .05$ * $p < .10$ (one-tailed tests)
Entries are maximum likelihood coefficients.
Standard errors are in parentheses.
Mean effects are in *italics*.
The dependent variable is whether the legislator supported or opposed Kennedy's stand.

more likely to support the president. Kennedy's electoral margin was far less helpful as a source of influence among southern Democrats. The Nixon-Kennedy race was more competitive in southern districts, where Kennedy's average victory margin over Nixon was 6 percent less than in northern Democratic districts.

Seniority conditions presidential support differently for the two parties. Senior Republicans were more disposed to support Kennedy than members who had served less than four or five terms. For Democrats, on the other hand, the number of terms served is not significant in the model. Ideology and incumbency advantage tap the effect of southerners' reticence to support the president. Nevertheless, seniority was substantively significant in other ways. The seniority system elevated many of the "safe-seat" southern Democrats to positions of considerable power on committees. Just as seat safety permitted them to openly oppose Kennedy's agenda on the floor, the autonomy they enjoyed from the president bolstered their ability to obstruct his policy objectives in committee. Ways and Means Committee chairman Wilbur Mills's blockage of Medicare is a quintessential example of the recalcitrance Kennedy faced from senior southern Democrats. Mills and other conservatives were determined to keep elements of the president's agenda from ever reaching floor consideration.

Public approval does not carry a strong impact on presidential support in either party across vote categories. Kennedy came into office quite popular and remained so for the entirety of the 87th Congress. His average approval was just under 74 percent during the period. At no point did evaluations of his job performance dip below 61 percent. Presidential support was driven primarily by localized factors, ideology, and the president's electoral popularity. Kennedy's popular approval did not mitigate southern Democrats' opposition by dint of their incumbency advantage, nor did it compensate for an extremely narrow popular electoral victory that robbed him of claims to a mandate.

The review of significant legislation, floor success, and legislative support for Kennedy emphasizes that the president proposed large-scale domestic change at a time when Congress was hardly inclined to look favorably on an activist program. Kennedy's ability to claim more than a modicum of independent policy success stemmed from his reliance on a fragile base of liberal Democrats in Congress, frequent compromise and hard-fought battles on Capitol Hill, and the manipulation of select procedural advantages in the House under unified control. Although progressives may have expressed disappointment with the pace of legislation in the 87th Congress, Kennedy's achievements were manifold and fairly extensive given the policy-making context of the closing years of the bipartisan conservative era.

His success also extends beyond his programmatic victories from 1961–63. He did not anticipate that Congress would complete many of his priorities in the first two years. His long-term legacy was to change the direction of the national policy debate. His steady stream of proposals was aimed at forcing the *consideration* of issues the conservative legislature would surely not have taken up on its own.[27] By thrusting this unwelcome agenda upon reticent members of Congress, Kennedy ensured that "a substantial foundation was being laid for the enactment of new programs in many policy areas. Therefore there was a significant effect on subsequent agenda management."[28] Legislative proposals that were defeated or never made it to the floor, including Medicare and civil rights legislation, were eventually adopted as part of President Johnson's Great Society. In this manner, some of Kennedy's priority issues that had languished in the 87th Congress were strategically "organized into" the legislative pipeline for Johnson. One thus may speculate that had Kennedy's term not been prematurely ended by an assassin's bullet, he would have been credited for many more substantial domestic policy successes. "A Congress that could withstand the power of presidential advocacy for two years," James L. Sundquist observes, "was bound to have difficulty in sustaining its resistance as it faced two more years of leadership and pressure."[29] Carrying on that leadership and persuasive effort fell to Lyndon Johnson under a radically different institutional and electoral context of unified government from 1965–68.

Lyndon Johnson and the Election of 1964: Prelude to the Great Society

Although bursts of extraordinary legislative output under the aegis of presidential leadership have been rare in the history of the American presidency, they have always been linked to unified party control of national institutions. Franklin Roosevelt's New Deal remains the definitive benchmark for the modern legislative presidency.[30] Only Lyndon Johnson's Great Society approximates such sweeping policy successes. Johnson's presidency is the unique example of extraordinarily strong positive legislative leverage in the postwar setting.

"War and peace; the nature and role of government; the morality and mercy of society; the quality of life—all were discussed in a campaign that will leave its mark behind in American life for a generation."[31] The controversy that swirled around the presidential election of 1964 often centered on Barry

Goldwater, the plainspoken and trenchant Republican standard-bearer. "The Democrats' treatment of Senator Goldwater as a person," says Stanley Kelly Jr., "reinforced their attempt to define the voter's choice as one between the policies of an extremist fringe and policies of the bipartisan center."[32] Their efforts were aided by Goldwater's curious remarks about nuclear weapons, his battle cry at the Republican nominating convention that "extremism in the defense of liberty is no vice," and his intimation that Social Security could be transformed into a voluntary system. Goldwater anticipated that a tide of "hidden" votes from a silent, conservative majority and a potential backlash against civil rights in the North and South would carry his candidacy to victory on election day.[33] That tide never materialized. Instead, the electoral tsunami for Lyndon Johnson and congressional Democrats left the GOP in tatters.

Johnson, Goldwater, and their running mates surely sensed that a malaise, however ill defined, was gripping the nation. Their respective approaches to remedy the melancholic state of the nation, however, could not have been farther apart. "Goldwater and Miller," Theodore White contends, "saw what was wrong as the government; and Johnson and Humphrey saw the government as the chief means of dealing with the wrong."[34] Johnson outlined the broad contours of his domestic agenda on the campaign trail in May, 1964. If a crisis of conscience was the source of the nation's weariness, to the former Senate leader from Texas, government action was the appropriate response: "The Great Society speech opened with the vision of a utopia with 'abundance and liberty' for all. There would be an end to poverty and racial injustice; knowledge would be readily available; and even leisure would involve, not boredom and restlessness, but a chance to build and reflect. Moreover, the 'desire for beauty' and 'hunger for community' would be served by 'the city of man.'"[35] Hope and optimism were the symbolic themes underlying the Great Society, as they had been during the New Deal. But Johnson's emphasis on poverty, the status of blacks and women, consumer rights, and environmental issues was not simply a matter of rhetoric. His articulation of the Great Society reflected resolution to carry out "a mammoth program of social reform."[36]

Johnson's electoral victory was a watershed. He achieved his landslide by reaching out to Republican voters and stressing a nonpartisan campaign in which he rarely mentioned Goldwater personally. Johnson captured 61 percent of the popular vote and 486 electoral votes. However, he paid a steep price at the polls in Dixie for his emphasis on civil rights. Goldwater carried the Deep South: Louisiana, Mississippi, Alabama, Georgia, and South Carolina (along with his home state of Arizona). So, while Democrats accrued forty-eight seats in the House and began the 89th Congress with a solid 295-

140 majority, Johnson's coattails were regionally based and most evident in northern constituencies. In the 212 northern districts where Johnson's vote share exceeded 60 percent, 166 (78 percent) returned Democratic legislators to the House. Moreover, forty-six of the forty-eight freshmen Democrats elected in 1964 were from constituencies outside the South.

The significance of the geography of Johnson's coattails is that the House's ideological balance shifted considerably in the president's favor. As the ranks of liberal Democrats swelled, the influence of southern conservatives waned.[37] Liberal Democrats in Congress, particularly freshmen, were indebted to the president for their electoral victories. Johnson also marshaled strong support in Republican districts. His personal appeal to Republican voters resulted in a large number of split districts around the country. Eighty percent of the districts that elected Republicans to Congress voted for Johnson.[38]

The electoral context of the 89th Congress paved the way for the nascent liberal activist period. Johnson's window of opportunity would be narrowed, however. His failure to grasp Americans' ambiguity about the war in Vietnam contributed to the heavy Democratic losses in the 1966 midterm elections. If his decisive electoral triumph represented an overwhelming endorsement of the Great Society in 1964, the loss of forty-eight Democratic seats two years later erased the party's gains and altered the policy-making environment on Capitol Hill. Former vice president Richard Nixon, who had campaigned indefatigably for GOP candidates, asserted that the Democratic losses were "the sharpest rebuff of a generation" and "a rebuke to the President's lack of credibility and lack of direction abroad."[39] It was also the case that because the Democrats had done so well in traditionally Republican districts in 1964, they had relatively more seats to lose in the midterm elections. Although Democrats retained a sizable numerical majority in the House (246-187), the minority's strengthened position implied greater opposition. The president thus was left with fewer resources to secure passage of legislation on controversial issues as his public approval steadily plummeted. To his benefit, however, much domestic legislation was already winding through the legislative process and party control edged it to fruition.

Lawmaking and Leadership under Lyndon Johnson

Johnson's ascension to the presidency following John F. Kennedy's assassination in 1963 precluded the traditional "Hundred Days" test of legislative productivity for an elected president. Johnson had no basis in 1963–64 to claim a mandate from the electorate. However, in finishing out Kennedy's truncated term, he drew upon public emotion over the slain president's memory and moved swiftly to lay the foundations of the Great Society. He would build on this foundation in the 89th and 90th Congresses once he had received a resounding endorsement for his domestic agenda from the electorate.

Perhaps the most far-reaching legislation adopted in 1963–64 was the Civil Rights Act of 1964. The bill's sinuous path has been traced in detail elsewhere, but the landmark legislation reflected Johnson's considerable legislative skill gained through years as Senate majority leader. He successfully worked with his party's leadership and reached across the aisle to Republican minority leader Everett Dirksen to circumvent conservatives' challenges.[40] Other bills inspired by Johnson included the Economic Opportunity Act of 1964 and the Food Stamp Act of 1964, beachheads in Johnson's "War on Poverty."[41]

The electoral and institutional context of unified government after 1964 facilitated considerably more policy innovation led by the president. Analysis of Mayhew's significant laws adopted during Johnson's full term reveals that his policy objectives dominated lawmaking. Many of the laws represented new programs targeted at urgent social issues. Others were continuing issues linked to Kennedy's unfinished agenda and expansions of existing programs. From Medicare in 1965 to the Truth-in-Lending Act of 1968, *all thirty-seven significant domestic laws were connected to the president's stated policy objectives.* The sum total of innovative legislation tied to Johnson's objectives would leave a lasting imprint on American social policy for decades.

Johnson's path-breaking domestic agenda, much of which emerged from the many task forces commissioned by the president, contributed to major strides in the areas of environmental regulation and consumer protection. Bills included a variety of new programs such as the Water Quality Act of 1965, the Food and Agriculture Act of 1965, the Fair Packaging and Labeling Act of 1966, the Air Quality Act of 1967, and the Wholesale Poultry Products Act of 1968.[42] Key elements of his War on Poverty and efforts to promote civil rights expanded federal responsibilities through the Voting Rights Act, the Housing and Urban Development Act of 1968, the Age Discrimination Act of 1967, and the Open Housing Act of 1968.[43] This body of legislation represented decisive agenda successes for the president.

Like Kennedy, Johnson also confronted a House seniority system that gave southern conservatives an advantage. However, the influx of new liberal members gave Johnson a greater edge. The adoption of a special twenty-one-day rule, which allowed committee chairs to petition the Speaker for floor consideration of legislation if the Rules Committee failed to provide a ruling within the three-week period, stifled the conservatives' ability to impede the president's agenda and helped break the influence of Rules Committee Chairman Howard Smith.[44]

Medicare's passage offers a substantive example of the blending of Johnson's coattails with the procedural advantages of party control of Congress. A continuing agenda item in Congress, this proposal for medical coverage for the elderly had originated with Kennedy but had languished in Wilbur Mills's Ways and Means Committee. The 1964 election brought forty-two more northern Democrats to the House and, combined with the loss of three conservative Republicans on the Committee, enabled the Democratic leadership to reconstitute party ratios and increase pressure to report the bill out. When House Resolution (HR) 6675 came to a floor vote, it was considered under a closed rule that prohibited amendments. The procedure ensured a favorable outcome for the administration, even if the final vote margin was narrow.[45]

Johnson's legislative skill and style should also not be underestimated. The president maintained good relations with House Speaker Carl Albert and Senate Majority Leader Mike Mansfield. He also made a concerted effort to bring Republican leaders into the administration's fold. The president met frequently with Charlie Halleck and Everett Dirksen, and also regularly called upon the Republican policy group that President Eisenhower had urged GOP members to form after the 1964 electoral debacle. Ironically, that group included Sen. Barry Goldwater.[46]

Although Johnson placed an experienced legislative team in the White House headed by Lawrence O'Brien, the president had no qualms about intervening directly in legislative debates. Reticent legislators were often subject to the "treatment," his infamous yet effective technique of direct persuasion through personal confrontation. House members sometimes objected to the president's tactics. During floor consideration of highway legislation in 1965, the ranking Republican on the House Public Works Committee lamented that he had "never before seen such pressures and arm twisting from the Executive Branch . . . as I have seen with respect to the highway beautification bill."[47] The bill passed, however, and on the same night that the president had requested.

As is to be expected in the course of the give-and-take of the legislative process, there were instances in which Johnson had to compromise. In establishing the Department of Transportation in 1966, for example, Congress refused to give the president maritime control, but it adopted the basic framework of the administration proposal.[48] Nor was congressional action quick in every case. Passage of Johnson's proposal for an income tax surcharge in 1968 was delayed for ten months. His request to establish a national scenic trails system stalled in Congress for almost three years before passing in the last year of his term.[49] Nevertheless, none of these caveats detracts from the essential point that Johnson's policy objectives formed the core of the shared agenda between the branches. Legislative action on these issues allowed both the president and the congressional majority to claim credit for many far-reaching policies.

An unparalleled synergy developed between the branches during Johnson's term that has rarely been repeated, even if Congress sometimes went beyond the president's legislative proposals. The regulations passed by Congress in the Clean Waters Restoration Act of 1966 were more stringent than those Johnson had sought.[50] Johnson's stance on traffic safety legislation in 1966 was more reserved than the provisions Congress actually passed.[51] Yet in only a single case did Johnson express serious misgivings about the form of legislation ultimately adopted: He objected to select provisions in the Omnibus Crime and Safe Streets Act of 1968 that allowed wiretapping, but ultimately signed the bill.[52]

Johnson's Success and Support in Congress

A closer examination of Johnson's roll-call success rate and the factors weighing on individual legislators' support of his policy stands stresses the importance of the electoral legitimization of his agenda in 1964. Particularly on close votes, Johnson's strong electoral bond with liberal Democrats played an integral role in defining the contours of support from his copartisans. His tumbling public approval over U.S. military involvement in Southeast Asia weakened his ability to rally the support of a diminished Democratic Party base after the midterm losses of 1966. His roll-call success rate remained high, however, because he was able to retain the support of his liberal copartisans

Table 6.4
Johnson's Legislative Success Rate,
89th and 90th Congresses*

	Close Votes		Nonclose Votes	
	89th Congress [n=8]	90th Congress [n=16]	89th Congress [n=43]	90th Congress [n=59]
Overall	100.0% (8)	81.3% (13)	97.7% (42)	79.7% (47)
Democratic Party	100.0% (8)	68.8% (11)	100.0% (43)	86.4% (51)
Republican Party	12.5% (1)	31.3% (5)	30.2% (13)	47.4% (28)

* Entries are the number and percentage of votes on which the president gained a majority overall and by party.

in Congress on domestic affairs. On occasion he also compromised with Republicans on less controversial issues that split Democrats.

Johnson's position prevailed on all eight of the close votes in the 89th Congress. A number of issues in this set of votes crosses over with Mayhew's significant laws, including the model cities program, public works, and funding for the Department of Housing and Urban Development. There were twice as many close votes in the 90th Congress as Johnson faced more floor challenges to his positions from both Republicans and conservative Democrats, whose support waned after the party's seat losses in 1966. The president frequently took positions only on motions to recommit (kill) bills and "stayed quiet" on the legislation that he favored, letting House leaders rally the rank-and-file. Among the close votes in 1967–68 were a proposed 5 percent cut to the national budget, the model cities program, funding for the arts and humanities, and open housing. Republican support carried the president's positions to victory when Democrats were internally divided on supplemental appropriations for school assistance, his narcotics bureau reorganization proposal, and an increase in funding and the scope of aid to Appalachia.

Johnson's pattern of success was repeated on nonclose votes over the course of his term. He lost only one vote in the 89th Congress, a supplemental appropriations bill, yet his overall success rate declined 18 percent in the 90th Congress. Johnson did garner greater GOP support on the subset of less controversial issues, winning a majority of Republicans on just less than a third of votes in the 89th Congress and just less than half of votes in the 90th Congress. Republican support was helpful on occasion either because of southern Democrats' opposition or because of absences. Two such examples were votes on federal mediation of a railway labor dispute (1967) and on the National Foundation for the Arts (1968).

Analysis of legislators' support of Johnson's positions shows that his coattails played an important role in bolstering Democratic support on the most controversial elements of his agenda. The mean effect of Johnson's electoral popularity was nearly 43 percent on close votes in the 89th Congress. His electoral connection was strongest with northern Democrats. Johnson's average district-level victory over Goldwater in 1964 was 35 percent in northern districts and only 5 percent in the thirteen Dixie states.[53] A thirty-point margin in the president's electoral popularity raises the likelihood of support by a northern Democrat 7.5 percent. The data confirm that Johnson's national electoral triumph proved most helpful in solidifying liberal Democrats' support.

Evidence of the regional divide among Democrats over Johnson's liberal agenda is borne out in the role ideology played in presidential support.

Table 6.5
Logistic Regression Estimation of Democrats' Domestic Policy Support for Johnson, 89th and 90th Congresses

	Close Votes		Nonclose Votes	
	89th Congress	90th Congress	89th Congress	90th Congress
Johnson's Margin	1.18****	.38**	.69****	.37****
of Victory 1964 (%)	(.30)	(.18)	(.16)	(.10)
	42.60	*16.00*	*12.30*	*13.70*
Legislator's Margin	−.33*	.16	−.43****	−.17**
of Victory (%)	(.22)	(.13)	(.13)	(.07)
	−6.90	*3.60*	*−4.50*	*−3.30*
Legislator's Terms	.04***	−.01	.013*	.00
Served	(.02)	(.01)	(.009)	(.01)
	17.60	*−4.20*	*2.80*	*1.60*
Democratic Leaders	.15	.09	.26	.17****
	(.30)	(.09)	(.26)	(.05)
	3.00	*2.20*	*2.90*	*11.80*
Committee Chairs	−.58**	−.00	−.20*	.04
	(.26)	(.16)	(.15)	(.09)
	−13.00	*−.10*	*−2.10*	*.90*
Ideology	−3.77****	−.15	−5.61****	−2.45****
	(.34)	(.21)	(.20)	(.12)
	−80.30	*−4.50*	*−75.70*	*−59.70*
Public Approval	−.00	.11****	.04****	.09****
of the President	(.01)	(.01)	(.00)	(.01)
	−.80	*36.90*	*10.00*	*31.10*
Constant	.60*	−4.17****	−.28	−3.28****
	(.44)	(.44)	(.22)	(.25)
Number of Cases	1,893.00	3,077.00	8,671.00	11,714.00
−2 × Log Likelihood	1,956.97	3,909.14	5,797.08	12,821.56
Model χ^2	427.17****	135.28****	2,372.42****	1,538.23****
Pseudo-R^2	.18	.03	.29	.11
Cases Correctly Predicted (%)	.79	.62	.87	.74

**** p < .001   *** p < .01   ** p < .05   * p < .10 (one-tailed tests)
Entries are maximum likelihood coefficients.
Standard errors are in parentheses.
Mean effects are in *italics.*
The dependent variable is whether the legislator supported or opposed Johnson's stand.

Sixty-four percent of the Democrats with ideological scores above the party median—the conservative wing of the party—were from the South. The negative slope of the coefficients in the models for close and nonclose votes shows that Johnson's support came from liberal legislators from northern constituencies who had scores well below the party median. The net impact of ideology for Johnson's legislative support is similar to that for Kennedy. The key difference, of course, was that Johnson had a much larger liberal cohort from which to draw support at the outset of his term.

The larger core of liberal Democrats mitigated resistance to the president's

Table 6.6
Logistic Regression Estimation of Republicans' Domestic Policy Support for Johnson, 89th and 90th Congresses

	Close Votes		Nonclose Votes	
	89th Congress	90th Congress	89th Congress	90th Congress
Johnson's Margin	−.17	.29	1.01****	.14
of Victory 1964 (%)	(.59)	(.32)	(.25)	(.16)
	−3.70	7.40	22.80	3.90
Legislator's Margin	−.39	.17	−.15	−.01
of Victory (%)	(.68)	(.26)	(.30)	(.13)
	−5.30	4.00	−2.90	−.30
Legislator's Terms	.03	−.02*	−.01	.01
Served	(.03)	(.01)	(.01)	(.01)
	11.20	−7.60	−4.30	.60
Republican Leaders	−.21	−.01	.04	.11***
	(.22)	(.06)	(.07)	(.04)
	−3.00	−1.40	3.60	10.40
Ranking Committee	−.34	−.11	−.07	.04
Members	(.30)	(.17)	(.11)	(.08)
	−4.70	−2.50	−1.50	1.00
Ideology	−3.23****	−.35	−4.97****	−3.14****
	(.68)	(.33)	(.30)	(.17)
	−46.40	−7.90	−79.50	−63.30
Public Approval	.01	−.15****	.02****	.03****
of the President	(.01)	(.01)	(.00)	(.01)
	5.10	−50.30	10.30	14.50
Constant	−2.36****	6.09****	−1.76****	−1.45****
	(.67)	(.54)	(.23)	(.23)
Number of Cases	956.00	2,402.00	4,450.00	9,283.00
−2 × Log Likelihood	901.44	3,027.04	5,182.28	12,308.50
Model χ^2	40.61****	182.20****	668.96****	558.06****
Pseudo-R^2	.04	.06	.11	.04
Cases Correctly Predicted (%)	.81	.64	.70	.60

**** $p < .001$ *** $p < .01$ ** $p < .05$ * $p < .10$ (one-tailed tests)
Entries are maximum likelihood coefficients.
Standard errors are in parentheses.
Mean effects are in *italics*.
The dependent variable is whether the legislator supported or opposed Johnson's stand.

agenda from factions within the Democratic leadership as well as from congressional copartisans with safe seats. Southern Democrats outnumbered northern Democrats as committee chairmen by a two-to-one margin. Committee chairs were 13 percent less likely to support Johnson on close votes. Seat safety also carried a sizable, though weaker, negative impact. A legislator who ran unopposed in 1964 was about 7 percent and 5 percent less likely to vote with Johnson on close and nonclose votes, respectively, in the 89th Congress. Twenty-eight of the thirty-five Democrats with electoral margins better than 90 percent were from the South.

Among Republicans, the negative slope of the ideology coefficient shows that Johnson drew the bulk of his support from moderate to liberal members. The impact of ideology is strongest on nonclose votes across time. There is also evidence that on this set of less controversial votes, the president's electoral popularity played an important, though smaller role compared to Democrats. Fifty-seven of the seventy-one GOP House members with ideological scores below the party median (the more liberal members) hailed from the Northeast and Midwest, where Johnson had been popular in 1964. On issues that lacked high-profile controversy, this pool of moderate legislators came under constituency pressure to follow the president's policy lead in the absence of leadership opposition to the president's stands. Johnson, unlike Kennedy—or Carter and Clinton, his Democratic successors under unified government—had a much stronger basis to rally bipartisan support for his legislative stands on the basis of his widespread electoral popularity.

The strong impact of Johnson's public approval on individual legislators' floor support highlights the link between his declining success rate in the domestic realm and foreign policy. As the war in Vietnam raged on, the problem for Johnson was "the inability to decide at what point the emotional and abnormally visible antiwar movement might be speaking for a majority of America."[54] The most damning indictment of Johnson's use of polling data suggests that the president failed to grasp the tenuous nature of public support for the conflict and attempted to justify decisions rather than gauge support for policy alternatives.[55]

There is some evidence that the effect of public approval on presidential support differed by party and by vote type. The backlash against the war in Vietnam and Johnson's subsequent decision not to seek reelection in 1968 visibly affected congressional support in the 90th Congress. For Democrats, Johnson's approval had a larger effect in the latter half of his term. The difference in the predicted probability of Democrats' support for close votes in the analysis taken at Johnson's highest level of approval of 52 percent in June, 1967, and his lowest level of 35 percent in September, 1968, is nearly 37 percent. Johnson's tumbling approval carried an almost equivalent impact on nonclose votes in the 90th Congress.

The analysis suggests that national factors became an increasingly important determinant of Democratic support after the severe losses the party incurred in the 1966 midterm elections. Legislators looked to their own fortunes in the next electoral cycle—fortunes in which the president had no stake after his announcement in March, 1968, that he would not seek reelection. The conundrum they faced was to judge constituency support of the lame-duck chief executive. Democrats approached support for Johnson, particularly on controversial issues, in light of the solidification of the public's misgivings about the conflict in Vietnam. As the court of public opinion turned against the president, his legislative stands became more vulnerable to Democratic defections.

Public approval carried much less of an impact on Republican support. Public opinion had a strong inverse effect on close votes in the 90th Congress. Johnson faced the most intense opposition from Republicans following the midterm elections, which netted the GOP substantial gains. His approval ratings in the 90th Congress were highest just after the election, but were largely irrelevant to an emboldened minority, which had been encouraged to mount challenges to the president's agenda. For example, two of the high-profile votes—those on the national debt and a 5 percent cut in the federal budget—occurred early in 1967. Public approval had little bearing as the GOP attempted to present an alternative agenda.

Summary

This comparison of Kennedy and Johnson stresses two general points about party control of national institutions in the postwar era. First, unified government yields far greater executive-legislative synergy on domestic legislation and provides the president with more opportunities for agenda leadership. It is worth noting that all of the significant domestic laws passed from 1961–68 were linked to the president's stated policy objectives. Unlike presidents operating under divided control, Kennedy and Johnson did *not* engage in veto politics to fend off elements of a congressionally initiated agenda. Their leadership focused on spurring Congress to action and preventing conservative forces from thwarting their legislative agenda. They sought to cultivate and manage an agenda of *shared policy objectives.*

The second point of the Kennedy-Johnson comparison is that the magnitude of positive leverage is contingent upon the particular electoral and institutional context of unified government. Kennedy's weaker leverage derived from the particular structure of voting coalitions in Congress, an entrenched conservative membership with incumbency advantage, and a lack of coattails. Johnson's election in 1964 was a "legitimizing event" for a sweeping presidential domestic agenda. His landslide victory gave him strong coattails among members of both parties and a working legislative majority of liberal Democrats who looked to him for policy leadership. The sum total of the policymaking environment yielded an abundance of new policies, large-scale change, and significant autonomous policy successes for the president.

Perhaps Kennedy's greatest success was to change the nature of internal debate in Congress during his brief tenure in the White House. Johnson's long-term legacy was to structure the national debate about social policy in the United States for decades after he left office. Johnson's legislative triumphs remain the subject of great controversy. At the tip of the iceberg are indictments that his domestic agenda yielded the inflation of the 1970s by failing to raise adequate revenues for the twin objectives of expanding social programs and maintaining military intervention in Vietnam.[56] Conservatives contend that Johnson's War on Poverty exacerbated rather than ameliorated the plight of the urban poor by creating a cycle of dependency on federal aid. The experimental nature of some programs during the period failed or fell into disarray later because they were adopted with haste, particularly as Johnson became preoccupied with surpassing FDR's legislative record.[57] In addition, the portrait of the adroit legislative leader and social reformer in the domestic realm is juxtaposed with the image of a commander in chief psychologically crippled by the conflict in Vietnam. To draw from Stephen Skowronek's view: "The 'tragedy of Lyndon Johnson' is a drama without parallel in modern American politics. It is the story of a master politician who self-destructed at the commanding heights, of an over-arching political consensus shattered in a rush of extraordinary achievements, of a superpower that squandered its resources in a remote conflict with people struggling on the fringes of modernity."[58]

Such critiques of Johnson notwithstanding, the confluence of contextual factors surrounding unified government from 1965–68 furnished the president with an opportunity to approximate, albeit imperfectly, the "textbook model" of chief legislator. "Party government" advocates have anxiously anticipated similar electoral, institutional, and environmental preconditions that might give rise to the type of legislative leadership Johnson was able to exert. If American politics may be likened to a drama, however, Samuel Beckett's play *Waiting for Godot* takes on a certain prescience. Such conditions, as the Carter and Clinton experiences make clear, have not materialized. Consequently, scholars who approach the question of party control of national institutions from the perspective of lawmaking productivity continue to posit that unified government makes little difference.

Reconciling the "party government" and "legislative productivity" views, as chapter 7 clarifies, requires a shift in perspective to the ways in which single-party control *did* matter for Carter and Clinton. The policy-making environment was less amenable to autonomous presidential *direction* of the shared agenda in a time of much greater competition for scarce resources and stronger congressional agenda-setting capacity. Missing from the Carter and Clinton presidencies were decisive electoral victories, weak organizational features in Congress, and strong deference to the president's policy objectives. The independent policy successes of Carter and Clinton were consequently more limited compared to Johnson. Their successes often involved scaling back programs, deregulation, or making incremental adjustments to existing programs. Yet, a frequently overlooked element to their legislative successes is their facilitation of efforts to pass longstanding party policy objectives and elements of the continuing agenda of Democratic majorities in Congress. It is essential not to lose sight of how such a leadership style qualitatively contrasts with presidents' legislative strategy and leadership during recent periods of divided control.

7 Carter, Clinton, and Unified Government in the Postreform/Party-Unity Era

JIMMY CARTER'S AND BILL CLINTON'S legislative presidencies are frequently noted for what they failed to achieve rather than what they accomplished.[1] Writing of Carter's first two years, David Mayhew observes that "despite Democratic majorities of 62–38 in the Senate and 292–143 in the House," the 95th Congress "proved to be a cemetery for liberal aspirations."[2] Mayhew cites the failure of national health insurance, consumer protection, welfare reform, campaign finance, and criminal law. Similarly, Clinton's high-profile defeats on health care reform and economic stimulus in the 103d Congress led Mayhew to the conclusion that unified control of national institutions did not matter very much.[3]

Unified government *did* indeed matter to the type of leadership that Carter and Clinton were able to exert, but in ways that scholars focused on legislative productivity have failed to recognize. The character of Carter's and Clinton's involvement on significant legislation contrasted sharply with the veto leverage presidents have wielded under divided control in the postreform/party-unity era. At the same time, their weaker positive leverage over Congress entailed a limited basis for *directing* the congressional agenda.

Both of their floor success rates remained high and the majority of significant legislation were linked to their stated policy objectives, yet the circumstances of unified government mandated a more jointly participatory and cooperative effort, with congressional leaders playing a vital role. Carter and Clinton had less autonomous policy success than Lyndon Johnson. They struggled to fit their policy priorities within the context of a better organized, more unified, and self-assured governing majority of their copartisans. Compared to Johnson, their role shifted somewhat more to cultivating a shared agenda with Congress. They frequently lent support to continuing congressional policy priorities while trying to manage difficult economic challenges. In many ways, this form of legislative success is more analogous to Kennedy's experience in terms of modifying, consolidating, and sometimes extending extant domestic programs on an incremental basis.

The Electoral and Policy-Making Context:
Carter and Congress, 1977–80

Jimmy Carter was elected in 1976 during the closing years of the liberal activist era. His defeat of Republican incumbent Gerald Ford restored Democratic Party dominance to both ends of Pennsylvania Avenue after eight years of divided control and protracted executive-legislative conflict. The Senate was firmly in Democratic hands, and the House majority was only three seats shy of what it had been for Lyndon Johnson in 1965. Although the prospects for more harmonious relations between the branches appeared strong, the paragon of Johnson's legislative leadership scarcely befits Carter's term.

In contrast to the last Democratic occupant of the White House, Carter's electoral connection with his majority in Congress was weak, the institutional setting of the legislature was far less deferential to presidential direction of the national agenda, and the policy-making environment of the mid- to late 1970s was marked by a recessionary economy. The economic downturn and the energy crisis compelled an emphasis on fine-tuning existing programs and responding to the pressing issues of inflation and unemployment rather than the unabashed growth of domestic programs. The type of legislative leadership Carter was capable of exerting was a product of these factors.

Carter garnered a narrow victory over Gerald Ford, and his virtually nonexistent coattails failed to cultivate strong ties with the governing majority. After trailing Carter by over 30 points early in the campaign, Ford rebounded to close the gap substantially by early October, 1976. The final outcome was determined by less than 2 percent of the popular vote. The election witnessed strong party loyalty in the electorate, with the poor state of the economy tipping the balance in Carter's favor.[4] Democrats gained only a single House seat and none in the Senate. Moreover, Carter's share of the two-party vote outpaced that of fewer than twenty House members. All told, incumbency advantage in Congress trumped presidential coattails.

Carter's "outsider" campaign and candidate-centered congressional campaigns combined to undermine a spirit of comity between him and the Democratic majority.

He was the first Democratic president to win the Oval Office following the McGovern-Fraser reforms, which marginalized the role of party leaders in choosing the nominee.[5] Tinsley Yarbrough suggests that if Democratic Party rules had "been of the pre-1972 variety, the congressional leaders Carter attacked [during the campaign] would have played key roles in the nomination process, and Carter would have pushed his outsider, anti-Washington theme at considerable risk."[6] His invectives against congressional incumbents and party leaders and his portrayal of politicians "inside the beltway" as being responsible for the "mess in Washington" may have suited the electorate's malaise following Watergate, but they damaged goodwill between the branches.[7] Congressional candidates' ability to finance and manage their own campaigns independent of the White House further undercut members' loyalty to Carter when they took up their positions on Capitol Hill.

There were other reasons Congress's institutional setting was not conducive to strong presidential policy leadership. Carter faced a more autonomous and assertive governing majority that scarcely resembled the "textbook" Congress of old.[8] The Democratic majority had shored up control of the legislative agenda and equipped itself with mechanisms to participate more fully and independently in policy making by the mid-1970s. Many of these reforms were undertaken as a means of combating Republican presidents' challenges to the achievement of the party's domestic policy objectives. "Democrats (and some Republicans)," Charles O. Jones notes, "came to think of themselves as an alternative government during Nixon's second administration."[9] Substantive changes in congressional capacity—and attitude—thus weakened Carter's institutional position.

The same Democrats who had championed internal reforms over the course of the Nixon-Ford years were reelected in droves in 1976. Carter, as Charles Jacob contends, faced a very "junior" House of Representatives.[10] Seventy-six of the seventy-eight freshmen elected in the Watergate class of 1974 were reelected in 1976. Ninety-six percent of incumbents were reelected in 1976, and sixty-seven freshmen joined their ranks. Nearly two-thirds of the House's Democratic majority had been elected since 1968 and so had never served with a president of their own party.[11] New leaders replaced the stalwarts of yesteryear and represented a cadre of activist liberals. "Tip" O'Neill and Robert Byrd occupied the top positions in the House and Senate, respectively. The waning of southern conservative influence in the party gave the Democratic Study Group a majority of liberals for the first time since its creation, although the conservative coalition remained powerful enough to occasionally derail legislation. "Without denying that the president and his legislative staff made fundamental mistakes when they first assumed office," Jon Bond and Richard Fleisher assert, "we should acknowledge that the Congress serving during the 1970s was not very interested in being led by a president—any president."[12]

Carter's "politics of the public good" fit uncomfortably with the continuing congressional agenda and frustrated, if not perplexed, many Democrats in Congress.[13] The majority's backlash against his vetoes of constituency projects "on principle" is the most often cited example of the administration's "lack of understanding" of Congress's internal workings. Moreover, critics attributed many of Carter's difficulties in building Capitol Hill coalitions to a lack of political skill, naïveté about the folkways of Washington, and a poorly organized legislative liaison office staffed by individuals with no national experience.[14] Carter may also have taken the dictum of "hitting the ground running" too far by inundating Congress with too many proposals and failing to signal his priorities at the outset of his term.

The president's early missteps in the legislative arena notwithstanding, high inflation, high unemployment, the deleterious effects of the Arab oil embargo on the domestic economy, and falling government revenues yielded a highly constrained policy-making environment. These vexing economic circumstances produced a setting that was favorable neither to large-scale change nor strong presidential management of the national legislative agenda. Roger Davidson contends that by the middle of his term, "deteriorating economic conditions and shifting attitudes had already caused President Carter to begin to curtail his legislative agenda."[15] The president's efforts to build supporting legislative coalitions were further complicated by congressional Democrats who were internally divided on the appropriate response to "stagflation."[16]

Select case studies of Carter's putatively flawed legislative presidency have tainted an understanding of the type of leadership he was able to exercise under these conditions of unified control. Carter's veto of water projects and the laborious passage of energy legislation are often considered major defeats and are portrayed as a basic reflection of the president's overall record.[17] However, such depictions are insufficiently nuanced to capture the complexity of Carter's legislative presidency. "The legacy of the Carter administration may be viewed as unsuccessful because many participants and scholars failed to grow comfortable with the president's style," Bond and Fleisher maintain, "and not because of the objective record of success."[18] Unified government *did* matter for Carter, but in ways scholars and observers have sometimes missed.

The incidence of single-party control provided the president both with a high floor success rate and some independent policy successes on significant legislation. Carter's role in securing passage of a large number of important laws was to locate and reinforce support for a shared agenda with the congressional majority and to help manage the federal response to difficult economic conditions. This type of legislative leadership accorded with the remarkably changed policy-making climate that characterized the mid- to late 1970s. In this regard, the institutional and electoral context of unified government bears a striking resemblance to the circumstances Clinton would face in the brief return to unified government in 1993–94.

Lawmaking and Leadership under Carter

Sixteen of the twenty significant domestic laws passed from 1977–80 were tied to Carter's stated policy objectives. The four remaining bills received the president's public support. The legislation falls into three broad categories of presidential involvement: Independent policy successes for Carter in the realm of deregulation, support for Congress's continuing agenda, and scaled-down versions of presidential proposals on controversial issues, including the economy, with which the two branches were forced to wrestle in light of poor economic conditions. It is in this latter category of legislation that Carter's dearth of autonomous leverage, Congress's more independent policy-making capacity, and the effect of organized interests on the shape of legislation were most evident.

Although deregulation fits less comfortably with the Democratic Party's traditional policy focus, Carter was not without considerable success on this central theme during his administration. Airline, trucking, and rail deregulation, as well as civil service reform, came closest to being independent policy successes for the president. Deregulation of the airline industry was a "top priority" for Carter, but his proposal ran into heated resistance from organized labor, a powerful Democratic constituency that feared job losses, and concerned leaders in smaller communities who feared the potential loss of airline service. As a result, Carter's proposal remained bottled up in committee for an extended period of time. In the final analysis, however, the president pushed the legislation through and got most of what he wanted in the bill. Supporters argued that it would increase industry competition by lifting controls over a seven-year period.[19]

Trucking and rail deregulation legislation gave these industries greater autonomy on price setting. Although unions initially opposed the trucking bill, they came to support congressional action on the president's proposal. The Interstate Commerce Commission's (ICC) easing of regulation convinced opponents that new legislation was more desirable than allowing the ICC to continue to take independent actions that might jeopardize industry interests.[20] The Staggers Rail Act of 1980 similarly reduced ICC oversight and allowed the rail industry more flexibility in pricing structures in exchange for removing industry exemptions from antitrust laws. Carter had called for the legislation in a special message to Congress. The resulting bill, which pitted the administration against consumer groups and energy producers, entailed some compromise by the president to fend off challenges by fellow Democrats.[21] Congress finally adopted almost all of Carter's plan for reorganizing the Civil Service Commission. The president did not procure provisions to curtail preferences for veterans, but the legislation represented the "most extensive revamping of the federal employment system since the civil service system was established in 1883" by creating the Office of Personnel Management, the Merit Systems Protection Board, and the Senior Executive Service.[22]

A large proportion of the legislation adopted by the 95th and 96th Congresses included issues that represented Congress's continuing agenda and the calibration of existing programs to current economic conditions. Carter's leadership role was sometimes to lend support for incremental changes, including legislation blocked during the Ford administration, and sometimes to jump-start Congress to reconsider select issues that had been put off the legislative calendar. For example, President Ford had twice vetoed the surface mining bill passed in 1977. Carter, who backed increased federal regulation of strip mining coal, provided reinforced support for the legislation and signed it upon passage. The Social Security tax increase of 1977 also represented a carryover issue from the Ford presidency. Government projections of trust fund shortfalls by 1979 prompted Carter to rework Ford's proposal. The bill ultimately relied on payroll taxes to supplement existing funds.[23] In similar fashion, the White House urged Congress to act on Clean Air Act amendments in 1977 after renewal of the legislation had stalled in the 94th Congress. The president lent his support to the broad bill, which strengthened the regulation of automobile emissions, set new standards for clean air in select areas like national parks, and called for new studies of air pollution.[24]

Other continuing items included Alaska lands, minimum wage, and banking legislation. Carter spurred Congress to take up the Alaska lands bill in 1977. Although the bill that was passed more than three years later did not contain many of the elements the president had sought, his support was a major reason the bill—which pitted developers against environmentalists—made it through Congress. Carter called passage of the legislation a "truly historic event" as it more than doubled the land area of U.S. national parks and wildlife refuges.[25] Adjusting the minimum wage in 1977 was a hard-fought victory for Congress and the administration, who were forced to hammer out an agreement acceptable to labor and civil rights groups. Although Congress rejected Carter's proposal to "index" the minimum wage to inflation, the president called the legislation a victory for workers. Step increases over a four-year period were projected to bring the wage above the poverty level by 1980.[26] Although congressional efforts to deregulate the banking industry can be traced to the Nixon administration, Carter and Congress were prompted to act on a broad bill when a federal appeals court ruled that federal regulatory agencies had overstepped their legal authority by allowing interest-bearing checking accounts.[27]

Much of the legislation adopted during Carter's term reflected uneasy compromise between the branches on a host of difficult issues concerning the economy. Although the legislation had strong ties to Carter's agenda, in light of the poor state of the economy and his lack of political capital, Congress often reshaped the proposals considerably. Opportunities for credit claiming were sometimes overshadowed by internal conflict in Congress as the national government struggled with ways to stabilize and manage a jittery economy, high inflation, and the oil crisis.

The 1977 tax cut and the government bailout of the Chrysler Corporation a year later are cases in point. The tax reduction began as part of Carter's economic stimulus plan. The president originally proposed rebates for low-income individuals, but later dropped the proposal after it encountered resistance in the Senate. Republicans championed a permanent tax reduction, and the Senate ultimately added business tax credits opposed by the president.[28] In the same way that George Bush's proposal to rescue the savings and loan industry had earned him precious little political mileage, federal loan guarantees for the ailing Chrysler Corporation did not yield a large credit-claiming payoff for Carter. The 1979 legislation came after months of discord in Congress. Carter ultimately accepted loan guarantees twice the amount he said the administration would support after economists issued gloomy forecasts for the American auto industry.[29]

Legislation aimed at easing the energy crisis was also a focus of presidential and congressional attention. As with elements of Carter's deregulation legislation, his policy stances upset various interest groups with ties to the Democratic base. His comprehensive energy package, a five-part proposal, took eighteen months to pass and narrowly survived several key votes and a Senate filibuster. Congress considerably altered the president's proposal, which affected coal, utility rates, energy conservation, and natural gas price controls. The energy program "had a wealth of natural opponents and no

strong supporters," forcing the administration to "mount a campaign to neu-
tralize the opposition while pleading for support on the grounds of national
prestige and loyalty to the president."[30] Carter's dilemma was that his institutional position and political capital were rather weak to make that argument
in light of the strength of organized interests poised to lobby Congress.

The effect of Carter's meager leverage is evident on other energy legislation
and a smattering of issues of importance to the president. In seeking the 1980
windfall profits tax levied on U.S. oil producers, the largest tax ever imposed
on a domestic industry, Carter angered consumer groups by including a proposal to lift government controls on oil prices. Congress responded by declining to include central elements of the president's plan in the final legislation. Rather than set up a special fund for the development of synthetic fuels
from the new tax, Congress placed the funds in the general revenue account.[31]
In a similar vein, the 1978 tax cut "bore little resemblance to the tax program
the president had proposed" earlier that year.[32] The administration was
unsuccessful in gaining a progressive tax cut in line with liberals' preferences.
Finally, both the establishment of the Department of Education in 1979 and
"Superfund" legislation were considerably scaled-down versions of the president's legislative requests. The Senate reshaped the education bill, which
took eighteen months to pass, and placed the two principal education interest
groups, the National Education Association and the American Federation of
Teachers, in opposition. Few of Carter's proposals for new programs were
adopted and only existing health, education, and welfare programs were
transferred to the new department. The lame-duck 96th Congress took up
emergency legislation in earnest to address toxic waste cleanups only after
Carter's successor, Ronald Reagan, indicated he was unopposed to such action. Congress dropped provisions regarding compensation for victims and
oil spills in order to pass the bill.[33]

Presidential involvement in significant lawmaking in the 95th and 96th
Congresses stressed Carter's positive legislative engagement but also his more
limited basis for autonomous influence. Carter and Congress faced the enormously difficult task of adjusting Great Society programs that came up for renewal in a time of daunting economic constraints. The innovative laws that
emerged were not of the caliber of the original Great Society legislation, but
they *were* either part of the president's stated policy objectives or received his
explicit support. His primary role often constituted mediation of the shared
agenda between the branches. The context of unified government did not
provide a basis for Carter to direct congressional lawmaking in the way that

Johnson had, but neither did it place him in the type of reactive position to which presidents have been relegated under divided control in the postreform/party-unity era.

Carter's Success and Support in the 95th and 96th Congresses

Carter maintained a relatively high success rate on floor votes from 1977–80. The notable exception is his victory ratio on close votes in the 95th Congress: he prevailed only half of the time. In most cases in this category, the president took positions in opposition to motions to recommit (kill) legislation pertaining to subjects ranging from consumer protection to education to the stabilization of commodities. Republicans joined with conservative Democrats to impede the creation of new programs. Carter's success rate with less controversial legislation was relatively stable owing both to strong Democratic and frequent Republican support. Only slightly more than a third of all votes pitted a majority of Democrats against a majority of Republicans.

An examination of the determinants of individual support for Carter's legislative positions emphasizes the importance of his ideological connection with his governing majority. The impact of his precarious electoral circumstances and the institutional context of a more independent Congress are also visible. Carter, like Clinton, was positioned most closely to his partisan base compared to other Democratic presidents. Table 7.2 shows that the president drew support from legislators with positions to the left of the party median, but the impact was relatively modest early in his term. On close votes in the 96th Congress, the difference in the likelihood of support from a legislator positioned ten points to the left of the median party score is only 4.3 percent. The impact of ideology on close votes mounted by nearly twenty points after the midterm elections as Congress and the president wrestled with issues such as

Table 7.1
Carter's Legislative Success Rate,
95th and 96th Congresses*

	95th Congress		96th Congress	
	Close Votes [n=10]	Nonclose Votes [n=33]	Close Votes [n=6]	Nonclose Votes [n=38]
Overall	50% (5)	87.9% (29)	83.3% (5)	65.8% (25)
Democratic Party	60% (6)	84.8% (28)	83.3% (5)	68.4% (26)
Republican Party	20% (2)	57.6% (19)	16.7% (1)	47.3% (18)

* Entries are the number and percentage of votes on which the president gained a majority overall and by party.

welfare reform, public works, and the national debt. The greater impact of ideology conveys a growing divide between liberal and moderate and conservative Democrats about the appropriate response to the poor state of the economy after the midterm elections in 1978.

Carter received relatively consistent support from Democratic leaders across vote categories. The impact of leadership support is about three times greater for close votes compared to less controversial legislation. Support from committee chairs was also greatest on close votes. The message of the data is clear. Democratic leaders were generally mindful of the president's

Table 7.2
Logistic Regression Estimation of Democrats' Domestic Policy Support for Carter, 95th and 96th Congresses

	95th Congress		96th Congress	
	Close Votes	Nonclose Votes	Close Votes	Nonclose Votes
Carter's Margin of Victory, 1976 (%)	2.18**** (.210) *52.90*	−.515**** (.160) *−12.00*	1.42**** (.267) *37.60*	−.104 (.143) *−2.70*
Legislator's Margin of Victory (%)	−.239* (.146) *−5.80*	.078 (.103) *3.50*	−.272* (.180) *−6.70*	.019 (.096) *.40*
Legislator's Terms Served	−.016* (.010) *−9.00*	−.006 (.007) *−2.50*	−.017 (.014) *−6.7*	−.000 (.007) *−.20*
Democratic Leaders	.588*** (.244) *29.80*	.618*** (.203) *11.40*	.913** (.485) *38.30*	.213** (.119) *12.60*
Committee Chairs	.265* (.178) *5.70*	−.013 (.115) *−.10*	.797**** (.247) *17.80*	.127 (.106) *2.80*
Ideology	−1.79**** (.212) *−43.1*	−3.79**** (.157) *−63.6*	−1.93**** (.231) *−62.7*	−1.03**** (.104) *−40.0*
Public Approval of the President	.017**** (.005) *12.20*	.035**** (.003) *11.40*	.000 (.004) *.30*	−.008*** (.003) *−4.70*
Constant	−.768*** (.268)	−.678**** (.150)	.217 (.190)	.932**** (.112)
Number of Cases	3,726.00	8,170.00	2,145.00	8,686.00
$-2 \times$ Log Likelihood	4,878.36	8,904.06	2,801.70	11,025.46
Model χ^2	271.74****	880.29****	156.25****	123.50****
Pseudo-R^2	.05	.09	.05	.01
Cases Correctly Predicted (%)	61.00	74.50	62.20	66.40

**** p < .001   *** p < .01   ** p < .05   * p < .10 (one-tailed tests)
Entries are maximum likelihood coefficients.
Standard errors are in parentheses.
Mean effects are in *italics.*
The dependent variable is whether the legislator supported or opposed Carter's stand.

Table 7.3
Logistic Regression Estimation of Republicans' Domestic Policy Support for Carter, 95th and 96th Congresses

	95th Congress		96th Congress	
	Close Votes	Nonclose Votes	Close Votes	Nonclose Votes
Carter's Margin	2.07****	−.172	2.01****	−.050
of Victory, 1976 (%)	(.213)	(.292)	(.288)	(.231)
	35.70	*−3.20*	*39.70*	*−1.00*
Legislator's Margin	−.174	−.157	−.619****	.034
of Victory (%)	(.149)	(.182)	(.184)	(.123)
	−4.20	*−3.90*	*−15.10*	*.90*
Legislator's Terms	.011	.009	.038***	−.026**
Served	(.009)	(.015)	(.014)	(.013)
	3.10	*2.70*	*22.20*	*−4.80*
Republican Leaders	−.143	.042	−.627**	.068
	(.151)	(.083)	(.331)	(.085)
	−11.80	*3.00*	*−39.20*	*6.90*
Ranking Minority	−.874****	−.025	−.923****	.044
Members	(.167)	(.115)	(.210)	(.108)
	−17.10	*−.50*	*−20.20*	*1.10*
Ideology	−1.80****	−5.28****	−2.38****	−2.44****
	(.218)	(.272)	(.251)	(.186)
	−33.60	*−72.50*	*−47.80*	*−49.80*
Public Approval	−.002	.027****	.009**	−.041****
of the President	(.005)	(.003)	(.004)	(.004)
	−1.90	*14.60*	*6.30*	*−26.10*
Constant	.103	−1.62****	−.316*	1.41****
	(.271)	(.196)	(.198)	(.148)
Number of Cases	3,600.00	4,130.00	2,037.00	5,063.00
−2 × Log Likelihood	4,721.02	5,186.40	2,588.04	6,684.22
Model χ^2	269.45****	517.76****	235.52****	315.48****
Pseudo-R^2	.05	.09	.08	.05
Cases Correctly Predicted (%)	62.20	64.70	61.80	60.10

**** p < .001   *** p < .01   ** p < .05   * p < .10 (one-tailed tests)
Entries are maximum likelihood coefficients.
Standard errors in parentheses.
Mean effects are in *italics*.
Dependent variable is whether the legislator supported or opposed Carter's stand.

positions and were supportive of his efforts to build winning coalitions. When Carter did not prevail on close votes, particularly in the first half of his term, the effect was due to the rank-and-file members' failure to follow the party leadership. Some of these members were junior; some were more conservative. The point is that the president and leaders of the governing majority encountered difficulties building coalitions on thorny economic matters.

Carter's dearth of coattails and the Democrats' incumbency advantage impeded strong unity on controversial legislation. The president's ability to convince moderate and conservative Democrats to support his stands pivoted on his electoral popularity on close votes. The impact of the president's district margin over Ford in 1976 surpasses ideology for the 95th Congress. Among Democrats elected in 1976, Carter defeated Ford in less than two-thirds of his copartisans' districts. His average margin over Ford in those districts was 12 percent (σ = 21). But his marginal coattails were thin. The president's share of the two-party vote surpassed the vote share of only 8 percent of his copartisans elected to the 95th Congress.

Incumbency advantage acted as a counterweight to presidential support on controversial votes among legislators from districts where Carter was unpopular. A Democrat who ran without opposition in 1976 was about 6 percent less likely to back the president's stands on close votes. And a ten-term member was 3.6 percent less likely to support Carter than a freshman. Carter's weak electoral victory and incumbency advantage for many moderate-to-conservative members did not generate strong loyalty.

Carter drew the bulk of his support in the GOP from moderate members positioned to the left of the party median. One-fifth of the Republicans in the 95th Congress were elected from split-districts that voted for Carter. The president's average victory over Ford in those districts was 7 percent (σ = 6). In districts carried by Ford, Carter's average loss was 14 percent (σ = 10). Carter's lack of electoral popularity in the lion's share of Republican districts solidified opposition to his stands on close votes. For Republican members from districts in which Carter sustained a loss of 10 percent, the likelihood of support on close votes in the 95th Congress drops by 7.3 percent. The effect is roughly equivalent in the 96th Congress. Republican opposition ossified in 1979–80 on high-profile votes for the debt and social programs. As the strong negative effects in table 7.3 show, Republican leaders and committee chairs became increasingly willing to challenge the majority. They were 20–40 percent less likely to support Carter on close votes in the 96th Congress. Seat safety bolstered rank-and-file opposition. Members who ran unopposed in 1978 were over 15 percent less likely to vote with the president.

Carter's job approval had a minimal impact on legislative support in either party. His public approval ranged from a high of 70 percent to a low of 28 percent for the votes in the analysis. The data show that the higher approval ratings earlier in his term seemingly shored up Democratic support somewhat, but there is no consistent pattern among Republicans. Nor did Carter's electoral popularity have any substantive impact on nonclose votes in either party. Positions in Congress were far more issue based. From environmental and regulatory topics to social legislation, Congress wrestled with a number of issues that carried over from the Nixon-Ford period. Legislators' ideology, incumbency, and the strength of Carter's coattails were more consistent predictors of presidential support.

The review of Carter's involvement in significant lawmaking and the factors that weighed on legislative support for his positions suggests that he often competed with an independent-minded governing majority to participate in the lawmaking process. Carter was most successful in garnering support for elements of the shared agenda that represented adjustments to the status quo. His role on much important legislation was to legitimize outstanding party objectives, lend support for incremental change, and cooperate with Congress in choosing the appropriate responses to an uneasy economy. Within these parameters, the president did have his share of agenda success in the sphere of regulation. An emphasis on scaling back government responsibility fit well with the resource constraints of the late 1970s but corresponded less well to traditional Democratic policy positions.

Carter's weak leverage over Congress was most evident on controversial legislation early in his term. His lack of coattails impeded building winning coalitions for new domestic programs or budgetary issues subject to partisan wrangling in Congress. A more independent and overwhelmingly junior membership of House Democrats was not always willing to follow the president's lead. Conservatives in the party retained enough clout and incumbency advantage alongside Republicans to occasionally thwart the president's stands. These features of the policy-making environment placed Congress on a far more equal footing with the president on domestic affairs than was the case for Lyndon Johnson at the outset of his term in 1965. Carter's proactive engagement in the legislative realm was based more on collaboration with, rather than direction of, the governing majority. In this regard, Carter shared much in common with the next Democratic president to win the White House some twelve years after he left the Oval Office.

Bill Clinton and Congress, 1993–94

The context of unified government in 1993–94 did not bode well for a "textbook model" of presidential legislative leadership any more than Carter's term had. The electoral and institutional circumstances surrounding Clinton early in his first term account for many of his legislative travails. Indefatigable controversy in Congress and the failure of several major presidential initiatives often overshadowed major legislative accomplishments. Setting the record straight on unified government and the legislative presidency in the postreform/party-unity era necessitates a closer analysis of the type of leadership Clinton was able to exercise.

Bill Clinton began his first term alongside a Democratic majority in 1993 under circumstances that were, in many ways, reminiscent both of Kennedy in 1961 and Carter in 1977. After a long period of divided party control of the presidency and Congress, the outlook for the new president appeared bright. Popular expectations ran high as he came to the White House, anxious to focus on domestic policy initiatives. Yet Clinton began his term with the smallest numerical majority of Democrats in both chambers since Harry Truman in 1949. He also won the 1992 election with only a plurality of the vote following a three-way election—scarcely a mandate for sweeping change in a policy-making environment marked by continuing federal deficits and economic recession.

Electoral links between the president and his Democratic majority were tenuous, at best, even though congressional Democrats in the 103d Congress were more ideologically homogeneous than at any other point in the postwar period. Clinton had purposefully distanced himself from congressional Democrats in the 1992 election by campaigning, like Carter, as an outsider. Voter concern with "gridlock" in the nation's capital and mounting public antipathy toward Congress were evidenced by the rise of the term-limit movement in many states. Voter anger was fueled by frustration with congressional incumbents who seemed to be tied endlessly to ethical scandals, exemplified by Jim Wright's resignation as Speaker of the House and members' abuse of the House bank. It is little wonder that when he accepted his party's nomination at the Democratic national convention, Clinton "took pains in his acceptance speech to disassociate himself from Congress, calling for an end to the 'brain-dead politics in Washington'—presumably at both ends of Pennsylvania Avenue."[34]

While billionaire Ross Perot's third-party candidacy was more damaging to incumbent George Bush than Clinton, his "antiestablishment," populist campaign robbed Clinton of a majority of the popular vote, leaving the new president with a 43 percent plurality. To complicate matters, Democrats lost ten seats in the House and made no gains in the Senate. The election was much more a repudiation of George Bush's handling of the economy than an endorsement of Clinton and his fellow Democrats. Clinton's marginal coattails were thin, though greater than for Carter. He ran ahead of just less than fifty Democrats in the House.

Given the influx of new members to the House (110) and Senate (12) on the heels of a record number of retirements, the only certain message of the 1992 congressional elections was voters' desire to "throw the rascals out." On balance, there was scarce evidence that the electorate had given the new president anything close to carte blanche for far-reaching domestic policy innovation. Economic issues were subject to wrangling among congressional Democrats because Congress, like the electorate in 1992, could not reach a consensus over what course of action to take to combat the sagging economy. The president found himself in the cross fire between unyielding opposition among Republicans, which his leadership style sometimes helped to cultivate, and skepticism among his copartisans on the economic recovery path to be followed. His outsider campaign and lack of coattails did little to shore up Democratic support on acrimonious economic issues when constituency pressures prevailed upon members. The result was sometimes a "failure of followership" as few Democrats felt a debt to Clinton for their election.[35]

Clinton also raised public expectations of legislative leadership during the campaign, tying his prospective leadership record to ambitious policy proposals emphasizing economic growth, welfare reform, and middle-class tax cuts. He suffered major setbacks when strategic miscalculations, such as the gays in the military issue and controversies over cabinet appointments, diverted public and congressional attention away from these policy objectives. He also endured several embarrassing defeats derived from a style of governance that excluded Republicans, who retaliated wherever possible, blocking procedural votes on crime legislation in the House and impeding passage of bills like "motor voter" with Senate filibusters.[36]

Of course, the most symbolic defeat for Clinton was the death of his comprehensive health care reform bill, which expired without a floor vote. The president invested precious time, resources, and political capital into reforming the nation's health care system. Yet the secretive "closed-door" process that gave birth to the complex proposal was roundly criticized as naïve for proffering unprecedented governmental control of the health care industry. The health care proposal mobilized the opposition of the pharmaceutical and insurance industries, as well as the professional medical establishment. The savvy media campaign launched by the bill's opponents increasingly fractured congressional Democrats, eventually sounding the death knell for substantive reform.[37] The net effect of the health care debacle was to edge out other administration priorities, like welfare reform, and create the perception that Clinton's presidency was foundering.

In retrospect, if one's vantage point shifts from what did *not* pass in the 103d Congress to what *did,* it becomes clear that Clinton and his Democratic copartisans built an impressive domestic policy record. The positive character of the president's involvement in significant policy accomplishments reflected an important level of mutuality between the branches. The shared agenda enabled Clinton to achieve some independent policy successes and jointly claim credit with his copartisans for several important laws. A central role he played was lending support to the continuing congressional agenda that George Bush had blocked. In other cases, partisan control allowed the president and Democrats to prevail on controversial legislation, if sometimes only narrowly, through minimum winning coalitions.

Lawmaking and Presidential Leadership under Clinton

Of the eleven significant laws that Mayhew lists for the 103d Congress, ten had ties to Clinton's stated policy objectives, and the single bill that did not—the California Desert Protection Act—was expressly supported by the president. Significant legislation in 1993–94 falls into three distinct categories: Several laws that may be considered independent policy successes for the president, legislation that represented the president's support for the continuing agenda of Congress, and laws that were part of the shared agenda between the branches and adopted with partisan support.

"Americorps" and "Goals 2000" were two innovative laws that reflected presidential campaign promises. The final bills followed the president's proposals very closely. The passage of Clinton's national service proposal, a domestic version of Kennedy's Peace Corps, allowed students to receive educational aid in exchange for community service. The bill was a major achievement following his inaugural call for a "season of service" by the nation's youth.[38] Congress also adopted the president's Goals 2000 initiative, a $427 million package of grants to states to encourage the adoption of national elementary and secondary educational standards.[39]

A larger core of the significant legislation passed by the 103d Congress and signed by the president reflected Congress's continuing agenda. Three of the four bills were connected to the president's stated policy objectives. In these cases, Clinton essentially lent support, and was eager to share credit with Congress, for issues blocked during twelve years of Republican control of the White House. Family leave and motor voter were early priorities of the Democratic Congress, symbolically designated HR 1 and HR 2, respectively. Clinton was not responsible for designing either law. The family leave bill, which guaranteed unpaid leave for workers needing to attend to family matters, was virtually indistinguishable from the bill vetoed by George Bush in the 102d Congress. Clinton signed the family leave legislation at a White House rose garden ceremony, seizing the occasion to declare the end of gridlock politics.[40] Motor voter, which mandated that states allow individuals to register to vote at local motor vehicle offices, won congressional approval after Senate

Democrats removed a provision that would have allowed individuals to register to vote at unemployment agencies. Clinton had vowed that he would have signed the motor voter legislation while on the campaign trail in 1992 after George Bush vetoed the measure. At a signing ceremony with much fanfare in the spring of 1993, Clinton proclaimed a victory for democracy in the bill, which putatively removed barriers to voting.[41]

Clinton also reinforced congressional efforts to adjust existing programs and confirmed his commitment to environmental matters. At the president's request and with Education Secretary Richard Riley's support, Congress passed legislation to replace the federal government's guarantee of student loans by private banks with a direct federal lending system. The new program provided more repayment options for students.[42] Clinton also publicly endorsed the California desert protection bill, the handiwork of Sen. Dianne Feinstein. The new national preserve in the Mojave Desert was the largest public lands protection bill since the 1980 Alaska Lands Act.[43]

The remaining significant laws passed during Clinton's watch represented presidential priorities shared with his copartisans. These bills were adopted only after extended partisan conflict and controversy. Clinton's crime bill and economic plan were characterized by brinksmanship and amounted to nearly Pyrrhic victories. The context of the 1992 election forced Clinton to compromise on a host of issues to persuade Congress—often by the thinnest of margins—to adopt the very basics of his proposals.

Clinton's economic plan is a case in point. The reconciliation bill that was eventually passed reduced the federal deficit by nearly $500 billion, with almost half the reduction in the form of a tax increase on wealthy individuals. The controversial package that was ultimately adopted came on the heels of the president's failed economic stimulus package and his decision to shirk a campaign promise to cut middle-class taxes and instead focus on deficit reduction. He was forced to retreat on a number of issues in order to eke out a victory with a minimum winning coalition in both chambers. Clinton's unpopular proposal to include a British thermal unit energy tax evoked the ire of Democrats under constituency pressure to oppose the increase. The administration's argument to recalcitrant Democrats that defeat of the bill might cripple the president's future prospects for governance fell largely on deaf ears in view of his weak coattails. Compelled by reticent moderate and conservative House Democrats to cede on the scope of the energy tax, the president also yielded on greater cuts to domestic programs than he originally desired. Clinton's exhaustive lobbying effort produced the barest victory in the House. He later drew the fury of representatives who had voted for the bill when the

Senate all but removed the energy tax provisions. The omnibus bill, which captured not a single Republican vote and led to a number of Democratic defections, was finally adopted when Vice President Al Gore broke a tie vote in the Senate.[44]

Gun control and anticrime legislation also proved a difficult row to hoe for the president, in large part due to intense Republican opposition. The Brady Bill, which required a five-day waiting period for the purchase of handguns and a background check on the purchaser, was adopted only after being separated out from the president's omnibus crime proposal and surviving a Republican-sponsored filibuster. Clinton had to yield to Republicans who wanted a four-year "sunset" on the waiting period in order to get legislative action.[45] His broad proposal for anticrime legislation also became mired in a myriad of internal congressional conflicts. The proposal was broken into several smaller bills. To placate conservatives, the legislation included tougher penalties for criminals, including drug trafficking and violence against women. To satisfy liberals, preventive measures, including community policing, were included. Most controversial was the ban of certain automatic assault weapons, which led to a protracted partisan battle.[46]

"Congressional Democrats," according to Barbara Sinclair, "especially members of the House, who must run for reelection every two years, perceived their fate as tied to Clinton's legislative success."[47] But Clinton did not have the autonomous leverage to push forth his own comprehensive legislative agenda. Many of his legislative successes were part and parcel of support for longstanding party policy goals. On bills like family leave and motor voter, his role was to champion the legislation and reinforce congressional efforts through the bully pulpit. In other cases, divisive economic and social issues forced the president to compromise with Republicans and his copartisans in light of his weak institutional position. The president cultivated intraparty cohesion, and legislative support flowed from a strong ideological bond with congressional Democrats.

Clinton's Success and Support in the 103d Congress

Clinton's roll-call victory ratio was conditioned by strong party unity in Congress for his domestic policy stands. On the close votes in the analysis, the president had a perfect record overall. He failed to garner a majority of Democratic votes on just a single issue—space station appropriations—but received enough backing from Republicans to prevail. Eight of the nine votes in 1993–94, ranging from gun control (Brady Bill) to the budget, pitted a majority of Democrats against a majority of Republicans. Less controversial votes were also prone to strong partisan cohesion. Thirty of thirty-seven votes (81 percent) were party-unity votes.

A focus on the determinants of presidential support underscores a strong ideological bond between the president and the vast majority of his copartisans. The model for Democratic support in table 7.5 was estimated twice, alternating the president's district-level electoral margin and the ideological positions of legislators, due to the strong linear relationship between these two variables (r = -.74). Legislators' ideological stances were much more important for Democrats on close votes at the heart of the party agenda, much of which had been blocked during the Bush years.

Clinton drew strong support from his liberal base in Congress. But there is also evidence of the opposition among moderates that the president encountered. The average "cross-pressured" Democrat was positioned only eleven points to the right of the party median, but was 14 percent less likely to support the president on controversial votes compared to the median Democrat. Some of these Blue Dog Democrats, like Billy Tauzin of Louisiana and Mike Parker of Mississippi, switched parties after the Republican landslide in November, 1994. It is among this group of legislators that defections from the president's stands were most likely, sometimes cutting Clinton's winning legislative coalitions to a bare minimum.

It is important to emphasize that Clinton did not face a profound, regionally based ideological division among his copartisans the way Kennedy had. The mean ideological score for Democrats in the 103d Congress was -.24, some seven points farther to the left compared to the 87th Congress and with a reduction in the standard deviation of three points. The more solid anchoring of congressional Democrats on the left enabled Clinton to hold the liberal base together in most instances and prevail on key floor votes. On close votes, however, Clinton lost an average of sixty-three Democrats. These losses, in view of the Republicans' near unanimity in opposition to the president's stands, threatened the barest of legislative victories.

The waning group of conservative Democrats took particular issue with

Table 7.4
Clinton's Legislative Success Rate,
103d Congress*

	Close Votes [n=9]	Nonclose Votes [n=37]
Overall	100.0% (9)	89.2% (33)
Democratic Party	88.9% (8)	94.6% (35)
Republican Party	11.1% (1)	13.5% (5)

* Entries are the number and percentage of votes on which the president gained a majority overall and by party.

Table 7.5
Logistic Regression Estimation of Democrats' Domestic Policy Support for Clinton, 103d Congress

	Close Votes		Nonclose Votes	
Clinton's Margin	3.90****	———	1.52****	———
of Victory 1992 (%)	(.33)		(.17)	
	55.30		*19.50*	
Legislator's Margin	−1.40****	−.48**	−.71****	−.33***
of Victory (%)	(.27)	(.24)	(.15)	(.13)
	−27.10	*−8.30*	*−10.80*	*−4.70*
Legislator's Terms	.037***	.05****	.00	.00
Served	(.013)	(.01)	(.01)	(.01)
	13.70	*16.60*	*.10*	*.90*
Democratic Leaders	.58****	.35**	.29****	.19***
	(.14)	(.15)	(.07)	(.07)
	20.80	*15.30*	*11.00*	*8.20*
Committee Chairs	.24	−.22	.07	−.09
	(.25)	(.26)	(.12)	(.12)
	4.10	*−3.80*	*.30*	*1.30*
Ideology	———	−6.37****	———	−2.39****
		(.43)		(.20)
		−73.20		*−24.80*
Public Approval	.11****	.12****	.11****	.11****
of the President	(.01)	(.01)	(.01)	(.01)
	20.50	*20.90*	*22.10*	*22.10*
Constant	−4.50****	−4.46****	−3.67****	−4.15****
	(.62)	(.63)	(.35)	(.35)
Number of Cases	2,267.00	2,267.00	9,316.00	9,303.00
−2 × Log Likelihood	2,291.94	2,186.91	8,361.26	8,286.44
Model χ^2	258.22****	363.27****	339.69****	391.00****
Pseudo-R^2	.10	.14	.04	.05
Cases Correctly Predicted (%)	.75	.76	.82	.82

**** p < .001   *** p < .01   ** p < .05   * p < .10 (one-tailed tests)
Entries are maximum likelihood coefficients.
Standard errors are in parentheses.
Mean effects are in *italics*.
The dependent variable is whether the legislator supported or opposed Clinton's stand.

the president's fiscal positions. The support data suggest that Democratic defections may partially be explained by Clinton's outsider campaign and his lack of coattails. Although the effect is slighter in the model with ideology, legislators' seat safety is negatively related to support of the president. Members who ran unopposed were about 8 percent less likely to support Clinton compared to those who faced more competitive races. Part of the "failure of followership" can also be traced to younger Democrats. The effect is slight, but a freshman was 3.5 percent less likely to support the president compared to a five-term member. Over half the Democrats who defected on the close budget vote in 1993 and over three-fourths of those who voted against the

Table 7.6
Logistic Regression Estimation of Republicans' Domestic Policy Support for Clinton, 103d Congress

	Close Votes	Nonclose Votes
Clinton's Margin of Victory 1992 (%)	1.30**	.75***
	(.76)	(.28)
	8.30	*10.50*
Legislator's Margin of Victory (%)	.06	.09
	(.41)	(.15)
	.60	*2.20*
Legislator's Terms Served	.03	−.01
	(.03)	(.01)
	5.80	*−2.50*
Republican Leaders	.20*	−.02
	(.15)	(.06)
	10.00	*1.30*
Ranking Minority Members	−.25	−.08
	(.29)	(.10)
	−2.30	*−1.70*
Ideology	−5.31****	−6.51****
	(.78)	(.31)
	−59.90	*−86.20*
Public Approval of the President	−.29****	−.034****
	(.02)	(.007)
	−38.00	*−11.00*
Constant	11.25****	2.85****
	(.90)	(.36)
Number of Cases	1,540.00	6,432.00
−2 × Log Likelihood	1,082.85	7,475.44
Model χ^2	308.06****	738.75****
Pseudo-R^2	.22	.09
Cases Correctly Predicted (%)	.85	.71

**** p < .001　*** p < .01　** p < .05　* p < .10 (one-tailed tests)
Entries are maximum likelihood coefficients.
Standard errors are in parentheses.
Mean effects are in *italics*.
The dependent variable is whether the legislator supported or opposed Clinton's stand.

1994 budget had served three terms or less. First-term Democrats, many of whom ran much better than Clinton in their districts, did not want to see their victory margins diminished in the next election by voting for the president's controversial economic plans.[48] But Clinton needed their support, and many were able to extract a host of concessions from the president in exchange for their vote. As James Pfiffner explains: "few Democrats in Congress felt they owed their victory to him, and all of them garnered more votes than he did in their own districts (due to Ross Perot's candidacy). Combine the absence of gratitude with a lack of fear of a president with relatively low public approval ratings, and you have the formula for weak presidential influence on the Hill."[49]

The data do point to a strong constituency-based linkage undergirding the party cohesion on Clinton's policy stands among liberal Democrats. On close votes, a Democrat from a district where Clinton outpaced Bush by a margin of five points was 9 percent more likely to support the president's stands. However, legislators from districts that Bush carried in 1992 were more reserved in their support. Clinton failed to carry a total of fifty-two Democratic districts, and his loss to Bush averaged 8 percent. Over half of those districts were in the South. While Democratic defections must not be overstated, the fragile electoral connection between the president and a handful of conservative-leaning Democrats weakened his basis for strong, autonomous influence.

Clinton's electoral margin had only a moderate impact on Republicans across vote categories. His electoral popularity among split-district members of the opposition did not serve as a strong rallying point. In the 103d Congress there were some fifty Republicans from a smattering of districts around the country where Clinton prevailed over Bush. A third were from the Northeast, and Clinton's average victory was 7 percent. The president was sometimes able to garner the support of this handful of moderates. In the districts of the rest of the GOP membership, Clinton lost to Bush by an average of 12 percent. For most Republicans, the magnitude of the president's defeat confirmed constituent opposition to his agenda and translated both into scarce support and a willingness to challenge the president and the Democratic majority.

Clinton's eroding public approval in 1993–94 did not play much of a role on Republican support, but it contributed to Democratic defections in the second session of the 103d Congress. By 1994, as the president's approval dropped below the 40 percent threshold, his ability to marshal the support of reticent members of his own party grew thinner as the midterm elections approached. Democrats were over 20 percent more likely to vote against the president by the second session of the 103d Congress. There is an inverse relationship between Republican support and Clinton's national job approval rating that is indicative of policy-focused voting. Republican opposition was strongest when the president's approval was *highest* at the outset of the 103d Congress. Republicans marshaled unity against Clinton's agenda to sharpen the policy distinction between the parties as the 1994 elections neared.

Summary

Comparing Carter's and Clinton's experiences under unified government supports two central tenets of the framework of presidential leverage in political time. First, when the focus of analysis is shifted from the production of laws, per se, to the nature of the president's involvement in significant lawmaking, a fundamental distinction between periods of unified and divided government is evident. A consistent feature of unified government is that the overwhelming number of significant laws shows a connection with the president's stated policy objectives and proposals. Presidents are better able to cultivate a shared policy agenda with the governing majority in Congress. Vetoes and veto threats do not constitute the president's means of negotiating policy outcomes.

Second, the marginal electoral victories that Carter and Clinton sustained translated into weaker leverage over Congress and a diminished basis for independent policy successes. Narrow electoral victories did not constitute legitimizing events for the Carter and Clinton domestic agendas in the way that Johnson's landslide victory had in 1964. Election campaigns that stressed their outsider status yielded weaker connections between the branches and did not kindle deference to the president's objectives. Incumbency advantage in Congress further eroded their leverage over members at key junctures, and economic constraints complicated efforts to achieve consensus on domestic legislative affairs. The lack of strong electoral resources and their weaker institutional positions explains, to a remarkable degree, the qualitatively different form of legislative success they enjoyed.

The "continuous" nature and malleability of congressional lawmaking stressed by many scholars is of particular import for the type of legislative success from which presidents with weaker institutional positions have been able to profit under single-party control in recent decades.[50] The incidence of unified government under the conditions that Carter and Clinton confronted yielded more opportunities to encourage and reinforce support for shared policy objectives with their copartisans. The efficacy with which presidents can profit from this type of legislative success may depend in large part upon their ability to sell such accomplishments to the electorate. Judging from the voters' ouster of Carter after one term and the Republicans' takeover of Congress in the 1994 midterm elections, the evidence suggests that neither Carter nor Clinton was particularly adept at securing an advantage from these often considerable legislative outcomes. Part of the problem may have stemmed from the polemic over their efforts at bold policy departures in a time of fiscal restraint. The failure of Carter's welfare reform plan and Clinton's health care plan drew attention away from other significant accomplishments. In addition, laborious issues on which the president ultimately prevailed with some compromise—such as energy legislation for Carter and the 1993 budget for Clinton—were so costly in terms of the political capital they expended and unfavorable media coverage the issues received that controversy eclipsed achievement.

The sum of evidence in this chapter stresses that while the LBJ model does not apply to the Carter and Clinton legislative presidencies, unified government from 1977–80 and in 1993–94 *did* afford each president opportunities for a different form of proactive leadership. For Carter and Clinton, weaker positive leverage provided a limited basis for substantial independent direction of Congress. Their achievements were partly the result of their efforts to impart credibility to party objectives and use the levers of the presidency to reinforce support for the passage of select issues. Such leadership undoubtedly contrasts with the veto-laden approaches that presidents have had to take with opposition majorities in Congress in the most recent era of divided government—and is not inconsequential to the policy legacies presidents leave behind.

8 Conclusion

AT THE END OF THIS JOURNEY through presidents' experiences under unified and divided party control of national institutions we are now in a better position to return to the two fundamental issues posed in the introduction. The first goal was to reconcile the normative claims of party government advocates about the importance of unified government for presidential leadership with chief executives' actual legislative records. The second goal was to grasp presidents' strategic response to the condition of divided government across time.

Systematic empirical analysis underscores the subtle yet consistent ways in which unified government has facilitated positive presidential engagement of Congress. High floor success rates and agenda synergy are common characteristics of single-party control. Presidents have sometimes been able to provide agenda leadership on their own set of preferred objectives. At other times, their role has been to cultivate support for and advance continuing agendas in Congress. From the vantage point of the White House, party control of Congress certainly *does* matter.

There has been far more diversity in presidential strategy and success in times of divided government. The impact of split-party control on the legislative presidency today is qualitatively different compared to the 1950s. Chapters 1–4 emphasized how presidents were frequently able to engage in cross-party coalition building, maintain relatively high floor success rates, and sometimes provide agenda leadership in the earlier decades of the postwar era. In the closing decades of the twentieth century, presidents' floor success rates have fallen dramatically. Congressional majorities now set more of the policy agenda. In light of the obstacles presidents face in building winning legislative majorities, post-passage and preemptive veto politics have become routine on domestic policies of national import.

The variable effect of divided government on the modern legislative presidency is best understood through the lens of political time. An emphasis on the particular electoral, institutional, and environmental contexts within which split-party control has occurred provides a firmer basis for meaningful comparisons of presidents' experiences. Superficially similar partisan configurations of the presidency and Congress have often appeared to have little in common during the last fifty years. Democratic Presidents Truman and Clinton, for example, faced Republican majorities in Congress, but their legislative presidencies bore little similarity in terms of veto leverage. Two-term Republican Presidents Eisenhower and Reagan were dealt the hand of divided government for a majority of their tenure, but Eisenhower was better able to sustain coalition-building leverage and higher floor success rates. Presidents Nixon and Bush confronted large Democratic majorities on Capitol Hill, but their strategies and the type of influence they could exert over legislative outcomes diverged significantly because of the electoral context and voting alignments in Congress.

The framework of presidential leverage in political time imposes an order on these complex and diverse cases of divided government. Subdividing periods of split-party control within distinct contextual eras in the postwar period relieves confusion about presidents' contrasting experiences. The approach sharpens our grasp of the conditions under which divided government has been most salient to the legislative presidency.

The central contribution of this book has been to show *how* and *why* presidents' success, strategy, and credit-claiming opportunities in the legislative realm have varied by degree across time. Broad trends in presidents' electoral resources, internal dynamics in Congress, agenda magnitude between the branches, and the larger policy-making environment have conditioned presidents' strategic modes of engagement. A multifaceted interpretation of presidential success that considers floor victory rates, leadership of and support for landmark domestic initiatives, and negotiation with opposition majorities through the veto power crystallizes fundamental differences in presidents' leadership of Congress between periods of unified and divided party control.

Several common threads run through the Kennedy, Johnson, Carter, and Clinton cases of unified government. These presidents had the most consistently high floor success rates. The significant domestic laws identified by Mayhew showed a consistent linkage to presidents' stated policy objectives.[1] A stronger shared policy agenda between the branches created more opportunities for joint credit claiming and the attainment of partisan policy objectives. All of these presidents differed in terms of their autonomous influence over Congress and their ability to garner substantial independent policy successes, but only Lyndon Johnson's term—which began with an electoral landslide and strong coattails—comes close to resembling the *beau idéal* of presidential direction of the national agenda.

Nevertheless, scholars have overlooked how unified government has facilitated presidential legislative leadership in important ways, even if single-party control typically resembled neither Johnson's term nor a hybrid form of "responsible party government" within our separated institutional structure. As the case studies of Kennedy, Carter, and Clinton showed, these presidents had weak positive leverage over Congress. They had only a moderate basis for pursuing an independent policy agenda. A nuanced interpretation of their role on legislative outcomes, however, underscores that some of their greatest successes were on "promising issues" that had been percolating in Congress.[2] They co-opted elements of continuing agendas on Capitol Hill and lent support and legitimacy to efforts to pass longstanding party objectives, including the extension and modification of existing programs. They were occasionally able to achieve some of their own independent policy objectives. Finally, they used the media spotlight on the presidency to boast publicly of policies of national import passed under single-party control.

Periods of divided government have evinced far greater diversity in presidential strategy, success, and opportunities for independent agenda leadership and joint credit claiming with Congress. Presidential-congressional concurrence on floor outcomes was more common in the early eras of the postwar period. Presidents were able to employ a mixed strategy in the legislative realm. Stronger coattails, weaker congressional organization, and less party polarization on Capitol Hill enabled chief executives to exert a fair bit of positive leverage when they chose to intervene. Autonomous influence over Congress varied, but Presidents such as Eisenhower, and to a lesser degree Nixon, could engage in agenda leadership, claim some independent policy successes, and lend support to congressional lawmaking. Only infrequently did they turn to vetoes and veto threats to shape significant legislative outcomes. During select periods of divided government in the postwar setting, the dynamics of presidential-congressional bargaining sometimes looked similar to those under unified conditions. Party control of Congress seemed less significant to presidential leadership.

When executive-legislative dynamics in the bipartisan conservative and liberal activist periods are juxtaposed with those in the postreform/party-unity era, the assertion that divided government is of little consequence to presidents is untenable. Recent presidents' successes in the legislative sphere have frequently been linked to Article I, Section 7, of the Constitution. Reliance on veto leverage is the product of a broadly contested agenda between the branches driven largely by opposition majorities' policy objectives. Presidential-congressional concurrence has been diminished by stronger institutional parties in Congress, more assertive leadership, and the sharpening of policy distinctions between Democrats and Republicans. Weakened electoral ties between the president and opposition party in Congress have decreased presidents' sway over those members' voting decisions. Presidents' floor success rates have plummeted as congressional majorities have given short shrift to presidents' preferred agendas. Significant legislation shows far fewer connections to presidents' stated policy objectives. This scenario has complicated and narrowed presidents' credit-claiming opportunities. Interbranch conflict has often overshadowed policy accomplishments. Presidents choose to stay quiet more frequently and intervene in lawmaking on a more selective basis.

Divided government in the postreform/party-unity era entails significant challenges for presidents. Veto leverage conflicts with conceptions about the legislative presidency based on forceful agenda leadership of Congress. Americans, as Michael Nelson notes, are "theoretical congressionalists" and "operational presidentialists."[3] Voters like the idea of congressional deliberation and debate, but they admire chief executives who take charge of legislative affairs. If the shared nature of lawmaking between the branches can be conceptualized as a "tandem cycle," the problem is that chief executives often peddle at the rear nowadays.[4] The old adage that "the president proposes and Congress disposes" has frequently been reversed. Opposition majorities in Congress have steered the course of the legislative agenda away from the direction preferred by the White House, whether presidents like Clinton have had larger independent agendas or presidents like Bush (senior) have had smaller ones. Presidents have sought to put the breaks on the cycle, using vetoes and threats to place boundaries on the range of acceptable outcomes to reassert control over policy outcomes. Their need to fend off the majority's agenda and recast the national policy debate places a greater emphasis on rhetorical skills and manipulation of the levers of the public presidency, even as high public job approval scarcely aids legislative support in the opposition majority.

Presidents face other constraints in the legislative realm in the postreform/ party-unity era, whether party control is unified or divided. Less deferential and more policy-focused majorities in Congress complicate presidential efforts to autonomously influence lawmaking when single-party control prevails. Presidents' greatest resource for legislative success—their copartisans' cohesion in Congress—can sometimes be their biggest constraint. Intense policy conflict between the parties on Capitol Hill has produced less room for presidents to find a middle course of action acceptable to both sides. Heightened interparty dissension may render policy outcomes unstable, thus complicating presidents' efforts to build legislative majorities.[5]

President Clinton faced such dilemmas on several occasions during his two terms. To get legislative action in the 103d Congress, he often made concessions to an intransigent Republican opposition and tried to position himself in the center. But these concessions, James P. Pfiffner notes, "were also cited as his weaknesses. At what point is willingness to compromise seen as 'caving in' to the opposition? After how many calls and personal appeals is the president 'overexposed' and in danger of devaluing the currency of personal presidential appeals?"[6] Clinton's ultimate compromises on the budget and welfare reform in the 104th Congress similarly drew rebukes from members of his own party under divided government. The loss of partisan support under divided government has the potential to undercut the president's veto leverage.

Future assessments of George W. Bush's legislative presidency must certainly take into account the types of challenges he may confront in light of the current policy-making environment. Party margins will likely remain narrow and relations between the branches tentative, whether party control of Congress remains split between the chambers or Republicans or Democrats manage to gain full control of Capitol Hill. Either way, Bush cannot stray too far from the locus of support from his conservative party base in Congress. This imperative may confound his bid to make good on a campaign pledge to bring Democrats and Republicans together to forge policy consensus.

Bush's first year has not yet come to a close at the time of this writing, but his legislative strategy and the type of leverage he has been able to exert are consistent with the expectations of the theoretical framework. The main characteristics of the postreform/party-unity era continued upon the first presidential election of the new millennium. With nonexistent coattails in the 2000 election and having declined to campaign with congressional Republicans, Bush's meager electoral connection to members of Congress in either party did not provide a strong basis for positive leverage from the outset of his term. He has championed a modest domestic agenda centered on the Republican leitmotiv of tax cuts for which he received mostly partisan support. He has counted on the thin Republican majority in the House to push his policy objectives and has selectively employed veto threats to keep activism by the Democratic-controlled Senate in check. Partisan voting in Congress remains at high levels, and the disappearance of the federal budget surplus may only lead to greater dissent between the parties over policy priorities. Continued fiscal constraint suggests incremental adjustments to the status quo on domestic policy and only a limited number of nationally significant laws.

In contemplating the future shape of presidential-congressional relations following the 2000 elections, it is striking how poorly the FDR and LBJ models of presidential influence coincide with current conditions. The ways in which presidents negotiate legislative outcomes *does* pivot on the partisan arrangement of national institutions. However, at the current historical juncture, the context of unified government will offer presidents a stronger basis for the promotion of shared policy goals with their congressional copartisans than autonomous agenda control. Divided government, by contrast, will yield a stronger foundation for veto leverage to fight off the contested agenda. Split control of Congress in 2001–2002 places Pres. George W. Bush in an uneasy set of circumstances that reflects a closely divided electorate.

Shifting the paradigm of presidential power from the conditional influence of the postreform/party-unity era back to stronger positive leverage will require an electoral legitimization of future presidents' agendas and a strong working majority on Capitol Hill. The essential problem for presidents may be that institutional partisanship has outpaced partisanship in the electorate. As party government in Congress grows stronger and partisan attachment among voters remains comparatively weak, "the mixing of these contrary movements of party at the different organizational levels plays havoc with the president's legislative goals, especially when party control of the national government is divided."[7] Notwithstanding a major partisan realignment of the electorate that enables one or the other party to gain a dominant position at both ends of Pennsylvania Avenue, current circumstances of divided government suggest the persistence of "low opportunity" presidents in the legislative sphere.[8]

Forging Ahead: Future Research on Divided Government

Divided government is *not* irrelevant to American chief executives. This research has emphasized that scholars must adopt a multifaceted perspective on the effects of party control of national institutions. Much work remains to be done beyond this book's focus on the legislative presidency in the domestic policy realm. Promising avenues of inquiry include the application of political time to other facets of institutional politics.

One area of research that deserves more careful consideration is the effect of party control on executive-legislative dynamics on foreign policy issues across time. There has been a growing consensus that partisan cleavages have spilled over to politics beyond the water's edge. The long-term impact of the

Vietnam War experience and the new issues that have emerged with the ending of the Cold War have diminished traditionally greater congressional deference to the president in the realm of foreign affairs, eroding the basis for Wildavsky's "two presidencies thesis."[9] Presidents can no longer expect to prevail in Congress more often on foreign policy compared to domestic policy. When the pre- and post-Vietnam periods are compared, there has been a significant decline in congressional support for presidents' foreign policy stands.[10]

Roughly one-sixth of all the laws Mayhew counts from 1947–96 pertain to foreign policy. An explicit focus on significant foreign policy legislation across time might show considerable variation in presidential leadership—but with different explanations driving such variation compared to this book's focus on domestic policy. Drawing distinctions between types of foreign policy matters (treaties, military force, trade, humanitarian assistance, peacekeeping) and the role of presidential leadership could help clarify to what degree the "two presidencies" has actually declined, and in what form the phenomenon may still persist. Perhaps presidents were more capable of independent policy successes in the sphere of treaties and disarmament during the Cold War. In the post–Cold War environment, the shift toward globalization and trade politics may have narrowed the basis for presidential autonomy as the line between domestic and foreign policies has become blurred.[11] How presidents like Clinton have managed continuing foreign policy agendas in Congress such as NAFTA and the GATT also deserves closer scrutiny.

The impact of party control on extraelectoral and interinstitutional combat also merits closer analysis. Some scholars have argued that President Clinton's impeachment was the culmination of a trend toward continuous institutionalized strife between the parties. Divided government and intense partisan conflict in the last quarter century may have prompted the parties to engage more frequently in "politics by other means."[12] Indeed, Mayhew's focus on the *number* of congressional investigations of the executive branch may fail to convey *qualitative changes* in the motives for such investigations and the tenor of those investigations over time.[13] Attention to congressional oversight of the executive branch, the use of special prosecutors, and indictments and convictions of officials might suggest a far greater effect of divided party control now compared to prior eras.

Finally, scholars should be encouraged to theorize about executive-legislative relations and divided government from a comparative perspective. A focus on divided government in the states and the impact on gubernatorial legislative leadership is one possibility.[14] Another is to look beyond the United

States to other presidential or mixed systems. The proportional electoral systems of various Western European countries have often produced parliamentary arrangements in which the executive's party does not possess a majority in the legislature. Coalition governments may be conceptualized as a form of divided government.[15]

The American case of divided government is often perceived as unique because of the constitutional separation of powers. Yet the French Fifth Republic has a separated institutional structure with important similarities to the United States—including independent elections of the president and legislators and several experiences with divided government in recent decades. French presidents' strategic adaptation to *cohabitation* or split-party control of the presidency and legislature under both Socialist president François Mitterand and center-right president Jacques Chirac would seem a fruitful point of departure.[16] Perhaps French presidents who have confronted divided government have been able to divert their efforts to foreign affairs in a way American presidents have not in the post–Cold War era. The French constitution gives presidents a decisively preponderant role in foreign affairs, and both Mitterand and Chirac played instrumental roles in the development of the political and economic institutions of the European Union.

Divided government will continue to be a legitimate and probable electoral outcome in America's separated system. Some have proposed "sorting out" presidential functions to improve governance.[17] Others have gone farther by suggesting that constitutional change preclude the occurrence of split-party control.[18] Yet the perspective of political time emphasizes that the resilience of the first and second branches of our national government must not be underestimated. Congress and the presidency are remarkably able to adapt to changing policy-making contexts and shifts in the balance of influence and power between the branches. "Our Constitution is so simple and practical," Franklin Roosevelt noted, "that it is possible always to meet extraordinary needs by changes in emphasis and arrangement without loss of essential form."[19]

The story of divided government and presidential leverage in the last half of the twentieth century bears out such wisdom. Recognizing how future presidents may be compelled to negotiate with Congress, and the moderate type of policy success to which they are able to lay claim, is a critical step in grasping both the limits and the opportunities of the legislative presidency at the turn of the new century. Surely this is a prerequisite for any meaningful dialogue on electoral and institutional reform.

Mayhew's Significant Domestic Laws

80th Congress (Truman)   223

Taft–Hartley Labor-Management Relations Act, 1947
Portal-to-Portal Act, 1947
Twenty-second Amendment (limits president to two terms)
Federal Insecticide, Fungicide, and Rodenticide Act, 1947
Income tax cut, 1948
Water Pollution Control Act, 1948
Hope–Aiken Agricultural Act, 1948

81st Congress (Truman)

Housing Act, 1949
Minimum wage increase, 1949
Agricultural Act, 1949
Social Security expansion, 1950
National Science Foundation Act, 1950
McCarran Internal Security Act, 1950
Tax increase, 1950
Excess Profits Tax, 1950

82d Congress (Truman)

Tax increase, 1951
Social Security increase, 1952
McCarran–Walter Immigration and Nationality Act, 1952

83d Congress (Eisenhower)

Tidelands Oil Act, 1953
Tax schedule revision, 1954
Social Security expansion, 1954
Saint Lawrence Seaway approved 1954

Communist Control Act, 1954
Atomic Energy Act, 1954
Agricultural Act, 1954
Housing Act, 1954

84TH CONGRESS (EISENHOWER)

Minimum wage increase, 1955
Agricultural Act, 1956
Federal Aid for Highways Act, 1956
Upper Colorado River Project authorized, 1956

85TH CONGRESS (EISENHOWER)

Civil Rights Act, 1957
Price–Anderson Nuclear Industry Indemnity Act, 1957
Alaska Statehood, 1958
National Aeronautics and Space Administration Act, 1958
National Defense Education Act, 1958
Agricultural Act, 1958
Social Security increase, 1958
Transportation Act, 1958
Food Additives Act amendments, 1958

86TH CONGRESS (EISENHOWER)

Landrum–Griffin Labor Reform Act, 1959
Housing Act, 1959
Hawaii Statehood, 1959
Civil Rights Act, 1960
Kerr–Mills Aid for the Medically Needy Aged Act, 1960

87TH CONGRESS (KENNEDY)

Housing Act, 1961
Minimum wage increase, 1961
Social Security increase, 1961
Area Redevelopment Act, 1961
Agricultural Act, 1961
Manpower Development and Training Act, 1962
Communications Satellite Act, 1962
Drug Regulation

Revenue Act of 1962
Public Welfare Act amendments, 1962

88TH CONGRESS (KENNEDY/JOHNSON)

Higher Education Facilities Act, 1963
Aid for the Mentally Ill and Retarded
Aid to Medical Schools
Clean Air Act, 1963
Equal Pay Act, 1963
Civil Rights Act, 1964
Economic Opportunity Act, 1964
Tax cut, 1964
Urban Mass Transportation Act, 1964
Wilderness Act, 1964
Cotton and Wheat Commodities Programs, 1964

89TH CONGRESS (JOHNSON)

Medical care for the aged, 1965
Voting Rights Act, 1965
Elementary and Secondary Education Act, 1965
Department of Housing and Urban Development established, 1965
Appalachian Regional Development Act, 1965
Regional Medical Centers for Heart Disease, Cancer, and Stroke established, 1965
Highway Beautification Act, 1965
Immigration reform, 1965
National Foundation of the Arts and Humanities established, 1965
Higher Education Act, 1965
Housing and Urban Development Act, 1965
Excise Tax Reduction Act, 1965
Motor Vehicle Air Pollution Control Act, 1965
Water Quality Act, 1965
Food and Agriculture Act, 1965
Department of Transportation established, 1966
Clean Waters Restoration Act, 1966
Air pollution control, 1966
Traffic Safety Act, 1966
Fair Packaging and Labeling Act, 1966

Minimum wage increase, 1966
Demonstration cities program, 1966

90TH CONGRESS (JOHNSON)

Social Security increase, 1967
Public Broadcasting Act, 1967
Air Quality Act, 1967
Wholesome Meat Act, 1967
Age Discrimination Act, 1967
Open Housing Act, 1968
Housing and Urban Development Act, 1968
Gun Control Act, 1968
Omnibus Crime Control and Safe Streets Act, 1968
Income tax surcharge, 1968
Central Arizona Project authorized, 1968
National scenic trails system established, 1968
National Gas Pipeline Safety Act, 1968
Wholesome Poultry Products Act, 1968
Truth-in-Lending Act, 1968

91ST CONGRESS (NIXON)

Coal Mine Safety Act, 1969
Social Security increase, 1969
Tax Reform Act, 1969
National Environmental Policy Act, 1969
Organized Crime Control Act, 1970
Postal Reorganization Act, 1970
Voting Rights Act extension, 1970
Clean Air Act, 1970
Water Quality Improvement Act, 1970
Cigarette advertising on radio and television banned, 1970
Occupational Safety and Health Act, 1970
Rail Passenger Service Act, 1970
Omnibus Crime Control Act, 1970
Narcotics Control Act, 1970
Agricultural Act, 1970
Airport and Airway Development Act, 1970
Urban Mass Transportation Assistance Act, 1970
Economic Stabilization Act, 1970

Food Stamps Program expanded, 1970
Unemployment compensation expanded, 1970

92D CONGRESS (NIXON)

Social Security increase, 1971
Tax reduction, 1971
National Cancer Act, 1971
Emergency Employment Act, 1971
Twenty-sixth Amendment (voting age lowered to eighteen), 1971
Federal Election Campaign Act, 1972
Water Pollution Control Act, 1972
State and Local Fiscal Assistance Act, 1972
Social Security increase
Equal Rights Amendment to the Constitution, 1972
Pesticide Control Act, 1972
Consumer Product Safety Act, 1972
Equal Employment Opportunity Act, 1972
Supplemental Security Income program approved, 1972
Higher Education Act, 1972

93D CONGRESS (NIXON/FORD)

Federal Aid Highway Act, 1973
Agricultural and Consumer Protection Act, 1973
Comprehensive Employment and Training Act, 1973
Social Security increase, 1973
District of Columbia home rule, 1973
Trans-Alaskan oil pipeline, 1973
Regional Rail Reorganization Act, 1973
Aid for development of Health Maintenance Organizations, 1973
Emergency Petroleum Allocation Act, 1973
Employment Retirement Income Security Act, 1974
Federal Election Campaign Act, 1974
Minimum wage increase, 1974
Congressional Budget and Impoundment Control Act, 1974
Freedom of Information Act amendments, 1974
Nuclear Regulatory Commission and Energy Research and Development
    Administration established, 1974.
Magnuson–Moss Product Warranty Act, 1974
National Health Planning and Resources Development Act, 1974

National Mass Transportation Assistance Act, 1974
Housing and Community Development Act, 1974

94TH CONGRESS (FORD)

Energy Policy and Conservation Act, 1975
Voting Rights Act extension, 1975
New York City bailout, 1975
Repeal of fair-trade laws, 1975
Tax Reduction Act, 1975
Securities Act amendments, 1975
Unemployment compensation overhaul, 1976
Copyright law revision, 1976
Toxic Substances Control Act, 1976.
Tax Reform Act, 1976
Railroad Vitalization and Regulatory Reform Act, 1976
National Forest Management Act, 1976
Federal Land Policy and Management Act, 1976
Resource Conservation and Recovery Act, 1976

95TH CONGRESS (CARTER)

Social Security tax increase, 1977
Tax cut, 1977
Minimum wage hike, 1977
Surface Mining Control and Reclamation Act, 1977
Food and Agriculture Act, 1977
Clean Water Act, 1977
Clean Air Act amendments, 1977
Tax revision, 1978
Comprehensive energy package, 1978
Civil Service Reform Act, 1978
Airline deregulation, 1978

96TH CONGRESS (CARTER)

Chrysler Corporation bailout, 1979
Department of Education, 1979
Depository Institutions and Monetary Control Act, 1980
Trucking deregulation, 1980
Staggers Rail Act, 1980
Windfall profits tax on oil, 1980

Synthetic fuels program, 1980
Alaska lands preservation, 1980
Toxic waste Superfund, 1980

97TH CONGRESS (REAGAN)

Economic Recovery Tax Act, 1981
Omnibus Budget Reconciliation Act, 1981
Agricultural and Food Act, 1982
Transportation Assistance Act, 1982
Tax Equity and Fiscal Responsibility Act, 1982
Voting Rights Act extension, 1982
Nuclear Waste Repository Act, 1982
Garn–St. Germain Depository Institutions Act, 1982
Job Training Partnership Act, 1982

98TH CONGRESS (REAGAN)

Martin Luther King's birthday declared a legal holiday, 1983
Social Security Act amendments, 1983
Antirecession jobs measure, 1983
Anticrime package, 1984
Deficit reduction measure, 1984
Cable Communications Policy Act, 1984

99TH CONGRESS (REAGAN)

Balanced Budget and Emergency Deficit Control Act, 1985
Food Security Act, 1985
Tax Reform Act, 1986
Immigration Reform and Control Act, 1986
Antinarcotics measure, 1986
Cleanup of toxic waste dumps
Omnibus Water Projects Act, 1986

100TH CONGRESS (REAGAN)

Water Quality Act, 1987
Surface Transportation Act, 1987
Balanced Budget and Emergency Deficit Control Reaffirmation Act, 1987
Housing and Community Development Act, 1987
McKinney Homeless Assistance Act, 1987
Catastrophic Health Insurance for the Aged Act, 1988

Family Support Act, 1988
Antidrug-abuse act, 1988
Civil Rights Restoration Act, 1988
Japanese–American reparations, 1988

101ST CONGRESS (BUSH)

Minimum wage hike, 1989
Savings-and-loan bailout, 1989
Deficit Reduction Act, 1990
Americans with Disabilities Act, 1990
Clean Air Act, 1990
Child care package, 1990
Immigration Act, 1990
National Affordable Housing Act, 1990
Agriculture Act, 1990

102D CONGRESS (BUSH)

Surface Transportation Act
Civil Rights Act
Omnibus Energy Act
Regulation of cable television rates
California water policy reform

103D CONGRESS (CLINTON)

Omnibus Deficit Reduction Act
Family and Medical Leave Act
Motor Voter Act
National Service Act (Americorps)
Reform of college-student loan financing
Brady Bill
Goals 2000 (education)
Omnibus Crime Act
California Desert Protection Act

104TH CONGRESS (CLINTON)

Curb on unfunded mandates
Congressional Accountability Act, 1995
Levin–Cohen Lobbying Reform Act, 1995
Antiterrorism Act, 1995

Curb on stockholder lawsuits
Welfare Reform Act, 1996
Agriculture deregulation
Line-Item Veto Act, 1996
$24 billion in spending cuts for fiscal 1996
Kassebaum–Kennedy Health Insurance Portability and Accountability
    Act, 1996
Illegal Immigration Reform and Immigrant Responsibility Act, 1996
Minimum wage increase
Overhaul of pesticide regulation legislation
Overhaul of safe drinking water regulation legislation

Modeling Congressional
Support for the President

The case studies in chapters 2–7 examine patterns of coalitional support for each president by party. The variables stressed in the individual-level model are closely related to the aggregate analysis of presidential floor success in chapter 1, but tap elements of presidential influence in Congress impossible to measure with aggregate data. The model of legislative support follows Edwards's rationale that "To investigate most theoretically significant questions about presidential success in Congress it is best to begin with data at the individual level. These are more suited to explanation than aggregate measures."[1] The model gauges the impact of the president's electoral resources, popular approval, incumbency advantage and leadership support in Congress, and ideology on members' decisions to support the president's policy stands. The objective is to explicate the factors subtending presidents' ability to craft partisan and cross-party support in Congress and extend the time-series analysis presented in chapter 1.

The dependent variable in the models is whether the legislator supported the president's expressed position on floor votes (coded one) or voted in opposition to the president's stand (coded zero). The annual single-issue votes used in chapter 1 were divided between *close* and *nonclose* votes to gauge the impact of electoral and institutional factors on legislators' voting decisions. Close or controversial votes were determined by a margin of 10 percent or less of all members voting. The outcomes of nonclose or less controversial votes were determined by a margin of between 11 percent and 89 percent. Lopsided votes on which more than 90 percent of the chamber voted together were purged from the analysis. Legislators' positions on the roll-call votes were pooled by party, yielding a total of 435 cases for each vote (assuming all House members voted).

Since the dependent variable is dichotomous, the most appropriate method to test the impact of the explanatory variables is logistic regression. The change in the likelihood of supporting the president is a probability function of the independent variables, and *not* a linear function as in ordinary least-squares regression.[2] Accordingly, the effect of each variable in the logistic regression equation cannot be interpreted directly from the coefficient. Instead, the "mean" or "first order" effect for each variable was calculated to evaluate its impact relative to the other variables. The mean effect reflects the change or difference in the predicted probability of support when the maximum and minimum values of the variable of interest are taken, holding all other variables constant at their mean or "natural" value.[3]

The rationales for the explanatory variables in the model coincide with the discussion of the time-series models in chapter 1. They are as follows:

Presidential electoral popularity. The president's electoral popularity is measured as the percent margin of victory over (coded plus), or loss to (coded minus), the opposing presidential candidate in the legislator's district. The impact of the president's electoral popularity should be strongest in the first two years of his term, matter most on controversial (close) votes, and have the greatest effect among his copartisans. The impact of presidential electoral popularity should be greatest in the bipartisan conservative and early liberal activist periods when coattails were more prevalent.

Legislators' seat safety and *terms served.* Legislators' own victory margins and the number of terms they have served in Congress are indicators of incumbency advantage. Seat safety is measured as the members' margin of victory percentage over their opponents in the last congressional race. The number of terms served was taken from the *Congressional Directory.* Both variables should be negatively related to support of the president among members of the opposition majority under divided control. Incumbency advantage gives members of the opposition little reason to shirk the party line when the president takes positions against legislation favored by the majority party's leadership. High levels of seat safety should also negatively affect the president's task of building support for controversial legislation in his own party under unified control. Incumbency advantage curbs members' fear of electoral retaliation for failing to support the president's policy stands.

Leadership. Dummy variables for committee chairs and ranking committee members are employed alongside a scaled measure for party leaders. The leadership variable was coded four for majority/minority leaders, three for majority/minority whips, two for conference leaders, and one for deputy/regional whips. The Speaker was excluded since he rarely casts floor votes. Obviously, party leadership organizations were less developed in the bipartisan conservative era.[4] The effect of the leadership variables should be most pronounced in the liberal activist and postreform/party-unity eras following organizational changes in Congress and the expansion of the whip system. Leadership support from the president's copartisans was strongest under unified *and* divided government in the liberal activist and postre-form/party-unity eras. Since the 1980s, party leaders faced with divided government have been far less inclined to support presidents as opposition majorities have come to set more of the agenda.

Legislators' ideology. DW-NOMINATE scores were used to calculate members' ideological placement above or below the party median. Members with scores higher than the party median are more conservative; members with scores lower than the party median are more liberal. This measure conveys critical information about the relative consistency of legislative support presidents have drawn from ideological factions within each party. Ideology should play a diminished role under divided government in the bipartisan conservative and liberal activist periods with Republicans in the White House. Polarization around the president's stands should be far more visible in the postreform/party-unity era of divided government (see fig. 1.2).

President's job approval. The president's monthly job approval measure is included in the model using the Gallup Poll's measure as close to the time of the vote as possible. The president's public approval may have a greater bearing on less controversial votes. Members may not feel the same levels of constituency pressure as for close votes and may turn to the president's job approval as a voting cue. Public approval should matter less on controversial votes. A *negative* relationship between the president's approval and legislative support may be anticipated for members of the opposition party.[5] With a stronger constituency basis to legislators' voting in the last two decades, members of the opposition are far more likely to eschew consideration of the president's standing in the polls and turn to district-level electoral and constituency cues for their voting decisions—particularly as the party leadership has set more of the agenda.

PRESIDENTIAL POSITION VOTES, 80TH HOUSE

BILL NO.	DATE	YEAS	NAYS	237
HR 2102	March 4, 1947	243	110	
HJ RES 146	March 21, 1947	287	54	
HR 3203	May 1, 1947	205	182	
HR 3601	May 28, 1947	315	38	
HR 1	June 2, 1947	220	99	
HR 2030	June 4, 1947	320	79	
HR 49	June 30, 1947	195	133	
HR 3950	July 8, 1947	302	112	
HR 3813	July 15, 1947	289	102	
HR 1639	July 17, 1947	203	188	
HR 29	July 21, 1947	290	112	
SJ RES 167	December 19, 1947	282	73	
HR 4790	February 2, 1948	297	120	
HJ RES 296	February 28, 1948	275	52	
S 2182	March 16, 1948	251	132	
HR 221	May 11, 1948	271	53	
HR 6396	June 11, 1948	289	91	
HR 6959	June 18, 1948	318	90	
SJ RES 157	August 5, 1948	264	97	

Notes

Introduction

1. Paul J. Quirk and Bruce Nesmith, "Divided Government and Policy Making: Negotiating the Laws," in *The Presidency and the Political System,* ed. Michael Nelson, 533.

2. Morris Fiorina, *Divided Government;* Gary C. Jacobson, *The Electoral Origins of Divided Government: Competition in U.S. House Elections, 1946–1988;* John R. Petrocik, "Divided Government: Is It All In The Campaigns?" In *The Politics of Divided Government,* ed. Gary W. Cox and Samuel Kernell; Sarah Binder, "The Dynamics of Legislative Gridlock, 1947–96," *American Political Science Review* 93 (1999): 519–34; John J. Coleman, "Unified Government, Divided Government, and Party Responsiveness," *American Political Science Review* 93 (1999): 821–36; Roger H. Davidson, "Invitation to Struggle: An Overview of Legislative-Executive Relations," *Annals of the American Academy of Political and Social Science* 499 (1988): 9–21; Sean Q. Kelly, "Divided We Govern? A Reassessment," *Polity* 25 (1993): 475–84; Keith Krehbiel, *Pivotal Politics: A Theory of U.S. Lawmaking;* David R. Mayhew, *Divided We Govern: Party Control, Lawmaking, and Investigations 1946–1990.*

3. Paul C. Light, *The President's Agenda: Domestic Policy Choice from Kennedy to Clinton;* Steven A. Shull, ed., *The Two Presidencies: A Quarter Century Assessment;* Aaron Wildavsky, "The Two Presidencies," in *Perspectives on the Presidency,* ed. idem.

4. David W. Rohde, *Parties and Leaders in the Postreform House.*

5. Barbara Sinclair, "The Emergence of Strong Leadership in the 1980s House of Representatives," *Journal of Politics* 54 (1992): 657–84; idem., "Hostile Partners: The President, Congress, and Lawmaking in the Partisan 1990s," in *Polarized Politics: Congress and the President in a Partisan Era,* ed. Jon R. Bond and Richard Fleisher.

6. Mayhew, *Divided We Govern,* 35.

7. Mark A. Peterson, *Legislating Together: The White House and Capitol Hill from Eisenhower to Reagan.*

8. Terry M. Moe, "The Politicized Presidency," in *The New Direction in American Politics,* ed. John E. Chubb and Paul E. Peterson.

9. Clinton Rossiter, *The American Presidency.*

10. William E. Leuchtenburg, *In the Shadow of FDR: From Harry Truman to Bill Clinton.*

11. James Pfiffner, "Divided Government and the Problem of Governance," in *Divided Democracy: Cooperation and Conflict Between the President and Congress,* ed. James A. Thurber, 49.

12. Charles Cameron, *Veto Bargaining: Presidents and the Politics of Negative Power;* George C. Edwards III, Andrew Barrett, and Jeffrey Peake, "The Legislative Impact of Divided Government," *American Journal of Political Science* 41 (1997): 545–63; Richard A. Watson, *Presidential Vetoes and Public Policy.*

13. James L. Sundquist, "Needed: A Political Theory for the New Era of Coalition Government in the United States," *Political Science Quarterly* 10 (1988): 613–35; Gary W. Cox and Samuel Kernell, eds., *The Politics of Divided Government,* 4–8.

14. John B. Gilmour, *Strategic Disagreement: Stalemate in American Politics.*

15. Sundquist, "Needed"; Lloyd N. Cutler, "To Form a Government," *Foreign Affairs* 59 (1988): 126–43.

16. Davidson, "Invitation to Struggle," 21.

17. Binder "Dynamics of Legislative Gridlock"; Coleman, "Unified Government"; Gregory R. Thorson, "Divided Government and the Passage of Partisan Legislation, 1947–1990," *Political Research Quarterly* 51 (1998): 751–64.

18. Charles O. Jones, *The Presidency in a Separated System*. Washington, D.C.: Brookings Institution, 1994.

19. Stephen Skowronek, *The Politics Presidents Make: Leadership from John Adams to George Bush*.

20. David A. Crockett, "The President as Opposition Leader," *Presidential Studies Quarterly* 30 (2000): 245–74; Lawrence C. Dodd, "A Theory of Congressional Cycles: Solving the Puzzle," in *Congress and Policy Change*, ed. Gerald C. Wright Jr., Leroy N. Rieselbach, and Lawrence C. Dodd; Jean R. Schroedel, *Congress, the President, and Policymaking: A Historical Analysis;* Skowronek, *Politics Presidents Make;* Jeffrey K. Tulis, *The Rhetorical Presidency*.

21. Kenneth E. Collier, *Between the Branches: The White House Office of Legislative Affairs;* Charles O. Jones, *Passages to the Presidency: From Campaigning to Governing;* James P. Pfiffner, *The Strategic Presidency: Hitting the Ground Running*.

22. Richard Neustadt, *Presidential Power and the Modern Presidents*.

23. Barbara Sinclair, "Studying Presidential Leadership," in *Researching the Presidency: Vital Questions, New Approaches*, ed. George C. Edwards III, John H. Kessel, and Bert A. Rockman. Sinclair posits that the budget deficits of the 1980s created greater competition for agenda space and precluded the type of individual policy entrepreneurship that Democrats had been able to exercise in the 1970s. In light of a more ideologically homogenous membership, rank-and-file members gave leaders the necessary procedural tools to ensure favorable outcomes. Leaders sought to ward off floor challenges to legislation by the Republican minority.

24. See Terry M. Moe, "Presidents, Institutions, and Theory," in *Researching the Presidency*, ed. Edwards, Kessel, and Rockman.

25. Light, *President's Agenda*.

26. Samuel Kernell, *Going Public: New Strategies of Presidential Leadership*.

27. Richard Born, "Reassessing the Decline of Presidential Coattails: U.S. House Elections from 1952–80," *Journal of Politics* 46 (1984): 60–79.

28. Harold W. Stanley and Richard G. Niemi, *Vital Statistics on American Politics, 1999–2000*.

29. Light, *President's Agenda*.

30. Paul Brace and Barbara Hinckley, *Follow the Leader: Opinion Polls and the Modern Presidents*.

31. Charles Press, "Presidential Coattails and Party Cohesion," *Midwest Journal of Political Science* 7 (1963): 320–35.

32. James E. Campbell and Joe A. Sumners, "Presidential Coattails in Senate Elections," *American Political Science Review* 84 (1990): 521.

33. George C. Edwards III, "Presidential Influence in the House: Presidential Prestige as a Source of Presidential Power," *American Political Science Review* 70 (1976): 104–106.

34. Richard F. Fenno, *Home Style: House Members in Their Districts*.

35. Light, *President's Agenda*, 28.

36. Alan I. Abramowitz, "Incumbency, Campaign Spending, and the Decline of Competition in U.S. House Elections," *Journal of Politics* 53 (1991): 34–56; John R. Alford and John R. Hibbing, "Increased Incumbency Advantage in the House," *Journal of Politics* 43 (1981): 1042–61; Barbara Hinckley, "Incumbency and the Presidential Vote in Senate Elections: Defining Parameters of Subpresidential Voting," *American Political Science Review* 64 (1970): 836–42; Gary C. Jacobson, "The Marginals Never Vanished: Incumbency and Competition in Elections to the U.S. House of Representatives, 1952–1982," *American Journal of Political Science* 31 (1987): 126–41.

37. Stanley and Niemi, *Vital Statistics*.

38. Fiorina, *Divided Government*.

39. Walter Dean Burnham, "American Politics in the 1970s: Beyond Party?" In *The American Party Systems: Stages of Political Development*, ed. William Nisbet Chambers and idem.; Randall L. Calvert and John A. Ferejohn, "Coattail Voting in Recent Presidential Elections," *American Political Science Review* 77 (1983): 407–19; James E. Campbell, "Predicting Seat Gains from Presidential Coattails," *American Journal of Political Science* 30 (1986): 165–83; George C. Edwards III, "The Impact of Presidential Coattails on Outcomes of Congressional Elections," *American Politics Quarterly* 7 (1979): 94–108.

40. On theories of voters' attempts to "balance" the parties, see Fiorina, *Divided Government;* Jacobson, *Electoral Origins of Divided Government;* Paul Frymer, Thomas P. Kim, and Terri L. Bimes, "Party Elites, Ideological Voters, and Divided Party Government," *Legislative Studies Quarterly* 22 (1997): 195–216; Paul Frymer, "Ideological Consensus within Divided Government," *Political Science Quarterly* 109 (1994): 287–311.

   On dealignment and split-ticket voting, see Walter Dean Burnham, *Critical Elections and the Mainsprings of American Politics;* Russell J. Dalton and Martin P. Wattenberg, "The Not So Simple Act of Voting," in *Political Science: The State of the Discipline II*, ed. Ada W. Finifter; Sean Q. Kelly, "Punctuated Change and the Era of Divided Government," in *New Perspectives on American Politics*, ed. Lawrence C. Dodd and Calvin Jillson; Everett C. Ladd, "Like Waiting for Godot: The Uselessness of 'Realignment' for Understanding Change in Contemporary American Politics," in *The End of Realignment? Interpreting American Electoral Eras*, ed. Byron E. Shafer; John R. Petrocik and Joseph Doherty, "The Road to Divided Government: Paved without Intention," in *Divided Government*, ed. Peter F. Galderisi; Martin P. Wattenberg, *The Decline of American Political Parties, 1952–1996*.

   On this rise of candidate-centered campaigns and media-centered politics see John H. Aldrich, "Presidential Campaigns in Party- and Candidate-Centered Eras," in *Under the Watchful Eye: Managing Presidential Campaigns in the Television Era*, ed. Matthew D. McCubbins; Everett C. Ladd, "1996 Vote: The 'No Majority' Realignment Continues," *Political Science Quarterly* 112 (1997): 1–28; Nelson W. Polsby and Aaron B. Wildavsky, *Presidential Elections: Strategies and Structures of American Politics;* Matthew D. McCubbins, "Party Decline and Presidential Campaigns in the Television Age," in *Under the Watchful Eye: Managing Presidential Campaigns in the Television Era*, ed. idem.; Barbara G. and Stephen A. Salmore, *Candidates, Parties, and Campaigns: Electoral Politics in America;* Kathryn Dunn Tenpas, *Presidents as Candidates: Inside the White House for the Presidential Campaign*, 188–93.

41. Gary C. Jacobson, "Party Polarization in National Politics: The Electoral Connection," in *Polarized Politics*, ed. Bond and Fleisher.

42. Paul J. Quirk, "What Do We Know and How Do We Know It? Research on the Presidency," in *Political Science: Looking to the Future*, vol. 4, *American Institutions*, ed. William J. Crotty, 47.

43. Duane M. Oldfield and Aaron B. Wildavsky, "Reconsidering the Two Presidencies," *Society* 26 (1989): 54–59.

44. Richard Fleisher and Jon R. Bond, "Congress and the President in a Partisan Era," in *Polarized Politics*, ed. idem.

45. Nelson Polsby, Miriam Gallagher, and Barry Spencer Rundquist, "The Growth of the Seniority System in the U.S. House of Representatives," *American Political Science Review* 63 (1969): 787–807.

46. Melissa P. Collie, "Universalism and the Parties in the U.S. House: 1921–80," *American Journal of Political Science* 32 (1988): 865–83; Barry R. Weingast, "A Rational Choice Perspective on Congressional Norms," *American Journal of Political Science* 23 (1979): 245–62.

47. James MacGregor Burns, *The Deadlock of Democracy: Four-Party Politics in America*. See also Jon R. Bond and Richard Fleisher, *The President in the Legislative Arena*. Bond and Fleisher call these moderate legislators "cross-pressured" because their ideological positions are closer to the median of the other party than to their own party.

48. James T. Patterson, *Congressional Conservatism and the New Deal: The Growth of the Conservative Coalition in Congress, 1933–1939;* Mack C. Shelley III, *The Permanent Majority: The Conservative Coalition in the United States Congress.*

49. See Robert D. Loevy, "The Presidency and Domestic Policy: The Civil Rights Act of 1964," in *Understanding the Presidency,* ed. James P. Pfiffner and Roger H. Davidson.

50. Fred I. Greenstein, *The Hidden-Hand Presidency: Eisenhower as Leader.*

51. Mayhew, *Divided We Govern,* 121.

52. Lawrence C. Dodd and Bruce I. Oppenheimer, "The House in Transition," in *Congress Reconsidered,* ed. idem., 29.

53. Rohde, *Parties and Leaders,* 20–23; Fiona M. Wright, "The Caucus Reelection Requirement and the Transformation of House Committee Chairs, 1959–94," *Legislative Studies Quarterly* 15 (2000): 469–80.

54. Lawrence C. Dodd, "The Expanded Roles of the House Democratic Whip System: The 93d and 94th Congresses," *Congressional Studies* 7 (1979): 32.

55. James L. Sundquist, *The Decline and Resurgence of Congress,* 387.

56. Robert L. Peabody, "House Party Leadership: Stability and Change," in *Congress Reconsidered,* ed. Dodd and Oppenheimer, 258.

57. Sinclair, "Emergence of Strong Leadership."

58. Rohde, *Parties and Leaders,* 83–118.

59. Roger H. Davidson, Walter J. Oleszek, and Thomas Kephart, "One Bill, Many Committees: Multiple Referrals in the U.S. House of Representatives," *Legislative Studies Quarterly* 13 (1988): 3–28.

60. Paul S. Herrnson and Kelly D. Patterson, "Toward a More Programmatic Democratic Party? Agenda-Setting and Coalition Building in the House of Representatives," *Polity* 27 (1995): 607–28.

61. Joseph Cooper and David W. Brady, "Institutional Context and Leadership Style: The House from Cannon to Rayburn," *American Political Science Review* 75 (1981): 415.

62. Keith T. Poole and Howard Rosenthal, "The Polarization of American Politics," *Journal of Politics* 46 (1984): 1061–79.

63. Charles S. Bullock and David W. Brady, "Party, Constituency, and Roll-Call Voting in the U.S. Senate," *Legislative Studies Quarterly* 8 (1983): 29–43; Robert S. Erikson, "Roll Calls, Reputations, and Representation in the U.S. Senate," *Legislative Studies Quarterly* 15 (1990): 623–42.

64. Rohde, *Parties and Leaders;* Barbara Sinclair, "House Majority Party Leadership in an Era of Legislative Constraint," in *The Postreform Congress,* ed. Roger H. Davidson.

65. Charles S. Bullock, "The Impact of Changing the Racial Composition of Congressional Districts on Legislators' Roll Call Behavior," *American Politics Quarterly* 23 (1995): 141–58.

66. Gary W. Cox and Matthew D. McCubbins, "Bonding, Structure, and the Stability of Political Parties: Party Government in the House," *Legislative Studies Quarterly* 19 (1994): 215–31.

67. Barbara Sinclair, "Trying to Govern Positively in a Negative Era: Clinton and the 103d Congress," in *The Clinton Presidency: First Appraisals,* ed. Colin Campbell, S.J., and Bert A. Rockman, 113.

68. William W. Lammers and Michael A. Genovese, *The Presidency and Domestic Policy: Comparing Leadership Styles, FDR to Clinton.*

69. George C. Edwards III, *At the Margins: Presidential Leadership of Congress.*

70. This term is borrowed from Lyn Ragsdale, *Vital Statistics on the Presidency: Washington to Clinton.*

71. Bond and Fleisher, *President in the Legislative Arena,* 670–78.

72. A focus exclusively on the development and fortune of the president's agenda is less useful to comprehending the impact of party control on the legislative presidency. On position taking, see

Cary R. Covington, J. Mark Wrighton, and Rhonda Kinney, "A 'Presidency-Augmented' Model of Presidential Success on House Roll Call Votes," *American Journal of Political Science* 39 (1995): 1001–24; George C. Edwards III and Andrew Barrett, "Presidential Agenda Setting in Congress," in *Polarized Politics*, ed. Bond and Fleisher; Jones, *Presidency in a Separated System;* Peterson, *Legislating Together;* Wayne P. Steger, "Presidential Policy Initiation and the Politics of Agenda Control," *Congress and the Presidency* 24 (1997): 17–36; Stephen J. Wayne, *The Legislative Presidency.*

On cue giving by the president, see Aage R. Clausen, *How Congressmen Decide: A Policy Focus;* Donald R. Matthews and James A. Stimson, *Yeas and Nays: Normal Decision-Making in the U.S. House of Representatives;* John L. Sullivan, L. Earl Shaw, Gregory E. McAvoy, and David G. Barnum, "The Dimensions of Cue-Taking in the House of Representatives: Variation by Issue Area," *Journal of Politics* 55 (1993): 975–97.

73. Thomas E. Cronin and Michael A. Genovese, *Paradoxes of the American Presidency,* 179.

74. Barbara Sinclair, *Legislators, Leaders, and Lawmaking: The U.S. House of Representatives in the Postreform Era;* R. Douglas Arnold, *The Logic of Congressional Action,* 99–108; Randall B. Ripley, *Majority Party Leadership in Congress.*

75. Dodd, "Expanded Roles"; Richard S. Conley, "Presidential Influence and Minority Party Liaison on Veto Overrides: New Evidence from the Ford Presidency," *American Politics Research* 30 (2002): 34–65.

76. Collier, *Between the Branches;* Eric L. Davis, "Congressional Liaison: The People and the Institutions," in *Both Ends of the Avenue: The Presidency, the Executive Branch, and Congress in the 1980s,* ed. Anthony King.

77. Only one vote per year per discrete issue on which the president took a stand was included in the data set to measure presidential floor success. Where possible, *Congressional Quarterly*'s "key vote" was included. Key votes are an appropriate measure of conflictual and important votes in Congress. See Steven A. Shull and James Vanderleeuw, "What Do Key Votes Measure?" *Legislative Studies Quarterly* 12 (1987): 573–82. When multiple roll-call votes took place on the same or related issues, the president's position on the final vote—typically the conference report (or motion to recommit the bill)—was included. This strategy surmounts a major shortcoming of *Congressional Quarterly*'s other measures, including the yearly "boxscore," by avoiding multiple votes on the same subject that can skew concurrence rates. The 116 separate roll-call votes taken in the Senate on the 1964 Civil Rights Act is an extreme example. On problems with roll-call measures, see Bond and Fleisher *President in the Legislative Arena,* 54–66. See also George C. Edwards III, "Measuring Presidential Success in Congress: Alternative Approaches," *Journal of Politics* 47 (1985): 667–85.

78. Andrew J. Taylor, "Domestic Agenda Setting, 1947–1994," *Legislative Studies Quarterly* 23 (1998): 373–97.

79. Presidential and congressional agendas evolve from many sources—campaign promises, interest groups, actors in the federal system, to name just a few. The Domestic Council is perhaps one of the most important actors within the executive branch in the crafting of the president's agenda. See Shirley A. Warshaw, *The Domestic Presidency: Policy Making in the White House;* Wayne, *Legislative Presidency.*

To be sure, these data do not speak to the subtler question of the origination of legislative ideas, nor do they relay information about agenda items given primacy by the "inside-the-beltway" policy community (see Frank R. Baumgartner and Bryan D. Jones, *Agendas and Instability in American Politics;* John W. Kingdon, *Agendas, Alternatives, and Public Policies*). But these are not the most important criteria for the purposes of this analysis. The goal is instead to measure the magnitude and interrelation of presidential and congressional agendas.

80. Taylor, "Domestic Agenda Setting"; Jones, *Presidency in a Separated System;* Ronald C. Moe and Steven C. Teel, "Congress as Policy-Maker: A Necessary Reappraisal," *Political Science Quarterly* 85 (1970): 443–70.

81. Russell Renka, "Comparing Presidents Kennedy and Johnson as Legislative Leaders," *Presidential Studies Quarterly* 15 (1985): 806–25.

82. Light, *President's Agenda;* Jones, *Presidency in a Separated System,* 147–81.

83. Sinclair, "Hostile Partners," 143.

84. Steger, "Presidential Policy Initiation," 18.

85. Erwin C. Hargrove and Michael Nelson, *Presidents, Politics, and Policy,* 272.

86. Roger H. Davidson, "The Presidency in Congressional Time," in *Rivals for Power: Presidential-Congressional Relations,* ed. James A. Thurber. Davidson posits that the "postreform" and "partisan conservative" eras extend from 1979–92 and 1993 to the present, respectively. I combined the two eras for the purposes of this study because they share much in common from the perspective of presidential electoral resources and Congress's internal organization.

87. Ibid., 29.

88. Ibid., 32.

89. Ibid., 40.

90. Jones, *Presidency in a Separated System,* 176.

91. A. James Reichley, *Conservatives in an Age of Change: The Nixon and Ford Administrations.*

92. Clinton's support for the North American Free Trade Agreement (NAFTA) and the General Agreement on Tariffs and Trade (GATT) are prime examples in the realm of international trade. Domestic laws are examined in chapter 5.

93. Gary King, "The Methodology of Presidential Research," in *Researching the Presidency,* ed. Edwards, Kessel, and Rockman.

94. Binder, "Dynamics of Legislative Gridlock."

Chapter 1.   The Legislative Presidency and Eras of Congress

1. Mayhew, *Divided We Govern,* 52–73.

2. This phrase is borrowed from Cary R. Covington, "'Staying Private': Gaining Congressional Support for Unpublicized Presidential Preferences on Roll Call Votes," *Journal of Politics* 49 (1987): 737–55.

3. Edwards, *At the Margins.*

4. Light, *President's Agenda;* James P. Pfiffner, *The Modern Presidency.*

5. Ragsdale, *Vital Statistics,* 360–61.

6. Lyn Ragsdale and Jerrold Rusk, "Elections and Presidential Policymaking," in *Presidential Policymaking: An End-of-Century Assessment,* ed. Steven A. Shull.

7. The Durbin-Watson statistic of 2.05 indicates the absence of serial correlation. Plotting the error terms in the model also did not reveal the presence of serial correlation. An autoregression of the time-series data using the Cochrane-Orcutt method did not significantly change the impact of the coefficients in the ordinary least squares model in Table 1.2.

8. Light, *President's Agenda;* Thomas E. Cronin, *The State of the Presidency.*

9. Pfiffner, *Strategic Presidency.*

10. Brad Lockerbie, Stephen Borrelli, and Scott Hedger, "An Integrative Approach to Modeling Presidential Success in Congress," *Political Research Quarterly* 51 (1998): 155–72.

11. Bond and Fleisher, *President in the Legislative Arena;* idem., "The President in a More Partisan Legislative Arena," *Political Research Quarterly* 49 (1996): 729–48.

    The model downplays a "presidency-centered" perspective focused on the president's personal attributes and "skill" in light of difficulties of quantifying such measures (see James David Barber, *The Presidential Character*). The case studies that follow this chapter consider the question of skill in a more appropriate fashion.

12. Terry Sullivan, "The Bank Account Presidency: A New Measure of Evidence on the Temporal Path of Presidential Influence," *American Journal of Political Science* 35 (1991): 686–723.

13. Jeffrey R. Cohen, "The Impact of the Modern Presidency on Presidential Success in the U.S. Congress," *Legislative Studies Quarterly* 7 (1982): 515–32; Light, *President's Agenda.*

14. Keith T. Poole and Howard Rosenthal, *Congress: A Political-Economic History of Roll Call Voting;* idem., "Patterns of Congressional Voting," *American Journal of Political Science* 35 (1991): 228–78.

15. A simple hypothetical example highlights the calculation of the measure and its utility. Let us assume that a Republican president's ideological position is .10 on the DW-NOMINATE scale and the ideological placement of all Democrats in the opposition majority in Congress averages –.20, with a standard deviation of .10. The president-majority party ideological distance score is equal to [(.10)–(–.20)]/(.10), or an absolute value of 3.00. In other words, the president's ideological position is located three standard deviations away from the position of the governing majority. In this example, there is a good bit of variation in the governing majority's positions that might facilitate the president's ability to construct supporting policy coalitions. If the majority were more homogenous in its ideological positions and the corresponding standard deviation lower, the expectation is that the president would have a harder time swaying members of the opposition. Let us assume, then, that the standard deviation drops to .05, suggesting a more internally consistent set of preferences in the majority. The president–majority party ideological distance score is equal to [(–.20)–(.10)]/(.05), or an absolute value of six standard deviations from the mean of the majority party.

16. Bond and Fleisher, *President in the Legislative Arena;* Kenneth E. Collier and Terry Sullivan, "New Evidence Undercutting the Linkage of Approval with Presidential Support and Influence," *Journal of Politics* 57 (1995): 197–209; Brace and Hinckley, *Follow the Leader;* Edwards, *At the Margins;* Douglas Rivers and Nancy Rose, "Passing the President's Program: Public Opinion and Presidential Influence in Congress," *American Journal of Political Science* 29 (1985): 183–96; Harvey G. Zeidenstein, "Varying Relationships Between President's Popularity and Their Legislative Success: A Futile Search for Patterns," *Presidential Studies Quarterly* 13 (1983): 530–49.

17. Lockerbie, Hedger, and Borelli, "An Integrative Approach," 161.

18. Kernell, *Going Public.*

19. Sullivan, "Bank Account Presidency."

20. There is no evidence of substantial multicollinearity in the model. Simple correlation coefficients (Pearson's *r*) between the independent variables were no higher than .50 in a single case. Variance inflation factors in the model also did not reveal the presence of multicollinearity.

21. Frymer, "Ideological Consensus within Divided Government," 287–311.

22. Edwards, *At the Margins.*

23. The results of a separate regression (not shown) in which the president's coattails the first year are interacted with his yearly public approval show a positive and statistically significant relationship. The model predicts that the combination of Lyndon Johnson's 63 percent approval and strong coattails in 1965 raised his annual success by over 10 percent. Johnson's situation was exceptional: he began his term after a landslide election and rode high in the polls his first year. Most other presidents have been less fortunate. Carter's first-year approval averaged 62 percent, but his coattails were quite short. In 1993, Clinton ran ahead of twice as many Democrats as Carter had in 1976, but his public approval averaged only 49 percent his first year as a result of early and numerous controversies.

24. Donald F. Kettle, "Presidential Management of the Economy," in *Understanding the Presidency,* ed. Pfiffner and Davidson.

25. Brace and Hinckley, *Follow the Leader,* 25.

26. David W. Rohde, "Electoral Factors, Political Agendas, and Partisanship in Congress," in *The Postreform Congress,* ed. Roger H. Davidson; Roger H. Davidson, "Senate Leaders: Janitors for an Untidy Chamber?" in *Congress Reconsidered,* ed. Dodd and Oppenheimer; Samuel C. Patterson, "Party Leadership in the U.S. Senate," in *The Changing World of the U.S. Senate,* ed. John R. Hibbing.

27. Burdett A. Loomis, *The Contemporary Congress,* 147.

28. Stanley and Niemi, *Vital Statistics,* 211.

29. Norman J. Ornstein, Robert L. Peabody, and David W. Rohde, "The U.S. Senate: Toward the

21st Century," in *Congress Reconsidered,* ed. Dodd and Oppenheimer; Barbara Sinclair, *The Transformation of the U.S. Senate.*

30. Correlations between the independent variables and analysis of tolerances in the model do not indicate the presence of multicollinearity.

31. The negative effect is slightly weaker compared to the House because of somewhat greater ideological diversity within each party and Republican control of the Senate from 1981–86.

32. Sinclair, "Hostile Partners," 145.

33. Ibid., 145.

34. The impact of divided government on legislation that does *not* pass is an important issue into which scholars have begun to inquire (see Edwards, Barrett, and Peake, "Legislative Impact of Divided Government," 545–63). The focus of this research, however, is on legislation that *did* pass, whether that legislation had a connection with the president's policy objectives, and the type of leadership the president exercised.

35. I am grateful to David R. Mayhew for providing me a list of significant legislation in 1995–96.

36. Sinclair, "Emergence of Strong Leadership," 657–84; Taylor, "Domestic Agenda Setting," 373–97.

37. Because *Congressional Quarterly* did not begin keeping track of presidential positions on roll-call votes until 1953, it is impossible to ascertain Truman's stands on the roll calls for the other significant legislation passed by the 80th Congress.

38. Richard S. Conley, "Democratic Presidents and Divided Government: Truman and Clinton Compared," *Presidential Studies Quarterly* 30 (2000): 222–44.

39. Peterson, *Legislating Together,* 77.

40. Joan Hoff, *Nixon Reconsidered.*

41. *Congressional Quarterly Almanac* 1970, 430–35.

42. James M. Cannon, "Gerald R. Ford, Minority Leader of the House of Representatives, 1965–73," in *Masters of the House: Congressional Leadership over Two Centuries,* ed. Roger H. Davidson, Susan Webb Hammond, and Raymond W. Smock.

43. These bills include the Toxic Substances Control Act, National Forest Management Act, Federal Land Policy and Management Act, and Resource Conservation and Recovery Act—all adopted in 1976.

44. *Congressional Quarterly Almanac,* 1975, 446.

45. *Public Papers of the Presidents of the United States: Jimmy Carter,* 1977, 1:36–46.

46. Max Friedersdorf, quoted in Reichley, *Conservatives in an Age of Change,* 323.

47. Cameron, *Veto Bargaining.*

48. Mayhew, *Divided We Govern,* 118.

49. Jones, *Presidency in a Separated System,* 273.

50. Thorson, "Divided Government," 751–64.

Chapter 2.   Truman, Eisenhower, and Divided Government

1. Greenstein, *Hidden-Hand Presidency.*

2. Davidson, "Presidency in Congressional Time."

3. Leuchtenburg, *In the Shadow of FDR,* 1–40.

4. Alonzo L. Hamby, "The Liberals, Truman, and FDR as Symbol and Myth," *Journal of American History* 56 (1970): 859–67.

5. *Public Papers of the Presidents of the United States: Harry Truman,* 1945, 1:263–309.

6. Mary H. Blewitt, "Roosevelt, Truman, and the Attempt to Revive the New Deal," in *Harry S. Truman and the Fair Deal,* ed. Alonzo L. Hamby, 82.

7. Patterson, *Congressional Conservatism;* Milton Plesur, "The Republican Comeback of 1938," *Review of Politics* 24 (1962): 525–62.

8. Samuel Kernell, "Presidential Popularity and Negative Voting: An Alternative Explanation of the Midterm Congressional Decline of the President's Party," *American Political Science Review* 71 (1977): 44–66; Edward R. Tufte, "Determinants of the Outcomes of Midterm Congressional Elections," *American Political Science Review* 69 (1975): 812–26; Robert S. Erikson, "The Puzzle of Midterm Loss," *Journal of Politics* 50 (1988): 1011–29.

9. Felix Belair Jr., "Scarcities Swell Tide of GOP in the Midwest," *New York Times,* Oct. 6, 1946, E10.

10. "The Republican 'Mandate' and '48," *New York Times Magazine,* Jan. 19, 1947, 52.

11. Richard Neustadt, "Congress and the Fair Deal: A Legislative Balance Sheet," in *Harry S. Truman and the Fair Deal,* ed. Alonzo L. Hamby, 23–24.

12. Samuel Kernell, "Facing an Opposition Congress: The President's Strategic Circumstance," in *Politics of Divided Government,* ed. Cox and Kernell, 99.

13. Rowe memo, 12–13, quoted in Gary A. Donaldson, "Who Wrote the Clifford Memo? The Origins of Campaign Strategy in the Truman Administration," *Presidential Studies Quarterly* 23 (1993): 751.

14. *Congressional Quarterly Almanac,* 1947, 297.

15. *Congressional Quarterly Almanac,* 1948, 58.

16. Harvard Sitkoff, "Years of the Locust: Interpretations of Truman's Presidency Since 1965," in *The Truman Period as a Research Field: A Reappraisal, 1972,* ed. Richard S. Kirkendall, 91.

17. Conley, "Democratic Presidents and Divided Government," 222–44.

18. Seymour Z. Mann, "Policy Formulation in the Executive Branch: The Taft-Hartley Experience," *Western Political Quarterly* 13 (1960): 597–608.

19. R. Alton Lee, *Truman and Taft-Hartley: A Question of Mandate,* 95.

20. Benjamin Aaron, "Amending the Taft-Hartley Act: A Decade of Frustration," *Industrial Labor Relations Review* 11 (1958): 327–38; Gerald Pomper, "Labor and Congress: The Repeal of Taft-Hartley," *Labor History* 2 (1961): 323–43.

21. The author calculated Roosevelt's margin of victory. County-level electoral returns were matched to congressional districts. In a few rare cases for metropolitan districts (e.g., New York, Chicago, and Los Angeles) Roosevelt's victory margin was estimated because the same county traversed more than one district. In these cases his victory margin in the overlapping counties was averaged.

22. Susan M. Hartmann, *Truman and the 80th Congress,* 1971, 18.

23. R. Alton Lee, "The Turnip Session of the Do-Nothing Congress: Presidential Campaign Strategy," *Southwestern Social Science Quarterly* 44 (1963): 256–67.

24. See James L. Sundquist, *Politics and Policy: The Eisenhower, Kennedy, and Johnson Years.*

25. *Public Papers of the Presidents of the United States: Dwight Eisenhower,* 1954, 1:246.

26. George H. Mayer, *The Republican Party, 1854–1964,* 496–98.

27. Barton J. Bernstein, "The Election of 1952," in *History of American Presidential Elections, 1789–1968,* ed. Arthur M. Schlesinger Jr., Fred L. Israel, and William Hansen, 4:3247–48.

28. Cornelius P. Cotter, "Eisenhower as Party Leader," *Political Science Quarterly* 98 (1983): 259.

29. Joseph M. Dailey, "The Reluctant Candidate: Dwight Eisenhower in 1951," in *Dwight D. Eisenhower: Soldier, President, Statesman,* ed. Joann Krieg, 6–7.

30. Merlo J. Pusey, *Eisenhower the President,* 27.

31. Bernstein, "Election of 1952," 3219–24.

32. Richard L. Guylay, "Eisenhower's Two Presidential Campaigns, 1952 and 1956," in *Dwight D. Eisenhower,* ed. Krieg, 22–23; Elmo Richardson, *The Presidency of Dwight D. Eisenhower,* 22–23.

33. Chester J. Pach Jr. and Elmo Richardson, *The Presidency of Dwight D. Eisenhower,* rev. ed., 27.

34. *Congressional Quarterly Almanac,* 1954, 712.

35. Pach and Richardson, *Presidency of Dwight D. Eisenhower,* 72.

36. Malcolm Moos, "The Election of 1956," in *History of American Presidential Elections, 1789–1968,* ed. Schlesinger, Israel, and Hansen, 4:3341.

37. Ibid., 4:3350–54.

38. Herbert B. Asher, *Presidential Elections and American Politics: Voters, Candidates, and Campaigns since 1952,* 151.

39. *Congressional Quarterly Almanac,* 1958, 715.

40. Cotter, "Eisenhower as Party Leader," 259.

41. Sidney M. Milkis and Michael Nelson, *The American Presidency: Origins and Development, 1776–1993,* 311–12.

42. Stephen Hess, *Organizing the Presidency,* 66.

43. Greenstein, *Hidden-Hand Presidency,* 111.

44. Henry Z. Scheele, "Executive-Legislative Relations: Eisenhower and Halleck," in *Reexamining the Eisenhower Presidency,* ed. Shirley Anne Warshaw, 137.

45. Kenneth E. Collier, "Eisenhower and Congress: The Autopilot Presidency," *Presidential Studies Quarterly* 24 (1994): 320.

46. Philip G. Henderson, *Managing the Presidency: The Eisenhower Legacy—From Kennedy to Reagan,* 28; Scheele, "Executive-Legislative Relations," 141.

47. Pach and Richardson, *Presidency of Dwight D. Eisenhower,* 53.

48. *Congressional Quarterly Almanac,* 1954, 489.

49. Pach and Richardson, *Presidency of Dwight D. Eisenhower,* 56.

50. *Congressional Quarterly Almanac,* 1954, 188–91.

51. Gary W. Reichard, *The Reaffirmation of Republicanism: Eisenhower and the Eighty-Third Congress,* 156.

52. *Congressional Quarterly Almanac,* 1956, 399–400.

53. Ibid., 1958, 610–11.

54. Steger, "Presidential Policy Initiation," 19.

55. *Congressional Quarterly Almanac,* 1958, 599.

56. Ibid., 1957, 587.

57. Ibid., 1956, 375–92.

58. Ibid., 1959, 245–56.

59. *Public Papers of the Presidents of the United States: Dwight Eisenhower,* 1957, 1:546.

60. *Congressional Quarterly Almanac,* 1957, 569.

61. Ibid., 1960, 185–207.

62. Ibid., 1958, 159.

63. Greenstein, *Hidden-Hand Presidency.*

64. The models were estimated with STATA 6.0. The program automatically drops variables when an intolerable threshold of collinearity is reached. Nonetheless, all models in this and subsequent chapters were checked for signs of collinearity and are noted where appropriate. Tests included correlations (Pearson's r) between the independent variables and auxiliary R^2 tests (regressing the independent variables on each other).

Chapter 3.   Nixon and Divided Government

1. Mayhew, *Divided We Govern.*

2. Quirk and Nesmith, "Divided Government and Policy Making."

3. Charles O. Jones, "The Separated Presidency—Making It Work in Contemporary Politics," in *The New American Political System*, 2d ed., ed. Anthony King, 8–9.

4. David Broder, "Election of 1968," in *History of American Presidential Elections*, vol. 4, ed. Schlesinger, Israel, and Hansen; Theodore H. White, *The Making of the President, 1968*, 257–313; Lewis Chester, Godfrey Hodgson, and Bruce Page, *An American Melodrama*, 726.

5. John R. Greene, *The Limits of Power: The Nixon and Ford Administrations*, 23–24; Reichley, *Conservatives in an Age of Change*, 54.

6. Broder, "Election of 1968," 4:3705.

7. Asher, *Presidential Elections*, 185.

8. Glen Moore, "Richard Nixon: The Southern Strategy and the 1968 Presidential Election," in *Richard M. Nixon: Politician, President, Administrator*, ed. Leon Friedman and William F. Levantrosser; Reg Murphy and Hal Gulliver, *The Southern Strategy*.

9. *Congressional Quarterly Weekly Report*, Nov. 8, 1968, 3086.

10. Mayhew, *Divided We Govern*, 162.

11. John C. Whitaker, "Nixon's Domestic Policy: Both Liberal and Bold in Retrospect," *Presidential Studies Quarterly* 26 (1996): 131–32.

12. Timothy Conlan, *New Federalism: Intergovernmental Reform from Nixon to Reagan*.

13. *Congressional Quarterly Almanac*, 1969, 83A–86A; ibid., 1970, 110A–118A.

14. *Congress and the Nation*, 1969–72, 97.

15. George C. Edwards III, *Presidential Influence in Congress*, 127.

16. Charles O. Jones, "Presidential Negotiation with Congress," in *Both Ends of the Avenue*, ed. King, 114–15.

17. Davis, "Congressional Liaison," 64.

18. Wayne, *Legislative Presidency*, 159.

19. *Congressional Quarterly Almanac*, 1969, 735–46.

20. Ibid., 833–40.

21. *Congress and the Nation*, 1969–72, 78.

22. *Congressional Quarterly Almanac*, 1971, 430.

23. Ibid., 1970, 804–809.

24. Ibid., 1971, 425–25; ibid., 1972, 399–403.

25. *Congress and the Nation*, 1969–72, 581–83.

26. *Congressional Quarterly Almanac*, 1972, 141–50.

27. Ibid., 1970, 531–39.

28. Ibid., 675.

29. *Congress and the Nation*, 1969–72, 257–62.

30. *Congressional Quarterly Almanac*, 1970, 341–65.

31. Ibid., 192–99.

32. Ibid., 433.

33. Reichley, *Conservatives in an Age of Change*, 211–27.

34. *Congressional Quarterly Almanac*, 1970, 472.

35. Ibid., 1971, 555–63.

36. Ibid., 1972, 722.

37. Theodore R. Marmor and Martin Rein, "Reforming 'The Welfare Mess': The Fate of the Family Assistance Plan, 1969–72," in *Policy and Politics in America: Six Case Studies*, ed. Allan Sindler.

38. Reichley, *Conservatives in an Age of Change,* 85–86.

39. Jones, *Presidency in a Separated System,* 175.

40. Mayhew, *Divided We Govern,* 82.

41. Sundquist, *Decline and Resurgence of Congress,* chap. 8.

Chapter 4   Reagan and Divided Government

1. Thomas E. Mann and Norman J. Ornstein, eds., *The American National Elections of 1982;* Larry M. Schwab, *The Impact of Congressional Reapportionment and Redistricting.*

2. *Congressional Quarterly Weekly Report,* Nov. 6, 1982.

3. Gary C. Jacobson, "Congress: Politics After A Landslide Without Coattails," in *The Elections of 1984,* ed. Michael Nelson, 222.

4. Paul R. Abramson, John H. Aldrich, and David W. Rohde, *Change and Continuity in the 1984 Elections,* 249.

5. Charles E. Jacob, "The Congressional Elections," in *The Election of 1980: Reports and Interpretations,* ed. Gerald M. Pomper, 133.

6. *Congressional Quarterly Almanac,* 1986, 4-B.

7. Mark A. Bodnick, "'Going Public' Reconsidered: Reagan's 1981 Tax and Budget Cuts, and Revisionist Theories of Presidential Power," *Congress and the Presidency* 17 (1990): 13–28; Barbara Sinclair, "Agenda Control and Policy Success: The Case of Ronald Reagan and 97th House," *Legislative Studies Quarterly* 20 (1985): 291–314.

8. Paul J. Quirk, "Presidential Competence," in *The Presidency and the Political System,* ed. Michael Nelson.

9. John W. Sloan, "Meeting the Leadership Challenges of the Modern Presidency: The Political Skills and Leadership of Ronald Reagan," *Presidential Studies Quarterly* 26 (1996): 798–99.

10. Richard P. Nathan, "The Reagan Presidency in Domestic Affairs," in *The Reagan Presidency: An Early Assessment,* ed. Fred I. Greenstein, 52; Allen Schick, "How the Budget Was Won and Lost," in *President and Congress: Assessing Reagan's First Year,* ed. Norman J. Ornstein, 26.

11. *Congressional Quarterly Almanac,* 1981, 257.

12. *Congress and the Nation,* 1981–84, 43.

13. Ibid., 65–66.

14. Stephen J. Wayne, "Congressional Liaison in the Reagan White House: A Preliminary Assessment of the First Year," in *President and Congress,* ed. Ornstein, 58.

15. *Congressional Quarterly Almanac,* 1981, 103.

16. *Congress and the Nation,* 1981–84, 66.

17. *Congressional Quarterly Almanac,* 1981, 91.

18. Ibid., 1982, 29.

19. Ibid., 1984, 144.

20. Ibid., 1987, 608.

21. Ibid., 604–609.

22. *Congress and the Nation,* 1981–84, 698.

23. *Congressional Quarterly Almanac,* 1986, 92–106.

24. Ibid., 1988, 281–92.

25. Ibid., 349–64.

26. Ibid., 1983, 219–26.

27. Ibid., 600–602.

28. Ibid., 1988, 85.

29. Ibid., 1982, 374.

30. Ibid., 1986, 67.

31. Ibid., 1987, 506.

32. Ibid., 1982, 255.

33. Ibid., 42.

34. *Congress and the Nation,* 1985–88, 767.

35. *Congressional Quarterly Almanac,* 1983, 450–51.

36. Ibid., 1986, 506.

37. Ibid., 506–18.

38. Ibid., 1985, 517.

39. Ibid., 1986, 111.

40. Richard S. Conley and Amie Kreppel, "Toward a New Typology of Vetoes and Overrides," *Political Research Quarterly* 56: (2001).

41. *Congressional Quarterly Almanac,* 1987, 331.

42. Charles O. Jones, "A New President, A Different Congress, A Maturing Agenda," in *The Reagan Presidency and the Governing of America,* ed. Lester M. Salamon and Michael S. Lund, 283.

43. David W. Brady and Morris Fiorina, "The Ruptured Legacy: Presidential-Congressional Relations in Historical Perspective," in *Looking Back on the Reagan Presidency,* 272.

44. John B. Bader and Charles O. Jones, "The Republican Parties in Congress: Bicameral Differences," in *Congress Reconsidered,* ed. Dodd and Oppenheimer.

45. Sinclair, "House Majority Party Leadership"; idem., *Majority Party Leadership in the U.S. House.*

46. See William F. Connelly Jr. and John J. Pitney Jr., *Congress' Permanent Minority? Republicans in the U.S. House.*

47. Dilys M. Hill and Phil Williams, "The Reagan Legacy," in *The Reagan Presidency: An Incomplete Revolution?* ed. Dilys M. Hill, Raymond A. Moore, and Phil Williams, 233.

48. Jacobson, "Congress," 230.

Chapter 5.   Bush, Clinton, and Divided Government

1. Marcia Lynn Whicker, "Managing the Bush White House," in *The Bush Presidency: Triumphs and Adversities,* ed. Dilys M. Hill and Phil Williams.

2. Colin Campbell, "Presidential Leadership," in *Developments in American Politics,* ed. Gilliam Peele, Christopher J. Baily, and Bruce Cain, 103.

3. Dean C. Hammer, "The Oakeshottian President: George Bush and the Politics of the Present," *Presidential Studies Quarterly* 25 (1995): 301–13.

4. Michael Duffy and Dan Goodgame, *Marching in Place: The Status Quo Presidency of George Bush.*

5. Paul J. Quirk, "Domestic Policy: Divided Government and Cooperative Presidential Leadership," in *The Bush Presidency: First Appraisals,* ed. Colin Campbell, S. J., and Bert A. Rockman, 75.

6. Michael Foley, "The President and Congress," in *Bush Presidency,* ed. Hill and Williams, 54–59.

7. See Paul Brace and Barbara Hinckley, "George Bush and the Costs of High Popularity: A General Model with a Current Application," *P.S.: Political Science and Politics* 26 (1993): 501–506.

8. *Congressional Quarterly Almanac,* 1992.

9. *Congressional Quarterly Weekly Report,* Dec. 30, 1989.

10. *Congress and the Nation,* 1989–92, 118.

11. *Congressional Quarterly Almanac,* 1991, 138.

12. Ibid., 151.

13. *Congressional Quarterly Almanac,* 1990, 271.

14. *Congress and the Nation,* 1989–92, 482.

15. Ibid., 611; *Congressional Quarterly Almanac,* 1990, 548–51.

16. *Congress and the Nation,* 1989–92, 502–505.

17. *Congressional Quarterly Almanac,* 1990, 448.

18. Ibid., 474; 485.

19. *Congress and the Nation,* 1989–92, 513–18.

20. *Congressional Quarterly Almanac,* 1990, 323–51.

21. Ibid., 656.

22. *Congress and the Nation,* 1989–92, 705–708.

23. *Congressional Quarterly Almanac,* 1991, 256.

24. Ibid., 261.

25. Ibid., 1992, 171.

26. Terry Eastland, "Bush's Fatal Attraction: Anatomy of the Budget Fiasco," *Policy Review* 60 (1992): 20–24.

27. Barbara Sinclair, "Governing Unheroically (and Sometimes Unappetizingly): Bush and the 101st Congress," in *Bush Presidency,* ed. Campbell and Rockman, 178.

28. Jon R. Bond and Richard Fleisher, "Assessing Presidential Support in the House, II: Lessons from George Bush," *American Journal of Political Science* 36 (1992): 540.

29. *Congressional Quarterly Almanac,* 1990, 141–66.

30. George C. Edwards III, "Campaigning is Not Governing: Bill Clinton's Rhetorical Presidency," in *The Clinton Legacy,* ed. Colin Campbell, S.J., and Bert A. Rockman.

31. Tim Hames, "The U.S. Mid-term Election of 1994," *Electoral Studies* 14 (1995): 223–26.

32. Paul Brace and Laura Langer, "Interpreting the 1994 State Legislative Elections," *Spectrum: The Journal of State Government* 68 (1995): 6–13.

33. Gary C. Jacobson, "The 1994 House Elections in Perspective," *Political Science Quarterly* 111 (1996): 203–20.

34. James G. Gimpel, *Legislating the Revolution: The Contract with America in Its First 100 Days,* 3.

35. Clyde Wilcox, *The Latest American Revolution? The 1994 Elections and Their Implications for Governance;* Harold W. Stanley, "The Parties, the President, and the 1994 Midterm Elections," in *Clinton Presidency,* ed. Campbell and Rockman, 188–211.

36. Connelly and Pitney, *Congress' Permanent Minority?;* Jacobson, *Electoral Origins of Divided Government;* Gimpel, *Legislating the Revolution,* 8–10.

37. *Congressional Quarterly Almanac* 1996, 2:3–7.

38. Ibid., 6:3–24.

39. *Congressional Quarterly Weekly Report,* Aug. 3 1996, 2196.

40. Ibid., 2190.

41. *Congressional Quarterly Almanac,* 1994, 36–42.

42. Ibid., 1995, 1:39–44.

43. *Congress and the Nation,* 1993–96, 548.

44. *Congressional Quarterly Almanac,* 1996, 6:28–39.

45. Ibid., 1995, 8:6.

46. Ibid., *1996,* 7:3–9.

47. *Public Papers of the Presidents of the United States: William Clinton,* 1996, 3:1317.

48. *Congressional Quarterly Almanac,* 1995, 3:16.

49. Ibid., 1:31–35.

50. *Congressional Quarterly Weekly Report,* June 27, 1996, 1747–49.   See also M. V. Hood, Irwin L. Morris, and Grant W. Neeley, "Penny Pinching or Politics? The Line Item Veto and Military Construction Appropriations," *Political Research Quarterly* 52 (1999): 753–66.

51. *Congressional Quarterly Almanac,* 1996, 5:3–17.

52. Ibid., 5:18–26.

53. Ibid., 3:15.

54. Ibid., 1995, 2:92.

55. Russell L. Riley, "Party Government and the Contract with America," *P.S.: Political Science & Politics* 28 (1995): 704.

56. Pfiffner, *Modern Presidency,* 163–66.

57. Charles O. Jones, *The Minority Party in Congress.*

58. Gimpel, *Legislating the Revolution,* 22.

59. Kerry Mullins and Aaron B. Wildavsky, "The Procedural Presidency of George Bush," *Political Science Quarterly* 107 (1992): 31–62.

60. See Robert H. Durr, John B. Gilmour, and Christina Wolbrecht, "Explaining Congressional Approval," *American Journal of Political Science* 41 (1997): 175–207.

Chapter 6.   Kennedy, Johnson, and Unified Government

1. Sundquist, *Politics and Policy,* 481.

2. *Congressional Quarterly Weekly Report,* Nov. 11, 1960, 1849.

3. See Philip Converse, "Religion and Politics: The 1960 Fiction," in *Elections and the Political Order,* ed. Angus Campbell et al.

4. Carroll Kilpatrick, "The Kennedy Style and Congress," in *John F. Kennedy and the New Frontier,* ed. Aïda DiPace Donald, 52.

5. Theodore C. Sorensen, *Kennedy,* 342.

6. Tom Wicker, *JFK and LBJ: The Influence of Personality Upon Politics,* 90.
   Conservative southern Democratic committee chairs defeated some of Kennedy's more far-reaching domestic agenda items without a floor vote. Kennedy never brought a tax reduction proposal to spur the economy before the 87th Congress because he knew conservatives fearful of budget deficits and skeptical of Keynesian economics would block the measure (James N. Giglio, *The Presidency of John F. Kennedy,* 135). Kennedy's Medicare proposal was shelved by House Ways and Means Committee chairman Wilbur Mills of Arkansas, and a Senate amendment to a welfare bill in 1962 failed despite public support for the measure (ibid., 102–103). Kennedy blamed the Medicare defeat partially on Mansfield's lack of leadership (Ross K. Baker "Mike Mansfield and the Birth of the Modern Senate," in *First Among Equals: Outstanding Senate Leaders of the Twentieth Century,* ed. Richard A. Baker and Roger H. Davidson, 275). Yet even if the Senate amendment had been successful, conservatives on the House and Senate Finance Committees most likely would have defeated the measure in conference (Alan Rosenthal, *Toward Majority Rule in the United States Senate,* 1–2).

7. Richard Bolling, *House Out of Order,* 74.

8. *Congressional Quarterly Weekly Report,* Nov. 18, 1960, 1903–04; Jan. 6, 1961, 21

9. Kilpatrick, "Kennedy Style and Congress," 53.

10. Edwards and Barrett, "Presidential Agenda Setting in Congress," 118.

11. Rosenthal, *Toward Majority Rule,* 1962.

12. Milton C. Cummings Jr. and Robert L. Peabody, "The Decision to Enlarge the Committee on Rules: An Analysis of the 1961 Vote," in *New Perspectives on the House of Representatives,* ed.

Robert L. Peabody and Nelson W. Polsby; Neil MacNeil, *Forge of Democracy: The House of Representatives,* 410–48.

13. *Congressional Quarterly Almanac,* 1961, 247–56.

14. Ibid., 184–201.

15. Ibid., 513–18.

16. Ibid., 197–210.

17. Ibid., 482.

18. Ibid., 257–61.

19. Ibid., 1962, 482.

20. Barbara Kellerman, *The Political Presidency: Practice of Leadership from Kennedy through Reagan,* 57–88.

21. Michael Foley, *The New Senate: Liberal Influence on a Conservative Institution, 1959–1972,* 43.

22. *Congressional Quarterly Weekly Report,* Jan. 13, 1961, 32–42.

23. Ibid., May 12, 1961.

24. James Reston "Kennedy and the New Congress: A Striking Contrast," *New York Times,* Feb. 15, 1961, 34.

25. Light, *President's Agenda,* 62.

26. Sorensen, *Kennedy,* 345.

27. Arthur M. Schlesinger, *A Thousand Days: John F. Kennedy in the White House,* 710.

28. Jones, *Presidency in a Separated System,* 174.

29. Sundquist, *Politics and Policy,* 482–83.

30. James MacGregor Burns, *Roosevelt: The Lion and the Fox: 1882–1940;* Thomas Ferguson, "From Normalcy to New Deal: Industrial Structure, Party Competition and American Public Policy in the Great Depression," *International Organization* 38 (1984): 42–94; Pendleton Herring, "First Session of the Seventy-third Congress, March 9, 1933 to June 16, 1933," *American Political Science Review* 28 (1934): 65–83; Godfrey Hodgson, *All Things to All Men: The False Promise of the Modern American Presidency;* Sylvia Snowiss, "Presidential Leadership of Congress: An Analysis of Roosevelt's First Hundred Days," *Publius* 1 (1971): 59–87.

31. Theodore White, *The Making of the President 1964,* 294.

32. Stanley Kelly Jr., "The Presidential Campaign," in *The National Election of 1964,* ed. Milton C. Cummings Jr., 61.

33. Polsby, "Strategic Considerations," in ibid.

34. White, *Making of the President, 1964,* 313.

35. Vaughn Davis Bornet, *The Presidency of Lyndon B. Johnson,* 101.

36. Doris Kearns, *Lyndon Johnson and the American Dream,* 211.

37. Milton C. Cummings Jr., "Nominations and Elections for the House of Representatives," in *National Election of 1964,* ed. idem.

38. Edwards, *Presidential Influence in Congress,* 76.

39. *Congressional Quarterly Almanac,* 1966, 1388.

40. Loevy, "Presidency and Domestic Policy"; *Congressional Quarterly Almanac,* 1964, 338–80.

41. *Congressional Quarterly Almanac,* 1964, 208–29; 110–15.

42. *Congress and the Nation,* 1965–68, 496–97; 558–61; *Congressional Quarterly Almanac,* 1968, 395–99; 1967, 875–87.

43. *Congressional Quarterly Almanac,* 1968, 313–25; ibid., 1967, 658–59; ibid., 1968, 152–68.

44. Carl Albert, *The Presidency and Congress.*

45. *Congressional Quarterly Almanac,* 1965, 238.

46. Bornet, *Presidency of Lyndon B. Johnson,* 132–33.

47. *Congressional Quarterly Almanac,* 1965, 725.

48. Ibid., 1966, 773–74.

49. Ibid., 1968, 477–79, 263–78.

50. Ibid., 1966, 636–40.

51. Ibid., 281–85.

52. Ibid., 1968, 225–37.

53. The southern states are Alabama, Arkansas, Florida, Georgia, Louisiana, Mississippi, North Carolina, Oklahoma, South Carolina, Tennessee, Texas, and Virginia.

54. Bornet, *Presidency of Lyndon B. Johnson,* 257.

55. Bruce E. Altschuler, *LBJ and the Polls,* 38–60.

56. Bornet, *Presidency of Lyndon B. Johnson,* 242.

57. Irving Bernstein, *Guns or Butter: The Presidency of Lyndon Johnson,* 531; Kearns, *Lyndon Johnson,* 216–17.

58. Skowronek, *Politics Presidents Make,* 325.

Chapter 7.   Carter, Clinton, and Unified Government

1. Kellerman, *Political Presidency;* Michael Malbin, "Rhetoric and Leadership: A Look Backward at the Carter Energy Plan," in *Both Ends of the Avenue,* ed. King; Theda Skocpol, *Boomerang: Clinton's Health Security Effort and the Turn Against Government in U.S. Politics;* Robin Toner, "Health Care Reform: A Case Study," in *Back to Gridlock? Governance in the Clinton Years,* ed. James L. Sundquist.

2. Mayhew, *Divided We Govern,* 98.

3. David R. Mayhew, "The Return to Unified Party Control Under Clinton: How Much of a Difference in Lawmaking?" In *The New American Politics: Reflections on Political Change and the Clinton Administration,* ed. Bryan D. Jones.

4. Gerald M. Pomper, "The Presidential Election," in *The Election of 1976: Reports and Interpretations,* ed. Marlene M. Pomper, 65–73.

5. William J. Crotty, *Decisions for the Democrats: Reforming the Party Structure;* Jeane Kirkpatrick, *Dismantling the Parties: Reflections on Party Reform and Party Decline;* Nelson W. Polsby, *Consequences of Party Reform.*

6. Tinsley E. Yarbrough, "Carter and the Congress," in *The Carter Years: The President and Policy Making,* ed. M. Glenn Abernathy, Dilys M. Hill, and Phil Williams, 174–75.

7. See Betty Glad, *Jimmy Carter: In Search of the Great White House.*

8. Kenneth A. Shepsle, "The Changing Textbook Congress," in *Can the Government Govern?* ed. John E. Chubb and Paul E. Peterson.

9. Charles O. Jones, *The Trusteeship Presidency: Jimmy Carter and the United States Congress,* 59.

10. Charles E. Jacob, "The Congressional Elections and Outlook," in *The Election of 1976: Reports and Interpretations,* ed. Marlene M. Pomper, 86.

11. Jones, *Trusteeship Presidency,* 50.

12. Jon R. Bond and Richard Fleisher, "Carter and Congress: Presidential Style, Party Politics, and Legislative Success," in *The Presidency and Domestic Policies of Jimmy Carter,* ed. Herbert D. Rosenbaum and Alexej Ugrinsky, 296.

13. Erwin C. Hargrove, *Jimmy Carter as President: Leadership and the Politics of the Public Good.*

14. Marcia Lynn Whicker and Raymond A. Moore, *When Presidents Are Great;* Davis, "Congressional Liaison."

15. Davidson, "Presidency in Congressional Time," 40.

16. Barbara Sinclair, "Coping with Uncertainty: Building Coalitions in the House and Senate," in *The New Congress,* ed. Thomas E. Mann and Norman J. Ornstein.

17. Kellerman, *Political Presidency;* Malbin, "Rhetoric and Leadership."

18. Bond and Fleisher, "Carter and Congress," 293.

19. *Congressional Quarterly Almanac,* 1978, 496–504.

20. Ibid., 1980, 242–48.

21. Ibid., 248–55.

22. Ibid., 1978, 818–35.

23. Ibid., 1977, 161–72.

24. Ibid., 627–46.

25. Ibid., 1980, 575–84.

26. Ibid., 1977, 138–46.

27. Ibid., 1980, 275–77.

28. Ibid., 1977, 101–11.

29. Ibid., 1979, 285–92.

30. Ibid., 1978, 658.

31. Ibid., 1980, 473–77.

32. Ibid., 1978, 219.

33. Ibid., 1980, 584–93.

34. James Ceaser and Andrew Busch, *Upside Down and Inside Out: The 1992 Elections and American Politics,* 138.

35. Norman J. Ornstein, "Too Many 'Lone Rangers'," *Washington Post,* Sept. 2, 1994, A23.

36. Robert D. Novak, "Problems of a 'Nixonian Democrat'," *Washington Post,* Aug. 15, 1994, A19; *Congressional Quarterly Almanac,* 1994, 29–30.

37. Toner, "Health Care Reform," 32–34.

38. *Congress and the Nation,* 1993–96, 623–25.

39. *Congressional Quarterly Almanac,* 1993, 404.

40. Ibid., 389.

41. Ibid., 199.

42. *Congress and the Nation,* 1993–96, 625–27.

43. Ibid., 405–407.

44. *Congressional Quarterly Almanac,* 1993, 107–39.

45. Ibid., 302.

46. *Congress and the Nation,* 1993–96, 683–703.

47. Sinclair, "Trying to Govern Positively," 96.

48. Elizabeth Drew, *On the Edge: The Clinton Presidency,* 61.

49. James P. Pfiffner, "President Clinton and the 103d Congress: Winning Battles and Losing Wars," in *Rivals for Power,* ed. Thurber, 187.

50. Jones, *Presidency in a Separated System,* 182–207.

Chapter 8.   Conclusion

1. Mayhew, *Divided We Govern.*

2. Lammers and Genovese, *Presidency and Domestic Policy.*

3. Michael Nelson, "Evaluating the Presidency," in *The Presidency and the Political System,* ed. Michael Nelson.

4. Peterson, *Legislating Together.*

5. Fleisher and Bond, "Congress and the President."

6. Pfiffner, "President Clinton and the 103d Congress," 171.

7. Bruce I. Oppenheimer, "The Importance of Elections in a Strong Congressional Party Era: The Effect of Unified vs. Divided Government," in *Do Elections Matter?* 3d ed., ed. Benjamin Ginsberg and Alan Stone, 82.

8. Lammers and Genovese, *Presidency and Domestic Policy.*

9. Wildavsky, "Two Presidencies"; Anthony J. Eksterowicz, ed., *The Post–Cold War Presidency;* Oldfield and Wildavsky, "Reconsidering the Two Presidencies," 54–59.

10. Fleisher and Bond, "Congress and the President."

11. Ryan Barilleaux, "The President, 'Intermestic' Issues, and the Risks of Policy Leadership," *Presidential Studies Quarterly* 15 (1985): 754–67; Bayliss Manning, "The Congress, the Executive, and Intermestic Affairs: Three Proposals," *Foreign Affairs* 55 (1977): 306–20.

12. Benjamin Ginsberg and Martin Shefter, *Politics by Other Means: Politicians, Prosecutors, and the Press from Watergate to Whitewater.*

13. Mayhew, *Divided We Govern,* 8–33.

14. Fiorina, *Divided Government;* Laura A. Van Assendelft, *Governors, Agenda-Setting, and Divided Government.*

15. Michael Laver and Kenneth A. Shepsle, "Divided Government: America is Not 'Exceptional'," *Governance* 4 (1991): 250–69.

16. Thomas Christofferson, *The French Socialists in Power, 1981–1986: From Autogestion to Cohabitation;* Thierry Pfister, *Dans les coulisses du pouvoir: la comédie de la cohabitation.*

17. Hess, *Organizing the Presidency.*

18. James L. Sundquist, *Constitutional Reform and Effective Government.*

19. Franklin D. Roosevelt, Inaugural Address, 1933.

Appendix B.   Modeling Congressional Support for the President

1. Edwards, *At the Margins,* 33.

2. See Scott Menard, *Applied Logistic Regression Analysis.*

3. Tim Futing Liao, *Interpreting Probability Models: Logit, Probit, and Other Generalized Linear Models,* 16–21.

4. On the development of party leadership organizations in Congress, see Ripley, *Majority Party Leadership.*

5. See Edwards, *Presidential Influence in Congress,* 96–98.

Bibliography

Aaron, Benjamin. "Amending the Taft-Hartley Act: A Decade of Frustration." *Industrial*
    Labor Relations Review 11 (1958): 327–38.

Abramowitz, Alan I. "Incumbency, Campaign Spending, and the Decline of Competition
    in U.S. House Elections." *Journal of Politics* 53 (1991): 34–56.

Abramson, Paul R., John H. Aldrich, and David W. Rohde. *Change and Continuity in the
    1984 Elections.* Washington, D.C.: Congressional Quarterly, 1984.

Albert, Carl. *The Presidency and Congress.* Austin, Tex.: LBJ School of Public Affairs, 1979.

Aldrich, John H. "Presidential Campaigns in Party- and Candidate-Centered Eras." In *Un-
    der the Watchful Eye: Managing Presidential Campaigns in the Television Era,* ed.
    Matthew D. McCubbins. Washington, D.C.: Congressional Quarterly, 1992.

Alford, John R., and John R. Hibbing. "Increased Incumbency Advantage in the House."
    Journal of Politics 43 (1981): 1042–61.

Altschuler, Bruce E. *LBJ and the Polls.* Gainesville: University of Florida Press, 1990.

Arnold, R. Douglas. *The Logic of Congressional Action.* New Haven, Conn.: Yale University
    Press, 1990.

Asher, Herbert B. *Presidential Elections and American Politics: Voters, Candidates, and
    Campaigns since 1952.* Homewood, Ill.: Dorsey Press, 1980.

Bader, John B., and Charles O. Jones. "The Republican Parties in Congress: Bicameral
    Differences." In *Congress Reconsidered,* 5th ed., ed. Lawrence C. Dodd and Bruce I.
    Oppenheimer. Washington, D.C.: Congressional Quarterly, 1993.

Baker, Ross K. "Mike Mansfield and the Birth of the Modern Senate." In *First Among
    Equals: Outstanding Senate Leaders of the Twentieth Century,* ed. Richard A. Baker
    and Roger H. Davidson. Washington, D.C.: Congressional Quarterly, 1991.

Barber, James David. *The Presidential Character.* Englewood Cliffs, N.J.: Prentice Hall,
    1993.

Barilleaux, Ryan. "The President, 'Intermestic' Issues, and the Risks of Policy Leadership."
    Presidential Studies Quarterly 15 (1985): 754–67.

Baumgartner, Frank R. and Bryan D. Jones. *Agendas and Instability in American Politics.*
    Chicago: University of Chicago Press, 1993.

Bernstein, Barton J. "The Election of 1952." In *History of American Presidential Elections,
    1789–1968.* Vol. 4, ed. Arthur M. Schlesinger Jr., Fred L. Israel, and William P.
    Hansen. New York: McGraw-Hill, 1971.

Bernstein, Irving. *Guns or Butter: The Presidency of Lyndon Johnson.* New York: Oxford
    University Press, 1996.

Binder, Sarah A. "The Dynamics of Legislative Gridlock, 1947–96." *American Political Sci-
    ence Review* 93 (1999): 519–34.

Blewitt, Mary H. "Roosevelt, Truman, and the Attempt to Revive the New Deal." In *Harry S. Truman and the Fair Deal,* ed. Alonzo L. Hamby. Lexington, Mass.: D. C. Heath, 1974.

Bodnick, Mark A. "'Going Public' Reconsidered: Reagan's 1981 Tax and Budget Cuts, and Revisionist Theories of Presidential Power." *Congress and the Presidency* 17 (1990): 13–28.

Bolling, Richard. *House Out of Order.* New York: E. P. Dutton, 1965.

Bond, Jon R. and Richard Fleisher. *The President in the Legislative Arena.* Chicago: University of Chicago Press, 1990.

———. "Carter and Congress: Presidential Style, Party Politics, and Legislative Success." In *The Presidency and Domestic Policies of Jimmy Carter,* ed. Herbert D. Rosenbaum and Alexej Ugrinsky. Westport, Conn.: Greenwood Press, 1994.

———. "Assessing Presidential Support in the House II: Lessons from George Bush." *American Journal of Political Science* 36 (1992): 525–41.

———. "The President in a More Partisan Legislative Arena." *Political Research Quarterly* 49 (1996): 729–48.

———. "The Disappearing Middle and the President's Quest for Votes in Congress." *Presidency Research Group Report,* Newsletter of the Presidency Research Group of the American Political Science Association, fall, 2000, 6–9.

Born, Richard. "Reassessing the Decline of Presidential Coattails: U.S. House Elections from 1952–80." *Journal of Politics* 46 (1984): 60–79.

Bornet, Vaughn Davis. *The Presidency of Lyndon B. Johnson.* Lawrence: University Press of Kansas, 1983.

Brace, Paul, and Barbara Hinckley. *Follow the Leader: Opinion Polls and the Modern Presidents.* New York: Basic Books, 1992.

———. "George Bush and the Costs of High Popularity: A General Model with a Current Application." *P.S.: Political Science and Politics* 26 (1993): 501–506.

Brace, Paul, and Laura Langer. "Interpreting the 1994 State Legislative Elections." *Spectrum: The Journal of State Government* 68 (1995): 6–13.

Brady, David W. "A Reevaluation of Realignments in American Politics: Evidence from the House of Representatives." *American Political Science Review* 79 (1985): 28–49.

Brady, David W., and Morris P. Fiorina. "The Ruptured Legacy: Presidential-Congressional Relations in Historical Perspective." In *Looking Back on the Reagan Presidency,* ed. Larry Berman. Baltimore: Johns Hopkins University Press, 1990.

Broder, David. "Election of 1968." In *History of American Presidential Elections, 1789–1968,* ed. Arthur M. Schlesinger Jr., Fred L. Israel, and William P. Hansen. Vol. 4. New York: McGraw-Hill, 1971.

Bullock, Charles S. "The Impact of Changing the Racial Composition of Congressional Districts on Legislators' Roll Call Behavior." *American Politics Quarterly* 23 (1995): 141–58.

———, and David W. Brady. "Party, Constituency, and Roll-Call Voting in the U.S. Senate." *Legislative Studies Quarterly* 8 (1983): 29–43.

Burnham, Walter Dean. *Critical Elections and the Mainsprings of American Politics.* New York: Norton, 1970.

———. "American Politics in the 1970s: Beyond Party?" In *The American Party Systems: Stages of Political Development,* ed. William Nisbet Chambers and Walter Dean Burnham. New York: Oxford University Press, 1975.

Burns, James MacGregor. *Roosevelt: The Lion and the Fox: 1882–1940.* New York: Harcourt, Brace, Jovanovich, 1956.

———. *The Deadlock of Democracy: Four-Party Politics in America.* Englewood Cliffs, N.J.: Prentice-Hall, 1963.

Calvert, Randall L., and John A. Ferejohn. "Coattail Voting in Recent Presidential Elections." *American Political Science Review* 77 (1983): 407–19.

Cameron, Charles. *Veto Bargaining: Presidents and the Politics of Negative Power.* New York: Cambridge University Press, 2000.

Campbell, Colin. "Presidential Leadership." In *Developments in American Politics,* ed. Gilliam Peele, Christopher J. Baily, and Bruce Cain. New York: St. Martin's Press, 1992.

Campbell, James E. "Predicting Seat Gains from Presidential Coattails." *American Journal of Political Science* 30 (1986): 165–83.

———, and Joe A. Sumners. "Presidential Coattails in Senate Elections." *American Political Science Review* 84 (1990): 513–23.

Cannon, James M. "Gerald R. Ford, Minority Leader of the House of Representatives, 1965–73." In *Masters of the House: Congressional Leadership Over Two Centuries,* ed. Roger H. Davidson, Susan Webb Hammond, and Raymond W. Smock. Boulder, Colo.: Westview Press, 1998.

Ceaser, James, and Andrew Busch. *Upside Down and Inside Out: The 1992 Elections and American Politics.* Lanham, Md.: Rowman and Littlefield, 1992.

Chester, Lewis, Godfrey Hodgson, and Bruce Page. *An American Melodrama.* New York: Dell, 1969.

Christofferson, Thomas. *The French Socialists in Power, 1981–1986: From Autogestion to Cohabitation.* Newark: University of Delaware Press, 1991.

Clausen, Aage R. *How Congressmen Decide: A Policy Focus.* New York: St. Martin's Press, 1973.

Cohen, Jeffrey. "The Impact of the Modern Presidency on Presidential Success in the U.S. Congress." *Legislative Studies Quarterly* 7 (1982): 515–32.

Coleman, John J. "Unified Government, Divided Government, and Party Responsiveness." *American Political Science Review* 93 (1999): 821–36.

Collie, Melissa P. "Universalism and the Parties in the U.S. House: 1921–80." *American Journal of Political Science* 32 (1988): 865–83.

Collier, Kenneth E. *Between the Branches: The White House Office of Legislative Affairs.* Pittsburgh: University of Pittsburgh Press, 1997.

———. "Eisenhower and Congress: The Autopilot Presidency." *Presidential Studies Quarterly* 24 (1994): 309–25.

———, and Terry Sullivan. "New Evidence Undercutting the Linkage of Approval with Presidential Support and Influence." *Journal of Politics* 57 (1995): 197–209.

Congress and the Nation. Washington, D.C.: Congressional Quarterly, 1947–96.

Congressional Quarterly Almanac. Washington, D.C.: Congressional Quarterly, 1947–96.

Conlan, Timothy. *New Federalism: Intergovernmental Reform from Nixon to Reagan.* Washington, D.C.: Brookings Institution, 1988.

Conley, Richard S. "Democratic Presidents and Divided Government: Truman and Clinton Compared." *Presidential Studies Quarterly* 30 (2000): 222–44.

———. "Presidential Influence and Minority Party Liaison on Veto Overrides: New Evidence from the Ford Presidency." *American Politics Research* 30 (2002): 34–65.

——, and Amie Kreppel. "Toward a New Typology of Vetoes and Overrides: Legislative and Non-Legislative Goals with Implications for Presidential and Congressional Power." *Political Research Quarterly* 56: (2001).

Connelly, William F., Jr., and John J. Pitney Jr. *Congress' Permanent Minority? Republicans in the U.S. House.* Lanham, Md.: Rowman and Littlefield, 1994.

Converse, Philip. "Religion and Politics: The 1960 Fiction. In *Elections and the Political Order,* ed. Angus Campbell et al. New York: Wiley, 1966.

Cooper, Joseph, and David W. Brady. "Institutional Context and Leadership Style: The House from Cannon to Rayburn." *American Political Science Review* 75 (1981): 411–25.

Cotter, Cornelius P. "Eisenhower as Party Leader." *Political Science Quarterly* 98 (1983): 255–83.

Covington, Cary R. "'Staying Private': Gaining Congressional Support for Unpublicized Presidential Preferences on Roll Call Votes." *Journal of Politics* 49 (1987): 737–55.

——, J. Mark Wrighton, and Rhonda Kinney. "A 'Presidency-Augmented' Model of Presidential Success on House Roll Call Votes." *American Journal of Political Science* 39 (1995): 1001–24.

Cox, Gary W., and Matthew D. McCubbins. "Bonding, Structure, and the Stability of Political Parties: Party Government in the House." *Legislative Studies Quarterly* 19 (1994): 215–31.

Cox, Gary W., and Samuel Kernell, eds. *The Politics of Divided Government.* Boulder, Colo.: Westview Press, 1991.

Crockett, David A. "The President as Opposition Leader." *Presidential Studies Quarterly* 30 (2000): 245–74.

Cronin, Thomas E. *The State of the Presidency.* Boston: Little, Brown, 1975.

——, and Michael A. Genovese. *Paradoxes of the American Presidency.* New York: Oxford University Press, 1998.

Crotty, William J. *Decisions for the Democrats: Reforming the Party Structure.* Baltimore: Johns Hopkins University Press, 1978.

Cummings, Milton C., Jr. "Nominations and Elections for the House of Representatives." In *The National Election of 1964,* ed. Milton C. Cummings Jr. Washington, D.C.: Brookings Institution, 1966.

——, and Robert L. Peabody. "The Decision to Enlarge the Committee on Rules: An Analysis of the 1961 Vote." In *New Perspectives on the House of Representatives,* ed. Robert L. Peabody and Nelson W. Polsby. Chicago: Rand McNally, 1963

Cutler, Lloyd N. "To Form a Government." *Foreign Affairs* 59 (1988): 126–43.

Dailey, Joseph M. "The Reluctant Candidate: Dwight Eisenhower in 1951." In *Dwight D. Eisenhower: Soldier, President, Statesman,* ed. Joann P. Krieg. New York: Greenwood Press, 1987.

Dalton, Russell J., and Martin P. Wattenberg. "The Not So Simple Act of Voting." In *Political Science: The State of the Discipline II,* ed. Ada W. Finifter. Washington, D.C.: American Political Science Association, 1993.

Davidson, Roger H. "Senate Leaders: Janitors for an Untidy Chamber?" In *Congress Reconsidered,* ed. Lawrence C. Dodd and Bruce I. Oppenheimer. 3d ed. Washington, D.C.: Congressional Quarterly, 1985.

——. "Invitation to Struggle: An Overview of Legislative-Executive Relations." *Annals of the American Academy of Political and Social Science* 499 (1988): 9–21.

———. "The Presidency in Congressional Time." In *Rivals for Power: Presidential-Congressional Relations,* ed. James A. Thurber. Washington, D.C.: Congressional Quarterly, 1996.

———, Walter J. Oleszek, and Thomas Kephart. "One Bill, Many Committees: Multiple Referrals in the U.S. House of Representatives." *Legislative Studies Quarterly* 13 (1988): 3–28.

Davis, Eric L. "Congressional Liaison: The People and the Institutions." In *Both Ends of the Avenue: The Presidency, the Executive Branch, and Congress in the 1980s,* ed. Anthony King. Washington, D.C.: American Enterprise Institute, 1983.

Dodd, Lawrence C. "A Theory of Congressional Cycles: Solving the Puzzle." In *Congress and Policy Change,* ed. Gerald C. Wright Jr., Leroy N. Rieselbach, and Lawrence C. Dodd. New York: Agathon Press, 1986.

———. "The Expanded Roles of the House Democratic Whip System: The 93d and 94th Congresses." *Congressional Studies* 7 (1979): 27–56.

Dodd, Lawrence C., and Bruce I. Oppenheimer. "The House in Transition." In *Congress Reconsidered,* ed. Lawrence C. Dodd and Bruce I. Oppenheimer. New York: Praeger, 1977.

Donaldson, Gary A. "Who Wrote the Clifford Memo? The Origins of Campaign Strategy in the Truman Administration." *Presidential Studies Quarterly* 23 (1993): 747–54.

Drew, Elizabeth. *On the Edge: The Clinton Presidency.* New York: Simon and Schuster, 1994.

Duffy, Michael, and Dan Goodgame. *Marching in Place: The Status Quo Presidency of George Bush.* New York: Simon and Schuster, 1992.

Durr, Robert H., John B. Gilmour, and Christina Wolbrecht. "Explaining Congressional Approval." *American Journal of Political Science* 41 (1997): 175–207.

Eastland, Terry. "Bush's Fatal Attraction: Anatomy of the Budget Fiasco." *Policy Review* 60 (1992): 20–24.

Eksterowicz, Anthony J., ed. *The Post–Cold War Presidency.* Lanham, Md.: Rowman and Littlefield, 1999.

Edwards, George C., III. *Presidential Influence in Congress.* San Francisco: W. H. Freeman, 1980.

———. *At the Margins: Presidential Leadership of Congress.* New Haven, Conn.: Yale University Press, 1989.

———. "Campaigning is Not Governing: Bill Clinton's Rhetorical Presidency." In *The Clinton Legacy,* ed. Colin Campbell, S.J., and Bert A. Rockman. New York: Chatham House, 2000.

———. "Presidential Influence in the House: Presidential Prestige as a Source of Presidential Power." *American Political Science Review* 70 (1976): 101–13.

———. "The Impact of Presidential Coattails on Outcomes of Congressional Elections." *American Politics Quarterly* 7 (1979): 94–108.

———. "Measuring Presidential Success in Congress: Alternative Approaches." *Journal of Politics* 47 (1985): 667–85.

———, and Andrew Barrett. "Presidential Agenda Setting in Congress." In *Polarized Politics: Congress and the President in a Partisan Era,* ed. Jon R. Bond and Richard Fleisher. Washington, D.C.: Congressional Quarterly, 2000.

———, and Jeffrey Peake. "The Legislative Impact of Divided Government." *American Journal of Political Science* 41 (1997): 545–63.

Erikson, Robert S. "The Puzzle of Midterm Loss." *Journal of Politics* 50 (1988): 1011–29.

——. "Roll Calls, Reputations, and Representation in the U.S. Senate." *Legislative Studies Quarterly* 15 (1990): 623–42.

Fenno, Richard F. *Home Style: House Members in Their Districts.* Boston: Little, Brown, 1978.

Ferguson, Thomas. "From Normalcy to New Deal: Industrial Structure, Party Competition and American Public Policy in the Great Depression." *International Organization* 38 (1984): 42–94.

Fiorina, Morris. *Divided Government.* 2d ed. Boston: Allyn and Bacon, 1996.

Fleisher, Richard, and Jon R. Bond. "Congress and the President in a Partisan Era." In *Polarized Politics: Congress and the President in a Partisan Era,* ed. Jon R. Bond and Richard Fleisher. Washington, D.C.: Congressional Quarterly, 2000.

——. "Partisanship and the President's Quest for Votes." In *Polarized Politics: Congress and the President in a Partisan Era,* ed. Jon R. Bond and Richard Fleisher. Washington, D.C.: Congressional Quarterly, 2000.

——, Glenn S. Krutz, and Stephen Hanna. "The Demise of the Two Presidencies." *American Politics Quarterly* 28 (2000): 3–25.

Foley, Michael. *The New Senate: Liberal Influence on a Conservative Institution, 1959–1972.* New Haven: Yale University Press, 1980.

——. "The President and Congress." In *The Bush Presidency: Triumphs and Adversities,* ed. Dilys M. Hill and Phil Williams. New York: St. Martin's Press, 1994.

Frymer, Paul. "Ideological Consensus within Divided Government." *Political Science Quarterly* 109 (1994): 287–311.

——, Thomas P. Kim, and Terri L. Bimes. "Party Elites, Ideological Voters, and Divided Party Government." *Legislative Studies Quarterly* 22 (1997): 195–216.

Giglio, James N. *The Presidency of John F. Kennedy.* Lawrence: University of Kansas Press, 1991.

Gilmour, John B. *Strategic Disagreement: Stalemate in American Politics.* Pittsburgh: University of Pittsburgh Press, 1995.

Gimpel, James G. *Legislating the Revolution: The Contract with America in Its First 100 Days.* Boston: Allyn and Bacon, 1996.

Ginsberg, Benjamin, and Martin Shefter. *Politics by Other Means: Politicians, Prosecutors, and the Press from Watergate to Whitewater.* New York: W. W. Norton, 1999.

Glad, Betty. *Jimmy Carter: In Search of the Great White House.* New York: Norton, 1980.

Greene, John R. *The Limits of Power: The Nixon and Ford Administrations.* Bloomington: Indiana University Press, 1992.

Greenstein, Fred I. *The Hidden-Hand Presidency: Eisenhower as Leader.* Baltimore: Johns Hopkins University Press, 1982.

Guylay, L. Richard. "Eisenhower's Two Presidential Campaigns, 1952 and 1956." In *Dwight D. Eisenhower: Soldier, President, Statesman,* ed. Joann P. Krieg. New York: Greenwood Press, 1987.

Hamby, Alonzo L. "The Liberals, Truman, and FDR as Symbol and Myth." *Journal of American History* 56 (1970): 859–67.

Hames, Tim. "The U.S. Mid-term Election of 1994." *Electoral Studies* 14 (1995): 223–26.

Hammer, Dean C. "The Oakeshottian President: George Bush and the Politics of the Present." *Presidential Studies Quarterly* 25 (1995): 301–313.

Hargrove, Erwin C. *Jimmy Carter as President: Leadership and the Politics of the Public Good.* Baton Rouge: Louisiana State University Press, 1988.

——, and Michael Nelson. *Presidents, Politics, and Policy.* New York: Knopf, 1984.

Hartmann, Susan M. *Truman and the 80th Congress.* Columbia: University of Missouri Press, 1971.

Henderson, Philip G. *Managing the Presidency: The Eisenhower Legacy—From Kennedy to Reagan.* Boulder, Colo.: Westview Press, 1988.

Herring, Pendleton. "First Session of the Seventy-third Congress, March 9, 1933 to June 16, 1933." *American Political Science Review* 28 (1934): 65–83.

Herrnson, Paul S., and Kelly D. Patterson. "Toward a More Programmatic Democratic Party? Agenda-Setting and Coalition Building in the House of Representatives." *Polity* 27 (1995): 607–28.

Hess, Stephen. *Organizing the Presidency.* Washington, D.C.: Brookings Institution, 1988.

Hill, Dilys M., and Phil Williams. "The Reagan Legacy." In *The Reagan Presidency: An Incomplete Revolution?* ed. Dilys M. Hill, Raymond A. Moore, and Phil Williams. New York: St. Martin's Press, 1990.

Hinckley, Barbara. "Incumbency and the Presidential Vote in Senate Elections: Defining Parameters of Subpresidential Voting." *American Political Science Review* 64 (1970): 836–42.

Hodgson, Godfrey. *All Things to All Men: The False Promise of the Modern American Presidency.* New York: Simon and Schuster, 1980.

Hoff, Joan. *Nixon Reconsidered.* New York: Basic Books, 1994.

Hood, M. V., Irwin L. Morris, and Grant W. Neeley. "Penny Pinching or Politics? The Line Item Veto and Military Construction Appropriations." *Political Research Quarterly* 52 (1999): 753–66.

Jacob, Charles E. "The Congressional Elections and Outlook." In *The Election of 1976: Reports and Interpretations,* ed. Marlene M. Pomper. New York: David McKay, 1977.

——. "The Congressional Elections." In *The Election of 1980: Reports and Interpretations,* ed. Gerald M. Pomper. Chatham, N.J.: Chatham House, 1980.

Jacobson, Gary C. *The Electoral Origins of Divided Government: Competition in U.S. House Elections, 1946–1988.* Boulder, Colo.: Westview Press, 1990.

——. "Congress: Politics After A Landslide Without Coattails." In *The Elections of 1984,* ed. Michael Nelson. Washington, D.C.: Congressional Quarterly, 1984.

——. "The Marginals Never Vanished: Incumbency and Competition in Elections to the U.S. House of Representatives, 1952–1982." *American Journal of Political Science* 31 (1987): 126–41.

——. "The 1994 House Elections in Perspective." *Political Science Quarterly* 111 (1996): 203–20.

——. "Party Polarization in National Politics: The Electoral Connection." In *Polarized Politics: Congress and the President in a Partisan Era,* ed. Jon R. Bond and Richard Fleisher. Washington, D.C.: Congressional Quarterly, 2000.

Jones, Charles O. *The Minority Party in Congress.* Boston: Little, Brown, 1974.

——. *The Trusteeship Presidency: Jimmy Carter and the United States Congress.* Baton Rouge: Louisiana State University Press, 1988.

——. *The Presidency in a Separated System.* Washington, D.C.: Brookings Institution, 1994.

———. *Passages to the Presidency: From Campaigning to Governing.* Washington, D.C.: Brookings Institution Press, 1998.

———. "Presidential Negotiation with Congress." In *Both Ends of the Avenue: The Presidency, Executive Branch, and Congress in the 1980s,* ed. Anthony King. Washington, D.C.: American Enterprise Institute, 1983.

———. "A New President, A Different Congress, A Maturing Agenda." In *The Reagan Presidency and the Governing of America,* ed. Lester M. Salamon and Michael S. Lund. Washington, D.C.: The Urban Institute Press, 1984.

———. "The Separated Presidency—Making It Work in Contemporary Politics." In *The New American Political System,* 2d ed., ed. Anthony King. Washington, D.C.: AEI Press, 1990.

Kearns, Doris. *Lyndon Johnson and the American Dream.* New York: Harper and Row, 1976.

Kellerman, Barbara. *The Political Presidency: Practice of Leadership from Kennedy through Reagan.* New York: Oxford University Press, 1984.

Kelly, Sean Q. "Punctuated Change and the Era of Divided Government." In *New Perspectives on American Politics,* ed. Lawrence C. Dodd and Calvin Jillson. Washington, D.C: Congressional Quarterly, 1994.

———. "Divided We Govern? A Reassessment." *Polity* 25 (1993): 475–84.

Kelly, Stanley, Jr. "The Presidential Campaign." In *The National Election of 1964,* ed. Milton C. Cummings Jr. Washington, D.C.: Brookings Institution, 1966.

Kernell, Samuel. *Going Public: New Strategies of Presidential Leadership.* 3d ed. Washington, D.C.: Congressional Quarterly, 1997.

———. "Facing an Opposition Congress: The President's Strategic Circumstance." In *The Politics of Divided Government,* ed. Gary W. Cox and Samuel Kernell. Boulder, Colo.: Westview Press, 1991.

———. "Presidential Popularity and Negative Voting: An Alternative Explanation of the Midterm Congressional Decline of the President's Party." *American Political Science Review* 71 (1977): 44–66.

Kettle, Donald F. "Presidential Management of the Economy." In *Understanding the Presidency,* ed. James P. Pfiffner and Roger H. Davidson. New York: Longman, 1997.

Kilpatrick, Carroll. "The Kennedy Style and Congress." In *John F. Kennedy and the New Frontier,* ed. Aïda DiPace Donald. New York: Hill and Wang, 1966.

King, Gary. "The Methodology of Presidential Research." In *Researching the Presidency: Vital Questions, New Approaches,* ed. George C. Edwards III, John H. Kessel, and Bert A. Rockman. Pittsburgh: University of Pittsburgh Press, 1993.

Kingdon, John W. *Agendas, Alternatives, and Public Policies.* Boston: Little, Brown, 1995.

Kirkpatrick, Jeane. *Dismantling the Parties: Reflections on Party Reform and Party Decline.* Washington, D.C.: American Enterprise Institute, 1978.

Krehbiel, Keith. *Pivotal Politics: A Theory of U.S. Lawmaking.* Chicago: University of Chicago Press, 1998.

Ladd, Everett C. "Like Waiting for Godot: The Uselessness of 'Realignment' for Understanding Change in Contemporary American Politics." In *The End of Realignment? Interpreting American Electoral Eras,* ed. Byron E. Shafer. Madison: University of Wisconsin Press, 1991.

———. "1996 Vote: The 'No Majority' Realignment Continues." *Political Science Quarterly* 112 (1997): 1–28.

Lammers, William W., and Michael A. Genovese. *The Presidency and Domestic Policy: Comparing Leadership Styles, FDR to Clinton.* Washington, D.C.: Congressional Quarterly, 2000.

Laver, Michael, and Kenneth A. Shepsle. "Divided Government: America is Not 'Exceptional.'" *Governance* 4 (1991): 250–69.

Lee, R. Alton. *Truman and Taft-Hartley: A Question of Mandate.* Lexington: University of Kentucky Press, 1966.

———. "The Turnip Session of the Do-Nothing Congress: Presidential Campaign Strategy." *Southwestern Social Science Quarterly* 44 (1963): 256–67.

Leuchtenburg, William E. *In the Shadow of FDR: From Harry Truman to Bill Clinton.* Ithaca, N.Y.: Cornell University Press, 1993.

Liao, Tim Futing. *Interpreting Probability Models: Logit, Probit, and Other Generalized Linear Models.* Thousand Oaks, Calif.: Sage, 1994.

Light, Paul C. *The President's Agenda: Domestic Policy Choice from Kennedy to Carter.* Baltimore: Johns Hopkins University Press, 1982.

———. *The President's Agenda: Domestic Policy Choice from Kennedy to Clinton.* 3d ed. Baltimore: Johns Hopkins University Press, 1999.

Lockerbie, Brad, Stephen Borrelli, and Scott Hedger. "An Integrative Approach to Modeling Presidential Success in Congress." *Political Research Quarterly* 51 (1998): 155–72.

Loevy, Robert D. "The Presidency and Domestic Policy: The Civil Rights Act of 1964." In *Understanding the Presidency,* ed. James P. Pfiffner and Roger H. Davidson. New York: Longman, 1997.

Loomis, Burdett A. *The Contemporary Congress.* Boston: Bedford/St. Martin's, 2000.

MacNeil, Neil. *Forge of Democracy: The House of Representatives.* New York: David MacKay, 1963

Malbin, Michael. "Rhetoric and Leadership: A Look Backward at the Carter Energy Plan." In *Both Ends of the Avenue: The Presidency, the Executive Branch, and Congress in the 1980s,* ed. Anthony King. Washington, D.C.: American Enterprise Institute, 1983.

Mann, Thomas E., and Norman J. Ornstein, eds. *The American National Elections of 1982.* Washington, D.C.: American Enterprise Institute for Public Policy Research, 1983.

Mann, Seymour Z. "Policy Formulation in the Executive Branch: The Taft-Hartley Experience." *Western Political Quarterly* 13 (1960): 597–608.

Manning, Bayliss. "The Congress, the Executive, and Intermestic Affairs: Three Proposals." *Foreign Affairs* 55 (1977): 306–20.

Marmor, Theodore R., and Martin Rein. "Reforming 'The Welfare Mess': The Fate of the Family Assistance Plan, 1969–72." In *Policy and Politics in America: Six Case Studies,* ed. Allan P. Sindler. Boston: Little, Brown, 1973.

Matthews, Donald R., and James A. Stimson. *Yeas and Nays: Normal Decision-Making in the U.S. House of Representatives.* New York: Wiley, 1975.

Mayer, George H. *The Republican Party, 1854–1964.* New York: Oxford University Press, 1964.

Mayhew, David R. *Divided We Govern: Party Control, Lawmaking, and Investigations 1946–1990.* New Haven, Conn.: Yale University Press, 1991.

———. "The Return to Unified Party Control Under Clinton: How Much of a Difference in Lawmaking?" In *The New American Politics: Reflections on Political Change and the Clinton Administration,* ed. Bryan D. Jones. Boulder, Colo.: Westview Press, 1995.

McCubbins, Mathew D. "Party Decline and Presidential Campaigns in the Television Age." In *Under the Watchful Eye: Managing Presidential Campaigns in the Television Era,* ed. Mathew D. McCubbins. Washington, D.C.: Congressional Quarterly, 1992.

McKay, David. "Divided and Governed? Recent Research on Divided Government in the United States." *British Journal of Political Science* 24 (1994): 517–34.

Menard, Scott. *Applied Logistic Regression Analysis.* Thousand Oaks, Calif.: Sage, 1995.

Milkis, Sidney M., and Michael Nelson. *The American Presidency: Origins and Development, 1776–1993,* 2d ed. Washington, D.C.: Congressional Quarterly, 1994.

Moe, Ronald C., and Steven C. Teel. "Congress as Policy-Maker: A Necessary Reappraisal." *Political Science Quarterly* 85 (1970): 443–70.

Moe, Terry M. "The Politicized Presidency." In *The New Direction in American Politics,* ed. John E. Chubb and Paul E. Peterson. Washington, D.C.: Brookings Institution, 1985.

———. "Presidents, Institutions, and Theory." In *Researching the Presidency: Vital Questions, New Approaches,* ed. George C. Edwards III, John H. Kessel, and Bert A. Rockman. Pittsburgh: University of Pittsburgh Press, 1993.

Moore, Glen. "Richard Nixon: The Southern Strategy and the 1968 Presidential Election." In *Richard M. Nixon: Politician, President, Administrator,* ed. Leon Friedman and William F. Levantrosser. Westport, Conn.: Greenwood Press, 1991.

Moos, Malcolm. "The Election of 1956." In *History of American Presidential Elections, 1789–1968,* ed. Arthur M. Schlesinger Jr., Fred L. Israel, and William P. Hansen. Vol. 4. New York: McGraw-Hill, 1971.

Mullins, Kerry, and Aaron B. Wildavsky. "The Procedural Presidency of George Bush." *Political Science Quarterly* 107 (1992): 31–62.

Murphy, Reg, and Hal Gulliver. *The Southern Strategy.* New York: Charles Scribner's Sons, 1971.

Nathan, Richard P. "The Reagan Presidency in Domestic Affairs." In *The Reagan Presidency: An Early Assessment,* ed. Fred I. Greenstein. Baltimore: Johns Hopkins University Press, 1983.

———. "A Retrospective on Richard M. Nixon's Domestic Policies." *Presidential Studies Quarterly* 26 (1996): 155–64.

Nelson, Michael. "Evaluating the Presidency." In *The Presidency and the Political System.* 4th ed., ed. Michael Nelson. Washington, D.C.: Congressional Quarterly, 1995.

Neustadt, Richard. *Presidential Power and the Modern Presidents.* New York: Free Press, 1960.

———. "Congress and the Fair Deal: A Legislative Balance Sheet." In *Harry S. Truman and the Fair Deal,* ed. Alonzo L. Hamby. Lexington, Mass.: D. C. Heath, 1974.

New York Times and *New York Times Magazine.*

Novak, Robert D. "Problems of a 'Nixonian Democrat'." *Washington Post,* August 15, 1994, A19.

Oldfield, Duane M., and Aaron B. Wildavsky. "Reconsidering the Two Presidencies." *Society* 26 (1989): 54–59.

Oppenheimer, Bruce I. "The Importance of Elections in a Strong Congressional Party Era: The Effect of Unified vs. Divided Government." In *Do Elections Matter?* ed. Benjamin Ginsberg and Alan Stone. 3d ed. Armonk, N.Y.: M. E. Sharpe, 1996.

Ornstein, Norman J. "Too Many 'Lone Rangers'." *Washington Post,* September 2, 1994, A23.

———, Robert L. Peabody, and David W. Rohde. "The U.S. Senate: Toward the 21st Century." In *Congress Reconsidered,* ed. Lawrence C. Dodd and Bruce I. Oppenheimer. 6th ed. Washington, D.C.: Congressional Quarterly, 1997.

Pach, Chester J., Jr., and Elmo Richardson. *The Presidency of Dwight D. Eisenhower.* Rev. ed. Lawrence: University Press of Kansas, 1991.

Patterson, James T. *Congressional Conservatism and the New Deal: The Growth of the Conservative Coalition in Congress, 1933–1939.* Lexington: University of Kentucky Press, 1967.

Patterson, Samuel C. "Party Leadership in the U.S. Senate." In *The Changing World of the U.S. Senate,* ed. John R. Hibbing. Berkeley, Calif.: Institute of Governmental Studies Press, 1990.

Peabody, Robert L. "House Party Leadership: Stability and Change." In *Congress Reconsidered,* ed. Lawrence C. Dodd and Bruce I. Oppenheimer. 3d ed. Washington, D.C.: Congressional Quarterly, 1985.

Peterson, Mark A. *Legislating Together: The White House and Capitol Hill from Eisenhower to Reagan.* Cambridge, Mass.: Harvard University Press, 1990.

Petrocik, John R. "Divided Government: Is It All In The Campaigns?" In *The Politics of Divided Government,* ed. Gary W. Cox and Samuel Kernell. Boulder, Colo.: Westview Press, 1991.

———, and Joseph Doherty. "The Road to Divided Government: Paved without Intention." In *Divided Government,* ed. Peter F. Galderisi. Lanham, Md.: Rowman and Littlefield, 1996.

Pfiffner, James P. *The Strategic Presidency: Hitting the Ground Running.* 2d ed. Lawrence: University of Kansas Press, 1996.

———. *The Modern Presidency.* 3d ed. Boston: Bedford/St. Martin's, 2000.

———. "Divided Government and the Problem of Governance." In *Divided Democracy: Cooperation and Conflict Between the President and Congress,* ed. James A. Thurber. Washington, D.C.: Congressional Quarterly, 1991.

———. "President Clinton and the 103d Congress: Winning Battles and Losing Wars." In *Rivals for Power: Presidential-Congressional Relations,* ed. James A. Thurber. Washington, D.C.: Congressional Quarterly, 1996.

Pfister, Thierry. *Dans les coulisses du pouvoir: la comédie de la cohabitation.* Paris: A. Michel, 1986.

Plesur, Milton. "The Republican Comeback of 1938." *Review of Politics* 24 (1962): 525–62.

Polsby, Nelson W. *Consequences of Party Reform.* New York: Oxford University Press, 1983.

———. "Strategic Considerations." In *The National Election of 1964,* ed. Milton C. Cummings Jr. Washington, D.C.: Brookings Institution, 1966.

———, and Aaron B. Wildavsky. *Presidential Elections: Strategies and Structures of American Politics,* 9th ed. Chatham, N.J.: Chatham House, 1996.

Polsby, Nelson, Miriam Gallagher, and Barry Spencer Rundquist. "The Growth of the Seniority System in the U.S. House of Representatives." *American Political Science Review* 63 (1969): 787–807.

Pomper, Gerald M. "The Presidential Election." In *The Election of 1976: Reports and Interpretations,* ed. Marlene M. Pomper. New York: David McKay, 1977.

———. "Labor and Congress: The Repeal of Taft-Hartley." *Labor History* 2 (1961): 323–43.

Poole, Keith T., and Howard Rosenthal. *Congress: A Political-Economic History of Roll Call Voting.* New York: Oxford University Press, 1997.

———. "The Polarization of American Politics." *Journal of Politics* 46 (1984): 1061–79.

———. "Patterns of Congressional Voting." *American Journal of Political Science* 35 (1991): 228–78.

Press, Charles. "Presidential Coattails and Party Cohesion." *Midwest Journal of Political Science* 7 (1963): 320–35.

Public Papers of the Presidents of the United States. Washington, D.C.: GPO, 1947–98.

Pusey, Merlo J. *Eisenhower the President.* New York: Macmillan, 1956.

Quirk, Paul J. "Domestic Policy: Divided Government and Cooperative Presidential Leadership." In *The Bush Presidency: First Appraisals,* ed. Colin Campbell, S.J., and Bert A. Rockman. Chatham, N.J.: Chatham House, 1991.

———. "What Do We Know and How Do We Know It? Research on the Presidency." In *Political Science: Looking to the Future.* Vol. 4, *American Institutions,* ed. William J. Crotty. Evanston, Ill.: Northwestern University Press, 1991.

———. "Presidential Competence." In *The Presidency and the Political System,* ed. Michael Nelson. Washington, D.C.: Congressional Quarterly, 1995.

———, and Bruce Nesmith. "Divided Government and Policy Making: Negotiating the Laws." In *The Presidency and the Political System,* ed. Michael Nelson. Washington, D.C.: Congressional Quarterly, 1995.

Ragsdale, Lyn. *Vital Statistics on the Presidency: Washington to Clinton.* Washington, D.C.: Congressional Quarterly, 1996.

———, and Jerrold Rusk. "Elections and Presidential Policymaking." In *Presidential Policymaking: An End-of-Century Assessment,* ed. Steven A. Shull. Armonk, N.Y.: M. E. Sharpe, 2000.

Reichard, Gary W. *The Reaffirmation of Republicanism: Eisenhower and the Eighty-Third Congress.* Knoxville: University of Tennessee Press, 1975.

Reichley, A. James. *Conservatives in an Age of Change: The Nixon and Ford Administrations.* Washington, D.C.: Brookings Institution, 1981.

Renka, Russell. "Comparing Presidents Kennedy and Johnson as Legislative Leaders." *Presidential Studies Quarterly* 15 (1985): 806–25.

Reston, James. "Kennedy and the New Congress: A Striking Contrast." *New York Times,* February 15, 1961, 34.

Richardson, Elmo. *The Presidency of Dwight D. Eisenhower.* Lawrence: Regents Press of Kansas, 1979.

Riley, Russell L. "Party Government and the Contract with America." *PS: Political Science & Politics* 28 (1995): 703–707.

Ripley, Randall B. *Majority Party Leadership in Congress.* Boston: Little, Brown, 1969.

———. "The Party Whip Organizations in the United States House of Representatives." *American Political Science Review* 58 (1964): 561–76.

Rivers, Douglas, and Nancy Rose. "Passing the President's Program: Public Opinion and Presidential Influence in Congress." *American Journal of Political Science* 29 (1985): 183–96.

Rohde, David W. *Parties and Leaders in the Postreform House.* Chicago: University of Chicago Press, 1991.

———. "Electoral Factors, Political Agendas, and Partisanship in Congress." In *The Postreform Congress,* ed. Roger H. Davidson. New York: St. Martin's Press, 1992.

Rosenthal, Alan. *Toward Majority Rule in the United States Senate.* Eagleton Institute Cases in Practical Politics. New Brunswick, N.J.: McGraw-Hill, 1962.

Rossiter, Clinton. *The American Presidency.* New York: Harcourt, Brace, 1960.

Salmore, Barbara G., and Stephen A. Salmore. *Candidates, Parties, and Campaigns: Electoral Politics in America.* Washington, D.C.: Congressional Quarterly, 1989.

Scheele, Henry Z. "Executive-Legislative Relations: Eisenhower and Halleck." In *Reexamining the Eisenhower Presidency,* ed. Shirley Anne Warshaw. Westport, Conn.: Greenwood Press, 1993.

Schick, Allen. "How the Budget Was Won and Lost." In *President and Congress: Assessing Reagan's First Year,* ed. Norman J. Ornstein. Washington, D.C.: American Enterprise Institute, 1982.

Schlesinger, Arthur M. *A Thousand Days: John F. Kennedy in the White House.* Boston: Houghton, Mifflin, 1965.

Schroedel, Jean R. *Congress, the President, and Policymaking: A Historical Analysis.* Armonk, N.Y.: M. E. Sharpe, 1994.

Schwab, Larry M. *The Impact of Congressional Reapportionment and Redistricting.* Lanham, Md.: University Press of America, 1988.

Shelley, Mack C., III. *The Permanent Majority: The Conservative Coalition in the United States Congress.* University: University of Alabama Press, 1983.

Shepsle, Kenneth A. "The Changing Textbook Congress." In *Can the Government Govern?* ed. John E. Chubb and Paul E. Peterson. Washington, D.C.: Brookings Institution, 1989.

Shull, Steven A., ed. *The Two Presidencies: A Quarter Century Assessment.* Chicago: Nelson Hall, 1991.

———, and James Vanderleeuw. "What Do Key Votes Measure?" *Legislative Studies Quarterly* 12 (1987): 573–82.

Sinclair, Barbara. *Majority Party Leadership in the U.S. House.* Baltimore: Johns Hopkins University Press, 1983.

———. *The Transformation of the U.S. Senate.* Baltimore: Johns Hopkins University Press, 1989.

———. *Legislators, Leaders, and Lawmaking: The U.S. House of Representatives in the Postreform Era.* Baltimore: Johns Hopkins University Press, 1995.

———. "Coping with Uncertainty: Building Coalitions in the House and Senate." In *The New Congress,* ed. Thomas E. Mann and Norman J. Ornstein. Washington, D.C.: American Enterprise Institute, 1981.

———. "Governing Unheroically (and Sometimes Unappetizingly): Bush and the 101st Congress." In *The Bush Presidency: First Appraisals,* ed. Colin Campbell, S.J., and Bert A. Rockman. Chatham, N.J.: Chatham House Publishers, 1991.

———. "House Majority Party Leadership in an Era of Legislative Constraint." In *The Postreform Congress,* ed. Roger H. Davidson. New York: St. Martin's Press, 1992.

———. "Studying Presidential Leadership." In *Researching the Presidency: Vital Questions, New Approaches,* ed. George C. Edwards III, John H. Kessel, and Bert A. Rockman. Pittsburgh: University of Pittsburgh Press, 1993.

———. "Trying to Govern Positively in a Negative Era: Clinton and the 103d Congress." In *The Clinton Presidency: First Appraisals,* ed. Colin Campbell, S.J., and Bert A. Rockman. Chatham, N.J.: Chatham House, 1996.

———. "Hostile Partners: The President, Congress, and Lawmaking in the Partisan 1990s." In *Polarized Politics: Congress and the President in a Partisan Era,* ed. Jon R. Bond and Richard Fleisher. Washington, D.C.: Congressional Quarterly, 2000.

————. "Agenda Control and Policy Success: The Case of Ronald Reagan and 97th House." *Legislative Studies Quarterly* 20 (1985): 291–314.

————. "The Emergence of Strong Leadership in the 1980s House of Representatives." *Journal of Politics* 54 (1992): 657–84.

Sitkoff, Harvard. "Years of the Locust: Interpretations of Truman's Presidency Since 1965." In *The Truman Period as a Research Field: A Reappraisal, 1972,* ed. Richard S. Kirkendall. Columbia: University of Missouri Press, 1974.

Skocpol, Theda. *Boomerang: Clinton's Health Security Effort and the Turn Against Government in U.S. Politics.* New York: Norton, 1996.

Skowronek, Stephen. *The Politics Presidents Make: Leadership from John Adams to George Bush.* Cambridge, Mass.: Harvard University Press, 1993.

Sloan, John W. "Meeting the Leadership Challenges of the Modern Presidency: The Political Skills and Leadership of Ronald Reagan." *Presidential Studies Quarterly* 26 (1996): 795–804.

Snowiss, Sylvia. "Presidential Leadership of Congress: An Analysis of Roosevelt's First Hundred Days." *Publius* 1 (1971): 59–87.

Sorensen, Theodore C. *Kennedy.* New York: Harper and Row, 1965.

Spitzer, Robert J. *The Presidential Veto: Touchstone of the American Presidency.* Albany: State University Press of New York, 1988.

Stanley, Harold W. "The Parties, the President, and the 1994 Midterm Elections." In *The Clinton Presidency: First Appraisals,* ed. Colin Campbell, S.J., and Bert A. Rockman. Chatham, N.J.: Chatham House, 1996.

————, and Richard G. Niemi. *Vital Statistics on American Politics, 1999–2000.* Washington, D.C.: Congressional Quarterly, 2000.

Steger, Wayne P. "Presidential Policy Initiation and the Politics of Agenda Control." *Congress and the Presidency* 24 (1997): 17–36.

Sullivan, John L., L. Earl Shaw, Gregory E. McAvoy, and David G. Barnum. "The Dimensions of Cue-Taking in the House of Representatives: Variation by Issue Area." *Journal of Politics* 55 (1993): 975–97.

Sullivan, Terry. "The Bank Account Presidency: A New Measure of Evidence on the Temporal Path of Presidential Influence." *American Journal of Political Science* 35 (1991): 686–723.

Sundquist, James L. *Politics and Policy: The Eisenhower, Kennedy, and Johnson Years.* Washington, D.C.: Brookings Institution, 1968.

————. *The Decline and Resurgence of Congress.* Washington, D.C.: Brookings Institution, 1981.

————. *Constitutional Reform and Effective Government.* Washington, D.C.: Brookings Institution, 1986.

————. "Needed: A Political Theory for the New Era of Coalition Government in the United States." *Political Science Quarterly* 10 (1988): 613–35.

Taylor, Andrew J. "Domestic Agenda Setting, 1947–1994." *Legislative Studies Quarterly* 23 (1998): 373–97.

Tenpas, Kathryn Dunn. *Presidents as Candidates: Inside the White House for the Presidential Campaign.* New York: Garland, 1997.

Thorson, Gregory R. "Divided Government and the Passage of Partisan Legislation, 1947–1990." *Political Research Quarterly* 51 (1998): 751–64.

Toner, Robin. "Health Care Reform: A Case Study." In *Back to Gridlock? Governance in the Clinton Years,* ed. James L. Sundquist. Washington, D.C.: Brookings Institution, 1995.

Tufte, Edward R. "Determinants of the Outcomes of Midterm Congressional Elections." *American Political Science Review* 69 (1975): 812–26.

Tulis, Jeffrey K. *The Rhetorical Presidency.* Princeton, N.J.: Princeton University Press, 1987.

Van Assendelft, Laura A. *Governors, Agenda-Setting, and Divided Government.* Lanham, Md.: University Press of America, 1997.

Warshaw, Shirley Anne. *The Domestic Presidency: Policy Making in the White House.* Boston: Allyn and Bacon, 1997.

Washington Post.

Wattenberg, Martin P. *The Decline of American Political Parties, 1952–1996.* Cambridge, Mass.: Harvard University Press, 1998.

Watson, Richard A. *Presidential Vetoes and Public Policy.* Lawrence: University of Kansas Press, 1993.

Wayne, Stephen J. *The Legislative Presidency.* New York: Harper and Row, 1978.

———. "Congressional Liaison in the Reagan White House: A Preliminary Assessment of the First Year." In *President and Congress: Assessing Reagan's First Year,* ed. Norman J. Ornstein. Washington, D.C.: American Enterprise Institute, 1982.

Weingast, Barry R. "A Rational Choice Perspective on Congressional Norms." *American Journal of Political Science* 23 (1979): 245–62.

Whicker, Marcia Lynn. "Managing the Bush White House." In *The Bush Presidency: Triumphs and Adversities,* ed. Dilys M. Hill and Phil Williams. New York: St. Martin's Press, 1994.

———, and Raymond A. Moore. *When Presidents Are Great.* Palo Alto, Calif.: Stanford University Press, 1988.

Whitaker, John C. "Nixon's Domestic Policy: Both Liberal and Bold in Retrospect." *Presidential Studies Quarterly* 26 (1996): 131–53.

White, Theodore H. *The Making of the President, 1964.* New York: Atheneum, 1965.

———. *The Making of the President, 1968.* New York: Atheneum, 1969.

Wicker, Tom. *JFK and LBJ: The Influence of Personality Upon Politics.* New York: Penguin Books, 1968.

Wilcox, Clyde. *The Latest American Revolution? The 1994 Elections and Their Implications for Governance.* New York: St. Martin's Press, 1995.

Wildavsky, Aaron B. "The Two Presidencies." In *Perspectives on the Presidency,* ed. Aaron Wildavsky. Boston: Little, Brown, 1975.

Wright, Fiona M. "The Caucus Reelection Requirement and the Transformation of House Committee Chairs, 1959–94." *Legislative Studies Quarterly* 15 (2000): 469–80.

Yarbrough, Tinsley E. "Carter and the Congress." In *The Carter Years: The President and Policy Making,* ed. M. Glenn Abernathy, Dilys M. Hill, and Phil Williams. New York: St. Martin's Press, 1984.

Zeidenstein, Harvey G. "Varying Relationships Between President's Popularity and Their Legislative Success: A Futile Search for Patterns." *Presidential Studies Quarterly* 13 (1983): 530–49.

Index

ISBN 1-58544-211-9